# CONSULTATION
# in PSYCHOLOGY

# CONSULTATION in PSYCHOLOGY

## A Competency-Based Approach

**Edited by** Carol A. Falender and Edward P. Shafranske

AMERICAN PSYCHOLOGICAL ASSOCIATION
Washington, DC

Published by
American Psychological Association
750 First Street, NE
Washington, DC 20002
https://www.apa.org

Order Department
https://www.apa.org/pubs/books
order@apa.org

In the U.K., Europe, Africa, and the Middle East, copies may be ordered from Eurospan
https://www.eurospanbookstore.com/apa
info@eurospangroup.com

Typeset in Meridien and Ortodoxa by Circle Graphics, Inc., Reisterstown, MD

Printer: Sheridan Books, Chelsea, MI
Cover Designer: Nicci Falcone, Gaithersburg, MD

**Library of Congress Cataloging-in-Publication Data**
Names: Falender, Carol A., editor. | Shafranske, Edward P., editor.
Title: Consultation in psychology : a competency-based approach /
  edited by Carol A. Falender and Edward P. Shafranske.
Description: Washington, DC : American Psychological Association, [2020] |
  Includes bibliographical references and index.
Identifiers: LCCN 2019014413 (print) | LCCN 2019014574 (ebook) |
  ISBN 9781433831416 (eBook) | ISBN 1433831414 (eBook) |
  ISBN 9781433830907 (pbk.) | ISBN 1433830906 (pbk.)
Subjects: LCSH: Psychiatric consultation. | Mental health consultation.
Classification: LCC RC455.2.C65 (ebook) | LCC RC455.2.C65 C64 2020 (print) |
  DDC 616.89—dc23
LC record available at https://lccn.loc.gov/2019014413

http://dx.doi.org/10.1037/0000153-000

*Printed in the United States of America*

10 9 8 7 6 5 4 3 2 1

# CONTENTS

Contributors     vii

**Introduction**     3
*Carol A. Falender and Edward P. Shafranske*

**I. FOUNDATIONS OF CONSULTATION PRACTICE**     9

1. **Consultation in Psychology: A Distinct Professional Practice**     11
*Carol A. Falender and Edward P. Shafranske*

2. **The Competency Framework: Best Practices in Consultation**     37
*Carol A. Falender and Edward P. Shafranske*

3. **Ethical, Legal, and Professional Issues in Consultation for Psychologists**     53
*Jeffrey E. Barnett*

4. **Consultation in Health Service Psychology: The Present and the Future**     71
*David J. Martin*

5. **Consultation in Interprofessional Practice and Collaboration**     87
*Patricia Arredondo*

6. **Can You See Me Now? Understanding Culture and Multicultural Phenomena as Essential to the Process of Consultation**     109
*William D. Parham*

## II. EXEMPLARS AND APPROACHES — 129

**7. Pediatric Consultation** — 131
Michael C. Roberts, Rebecca J. Johnson, and Christina M. Amaro

**8. Consultation in Medical Settings** — 151
Barbara Cubic

**9. Consultation in Leadership** — 169
Jennifer Wootten and Nadine J. Kaslow

**10. Consultation in Corporations and Organizations** — 187
Rodney L. Lowman

**11. School-Based Consultation** — 201
Markeda Newell, Carly Tindall, Kelsie Reed, and Scott Zwolski

**12. Consultation With Religious Professionals and Institutions** — 221
Thomas G. Plante

**13. Forensic Consultation** — 239
Jeffrey N. Younggren, Michael C. Gottlieb, and Cassandra L. Boness

**14. Custody Case Family Consultation** — 253
G. Andrew H. Benjamin and Florence W. Kaslow

**15. Consultation in Police and Public Safety Psychology** — 279
Cary L. Mitchell and Edrick H. Dorian

**16. Consultation Within the Military Setting** — 301
Christina L. Schendel and Carrie H. Kennedy

**Afterword: Advancing Consultation Practice** — 319
Carol A. Falender and Edward P. Shafranske

Index — 327
About the Editors — 343

# CONTRIBUTORS

**Christina M. Amaro, MA,** Clinical Child Psychology Program, University of Kansas, Lawrence

**Patricia Arredondo, EdD,** Arredondo Advisory Group, Phoenix, AZ; School of Leadership Studies, Fielding Graduate University, Santa Barbara, CA

**Jeffrey E. Barnett, PsyD, ABPP,** Department of Psychology, College of Arts and Sciences, Loyola University Maryland, Baltimore

**G. Andrew H. Benjamin, JD, PhD, ABPP,** Parenting Evaluation/ Training Program, University of Washington, Seattle

**Cassandra L. Boness, MA,** Department of Psychology, University of Missouri, Columbia

**Barbara Cubic, PhD,** Department of Family Medicine, West Virginia University School of Medicine, Morgantown

**Edrick H. Dorian, PsyD, ABPP,** Los Angeles Police Department, Los Angeles, CA

**Carol A. Falender, PhD,** Graduate School of Education and Psychology, Pepperdine University, Los Angeles, CA; Department of Psychology, University of California, Los Angeles

**Michael C. Gottlieb, PhD,** independent practice, Dallas, TX

**Rebecca J. Johnson, PhD, ABPP,** Children's Mercy Kansas City, Kansas City, MO; University of Missouri–Kansas City School of Medicine

**Florence W. Kaslow, PhD, ABPP,** Kaslow Associates, Palm Beach Gardens, FL; Department of Psychology, Florida Institute of Technology, Melbourne

**Nadine J. Kaslow, PhD, ABPP,** Department of Psychiatry and Behavioral Sciences, Emory University, Atlanta, GA

**Carrie H. Kennedy, PhD,** Psychological Health Center of Excellence, Falls Church, VA; Defense Health Agency, Falls Church, VA

**Rodney L. Lowman, PhD, ABAP,** Lowman & Richardson/Consulting Psychologists, San Diego, CA; California School of Professional Psychology, Alliant International University, San Diego, CA

**David J. Martin, PhD, ABPP,** independent consultant, Washington, DC

**Cary L. Mitchell, PhD,** Graduate School of Education and Psychology, Pepperdine University, Los Angeles, CA

**Markeda Newell, PhD,** School of Education, Loyola University Chicago, Chicago, IL

**William D. Parham, PhD, ABPP,** Department of Specialized Program in Professional Psychology, School of Education, Loyola Marymount University, Los Angeles, CA; National Basketball Players Association, New York, NY

**Thomas G. Plante, PhD, ABPP,** Department of Psychology, Santa Clara University, Santa Clara, CA; Department of Psychiatry and Behavioral Sciences, Stanford University School of Medicine, Stanford, CA

**Kelsie Reed, MEd,** PhD student, School of Education, Loyola University Chicago, Chicago, IL

**Michael C. Roberts, PhD, ABPP,** Office of Graduate Studies, University of Kansas, Lawrence

**Christina L. Schendel, PhD,** Psychological Health Center of Excellence, Falls Church, VA; Defense Health Agency, Falls Church, VA

**Edward P. Shafranske, PhD, ABPP,** Graduate School of Education and Psychology, Pepperdine University, Los Angeles, CA; School of Medicine, University of California, Irvine

**Carly Tindall, MEd,** PhD student, School of Education, Loyola University Chicago, Chicago, IL

**Jennifer Wootten, MD,** Department of Psychiatry and Behavioral Sciences, Emory University, Atlanta, GA

**Jeffrey N. Younggren, PhD, ABPP,** Department of Psychiatry and Behavioral Sciences, University of New Mexico, Albuquerque

**Scott Zwolski,** MEd student, School of Education, Loyola University Chicago, Chicago, IL

# CONSULTATION in PSYCHOLOGY

# Introduction

Carol A. Falender and Edward P. Shafranske

Consultation is a practice that plays an essential role in professional or health service psychology (HSP),[1] particularly in integrated care and interprofessional collaboration and in the evolving practice environments within the public and private sectors of society. Although it is most often used to enhance the quality of care in individual cases, consultation may also be directed to groups, including large health care, education, or other professional systems, such as departments of mental health, and in the corporate arena. No matter the area of their specialization, psychologists will undoubtedly engage in consultation in their careers, and for some, clinical neuropsychologists or school psychologists, for example, it will constitute a primary focus. Competence in consultation is therefore required for professional practice in HSP as recognized in accreditation standards (American Psychological Association, Commission on Accreditation, 2018), the blueprint for education and training (Health Service Psychology Education Collaborative, 2013), and competency benchmarks (Fouad et al., 2009). Although widely agreed on as a competency and requirement for practice, consultation has not been a central topic in the graduate trajectory and has had high variability in content when

---

[1]The term *health service psychology* reflects the newly adopted nomenclature. It refers to applied practice in the areas of clinical psychology, counseling psychology, and school psychology and is reflected in accreditation standards (American Psychological Association, Commission on Accreditation, 2018). We use *health service psychology* interchangeably with the commonly used term *professional psychology.*

http://dx.doi.org/10.1037/0000153-001
*Consultation in Psychology: A Competency-Based Approach*, C. A. Falender and E. P. Shafranske (Editors)

it has been the subject of a dedicated course (e.g., school consultation; Hazel, Laviolette, & Lineman, 2010).

The practice of HSP is remarkably diverse and comprehensive: It provides services to clients in a multiverse of settings (e.g., private practice, community agencies, schools, universities, military, medical centers and health care organizations) and addresses an array of medical, psychological, and behavioral problems. Recently, advances in psychological science as well as initiatives in integrated care have led to reconsideration of professional practice and to a broadened view of HSP, going beyond the traditional HSP focus on mental health (Belar, 2012, 2016; Health Service Psychology Education Collaborative, 2013). We envision the future of professional psychology as offering an expansive horizon of opportunities for the application of psychological science to address individual and societal needs in respect to health and behavior. Consultation is integral to this transition within HSP as service provision expands from the silos of individual treatment to increased interprofessional collaboration and engagement in integrated care.

As the role of psychologists has expanded so has the scope of clients. The term *client* may now refer to the individual, group, population, or organization as the recipient of intended services or program. In addition to consultation aimed to improve individual patient care, system-level consultation (including cost-effectiveness analysis) will contribute to large-scale efforts to enhance effectiveness and increase economic efficiencies in the changing health care environment (Mihalopoulos, Vos, Pirkis, & Carter, 2011). Such transformations of clinical services involving the implementation of evidence-based and other practices will require training and ongoing consultation to be successful (Barlow, Bullis, Comer, & Ametaj, 2013). Increasingly, applications of psychological science will take the form of consultation, such as offered in community-based programs of diversity training, public health and prevention, consultation to law enforcement agencies, and in unique niche areas, for example, consultation to the National Aeronautics and Space Administration, to enhance teamwork (Landon, Slack, & Barrett, 2018) and prepare crew members and their families for long-duration missions. Consultation will also be provided to enhance work and education environments and in areas of leadership and organizational development. Current and future practice in HSP will require competence in consultation, which is similar to other functional competencies in that it involves a unique set of knowledge, skills, and attitudes for its performance. Furthermore, psychologists will not only need to be prepared to offer consultation, they will need to know when to seek consultation (Belar, 2014), a task that implicitly requires knowledge of the limits of one's own professional competence.

This book presents a comprehensive and competency-based approach to the practice of consultation. It provides a foundation for effective practice, emphasizing ethics, culture, and interprofessional practice in multiple consultation settings. Building on this foundation, the chapters focus on a variety of consultation settings, including medical, forensic, school, corporate, professional leadership, family, religious, police, and military contexts. This volume will prepare graduate students, interns, postdoctoral fellows, and practicing psychologists to effectively and competently offer consultation in traditional and emerging areas of professional practice.

## FUNDAMENTAL PRINCIPLES IN COMPETENCY-BASED CONSULTATION

In our view, the effectiveness of consultation is based on adherence to a number of salient principles. Each principle contributes in its own way to orient and structure the process of consultation. Awareness of these foundational standards assists in the process of learning and developing competence in consultation, provides points of reference when making decisions in consultation, and supports reflective practice and self-assessment. These principles come from multiple sources, including (but not limited to) the consultation literature (e.g., the contributions of Gerard Caplan, William P. Erchul, and many others); our appreciation of the centrality of competence in education, training, professional practice, and continuous professional development (e.g., Nadine Kaslow's and others' groundbreaking leadership in the competency movement, accreditation standards, benchmarks, guidelines); the contributors to this volume; and our own personal experiences as consultants, educators, practitioners, and consumers of consultation. We offer the following principles for your consideration:

1. Consultation is a distinct professional practice.

2. Consultation involves an identifiable assemblage of knowledge, skills, and attitudes that are used in its performance.

3. The effectiveness of consultation is based on the competencies of the consultant (as an expert and as a consultant); the consultee (as a professional and as a consultee); and the development of a respectful, collaborative working relationship.

4. Although the consultant possesses greater expertise and experience than the consultee, the relationship between the consultant and consultee is nonhierarchical and collegial and is imbued with respect, including toward the multiple professions involved.

5. Consultation requires clear articulation of the objectives of the consultation and clarity of roles, which may be stated in a formal consultation contract.

6. The consultee bears the sole responsibility to decide whether or not (or to what extent) to follow the consultant's guidance and to implement the consultant's recommendations.

7. Consultation is conducted consistent with legal and ethical principles and codes of conduct of the professions represented and with consideration of multicultural diversity factors and contexts of the client, consultee, and consultant.

We are influenced by our belief that competence in consultation (or any professional practice) can be developed, sustained, and enhanced through education, thoughtful study, training, supervision, and consultation.

## OVERVIEW AND ORGANIZATION OF THE BOOK

The impetus for this book sprung from the (a) perceived need for a resource to support education and training (including continuous professional development) in consultation; (b) awareness of the expanding role of consultation in HSP practice; and (c) importance of furnishing a competency-based approach to consultation, taking into consideration ethical and multicultural dimensions of practice. Whereas psychologists are well prepared to provide direct clinical services to consumers, they are generally less prepared to serve as consultants because education and training has primarily focused on direct service. In addition, anecdotally, it appears that limited curricular attention has been placed on developing competencies used in professional-to-professional relationships, such as in consultation. In the emerging health care and applied psychology environment, psychologists will be increasingly called on to provide consultation in primary care, prevention, and clinical and other professional service areas. Consistent with these points, we believe that consultation is an extremely important and expanding area of professional practice, which will have significant impact on individuals, systems, and society at large.

Consultation, consistent with other professional practices, involves the use of knowledge, skills, and attitudes (or values) that are assembled to form competence. This competence-based framework is incorporated throughout the book and serves as the basic orientation to learning, practice, and self-assessment. Whether in training, continuous professional development, or preparation for engagement in consultation, it is essential to identify the domains of knowledge and the skills necessary to perform consultation effectively as well as to consider the attitudes and cultural context that informs the professional relationship.

The book consists of two major parts: Foundations of Consultation Practice and Exemplars and Approaches, and it closes with a chapter discussing the future of consultation. The chapters in the Foundations section provide an overview of the process of consultation, including (a) an introduction to consultation as a distinct professional practice; (b) consultation within the competency-based framework, which provides a blueprint for practice; (c) law and ethics in consultation; (d) an orientation to HSP and the role of consultation; (e) interprofessional practice; and (f) an understanding of culture and multicultural phenomena as essential throughout all forms of consultation practice. Read together, these chapters provide important background and theory and practical guidelines for developing a comprehensive understanding of consultation on which competence can be developed.

Part II provides examples of consultation practice that span a range of contexts, such as medical, educational, and religious settings; forensics; custody evaluations; law enforcement; military; and the corporate environment.[2] These chapters highlight the competencies and credentials that establish expertise in a given area of HSP, provide an overview of the contexts in which consultation is sought, and offer best practices and practical advice. These chapters do not intend to present an exhaustive survey of consultation niches, including, for example, sports psychology or rehabilitation psychology. Rather, the goal of these chapters is to encourage forward and imaginative thinking about the many situations in which psychology can benefit individual, group, and corporate clients, both in and outside of the traditional health service context.

For the psychologist who already is engaged in consultation or is considering expanding practice opportunities, and for doctoral students, interns, or fellows who are embarking on their careers, this book provides a foundation for competency-based practice and offers illustrations of core principles and practices for consultation success. We turn now to Chapters 1 and 2, which present a comprehensive overview of consultation in its many forms and a competency-based approach for effective professional practice.

## REFERENCES

American Psychological Association, Commission on Accreditation. (2018). *Standards of accreditation for health service psychology*. Retrieved from http://www.apa.org/ed/accreditation/about/policies/standards-of-accreditation.pdf

Barlow, D. H., Bullis, J. R., Comer, J. S., & Ametaj, A. A. (2013). Evidence-based psychological treatments: An update and a way forward. *Annual Review of Clinical Psychology*, *9*, 1–27. http://dx.doi.org/10.1146/annurev-clinpsy-050212-185629

Belar, C. D. (2012). Reflections on the future: Psychology as a health profession. *Professional Psychology: Research and Practice*, *43*, 545–550. http://dx.doi.org/10.1037/a0029633

Belar, C. D. (2014). Reflections on the Health Service Psychology Education Collaborative blueprint. *Training and Education in Professional Psychology*, *8*, 3–11. http://dx.doi.org/10.1037/tep0000027

Belar, C. D. (2016). Interprofessional education and training. In J. C. Norcross, G. R. VandenBos, D. K. Freedheim, & L. F. Campbell (Eds.), *APA handbook of clinical psychology: Education and profession* (Vol. 5, pp. 153–160). Washington, DC: American Psychological Association. http://dx.doi.org/10.1037/14774-010

Fouad, N. A., Grus, C. L., Hatcher, R. L., Kaslow, N. L., Hutchings, P. S., Madson, M., . . . Crossman, R. E. (2009). Competency benchmarks: A model for understanding and measuring competence in professional psychology across training levels. *Training and Education in Professional Psychology*, *3*(Suppl.), S5–S26. http://dx.doi.org/10.1037/a0015832

Hazel, C. E., Laviolette, G. T., & Lineman, J. M. (2010). Training professional psychologists in school-based consultation: What the syllabi suggest. *Training and Education in Professional Psychology*, *4*, 235–243. http://dx.doi.org/10.1037/a0020072

---

[2]All clinical case material has been altered to protect client confidentiality.

Health Service Psychology Education Collaborative. (2013). Professional psychology in health care services: A blueprint for education and training. *American Psychologist, 68,* 411–426. http://dx.doi.org/10.1037/a0033265

Landon, L. B., Slack, K. J., & Barrett, J. D. (2018). Teamwork and collaboration in long-duration space missions: Going to extremes. *American Psychologist, 73,* 563–575. http://dx.doi.org/10.1037/amp0000260

Mihalopoulos, C., Vos, T., Pirkis, J., & Carter, R. (2011). The economic analysis of prevention in mental health programs. *Annual Review of Clinical Psychology, 7,* 169–201. http://dx.doi.org/10.1146/annurev-clinpsy-032210-104601

# FOUNDATIONS OF
# CONSULTATION PRACTICE

# 1

# Consultation in Psychology

## A Distinct Professional Practice

Carol A. Falender and Edward P. Shafranske

Psychologists perform many professional responsibilities during the course of their training and careers. Increasingly, psychologists are called on to provide consultation both in traditional mental health practice and in diverse and ever-expanding professional and interprofessional settings. Although consultation draws on clinical expertise, it is a distinct professional practice that requires clear understanding of its aims and functions as well as the application of a unique set of skills.

This chapter provides an orientation to consultation in professional psychology. We begin by tracing the development of definitions and approaches to consultation, describe its types and distinctive features, and close with a discussion of the differences between consultation provided within health service psychology (HSP) and the specialty of consulting psychology, which includes industrial, organizational, and other forms of individual and corporate consultation. In keeping with our competency-based approach, comprehensive knowledge of consultation plays an essential role in its professional practice.

## DESCRIPTIONS AND DEFINITIONS OF CONSULTATION

The term *consultation* can be used in many different ways, as noted by Caplan (1970). It may be used generically to refer to any practice of a specialist—for example, medical consultation—or more narrowly described as a specialized

http://dx.doi.org/10.1037/0000153-002
*Consultation in Psychology: A Competency-Based Approach*, C. A. Falender and
E. P. Shafranske (Editors)

activity between two persons—for example, psychologists—in regard to a third person when consulting about a patient. Caplan (1970) defined *consultation* as

> a process of interaction between two professional persons—the consultant, who is a specialist, and the consultee, who invokes the consultant's help in regard to a work problem with which he is having some difficulty and which he has decided is within the other's area of specialized competence. (p. 19)

It is a planned, collaborative interaction arranged between professionals to address the needs of the client. Consultation aims to help the consultee work more effectively (Brown, Pryzwansky, & Schulte, 2011; Sears, Rudisill, & Mason-Sears, 2006) and to maintain, develop, and enhance the consultee's professional competence as well as mitigate the risks of clinical errors (Thomas, 2010).

In a broad sense, consultation involves a process of advisement that may extend to offering expert opinion and making professional recommendations but falls short of issuing a direction that *must* be followed (as would be the case in clinical or administrative supervision). Consultation may also be viewed more globally as "a diverse set of activities deployed in response to requests from individuals, groups, or organizations for information or guidance that could lead to change" (see Chapter 6, this volume, p. 110). Similarly, the *APA Thesaurus of Psychological Index Terms* provides the following description: "Advisory services offered by specialists in a particular field which may be client or colleague oriented or focus on policy setting, planning, and programs of an organization" (American Psychological Association [APA], n.d.-b). Consultants at times not only advise or recommend a plan of action but also may arrange or actively participate in its implementation per the client or consultee's request.

In their discussion of a preliminary framework for defining competencies in consultation and interprofessional practice (by the Consultation and Interdisciplinary Relationships Workgroup in 2002 at The Competencies Conference: Future Directions in Education and Credentialing in Professional Psychology in Scottsdale, Arizona), Arredondo, Shealy, Neale, and Winfrey (2004) proposed the following definition:

> Psychological Consultation focuses on the needs of individuals, groups, programs, and organizations. It refers to planned interactions between the professional psychologist (consultant) and one or more representatives of clients, colleagues, or systems (consultees) relative to a problem, person, area, or program. Psychological consultation is based on principles and procedures found within psychology and related disciplines in which a professional psychologist applies to his/her areas of expertise in response to the presenting needs and stated objectives of consultees. (p. 789)

Incorporating a competency orientation, we define *consultation* as

> a process of interaction between two or more professionals: the consultant, who is an expert or possesses particular competence in the area to be discussed, and the consultee, who has a particular work issue, question, or problem regarding assessment, treatment, intervention, management, organizational process, policy, or implementation of professional services. In competency-based consultation, the

consultee presents the consultation question(s) and supplies relevant background information, and the consultant identifies the requisite knowledge, skills, and attitudes within the consulting question and provides education, guidance, and direction. The consultant does not assume responsibility for the client. The consultee bears the full responsibility for the decision whether to adopt and implement the consultant's recommendations. At the consultee's request, the consultant may provide direct services to the client (i.e., individual, group, or organization), aligned with the objectives of the consultation and responsive to the client's needs.

This definition applies to consultation that primarily aims to enhance the consultee's competence and effectiveness in response to the client's needs. Ordinarily, the consultant does not have direct contact with the client; however, as included in our definition, there are situations in which the consultant, at the request of the consultee, provides services directly to the client to address the consultation issue. For example, in hospital-based consultation, the consultant may interview or evaluate the patient to provide additional assessment and to assist the consultee to arrive at an accurate diagnosis and treatment plan; in a corporate setting, a consulting psychologist may devise a survey to assess workplace morale or provide training to improve effectiveness and job satisfaction (see Chapter 10, this volume). No matter the focus of the consultation, we emphasize a competency-based approach that identifies the knowledge, skills, and attitudes involved in consultee's question and in the information, guidance, assessment, or interventions offered by the consultant as well as in the competencies used by the consultant.

## TYPES OF CONSULTATION

Consultation as practiced in HSP commonly takes the form of clinical case consultation; however, other types of consultation may be offered to address the consultee's questions and associated client needs. The various types are distinguished by the nature and focus of the consultation, which may include differences in clients, aims of the consultation, and the role and functions assumed by the consultant. These differences, which are summarized in Table 1.1, shape the nature of the consultation and determine the knowledge, skills, and attitudes required of the consultant. Clients may include individual clients in health care settings or leaders in community or corporate settings or may involve groups or organizations. Aims may vary, too. For example, consultation may be directed to improve individual patient care, to enhance effectiveness among professionals within a system via programs designed specifically to achieve that goal, or to improve community relations or business culture through intentional efforts, or to assess and augment the skills of individuals in leadership positions. The roles and functions of the consultant also must be adapted to align with the consultee's objectives. Generally, consultants offer their knowledge and experience to enable consultees to perform or enhance their effectiveness; however, they may also apply their expertise directly to the client through assessment,

**TABLE 1.1. Types of Consultation**

| Consultation features | Type | | | | | |
|---|---|---|---|---|---|---|
| | Client-focused clinical case consultation and interprofessional practice | Consultee-focused clinical case consultation | Consultee-focused professional development | Client-focused community organizational consultation | Consultee-focused community organizational consultation | Peer consultation |
| Client | Individual clinical case | Individual clinical case | In a clinical setting, professional development is aimed at specific client group (based on diagnosis or other category, e.g., age) or treatment modality to be applied to the general client population; in a nonclinical setting, professional development is aimed at clients whom the organization serves or interacts | Community or organization client(s) | Individual(s) within the organization responsible for its functioning and implementation of its mission | Professional peers |
| Objective | To enhance understanding of the client, including the client's presenting problems, diagnosis, and case formulation as well as to respond to consultee questions specific to the client | To enhance the consultee's professional competence specific to individual case | In a clinical setting, to enhance the consultee's professional competence (knowledge, skills, and attitudes); in a nonclinical setting, to increase consultee effectiveness to fulfill the organization's mission | To provide psychological knowledge responsive to the consultee's questions or consultation issues related to the community or organization's clients and the organization's mission with respect to its client(s) | Consultation focuses on enhancing the organization's ability to fulfill its mission | Professional peers voluntarily meet as a dyad or in a group to enhance professional competence, provide mutual support, and encourage positive collegial relationships |

| | | | | | | |
|---|---|---|---|---|---|---|
| Consultant role | Provides information and guidance with respect to client assessment, diagnosis, case conceptualization, and treatment or intervention or risk and case management plan and may include provision of services directly to the client, such as performing an evaluation of the client | Collaborates with the consultee to identify the nature of the clinical difficulties or issues, such as clinical competence (knowledge, skill(s), attitudes), motivation, treatment implementation, personal reactivity or theme interference, alliance, and outcomes and offers guidance and direction | Provides services that may include teaching, training, and ongoing consultation to enhance the consultee's knowledge, skills, and attitudes; in the clinical setting, services may include enhancing the consultee's ability to implement evidence-based treatments | Provides information and guidance relevant to the client and the community or organization's mission with respect to its client(s); the consultant may provide services, such as developing and conducting a needs assessment of the organization's client(s) | Provides services, such as education, training, leadership, team building, and interventions to address problems, barriers, or both, to enhance the organization's ability to fulfill its mission | Each member of the dyad or group assumes the roles of facilitator, consultee, and consultant in the group over time; participants offer knowledge, perspectives, reflections, and guidance with respect to the client, the intervention or treatment plan, and the interactional process between the "consultee" and the client and possibly the milieu; also provides professional support and feedback as indicated |
| Responsibility for decision making | Consultee, professional who bears primary patient responsibility on a collaborative treatment team, or both | Consultee | Consultee | Consultee | Consultee | Member of the group bearing legal or professional responsibility to the client |

intervention, and training and in interprofessional collaboration. The following are a few examples of different types of consultation:

- A pediatric neuropsychologist engages in interprofessional practice as part of a collaborative treatment team. She conducts an assessment and works with the patient's pediatrician to develop a treatment plan. She then provides input to the school for appropriate modifications (this is an example of client-focused clinical case consultation; see Chapter 7, this volume).

- A psychologist delivers an educational program and provides ongoing individual consultation to train mental health professionals (e.g., psychologists, social workers, licensed professional counselors) in an evidence-based treatment for posttraumatic stress disorder at a community clinic that serves an ethnically diverse clinical population (this is an example of consultee-focused professional development and interprofessional practice; see Chapter 5).

- The administration of an APA-accredited doctoral program in counseling psychology hires a psychologist consultant with expertise in law and ethics and experience in graduate education to review its policies and to provide a second opinion when considering the dismissal of a student (this is an example of consultee-focused consultation involving law and ethics; see Chapter 3).

- A clinical psychologist provides preemployment assessments of applicants to a law enforcement and safety department (this is an example of direct service provision to address the department's needs; see Chapter 15).

- A psychologist conducts a survey of a religious congregation and facilitates a retreat for the clergy and staff to discuss the findings and to establish priorities (this is an example of consultation involving service provision directly to the client; see Chapter 12).

- A chief executive officer seeks individual consultation to assist in her development as a leader and change agent (this is an example of consultee-focused corporate consultation; see Chapters 9 and 10).

- A clinical psychologist seeks consultation regarding clinical management of a challenging, at-risk client (this is an example of consultee-focused clinical case consultation involving ethics and law, see Chapter 3).

Given the varied needs of consultees (and their clients), consultation resists rigid categorization in its implementation or in the specific services that are offered. The categories presented illustrate general areas of consultation practice rather than offer an all-inclusive list of types of consultation.

## Client-Focused Clinical Case Consultation and Interprofessional Practice

*Clinical case consultation* (sometimes referred to as simply *case consultation*) has been a widely used and essential practice in health care (Gallessich, 1982).

The two general types of case consultation are client focused and consultee focused. In this section, we discuss client-focused case consultation.

*Client-focused case consultation* is aimed at helping the consultee develop a plan to address the client's needs (Caplan, 1970); therefore, the consultant may be seen as indirectly providing services to the client (Fredman, Papadopoulou, & Worwood, 2018). Note that in case consultation, the client is the person receiving treatment (i.e., the patient). In clinical settings, consultants bring their knowledge and expertise to assist in diagnosis and treatment planning. Consultation may be sought when additional information is needed (or is outside of the consultee's area of competence) or when problems occur in treatment that require expert opinion. In hospital settings—for example, in pediatrics—brief consultations with psychologists can occur at the point of initial evaluation and admission as part of the psychiatry consultation-liaison service (Lipsitt, 2016) or later as part of a treatment plan to deal with medication noncompliance or possible mental health diagnoses that will interfere with treatment interventions. Although the information and recommendations provided are directed to the individual case and for the client's benefit, the consultation may also contribute to the consultee's continuing education; however, this education is limited by the specificity of the case under consideration (Caplan & Caplan, 1993).

In client-focused consultation, the emphasis is on assessment of the client, albeit vicarious and limited, because the evaluation is derived from the information and observations provided by the consultee. In educational settings, it is not unusual for the consultee to include information assembled from observations of teachers, counselors, parents, and other collateral sources (Brown et al., 2011; see also Chapter 11, this volume). The focus remains centered on the client rather than on the consultee (as would be the case in consultee-focused case consultation). The consultee describes the purpose of the consultation and the questions or problems that have prompted the need for consultation and provides information, including background, observations, client-reported information, and test data, that are specifically relevant to the focus of consultation. Information may be de-identified to protect client privacy or it may be essential that it be identifiable, for example, in an interprofessional treatment team, and thus would require client knowledge and informed consent. It is essential that the objectives of the consultation and the consultee questions be clearly stated and that the information the consultee provides be delimited in scope for the consultation to be productive (for best practices, see Chapter 2). In some instances, the consultant may need to examine the client or administer a battery of tests to answer the address consultation questions, which often is the case in consultations conducted in medical settings. Although the assessment involves the patient and contributes to his or her care, the aim of the assessment is situated within consultation, and the consultant's primary obligation is to the consultee because the consultee (and not the consultant) has the responsibility for the case, clinical decision making, and patient welfare.

**Client-Focused Interprofessional Practice**

In the transformation from multidisciplinary to interprofessional practice, Belar (2016) compared the change from "parallel play" (p. 153), or the independent working of several disciplines on a clinical client or case, to *interprofessional*, a shift to interdisciplinary practice. Interprofessional practice describes multiple professions working together for the purposes of health care delivery and conveys "interactive, collaborative, team-based models of care in which professionals rely on one another to deliver quality care" (Belar, 2016, p. 154). This model is in contrast to the usual models of independent training of each profession without attention to or interaction with the others. In 2012, APA joined multiple other disciplines (e.g., pharmacy, nursing, medical colleges, dentistry) in endorsing *Core Competencies for Interprofessional Collaborative Practice* (Interprofessional Education Collaborative, 2016; Interprofessional Education Collaborative Expert Panel, 2011). APA adopted as policy specific established competencies for all health service psychologists in a blueprint for psychology education and training (Health Service Psychology Education Collaborative, 2013). The policy includes being knowledgeable about core competencies for interprofessional practice, ethics, communication, roles, and teamwork, applying those competencies in collaborative practice, and being knowledgeable about the outcomes literature and assessment of outcomes in health care delivery. APA joined the Interprofessional Education Collaborative in 2016 (APA, 2016). Additional competencies required for interprofessional behavior include communication skills, respectful interaction, altruism and caring, ethics, excellence, placing client care above hierarchies or professional issues, and accountability (adapted from Interprofessional Professionalism Collaborative, 2014). In this policy, as in our competency-based model, emphasis is on both processes *and* outcomes.

For all consultation practice, interprofessional practice competency is essential. Belar (2016) described barriers to such practice that are geographical, schedule related, and—we would add—strategic. Because professionals of different disciplines are housed separately and function on different schedules, coordination is difficult. Furthermore, faculty and supervisors may not be trained in interprofessional collaboration or may not see its proven or evidence-based value. Incorporating interprofessional practice into the vision of training and its essential competencies will require faculty and supervisor competence and a shift in practices away from silo-driven models. When working as part of an interdisciplinary treatment team in a hospital or other health care setting, it is essential to establish who has primary responsibility for the patient's care.

**Consultee-Focused Clinical Case Consultation**

In *consultee-focused clinical case consultation*, the aim is to understand and to remedy the consultee's work difficulties and enhance the consultee's effectiveness to meet his or her professional responsibilities to the client (Caplan, 1970, 2004). Selective attention is placed on the client, often including diagnosis, treatment plan, background, clinical interaction, and progress, to provide a context to understand the difficulties in the case. The emphasis is on "the professional work problems of the consultee, rather than on the condition of the client as a person in [his or her] own right" (Caplan & Caplan, 1993, p. 101). Such consultation may be sought when the consultee is experiencing a "work problem" (Caplan, 1970, p. 19) or when the consultee has limited experience with the clinical issues involved or implementation of the treatment protocol. Rather than conceptualizing such consultation issues summarily as consultee performance problems or deficits, we believe it is more useful to keep in mind and acknowledge the consultee's use of metacompetence in recognizing the limits of his or her competence and responding to the need to obtain consultation.

The consultation may focus on enhancing the consultee's knowledge and skills or may provide reassurance and bolster confidence in the consultee's abilities specific to the case. Obtaining a second opinion and consultation reflects professional judgment rather than deficiency. Also, given the proliferation (and advancement) of evidence-based assessment and treatments, it is likely that clinicians may wish to implement protocols that have received empirical support, though in which they have not received formal supervised training. Expert consultation in addition to continuing education, individual study, and training can provide the means for the consultee to implement cutting-edge treatments in an ethically responsible manner.

At times, problems can emerge in cases that compromise or challenge the consultee's objectivity and effectiveness and pose what Caplan (1970) identified as *theme interference*. Theme interference is akin to what is commonly referred to as *countertransference* and posits that the difficulties that the consultee is experiencing in the case are the result of the consultee's personal conflicts or reactions to the systemic context in which client and consultant are situated. These unconscious dynamics may result in subjective experiences of confusion, irritation, or "stuck-ness"; create false assumptions about the client; create pessimism about the likelihood of client improvement; and interfere with the consultee's use of his or her competence. The consultee incorrectly attributes the difficulties to the client and is unaware of his or her own contributions to the problem. Consultants draw attention to clinical factors, inconsistencies, and biases that appear to be negatively affecting the consultee's perception and performance but refrain from engaging in a therapeutic process with the consultee, although, in some instances, the consultant could empathically suggest that the consultee may wish to seek out personal assistance to manage the intensity of the emotional response or impact on the consultee's functioning. It is essential that the consultant not cross the boundary and conduct personal therapy to the consultee.

## Consultee-Focused Professional Development

*Consultee-focused professional development* is distinguished from other forms of consultation, given its focus on developing and enhancing competence that is intended to be applied across multiple cases, populations, or clients, rather than having a focus on a single client or individual. It may take the form of consultation with a consultee, who, in turn, has the responsibility of developing and implementing training to other professionals in the work environment. Or, the consultant may deliver education and training and develop and implement a program of continuing professional development.

Although formal continuing education and professional development are underrepresented in the consultation literature, we believe it is useful to place such activities under consultation, given the distinct need of ongoing individual or group consultation, to ensure skill development, for example, in the implementation of evidence-based treatments. This type of consultation is particularly relevant to HSP when considering the diminishing durability of professional knowledge (Neimeyer & Taylor, 2014) and the ethical requirement to maintain competence throughout one's professional career (see Standard 2.03 in *Ethical Principles of Psychologists and Code of Conduct* [APA, 2017a], which involves the incorporation and updating of new knowledge and skills). It is sobering to learn that informed opinion concludes that the "half-life"[1] of professional knowledge "was expected to decrease within the next decade from nearly 9 years to just over 7 years, with substantial variability across various specialties and proficiencies" (Neimeyer, Taylor, & Rozensky, 2012, p. 364) and to shrink in every area of specialization to as little as 5.61 years (in clinical health psychology) within a decade from now (Neimeyer, Taylor, Rozensky, & Cox, 2014, p. 92). These predictions underscore the importance of formal continuing education and consultation as components of lifelong learning (Neimeyer & Taylor, 2014; Taylor & Neimeyer, 2016).

Educational programs are generally sufficient to disseminate new knowledge; however, the development of competence requires supervised practice, including additional training and supervision or consultation (Herschell, Kolko, Baumann, & Davis, 2010; Herschell, Reed, Person Mecca, & Kolko, 2014; Jackson, Herschell, Schaffner, Turiano, & McNeil, 2017; McLeod et al., 2018). Web-based and face-to-face training, followed by *formal case consultation*, are recommended to become proficient in evidence-based treatments (Fritz et al., 2013). The evolving literature in implementation science suggests the relevance of two forms of consultation: *organizational intervention* for improving the social context of mental health services (Aarons et al., 2012; Raghavan, Bright, & Shadoin, 2008) and *ongoing clinical consultation*, which has consistently been identified as pivotal in the effective dissemination of evidence-based treatments (Edmunds, Beidas, & Kendall, 2013). The Longitudinal Education for Advanced Practice (LEAP) model (Kendall, Crane, & Phillips, 2018), a promising, science-informed theoretical model for clinician training, identifies the role of consultation in the development of procedural knowledge, which is integral to

---

[1]*Half-life* has been described as the length of time it takes a practicing professional—without any new learning—to become roughly half as knowledgeable or competent to practice, owing to the generation of new knowledge within the field (Dubin, 1972).

the ability to apply new knowledge and metacognitive skills to novel clinical situations (McLeod et al., 2018). Research and training in consultation aimed at professional development are essential to efforts to maintain competence and advance the professional practice.

### Client-Focused Community Organizational Consultation

Communities and organizations, including social services agencies, public institutions, and private companies, can also be the focus of consultation within HSP. Psychological consultation to industry with attention placed on work, human performance, organizational processes, teamwork, and leadership has historically been in the wheelhouse of consulting psychology. However, consultation focusing on wellness promotion in communities or organizations, antibullying campaigns in schools, or programs to address stigma within the public sector are examples of projects aligned with the clinical interests and expertise in HSP. Caplan's (1970) early contributions included "program-centered administrative consultation," which aimed to assist in the "area of planning and administration—how to develop a new program or to improve an existing one" (p. 33).

Psychological consultants bring psychological knowledge and expertise in assessment and intervention approaches to assist the consultee to develop a plan to fulfill the objectives of the agency, organization, government department, school, or religious institution initiating the program. This assistance may involve knowledge specific to the program's area of focus; in school-based antibullying campaigns, for example, child and adolescent development and social psychology would be two of the content domains relevant to such a project. Consultants might also assist in the development of materials and offer advice on intervention approaches specific to the intended clients or consumers of the services while being mindful of the community or cultural or diversity context. In some instances, consultants might serve as active contributors in the implementation of the program; in the preceding antibullying campaigns example, they might serve as presenters or guest speakers in a school- or community-based public health program.

### Consultee-Focused Community Organizational Consultation

Analogous to consultee-focused clinical case consultation, in *consultee-focused community organizational consultation*, the focus is on the consultee rather than on the client. Psychological consultation may be sought to enhance the effectiveness of program leadership, assist in team building, provide training to staff or volunteers who will be coordinating and implementing the program, or assist in the development of tools to evaluate the effectiveness of the program. Consultants may also be brought in to address conflicts within the program or barriers to its success. Consultation may be directed to a specific program or may focus more broadly on the organizational unit providing services within the community or within a company or public agency. The aim of consultation is to enable consultees to plan thoughtfully and to work collaboratively with competent leadership to accomplish the organization's mission and goals.

## Peer Consultation

Peer consultation is different from the types of consultation previously discussed. Consultation as formally defined involves consultation from an expert; however, *peer consultation* does not involve a formally designated expert; rather, it draws on the shared expertise within a group of professionals. As such, it should not be confused with formal consultation or group peer supervision (despite certain similarities; Shah & Rodolfa, 2016). Peer consultation is a distinct practice. Consultation groups may or may not have a leader and may have flexible and variable formats (Thomas, 2010). Such consultation groups allow for a fluid exchange of roles among members: informally constituting consultees and consultants and shifting functional relationships as learners and experts. Drawing on the competence constellation model (Johnson, Barnett, Elman, Forrest, & Kaslow, 2013), peer consultation groups offer the potential of forming "a cluster of relationships with people who take an active interest in and engage in action to advance a professional's well-being and professional competence" (Johnson et al., 2013, p. 343).

In consultation groups, the consultant may be one individual or each member may serve as consultants to the other group members. None assumes responsibility for the clients or cases presented, but each simply provides reflection and input. Composition of peer consultation groups include professionals potentially from a single discipline or a combination of psychology, medicine, mental health, and allied health professions who meet without a leader to discuss cases and learn from the expertise and perspective of others. Generally, peer consultation groups have a fixed membership; however, some are open. Also, technology-assisted peer consultation can be offered in rural settings and provides support and accessible networking and opportunities for professional growth while decreasing isolation (Paulson, Casile, & Jones, 2015).

In all settings, individuals comply with the ethical standards of their professions, ensuring for example, client confidentiality. Other consultation group rules may be formulated, including a respectful process, resolution of conflicts that might arise in the group, and cell phone use. Professional consultation groups are protective, enhance practice, provide valuable feedback, and potentially lead to a higher level of professional services (Knapp, VandeCreek, & Fingerhut, 2017). However, some concern might be warranted in that interpersonal factors, group dynamics, and the equal status of group members could interfere with the ability to be direct in communicating and in obtaining useful feedback and support. Given the possibility of providing critical or constructive feedback to participants who are presenting cases, fearing strain or rupture to relationships, being protective, or simply feeling the need to be socially correct and positive, accurate, constructive feedback may not be offered, and the effectiveness of the peer consultation would be compromised.

Agreement exists that postlicensure support of clinical work, self-care, and general maintenance of competence are needed. Peer consultation, a more personal, connected, and often case-specific process, may present a conduit to address and reduce impact of multiple challenges, including traumatic and challenging case presentations, societal and practice stressors, and emerging research and innovative practices. Peer consultation is perceived by psychologists queried to be an effective means of continuing professional development and a significant contributor to professional competence (Neimeyer, Taylor, & Cox, 2012). Peers may assist as a part of ethical decision making when faced with an ethical or clinical dilemma (Gottlieb, 2006). Peer consultation groups focusing on supervision competence may be particularly useful in supporting the development of supervisors (Granello, Kindsvatter, Granello, Underfer-Babalis, & Hartwig Moorhead, 2008). Consultation serves a number of important functions and is included in the APA Ethics Code (APA, 2017a) in multiple places, including Standard 2.01, Boundaries of Competence; a means to attain competence; and 4.06, confidentiality standards in consultation.

Internationally, peer consultation for psychologists is a regulatory requirement. The *Health Practitioner Regulation National Law Act 2009* of the Psychology Board of Australia requires each psychologist to complete and document 10 hours of peer consultation per year as part of that psychologist's mandatory continuing professional development. The board defined peer consultation as "supervision and consultation in individual or group format, for the purposes of professional development and support in the practice of psychology and includes a critically reflective focus on the psychologist's own practice" (Psychology Board of Australia, n.d., p. 3). In the United Kingdom, peer consultation is described as a part of working in teams for applied psychologists (The British Psychological Society, 2007). Because there is no requirement or structure in the United States beyond continuing education requirements for clinical supervision or support postlicensure, peer consultation is an excellent mechanism for maintaining and increasing competence, perspective, and lifelong learning.

## DISTINCTIVE FEATURES OF CONSULTATION

Consultation is distinguished from clinical supervision and other forms of education and training in HSP, as shown in Table 1.2. The quintessential difference between consultation and supervision concerns the legal responsibility for the client. The consultee bears the full responsibility for all decisions regarding the client, including incorporation of the information, opinion, and advice provided by the consultant in the client's care as well as decision making regarding the implementation of the consultant's recommendations. No matter the expertise or professional standing of the consultant or how convincing the consultant's claims are, the consultee has the responsibility to make an independent and informed decision regarding the client's care. There are multiple reasons

**TABLE 1.2. Comparisons of Clinical Supervision, Consultation, and Peer Consultation**

| Profession activity | Clinical supervision | Type of service — Consultation | Peer consultation or peer consultation group |
|---|---|---|---|
| Roles | Supervisor–supervisee | Consultant–consultee | Colleague(s) |
| Initiation | Supervisor is responsible for initiating and providing | Consultee initiates | Peer consultee or group members initiate |
| Agenda setting | Collaborative; however, supervisor has the obligation to ensure appropriate focus and use of supervision | Primary responsibility of consultee | By peer consultee or group members |
| Process | Collaborative; however, given the legal responsibility, supervisor has the obligation to facilitate a process that allows for overview and training | Collaborative; however, the consultee has the responsibility to ensure consultation questions are addressed | Collaborative |
| Personal reactions | Inquiry into supervisee's personal reactions should be initiated only when affecting client care | Consultant does not initiate inquiry into the consultee's personal reactions | Peer presenting as consultee initiates inquiry |
| Expertise | Supervisor has appropriate expertise to oversee conduct supervision | Consultant possesses competence and expertise appropriate to address the consultation questions | May include peers with similar or different levels of expertise |

| | | | |
|---|---|---|---|
| Hierarchy in relationship | Supervisor exercises authority over the supervisee and performs oversight and evaluative functions | Although the consultant's standing and expertise may suggest a hierarchical relationship, consultant and consultee are equals in the consultation process | Coequal peers, nonhierarchical in structure |
| Legal responsibility | Supervisor is responsible for the client's welfare and conduct of all services performed under supervision | Consultee has sole responsibility for the client | Peer consultee has sole responsibility for the client |
| Mandating requirements | Supervisor and supervisee | Consultee has sole responsibility because, ordinarily, the consultant has no direct contact with the client | Peer consultee has sole responsibility |
| Professional responsibility | Collaborative; however, the supervisor bears the legal and professional responsibilities | Collaborative; however, the consultant has the professional responsibility for the accuracy and relevance of the information conveyed and recommendations offered | Collaborative; however, the peer consultant has the professional responsibility for the accuracy and relevance of the information conveyed and recommendations offered |
| Decision making | Collaborative; however, the supervisor bears the legal responsibility for the conduct of the professional services | Consultee is solely responsible for decision making, including implementation of the consultant's recommendations | Peer consultee is solely responsible for decision making |
| Case management | Collaborative; however, the supervisor bears the legal responsibility for the conduct of the professional services | Consultee is solely responsible for decision making in case management | Peer consultee is solely responsible for decision making in case management |

for this determination of responsibility. The professional responsibility for the client is established in the consent to treatment agreed to by the client and is not suspended or altered by involvement of a consultant. The consultee has the responsibility to determine the use of the information provided in the consultant's report, including decisions regarding implementation of the consultant's recommendations.

Therefore, one might ask, Does the consultant bear any responsibility? The consultant, based on professional ethics and law, has the obligation to practice within his or her scope of practice, to accurately present his or her qualifications and expertise specific to the requirements of the consultation, and to conduct the examination or assessment in a competent manner by providing an informed opinion based on the consultant's qualifications and experience.

Also, consultants have limited knowledge and experience of the client, given the specificity of the consultation, and do not have the complete picture of the client, including history, background, context, and multicultural factors. Given these limitations, the consultant does not have sufficient experience of the client or a comprehensive understanding to make final clinical decisions regarding the client's treatment.

Confusion regarding the responsibility for the case may be caused by a number of factors. Given that the consultant is an expert (or possesses greater competence regarding the consultation issue), a misunderstanding or misattribution of hierarchical status may create confusion regarding who is responsible for clinical decision making. Although the consultant ordinarily has greater expertise (and perhaps professional standing) than the consultee, the consultee nevertheless has more comprehensive understanding of the case and bears the legal responsibility (and liability), given the client's informed consent. Also, the consultee may misapply the nature of consultation with an incorrect analogy to supervision. In supervision, the supervisor bears responsibility for client welfare and clinical decision making, is in a hierarchical position in respect to the supervisee, evaluates the supervisee, and directs the supervisee's work. Although the consultant possesses greater expertise, consultation is not supervision, and the aforementioned features of the power differential in supervision do not apply. The distinction between consultation and supervision provides clear guidance: The consultee bears the full responsibility for clinical decision making and client welfare.

When consultation is provided in the context of clinical training, trainees may become confused about the distinctions between consultation and supervision. Trainees may errantly assume that when their supervisors suggest they seek consultation with another member of the clinical faculty, they should implement the consultant's recommendations. The supervisee should be directed to bring the input and recommendations obtained in the consultation to the supervisor, who will then make the final determination regarding the implementation of the consultant's recommendations. It is extremely valuable for trainees to receive consultation as well as to provide consultation under direct supervision to assist in developing competence in consultation. We turn now to a more detailed discussion of legal and ethical considerations.

## LEGAL AND ETHICAL CONSIDERATIONS

Generally, consultants have limited liability compared with clinical supervisors. To ensure that limited liability, it is essential that the terms of the consultation be clear. Use of an agreement or contract provides clarity and reduces the likelihood of misunderstandings. The consultation contract does not have to be overly comprehensive; however, the consultant should ensure that the contract corresponds to what the consultation will actually entail. The consultant should clearly state that the decision whether to implement the consultation input lies solely with the consultee, ensuring that the statement corresponds to both the reality of the setting and the legal and ethical standards.

The consultation should be terminated if the limits of the consultant's competence or expertise are reached, the task is completed, or when the consultation does not correspond to the stated needs of the setting. An exception would be if the consultation contract were to be renegotiated. Unforeseen events may occur in the course of consultation. For example, in a school, a consultant might identify a suicidal or homicidal child, even though that was not the consultant's designated role. The agreement should have clarity that psychologists have the obligation to disclose particular information to the proper authorities and abide by legal and ethical standards and codes when functioning in the school setting (e.g., child abuse and duty to warn). It would be important to know the consultee's procedure for such instances and ensure that the consultee understands the consultant's professional responsibilities.

Consultants may incur peripheral involvement via their school, organization, or other consultation venue, which exposes them to legal risk or court cases (Brown et al., 2011). It is important to have clarity about privilege and its limits. In addition, the consultant should have knowledge of the laws governing the workplace in which the consultation occurs or intersects. Knowledge might include, for example, state and federal statutes as well as contextual laws for each setting (e.g., Health Insurance Portability and Accountability Act of 1996; Americans With Disabilities Act of 1990 [Falender, Collins, & Shafranske, 2009]; the Individuals With Disabilities Education Act of 1990).

The consultant should be sure that the consultee and consultant agree on the identification of the client in the consultation. This important aspect is well addressed in several chapters and should be a general part of consultation. In addition, consultants should address the issue that might arise if the interests of the organization do not coincide with that of the individual, for example, interests of child, teacher, or other leader in the setting. Furthermore, if, for example, an administrator initiated the consultation, the consultant should remain mindful of the task, ethical codes, and need to navigate and maintain integrity with the staff working under the administrator. Moreover, consultants should ensure that the consultation integrates organizational with individual staff priorities and values. If conflicts arise, the consultant should address them directly in the context of the consultation project because those conflicts may relate to the essence of the situation that prompted the consultation. The consultant should establish clarity regarding confidentiality. In some settings, client information may be disidentified, but in others, that is not possible. Consultants should consider need for client informed consent for consultation.

Temptations may arise that challenge ethical or legal standards; for example, there may be the temptation to become the decision maker rather than the person who fosters those skills in the consultee. Or, it might be tempting to extend consultation for financial gain or because the consultant has identified other areas to be addressed. Due to a lack of metacompetence, the consultant may be unaware of the limits of his or her ability to provide meaningful consultation and thus might find himself or herself consulting in areas outside of the agreed on area of consultation, losing objectivity (and this may not necessarily be related to multiple relationships) but resulting in failure to maintain the role of consultant and behaving like a leader or employee in the setting. In addition, the consultant may not build in evaluation procedures to ensure outcomes are consistently and regularly assessed and addressed.

Furthermore, if the consultant is working under supervision (as is the case of a trainee accruing hours for licensure), the supervisor of the consultation activity, as with any supervision, has the duty to ensure that the consultant is performing properly and within the agreed on parameters. Negligent supervision can result in direct liability to the supervisor of the consultation.

Consultation, consistent with all professional practices in HSP, involves careful consideration of contextual factors, including influences on the contents and conduct of the consultation, features of multicultural diversity and intersectionality affecting the client and consultee, the role of the sociocultural setting in which the consultation takes place, and potential use or misuse of the consultant's opinions or recommendations. Consideration of diversity and culture must be infused throughout the process of consultation (see Chapters 5 and 6, this volume).

The practice of consultation requires and is built on the expertise of the consultant. That requisite requires the consultant to practice within his or her scope of practice and to know the limits of his or her expertise. Although this is a requirement for all psychologists, it has particular consequence when a psychologist takes on the responsibility of providing *expert* opinion. Consultants need to be able to form an accurate appraisal of their competence and realistically determine the scope in which they are experts. Consultants are not experts in everything; indeed, such competence is unattainable. Skill in metacompetence (i.e., to know what one knows and does not know) is essential for ethical practice, particularly as a consultant. One must be mindful of *halo effects* in which a presumption is formed regarding the consultant's expertise outside of the competencies in which they have attained a high level of expertise. As health service psychologists expand into nontraditional areas, such as organizational consultation, it is important for them to recognize the limits of their education, training, and experience and to know those areas of consultation in which non-HSP psychologists may have particular expertise. We turn now to a brief discussion of history to elucidate the differences in orientation and training that are relevant to consultation practice.

## A HISTORICAL NOTE AND CAVEAT

The development and practice of consultation has been influenced by a number of interrelated historical, contextual, and discipline-specific factors. This volume focuses explicitly on consultation in HSP, which situates practice primarily within clinical, counseling, and school psychology specialties and, as such, is influenced by specific education and training requirements (e.g., accreditation standards), areas of practice, and career trajectories. Consulting psychology has existed in its own right as an applied practice, includes a unique history and development, comprises distinct competencies, and provides consultation generally outside of the clinical context and HSP (APA, 2017b; Hellkamp, 1993; Kilburg, 2016; O'Roark, 2007). Having familiarity with the differences in approach in HSP and consulting psychology is important, given the likely interface between consulting psychologists and health service psychologists, particularly when working with organizations and in corporate or health- or public service-related institutional settings. Although a detailed discussion of consulting psychology is outside of the scope of this chapter, the following presents a historical overview and highlights shared features and differences in approaches to consultation.

In 1897, at APA's 5th annual meeting, Lightner Witmer urged his academic colleagues to use their psychology to "throw light upon the problems that confronted humanity" (Witmer, 1897, p. 107, as cited in Benjamin, 2005, p. 5) and later called for training for a new profession: "that of a psychological expert" (Witmer, 1996, p. 249). This call echoed G. Stanley Hall's earlier call for a new psychology in education (Hall, 1894, as cited in Cautin & Baker, 2014, p. 18) and set the stage for the development of applied psychology, which would include both clinical practice and consultation, thus giving impetus to the emerging specialties of clinical psychology and consulting psychology. Interest in human behavior expanded beyond the academy, and its laboratories, and applied practice took root. Psychology broadened its scope to address societal issues and emergent needs, such as during times of war and its aftermath, as well as aimed to enhance its standing as a discipline and profession. Consultation was integral to these objectives.

Early in its history, APA (n.d.-a) was enjoined in debates about the qualifications of experts who provide authoritative opinions about human behavior, including commentary regarding America's entry into World War I. APA leadership convened the "Committee of Five" under the Whipple Resolution, which led to the formal recognition of clinical psychology and consulting psychology and eventuated in the formation of sections and, later, the establishment of the divisions of clinical psychology and consulting psychology. Although the fields of clinical psychology and consulting psychology were acknowledged, a review of history finds a divide between these two groups, despite common interests held in common.

Psychology experienced tremendous growth during and after World War II, including the founding of the American Association of Applied Psychology and the American Association of Clinical Psychologists. The leaders of APA, "realizing that the growth of applied psychology [outside of APA] represented a potential threat to its preeminence," reorganized the association during World War II. Under this reorganization plan, APA merged with other psychological organizations; the result was a broader association organized around "an increasingly diffuse conceptualization of psychology" (APA, n.d.-a). This development encouraged the creation of new divisions, which in turn became centers of influence and affiliation and resulted in a "pattern of progressive differentiation" in APA and within divisions (Dewsbury, 1997, p. 737).

The trajectories in the development of broadly conceived applied clinical psychology (today referred to as *health service psychology*) and consulting psychology were distinctive. Consultation based on clinical and educational theory, research, and application emphasized the model of a clinic that provides assessment and interventions primarily to individuals and families (Benjamin, 2005). With the impetus of community psychology (Bloom, 1973), efforts were extended to interventions and consultation to enhance the effectiveness of community-based clinics, public health initiatives, and mental health and social services agencies (see Caplan & Caplan, 1993, and Trickett, 1993, for further discussion of community-centered consultation). Increased specialization with HSP and the contexts in which consultation was offered—for example, schools, hospitals, criminal justice—played a role in shaping contemporary consultation practice. Consultation plays a central role in certain specialties in HSP, such as pediatric psychology or clinical neuropsychology, and psychologists trained in those specialties often obtain considerable discipline- or specialization-specific experience in consultation during the course of their clinical training, which results in a high degree of variability of experience and in expertise in consultation practice within HSP.

Any discussion of history would be incomplete without referencing the contributions of Gerald Caplan (1970; see also Caplan, Caplan, & Erchul, 1994; Erchul, 2009, 1993/2015). In his 1970 text *The Theory and Practice of Mental Health Consultation*, Caplan described the various types of consultation and the fundamentals of practice and established consultation as a professional practice. Relevant to this volume, Caplan applied consultation in multiple settings to individuals (e.g., clinical case consultation) as well as organizations (community-based organizations; see Chapter 2, this volume, for the application of Caplan's foundational principles).

Consulting psychology took a different path, based, in part, on its focus on the psychological aspects of work and organizational process. Kilburg (2016) reminded us that during the first 5 decades (1897–1947), clinical psychology was subsumed in the larger domain of applied psychology rather than primarily as a health care profession, a feature of history that is often overlooked (see also Benjamin, 2005; Capshew, 1999). Furthermore, "despite the successful rise and seeming domination of the health care version of clinical psychology, many clinically trained psychologists have contributed to the robust growth of a more generalist practice of applied psychology" (Kilburg, 2016, p. 526), such as found in consulting psychology and in the specialization of industrial-organizational psychology. These psychologists provide consultation to industry and in corporate settings; that consultation is especially related to work, human factors, human performance, organizational development, leadership, and emerging applications in coaching (APA, 2017b; Mahoney, Buboltz, Soper, Doverspike, & Simoneaux, 2008; O'Roark, 2007; Rigby, 1992). Consulting psychologists involve unique competencies and expertise in consultation.

When consultation in HSP is directed at systemic-level assessment and interventions aimed at organizational change, psychological training in HSP may be insufficient, and competencies found in consulting psychology may be required. Quoting from the original guidelines proposal of APA Division 13:

> Being an effective psychologist is not enough to be an effective consultant. There is a body of knowledge and skills unique to this particular application of psychology, and just graduating from a doctoral program in psychology does not [necessarily] prepare one to provide consultees with the best possible consulting services. (Kurpius, Fuqua, Gibson, Kurpius, & Froehle, 1995, p. 88)

Psychologists should be mindful of their competence and scope of practice in consultation (similar to their self-assessments in other areas of professional practice). Although most clinical psychology training programs do not expose students to the knowledge or skills used in organizational consulting—for example, technostructural and human process approaches and interventions—clinical psychologists can develop competence through formal education in non-psychology university departments or through continuing education programs (Kilburg, 2016). However, the transition from HSP to consulting psychology is not without its challenges. Liebowitz and Blattner (2015) provided comparisons between the two practice orientations and concluded that

> the field of consulting has become a magnet attracting many clinical psychologists into its fold. However, the field of clinical psychology is not organizational consulting. This career transition requires a basic shift in approach from clinical work to the practice of consulting (e.g., learning to sell one's services, doing homework on prospective clients, and dealing with rejection). This shift requires a self-assessment along lines that do not appear in clinical work but are revealed when consulting. (p. 159)

The intention of this historical note is to provide a context within which the reader can appreciate the various approaches to consultation existing within and outside of HSP.

## CONCLUSION

As we have discussed, consultation is a complex and highly diverse professional practice that serves many different kinds of clients in a range of settings. Consultation services aim to apply expertise to assist other professionals, advance care and welfare, and solve a variety of human problems through the perspective and resources of psychology as a science. No matter the specific nature of the consultation, competent practice is built on the principles discussed first in the book's Introduction, which emphasizes the importance of integrating a competency-based approach. Chapter 2 builds on these principles and the foundation of knowledge that is presented in this chapter.

## REFERENCES

Aarons, G. A., Glisson, C., Green, P. D., Hoagwood, K., Kelleher, K. J., Landsverk, J. A., Schoenwald, S., & the Research Network on Youth Mental Health. (2012). The organizational social context of mental health services and clinician attitudes toward evidence-based practice: A United States national study. *Implementation Science, 7,* 56–70. http://dx.doi.org/10.1186/1748-5908-7-56

American Psychological Association. (n.d.-a). *APA history.* Retrieved from http://www.apa.org/about/apa/archives/apa-history.aspx

American Psychological Association. (n.d.-b). *Consultation.* Retrieved from http://psycnet.apa.org/thesaurus/item?code=40680

American Psychological Association. (2016, February 22). *APA joins Interprofessional Education Collaborative* [Press release]. Retrieved from http://www.apa.org/news/press/releases/2016/02/interprofessional-education.aspx

American Psychological Association. (2017a). *Ethical principles of psychologists and code of conduct* (2002, Amended June 1, 2010, and January 1, 2017). Retrieved from http://www.apa.org/ethics/code/index.aspx

American Psychological Association. (2017b). *Guidelines for education and training at the doctoral and postdoctoral level in consulting psychology (CP)/organizational consulting psychology (OCP).* Retrieved from https://www.apa.org/about/policy/education-training.pdf

Americans With Disabilities Act of 1990, Pub. L. 101–336, 42 U.S.C. §§ 12101–12213.

Arredondo, P., Shealy, C., Neale, M., & Winfrey, L. L. (2004). Consultation and interprofessional collaboration: Modeling for the future. *Journal of Clinical Psychology, 60,* 787–800. http://dx.doi.org/10.1002/jclp.20015

Belar, C. D. (2016). Interprofessional education and training. In J. C. Norcross, G. R. VandenBos, D. K. Freedheim, & L. F. Campbell (Eds.), *APA handbook of clinical psychology: Education and profession* (Vol. 5, pp. 153–160). Washington, DC: American Psychological Association. http://dx.doi.org/10.1037/14774-010

Benjamin, L. T., Jr. (2005). A history of clinical psychology as a profession in America (and a glimpse at its future). *Annual Review of Clinical Psychology, 1,* 1–30. http://dx.doi.org/10.1146/annurev.clinpsy.1.102803.143758

Bloom, B. L. (1973). The domain of community psychology. *American Journal of Community Psychology, 1,* 8–11. http://dx.doi.org/10.1007/BF00881242

The British Psychological Society. (2007). *New ways of working for applied psychologists in health and social care: Working psychologically in teams.* Retrieved from http://www.wiltshirepsychology.co.uk/Working%20Psychologically%20in%20Teams.pdf

Brown, D., Pryzwansky, W. B., & Schulte, A. C. (2011). *Psychological consultation and collaboration: Introduction to theory and practice* (7th ed.). Upper Saddle River, NJ: Pearson.

Caplan, G. (1970). *The theory and practice of mental health consultation.* New York, NY: Basic Books.

Caplan, G. (2004). Recent advances in mental health consultation and collaboration. In N. M. Lambert, I. Hylander, & J. H. Sandoval (Eds.), *Consultee-centered consultation: Improving the quality of professional services in schools and community organizations* (pp. 21–35). Mahwah, NJ: Erlbaum.

Caplan, G., & Caplan, R. B. (1993). *Mental health consultation and collaboration.* Prospect Heights, IL: Waveland Press.

Caplan, G., Caplan, R. B., & Erchul, W. P. (1994). Caplanian mental health consultation: Historical background and current status. *Consulting Psychology Journal: Practice and Research, 46,* 2–12. http://dx.doi.org/10.1037/1061-4087.46.4.2

Capshew, J. H. (1999). *Psychologists on the march: Science, practice, and professional identity in America, 1929–1969.* New York, NY: Cambridge University Press.

Cautin, R. L., & Baker, D. B. (2014). A history of education and training in professional psychology. In R. L. Cautin, D. B. Baker, W. B. Johnson, & N. J. Kaslow (Eds.), *The Oxford handbook of education and training in professional psychology* (pp. 17–32). New York, NY: Oxford University Press.

Dewsbury, D. A. (1997). On the evolution of divisions. *American Psychologist, 52,* 733–741. http://dx.doi.org/10.1037/0003-066X.52.7.733

Dubin, S. S. (1972). Obsolescence or lifelong education: A choice for the professional. *American Psychologist, 27,* 486–498. http://dx.doi.org/10.1037/h0033050

Edmunds, J. M., Beidas, R. S., & Kendall, P. C. (2013). Dissemination and implementation of evidence-based practices: Training and consultation as implementation strategies. *Clinical Psychology: Science and Practice, 20,* 152–165. http://dx.doi.org/10.1111/cpsp.12031

Erchul, W. P. (2009). Gerald Caplan: A tribute to the originator of mental health consultation. *Journal of Educational and Psychological Consultation, 19,* 95–105. http://dx.doi.org/10.1080/10474410902888418

Erchul, W. P. (Ed.). (2015). *Consultation in community, school, and organizational practice. Gerald Caplan's contributions to professional psychology.* New York, NY: Routledge. (Original work published 1993)

Falender, C. A., Collins, C. J., & Shafranske, E. P. (2009). "Impairment" and performance issues in clinical supervision: After the 2008 ADA Amendments Act. *Training and Education in Professional Psychology, 3,* 240–249.

Fredman, G., Papadopoulou, A., & Worwood, E. (Eds.). (2018). *Collaborative consultation in mental health: Guidelines for the new consultant.* New York, NY: Routledge. http://dx.doi.org/10.4324/9781315696652

Fritz, R. M., Tempel, A. B., Sigel, B. A., Conners-Burrow, N. A., Worley, K. B., & Kramer, T. L. (2013). Improving the dissemination of evidence-based treatments: Facilitators and barriers to participating in case consultation. *Professional Psychology: Research and Practice, 44,* 225–230. http://dx.doi.org/10.1037/a0033102

Gallessich, J. (1982). *The profession and practice of consultation: A handbook for consultants, trainers of consultants, and consumers of consultation services.* San Francisco, CA: Jossey-Bass.

Gottlieb, M. C. (2006). A template for peer ethics consultation. *Ethics & Behavior, 16,* 151–162. http://dx.doi.org/10.1207/s15327019eb1602_5

Granello, D. H., Kindsvatter, A., Granello, P. F., Underfer-Babalis, J., & Hartwig Moorhead, H. J. (2008). Multiple perspectives in supervision: Using a peer consultation model to enhance supervisor development. *Counselor: Education and Supervision, 48,* 32–47. http://dx.doi.org/10.1002/j.1556-6978.2008.tb00060.x

Hall, G. S. (1894). The new psychology as a basis of education. *Forum, 17,* 710–720.

Health Insurance Portability and Accountability Act of 1996 (HIPAA), Pub. L. 104–191, 42 U.S.C. § 300gg, 29 U.S.C. §§ 1181–1183, and 42 U.S.C. §§ 1320d–1320d9.

Health Service Psychology Education Collaborative. (2013). Professional psychology in health care services: A blueprint for education and training. *American Psychologist, 68,* 411–426. http://dx.doi.org/10.1037/a0033265

Hellkamp, D. T. (1993). History of the Division of Consulting Psychology: 1972–1992. *Consulting Psychology Journal: Practice and Research, 45,* 1–8. http://dx.doi.org/10.1037/1061-4087.45.1.1

Herschell, A. D., Kolko, D. J., Baumann, B. L., & Davis, A. C. (2010). The role of therapist training in the implementation of psychosocial treatments: A review and critique with recommendations. *Clinical Psychology Review, 30,* 448–466. http://dx.doi.org/10.1016/j.cpr.2010.02.005

Herschell, A. D., Reed, A. J., Person Mecca, L., & Kolko, D. J. (2014). Community-based clinicians' preferences for training in evidence-based practices: A mixed-method study. *Professional Psychology: Research and Practice, 45,* 188–199. http://dx.doi.org/10.1037/a0036488

Individuals With Disabilities Education Act of 1990, Pub. L. 101–476, renamed the Individuals With Disabilities Education Improvement Act, codified at 20 U.S.C. §§ 1400–1482.

Interprofessional Education Collaborative. (2016). *Core competencies for interprofessional collaborative practice: 2016 update.* Washington, DC: Interprofessional Education Collaborative. Retrieved from https://nebula.wsimg.com/2f68a39520b03336b41038c370497473?AccessKeyId=DC06780E69ED19E2B3A5&disposition=0&alloworigin=1

Interprofessional Education Collaborative Expert Panel. (2011). *Core competencies for interprofessional collaborative practice: Report of an expert panel.* Washington, DC: Interprofessional Education Collaborative. Retrieved from https://nebula.wsimg.com/3ee8a4b5b5f7ab794c742b14601d5f23?AccessKeyId=DC06780E69ED19E2B3A5&disposition=0&alloworigin=1

Interprofessional Professionalism Collaborative. (2014). *Behaviors: Interprofessional professionalism behaviors.* Retrieved from http://www.interprofessionalprofessionalism.org/behaviors.html

Jackson, C. B., Herschell, A. D., Schaffner, K. F., Turiano, N. A., & McNeil, C. B. (2017). Training community-based clinicians in parent–child interaction therapy: The interaction between expert consultation and caseload. *Professional Psychology: Research and Practice, 48,* 481–489. http://dx.doi.org/10.1037/pro0000149

Johnson, W. B., Barnett, J. E., Elman, N. S., Forrest, L., & Kaslow, N. J. (2013). The competence constellation model: A communitarian approach to support professional competence. *Professional Psychology: Research and Practice, 44,* 343–354. http://dx.doi.org/10.1037/a0033131

Kendall, P. C., Crane, M. E., & Phillips, K. E. (2018). LEAPing ahead in clinical training. *Clinical Psychology: Science and Practice, 25,* e12261. http://dx.doi.org/10.1111/cpsp.12261

Kilburg, R. R. (2016). Consultation. In J. C. Norcross, G. R. VandenBos, D. K. Freedheim, R. Krishnamurthy, J. C. Norcross, G. R. VandenBos, & R. Krishnamurthy (Eds.), *APA handbook of clinical psychology: Applications and methods* (pp. 525–535). Washington, DC: American Psychological Association. http://dx.doi.org/10.1037/14861-028

Knapp, S. J., VandeCreek, L. D., & Fingerhut, R. (2017). Ethical decision making. In S. J. Knapp, L. D. VandeCreek, & R. Fingerhut, *Practical ethics for psychologists: A positive approach* (pp. 39–50). Washington, DC: American Psychological Association. http://dx.doi.org/10.1037/0000036-003

Kurpius, S. E. R., Fuqua, D. R., Gibson, G., Kurpius, D. J., & Froehle, T. C. (1995). An occupational analysis of consulting psychology: Results of a national survey. *Consulting Psychology Journal: Practice and Research, 47,* 75–88. http://dx.doi.org/10.1037/1061-4087.47.2.75

Liebowitz, B., & Blattner, J. (2015). On becoming a consultant: The transition for a clinical psychologist. *Consulting Psychology Journal: Practice and Research, 67,* 144–161. http://dx.doi.org/10.1037/cpb0000037

Lipsitt, D. R. (2016). *Foundations of consultation-liaison psychiatry: The bumpy road to specialization.* New York, NY: Routledge. http://dx.doi.org/10.4324/9781315695600

Mahoney, K. T., Buboltz, W. J., Soper, B., Doverspike, D., & Simoneaux, B. J. (2008). Content analysis of *Consulting Psychology Journal: Practice and Research* (Vols. 44–59). *Consulting Psychology Journal: Practice and Research, 60,* 246–258. http://dx.doi.org/10.1037/a0013137

McLeod, B. D., Cox, J. R., Jensen-Doss, A., Herschell, A., Ehrenreich-May, J., & Wood, J. J. (2018). Proposing a mechanistic model of clinician training and consultation. *Clinical Psychology: Science and Practice, 25,* e12260. http://dx.doi.org/10.1111/cpsp.12260

Neimeyer, G. J., & Taylor, J. M. (2014). Ten trends in lifelong learning and continuing professional development. In W. B. Johnson & N. J. Kaslow (Eds.), *The Oxford handbook of education and training in professional psychology* (pp. 214–234). New York, NY: Oxford University Press. http://dx.doi.org/10.1093/oxfordhb/9780199874019.013.010

Neimeyer, G. J., Taylor, J. M., & Cox, D. R. (2012). On hope and possibility: Does continuing professional development contribute to ongoing professional competence? *Professional Psychology: Research and Practice, 43,* 476–486. http://dx.doi.org/10.1037/a0029613

Neimeyer, G. J., Taylor, J. M., & Rozensky, R. H. (2012). The diminishing durability of knowledge in professional psychology: A Delphi Poll of specialties and proficiencies. *Professional Psychology: Research and Practice, 43,* 364–371. http://dx.doi.org/10.1037/a0028698

Neimeyer, G. J., Taylor, J. M., Rozensky, R. H., & Cox, D. R. (2014). The diminishing durability of knowledge in professional psychology: A second look at specializations. *Professional Psychology: Research and Practice, 45,* 92–98. http://dx.doi.org/10.1037/a0036176

O'Roark, A. M. (2007). The best of consulting psychology 1900–2000: Insider perspectives. *Consulting Psychology Journal: Practice and Research, 59,* 189–202. http://dx.doi.org/10.1037/1065-9293.59.3.189

Paulson, L. R., Casile, W. J., & Jones, D. (2015). Tech it out: Implementing an online peer consultation network for rural mental health professionals. *Journal of Rural Mental Health, 39,* 125–136. http://dx.doi.org/10.1037/rmh0000034

Psychology Board of Australia. (n.d.). *Guidelines on continuing professional development.* Retrieved from https://www.psychologyboard.gov.au/documents/default.aspx?record=WD10%2F271%5Bv3%5D&dbid=AP&chksum=e3E96c7g%2BS8Iw135bnsVPw%3D%3D

Raghavan, R., Bright, C. L., & Shadoin, A. L. (2008). Toward a policy ecology of implementation of evidence-based practices in public mental health settings. *Implementation Science, 3,* 26. http://dx.doi.org/10.1186/1748-5908-3-26

Rigby, W. K. (1992). History, 1924 to 1972, of the Division of Consulting Psychology. *Consulting Psychology Journal: Practice and Research, 44,* 2–8.

Sears, R. W., Rudisill, J. R., & Mason-Sears, C. (2006). *Consultation skills for mental health professionals.* Hoboken, NJ: Wiley.

Shah, S., & Rodolfa, E. (2016). Peer supervision and support. In J. C. Norcross, G. R. VandenBos, D. K. Freedheim, & L. F. Campbell (Eds.), *APA handbook of clinical psychology: Education and profession* (pp. 197–207). Washington, DC: American Psychological Association. http://dx.doi.org/10.1037/14774-013

Taylor, J. M., & Neimeyer, G. J. (2016). Continuing education and lifelong learning. In J. C. Norcross, G. R. VandenBos, D. K. Freedheim, & L. F. Campbell (Eds.), *APA handbook of clinical psychology: Education and profession* (pp. 135–152). Washington, DC: American Psychological Association. http://dx.doi.org/10.1037/14774-009

Thomas, J. T. (2010). *The ethics of supervision and consultation: Practical guidance for mental health professionals.* Washington, DC: American Psychological Association. http://dx.doi.org/10.1037/12078-000

Trickett, E. J. (1993). Gerald Caplan and the unfinished business of community psychology: A comment. In W. P. Erchul (Eds.), *Consultation in community, school, and organizational practice: Gerald Caplan's contributions to professional psychology* (pp. 163–175). Philadelphia, PA: Taylor & Francis.

Witmer, L. (1897). The organization of practical work in psychology. *Psychological Review, 4,* 116–117.

Witmer, L. (1996). Clinical psychology: Reprint of Witmer's 1907 article. *American Psychologist, 51,* 248–251. http://dx.doi.org/10.1037/0003-066X.51.3.248

# 2

# The Competency Framework

## Best Practices in Consultation

Carol A. Falender and Edward P. Shafranske

Consultation has been identified as one of the six functional competency domains in professional psychology (Rodolfa et al., 2005). It is a distinct professional practice that requires the competence of the consultant and the consultee and leads to the mutual creation of a collaborative and effective working relationship. It builds on the groundwork of the foundational competencies of (a) reflective practice–self-assessment, (b) scientific knowledge–methods, (c) relationships, (d) ethical–legal standards–policy, (e) individual–cultural diversity, and (f) interdisciplinary systems (Rodolfa et al., 2005), each of which is essential in consultation practice.

Our emphasis on consultation as a distinct practice underscores our position that a unique assemblage of knowledge, skills, and attitudes (KSA) is necessary. Transforming to competency-based consultation requires understanding of not simply competence but the structure and interrelationships of KSA and their role in the complex intentional formulation and implementation of the consultation process (e.g., relationship, content, multicultural factors).

Furthermore, the KSA used in consultation are not equivalent to the competencies used in other areas of applied psychology practice; therefore, it should not be assumed that competence is readily transferable simply by virtue of clinical expertise, for example, or assimilation (i.e., having received consultation from others). Consultation, like other competencies, requires education and training obtained in graduate school and clinical training (as required by the American Psychological Association's [APA's] *Standards of Accreditation for*

http://dx.doi.org/10.1037/0000153-003
*Consultation in Psychology: A Competency-Based Approach*, C. A. Falender and
E. P. Shafranske (Editors)

*Health Service Psychology*; APA, Commission on Accreditation, 2018) or, after licensure, through independent study, training, consultation, and supervised practice. In this chapter, we highlight the domains of KSA that are incorporated in consultation and present an outline or blueprint of consultation practice that incorporates a competency framework to support education and training and to furnish a reference tool or scaffold to identify best practices when providing consultation.[1] It is intended that this chapter be read with the other chapters in the Foundations of Consultation Practice (Part I) section to provide a comprehensive understanding of consultation.

## COMPETENCE IN CONSULTATION

Competence has always been relevant to the applied practice of psychology (Rubin et al., 2007); however, focus has been galvanized with the development of accreditation standards (Altmaier, 2003), the contemporary "zeitgeist of accountability for professionals" (Fouad & Grus, 2014, p. 105; Nelson, 2007), and the need for quality assurance (Altmaier, 2014) and objective assessment of outcomes in education (Roberts et al., 2005). Competence is among the "constellation of principles and values that inform psychology as a profession" (Falender & Shafranske, 2007, p. 232) and is a hallmark of effective consultation. Our approach is aligned with competency-based education and training (Hatcher et al., 2013) and affirms that competence is not attained simply by completing course work or clinical training but requires demonstration of the use of specific KSA essential to the practice of consultation.

There are many definitions of competence, such as by Epstein and Hundert (2002); however, for our purposes, we begin with Kaslow's (2004) perspective: "Competence refers to an individual's capability and demonstrated ability to understand and do certain tasks in an appropriate and effective manner consistent with the expectations for a person qualified by education and training in a particular profession or specialty" (p. 775). The consultant therefore must be qualified and possess expertise in the consultation subject area as well as understand and perform the tasks involved in the process of consultation. Furthermore, "competence is not an absolute . . . rather [it] reflects sufficiency of a broad spectrum of personal and professional abilities relative to a given requirement" (Falender & Shafranske, 2004, p. 5). In the context of consultation, given the varied nature of the presenting questions, issues, contexts, goals, and so on,

---

[1] Our recommendations are informed by many different sources, including the foundational contributions of Caplan (1970) and colleagues (e.g., Caplan & Caplan, 1993; Erchul, 1993); material drawn from specific areas of consultation practice, for example, school consultation (e.g., Brown, Pryzwansky, & Schulte, 2011; Erchul & Martens, 2010); consultation texts (e.g., Fredman, Papadopoulou, & Worwood, 2018; Scott, Royal, & Kissinger, 2015; Sears, Rudisill, & Mason-Sears, 2006); contributors to this volume; the theoretical and research literature; and our own experiences as consultants, consultees, and supervisors of consultation.

competence is based on the capability to fulfill the unique requirements of the specific consultation request. An expert might be highly suitable for one assignment and not the best fit for another; for example, a neuropsychology expert might be outstanding in hospital consultation but less so if contracted to serve as an expert witness in a legal proceeding, which often requires skills beyond clinical assessment. Therefore, competence is not static; rather, it is dynamic and reflects best practices adapted to unique situations.

It is possible, however, to identify a baseline of expected abilities in consultation at different stages of training and professional development. Competency benchmarks for consultation were originally published in 2009 (Fouad et al., 2009) and provide a useful start to consider essential components and behavioral anchors of competence. We view the elaboration of behavioral elements in the Fouad et al. (2009) document to be an essential component of benchmarks that provides behavioral exemplars (see Table 2.1).

## COMPETENCY FRAMEWORK: KNOWLEDGE, SKILLS, AND ATTITUDES

Competence can be understood in terms of the KSA, which are assembled in the conduct of consultation. The "molecular" approach to competence (Falender & Shafranske, 2004, 2009) focuses on the constituent components of consultation and provides specificity, which is useful in education, training, evaluation, and self-assessment. Although KSA can be viewed as separate components, they are interrelated and incorporated into the practice of consultation; for example, knowledge is integral to skills and attitudes affect every aspect of the process of consultation. The following blueprint uses the KSA involved in clinical case consultation to illustrate the application of the competency-based framework. The principles presented are generally applicable to other types of consultation; however, additional knowledge and skills are required in other forms of consultation. For example, additional skills are required when providing consultee-focused professional development, such as skills in oral presentation or lecturing or in the development of education and training materials. We follow the convention of KSA; however, we begin our discussion by focusing on attitudes in consultation practice.

### Attitudes

In addition to the knowledge and skills that make up competence, attitudes contribute to the conduct and outcomes of consultation. Values influence the nature of the interpersonal, professional, and interprofessional engagement. Ethical principles, such as those found in the APA (2017) *Ethical Principles of Psychologists and Code of Conduct*—that is, Principle A: Beneficence and Non-maleficence, Principle B: Fidelity and Responsibility, Principle C: Integrity, Principle D: Justice, and Principle E: Respect for People's Rights and Dignity—provide

**TABLE 2.1. Competency Benchmarks in Consultation**

*Consultation:* The ability to provide expert guidance or professional assistance in response to a client's needs or goals.

| Developmental level | | |
| --- | --- | --- |
| **A. Role of consultant** | | |
| **Readiness for practicum** | **Readiness for internship** | **Readiness for entry to practice** |
| Essential component: | Essential component: | Essential component: |
| No expectation for prepracticum level | Knowledge of the consultant's role and its unique features as distinguished from other professional roles (such as therapist, supervisor, teacher). | Determines situations that require different role functions and shift roles accordingly |
| | Behavioral anchor: | Behavioral anchor: |
| | • Articulates common and distinctive roles of consultant | • Recognizes situations in which consultation is appropriate |
| | • Compares and contrast consultation, clinical and supervision roles | • Demonstrates capability to shift functions and behavior to meet referral needs |
| **B. Addressing referral question** | | |
| **Readiness for practicum** | **Readiness for internship** | **Readiness for entry to practice** |
| Essential component: | Essential component: | Essential component: |
| No expectation for prepracticum level | Knowledge of and ability to select appropriate means of assessment to answer referral questions | Knowledge of and ability to select appropriate and contextually sensitive means of assessment/data gathering that answers consultation referral question |
| | Behavioral anchor: | Behavioral anchor: |
| | • Implements systematic approach to data collection in a consultative role | • Demonstrates ability to gather information necessary to answer referral question |
| | • Identifies sources and types of assessment tools | • Clarifies and refines referral question based on analysis/assessment of question |

**TABLE 2.1.** (*Continued*)

| C. Communication of findings | | |
| --- | --- | --- |
| **Readiness for practicum** | **Readiness for internship** | **Readiness for entry to practice** |
| Essential component: | Essential component: | Essential component: |
| No expectation for pre-practicum level | Identifies literature and knowledge about process of informing consultee of assessment findings | Applies knowledge to provide effective assessment feedback and to articulate appropriate recommendations |
| | Behavioral anchor: | Behavioral anchor: |
| | • Identifies appropriate approaches and processes for providing written and verbal feedback and recommendation to consultee | • Prepares clear, useful consultation reports and recommendations to all appropriate parties<br>• Provides verbal feedback to consultee of results and offers appropriate recommendations |
| D. Application of methods | | |
| **Readiness for practicum** | **Readiness for internship** | **Readiness for entry to practice** |
| Essential component: | Essential component: | Essential component: |
| No expectation for prepracticum level | Identifies and acquires literature relevant to unique consultation methods (assessment and intervention) within systems, clients, or settings | Applies literature to provide effective consultative services (assessment and intervention) in most routine and some complex cases |
| | Behavioral anchor: | Behavioral anchor: |
| | • Identifies appropriate interventions based on consultation assessment findings | • Identifies and implements consultation interventions based on assessment findings<br>• Identifies and implements consultation interventions that meet consultee goals |

*Note.* Adapted from "Competency Benchmarks: A Model for Understanding and Measuring Competence in Professional Psychology Across Training Levels," by N. A. Fouad, C. L. Grus, R. L. Hatcher, N. J. Kaslow, P. S. Hutchings, M. B. Madson, . . . R. E. Crossman, 2009, *Training and Education in Professional Psychology*, *3*(Suppl.), p. S20. Copyright 2009 by the American Psychological Association.

a fundamental orientation to professional service. Other attitudes and values dispositions shape consultation:

- Respect initiates the process of collaboration and the creation of an effective working relationship; it permeates all aspects of consulting.

- Valuing (and attending to) the relationship dimension in consultation strengthens the collaboration.

- Cultural humility allows both consultant and consultee to engage in thoughtful consideration of consultation issues and solutions without defensiveness or posturing and, from a cultural perspective, fosters open-ness, self-awareness, and a desire to understand the experience of the other and that person's personal, institutional, societal, and professional contexts. In addition, taking a stance of humility and "not knowing too quickly" (Fredman et al., 2018, p. 9) is helpful to build collaboration, par-ticularly when working with organizations.

- Valuing knowledge and practices derived from psychology as a discipline and science, including evidence-based practice as well as in interprofessional practice, and respect for profession-specific values, knowledge, skills, and contributions are all essential to consultation practice.

Certainly, other attitudes and values could be enumerated. For our purposes, this brief discussion is intended to simply focus attention on the underlying ethical, professional, and human values and attitudes that contribute to consultation.

## Knowledge

Knowledge of consultation as a distinct professional practice is a starting point in competent practice. Definitions and background provide the means to under-stand the unique features and objectives of consultation and to differentiate it from other professional practices (see Chapter 1, this volume). Both consultant and consultee should understand the following domains of knowledge for competent practice.

### Consultation as a Professional Practice
Consultation

- is a planned collaborative interpersonal process between two or more professionals;

- involves a work issue, question, or problem regarding assessment, treatment, intervention, ethics, management, policy, process, organization, or imple-mentation of professional services, or, broadly stated, any professional activity responsive to requests for consultation;

- comprises several types of consultation, each of which has different aims and involve different KSA (see Chapter 1 for explication);

- involves the provision of knowledge, opinion, guidance, and direction by a consultant (who is an expert or possesses particular competence in the area to be discussed) in response to the consultation questions or issues posed by the consultee;

- aims to assist and enable the consultee to effectively fulfill his or her responsibilities to the client; and

- provides direct services to the client in some instances and is responsive to the needs expressed by the consultee.

### Consultation as Situated in a Multicultural, Institutional, and Societal Context

Culture and context are embedded in every aspect of the consultation process from the institutional setting in which the consultation issues emerge to contextual factors incorporated in the subject area of the consultation, to the roles and interactions between consultant and consultee. The authors of Chapter 5 and Chapter 6 present an all-encompassing and nuanced discussion of the impact of culture and the critical importance of using a cultural lens throughout the process of consultation. All parties to the consultation need to be knowledgeable and mindful that

- consultation involves awareness and knowledge of contextual, multicultural, and diversity factors;

- consultation requires knowledge of multicultural theory, historical context, and the impacts of diversity and contextual factors, most particularly of the consultant but also of the context or setting of the consultee; and

- consultation in interprofessional practice requires knowledge of other professions, cultures of practice, and institutional contexts.

### Responsibilities in Consultation

- The practice of consultation is governed by professional ethics and law.

- Although clinical case consultation may contribute to a professional's continuing education, the focus and benefit of consultation is directed to the individual client.

- Distinct from supervision, the consultant does not assume responsibility for the client, nor is there a hierarchical relationship in which the consultee *must* implement what the consultant advises; to the contrary, the decision regarding implementation is the consultee's.

- The consultee bears the full responsibility for the decision whether to adopt and the implementation of the consultant's recommendations.

### Subject Area Knowledge

- The consultant possesses up-to-date, expert knowledge and experience in the specific area(s) that are the subjects of the consultation.

- The consultant incorporates knowledge of diversity, culture, and context when offering expert opinion and guidance.

**Skills**

The consultant and consultee together contribute to the success of the consultation by their use of specific skills and the ability to create a mutually respectful and collaborative working relationship. In the sections that follow, we highlight the skills that the consultant and consultee contribute during different phases of the consultation process.

### Initiation of Consultation

The consultee

- recognizes—through the use of reflection and metacompetence—the need for consultation, which may include identification of the necessity for advanced knowledge and guidance from an expert or assistance to address difficulties the consultee is experiencing or has identified in his or her work performance or context;

- identifies professionals possessing required expertise by soliciting referrals from colleagues, reviews psychologists (or other professionals) who hold advanced credentials such as board certification (e.g., American Board of Professional Psychology) or specialty board members (e.g., American Board of Clinical Neuropsychology), or reviews those involved in a professional society (e.g., American Psychology Law Society); and

- initiates contact with a potential consultant and presents a brief summary of the consultation issue and goals and inquiries about the consultant's experience and areas of expertise with respect to the consultation issue.

The consultant

- reflects on the consultation request and, using metacompetence, determines his or her suitability to provide consultation specific to the issues involved;

- is aware of the competencies and approaches used in consulting psychology, for example, in the specialization industrial-organizational psychology, and considers which approach offers the best fit with respect to the purpose of the consultation;

- potentially assists to frame or reframe the consultation question by refining context and adding considerations (Liebowitz & Blattner, 2015); and

- clearly states his or her experience, delimits areas and limits of expertise, and discusses the practical details of the consultation, such as availability, purpose, limits of confidentiality, fees, and setting, and prepares a consultation agreement or contract (see Appendix 2.1).

### Consultation Process

The consultant and the consultee

- arrange, on reaching agreement, for the formal consultation.

The consultee

- engages in an interactive process that is respectful, collegial, collaborative, and focused on the specifics of the consultation issues and
  - is mindful that he or she bears sole responsibility to determine whether the consultant's input is used and the recommendations implemented, and
  - maintains an active role in the process and asks relevant questions and provides information at the time and throughout to ensure the effectiveness of the process;

- prepares a summary or outline of the consultation issues—before the consultation session—including specific questions and a brief background appropriate and specific to the consultation issues:
  - understands that for the consultation to be efficient and effective, it is critical that the information presented to the consultant be concise and to the point, and
  - understands that lengthy digressions lead to a loss of focus and obscure the relevant and essential data that the consultant needs so that he or she can provide information and guidance that are accurate and responsive to the consultee's request.

The consultant

- engages in an interactive process that is respectful, collegial, collaborative, and focused on the specifics of the consultation issues:
  - reviews—before the consultation session—any materials, such as science-based literature and resources, that are relevant to the consultation issues, and prepares notes and any initial clarifying questions;
  - keeps the focus on the subject of the consultation and the consultee's questions;
  - is thoughtful and efficient;
  - checks in throughout the consultation session to obtain brief feedback to ensure that the consultation is on track and responsive (e.g., Am I providing the kind of information that is helpful? Are you clear and in agreement about how the questions are being addressed?); and
  - ensures that the consultee understands and takes responsibility for decision making regarding the consultant's input;

- follows all legal and ethical standards, including the following: performs services within the scope of practice; follows procedures, such as obtaining informed consent and a release of information; and complies with the Health Insurance Portability and Accountability Act of 1996 standards in clinical consultation when providing a direct service to the client;

- integrates a multicultural perspective throughout the consultation process, including
  - having a culturally attuned understanding of the relevant literature (and sensitivity to limitations and biases) that informs opinion and recommendations as well as ensures cultural humility;
  - attends to the cultural dimensions involved in the consultation; and
  - acquires knowledge of and is respectful of the roles, titles, and decorum in the institutional culture, such as military, police and public safety departments, religious organizations, schools;

- enhances collaboration and effectiveness when engaging in interprofessional practice by
  - displaying respect and interest in the perspectives of other professions; and
  - being knowledgeable and sensitive to the roles and cultures of the practice of other professions, such as using salutations like "Dr." versus first name; and

- is mindful when the consultation focuses on work-related difficulties or challenges that are impacting the consultant's professional performance to
  - maintain the role of consultant, which involves bringing knowledge and expertise to assist the consultee in identifying the sources of the "blocks" in the work performance (see the Consultee-Focused Clinical Case Consultation section in Chapter 1, this volume); and
  - not assume the role of psychotherapist or engage in diagnostic formulation or psychotherapeutic interventions, each of which would constitute boundary violations and practice outside of informed consent and the inherent limitations of consultation.

### Postconsultation

The consultee

- reflects on the input provided by the consultant and forms conclusions regarding the applicability of the guidance specific to the client and the institutional and cultural context, engages with colleagues and with stakeholders (as appropriate) during this process of decision making, and

- makes the decision regarding the use of the input received from the consultant and the implementation of the consultant's recommendations.

The consultant

- documents and maintains records of the consultation, including the contract (if used) and notes regarding the process, meetings, conclusions, and recommendations of the consultation; and

- schedules or suggests—if agreed on in advance or if the consultant views it as being optimal—a follow-up consultation with the consultee.

## APPLICATION OF THE COMPETENCY FRAMEWORK

In this chapter, we identify the KSA that are assembled in the performance of consultation. The intent is to provide an orientation to consultation that places emphasis on actual practice through the framework of competence as well as present a description of best practices.

When conducting, preparing for, or learning about consultation, this outline can serve to organize consultant and consultee responsibilities, increase awareness and knowledge of consultation as a dynamic process, and provide a checklist for self-assessment and planning.

## EDUCATION, TRAINING, AND CONTINUOUS PROFESSIONAL DEVELOPMENT IN CONSULTATION

Efforts to achieve a threshold of competence in consultation requires education and training in consultation as a distinct professional practice. This text and others provide resources to learn about best practices to support formal courses and training in the field. In keeping with models of competency-based education, we advocate that there be intentional and systematic training in consultation beginning in graduate school and throughout clinical training (e.g., practicum, internship, fellowship, specialized postdoctoral training). Such efforts should focus explicitly on the KSA that consultees and consultants contribute to the consultation process. We suggest that during training (e.g., during internship, consistent with APA accreditation standards), opportunities be provided to observe, receive, and provide consultation under supervision. We find it a necessity to train students to be effective and competent consultees, topics that are largely ignored during graduate education.

Supervised professional experience is required for competence to be developed, including supervision in program development or organizational consulting, areas outside of clinical case consultation (Gallessich, 1982). Competency-based clinical supervision (Falender & Shafranske, 2004, 2017) complements the competency approach presented in this volume. Supervision focuses observation, processes of monitoring and evaluation, and learning strategies on the domains of KSA discussed earlier. Rather than giving general feedback, supervisors using this approach provide evaluative feedback directed to a specific aspect of knowledge, skill, or attitude and offer guidance regarding learning strategies to enhance competence. Attention should also be directed to developing competence in interprofessional practice and collaboration, particularly in light of changes in the health care environment and the expanding roles within health service psychology.

Developing and maintaining competence in consultation poses the same challenges faced in other areas of professional practice. Given the expanding knowledge base in psychology (see the discussion on the half-life of knowledge in psychology in Chapter 1 of this volume), it is necessary for consultants to commit to ongoing self-directed learning, continuing education, and training to maintain and enhance expertise in the subject areas in which they provide consultation. Enhancing competence in the practice of consultation also requires dedicated effort and can be accomplished through study and through peer and expert consultation.

---

## APPENDIX 2.1
## CONSULTATION CONTRACT

Date: _____

Agreement between

_____ (Consultee) / _____ (Organization)

and _____ (Consultant)

Consultation question(s):

General scope of consultation:

What the Consultant is agreeing to do:

Who is making the consultation request:

Tentative proposed time frame for consultation:

Start date

End date

Specific tasks or responsibilities of the Consultant, including identification of services to be provided:

Evaluation (ongoing and summative) to be used:


Timing of evaluation(s)


Boundaries of consultation: to whom will the Consultant report or interface, issues of confidentiality within the setting or organization, individual(s) who will set the parameters of the consultation:


Consultee's responsibilities:


Organization's responsibilities:


The Consultee will provide input on the consultation issues, but the ultimate decision of whether to implement the Consultant's plans or proposals or input is the Consultee's. The Consultee is responsible for decisions.


Fees or payment to the Consultant:


Ability to terminate consultation (by either party), notice required, conditions under which termination could be immediate:


## REFERENCES

Altmaier, E. M. (2003). The history of accreditation of doctoral programs in psychology. In E. M. Altmaier (Ed.), *Setting standards in graduate education: Psychology's commitment to excellence in accreditation* (pp. 39–60). Washington, DC: American Psychological Association. http://dx.doi.org/10.1037/10568-002

Altmaier, E. M. (2014). Accreditation of education and training programs. In W. B. Johnson & N. J. Kaslow, *The Oxford handbook of education and training in professional psychology* (pp. 87–101). New York, NY: Oxford University Press.

American Psychological Association. (2017). *Ethical principles of psychologists and code of conduct* (2002, Amended June 1, 2010 and January 1, 2017). Retrieved from http://www.apa.org/ethics/code/index.aspx

American Psychological Association, Commission on Accreditation. (2018). *Standards of accreditation for health service psychology*. Retrieved from http://www.apa.org/ed/accreditation/about/policies/standards-of-accreditation.pdf

Brown, D., Pryzwansky, W. B., & Schulte, A. C. (2011). *Psychological consultation and collaboration. Introduction to theory and practice* (7th ed.). Upper Saddle River, NJ: Pearson.

Caplan, G. (1970). *The theory and practice of mental health consultation*. New York, NY: Basic Books.

Caplan, G., & Caplan, R. B. (1993). *Mental health consultation and collaboration*. Prospect Heights, IL: Waveland Press.

Epstein, R. M., & Hundert, E. M. (2002). Defining and assessing professional competence. *JAMA, 287*, 226–235. http://dx.doi.org/10.1001/jama.287.2.226

Erchul, W. P. (1993). Selected interpersonal perspectives in consultation research. *School Psychology Quarterly, 8*, 38–49. http://dx.doi.org/10.1037/h0088830

Erchul, W. P., & Martens, B. K. (2010). *School consultation: Conceptual and empirical bases of practice* (3rd ed.). New York, NY: Springer. http://dx.doi.org/10.1007/978-1-4419-5747-4

Falender, C. A., & Shafranske, E. P. (2004). *Clinical supervision: A competency-based approach*. Washington, DC: American Psychological Association.

Falender, C. A., & Shafranske, E. P. (2007). Competence in competency-based supervision practice: Construct and application. *Professional Psychology: Research and Practice, 38*, 232–240. http://dx.doi.org/10.1037/0735-7028.38.3.232

Falender, C. A., & Shafranske, E. P. (2009). Competence in competency-based supervision practice: Construct and application. *Professional Psychology: Research and Practice, 36*, 232–240. http://dx.doi.org/10.1037/0735-7028.38.3.232

Falender, C. A., & Shafranske, E. P. (2017). Competency-based clinical supervision: Status, opportunities, tensions, and the future. *Australian Psychologist, 52*, 86–93. http://dx.doi.org/10.1111/ap.12265

Fouad, N. A., & Grus, C. L. (2014). Competency-based education and training in professional psychology. In W. B. Johnson & N. J. Kaslow, *The Oxford handbook of education and training in professional psychology* (pp. 105–119). New York, NY: Oxford University Press.

Fouad, N. A., Grus, C. L., Hatcher, R. L., Kaslow, N. J., Hutchings, P. S., Madson, M. B., . . . Crossman, R. E. (2009). Competency benchmarks: A model for understanding and measuring competence in professional psychology across training levels. *Training and Education in Professional Psychology, 3*(Suppl.), S5–S26. http://dx.doi.org/10.1037/a0015832

Fredman, G., Papadopoulou, A., & Worwood, E. (Eds.). (2018). *Collaborative consultation in mental health: Guidelines for the new consultant*. New York, NY: Routledge. http://dx.doi.org/10.4324/9781315696652

Gallessich, J. (1982). *The profession and practice of consultation: A handbook for consultants, trainers of consultants, and consumers of consultation services*. San Francisco, CA: Jossey-Bass.

Hatcher, R. L., Fouad, N. A., Campbell, L. F., McCutcheon, S. R., Grus, C. L., & Leahy, K. L. (2013). Competency-based education for professional psychology: Moving from concept to practice. *Training and Education in Professional Psychology, 7*, 225–234. http://dx.doi.org/10.1037/a0033765

Health Insurance Portability and Accountability Act of 1996 (HIPAA), Pub. L. 104–191, 42 U.S.C. § 300gg, 29 U.S.C. §§ 1181–1183, and 42 U.S.C. §§ 1320d–1320d9.

Kaslow, N. J. (2004). Competencies in professional psychology. *American Psychologist, 59*, 774–781. http://dx.doi.org/10.1037/0003-066X.59.8.774

Liebowitz, B., & Blattner, J. (2015). On becoming a consultant: The transition for a clinical psychologist. *Consulting Psychology Journal: Practice and Research, 67*, 144–161. http://dx.doi.org/10.1037/cpb0000037

Nelson, P. D. (2007). Striving for competence in the assessment of competence: Psychology's professional education and credentialing journey of public accountability. *Training and Education in Professional Psychology, 1*, 3–12. http://dx.doi.org/10.1037/1931-3918.1.1.3

Roberts, M. C., Borden, K. A., Christiansen, M. D., & Lopez, S. J. (2005). Fostering a culture shift: Assessment of competence in the education and careers of professional psychologists. *Professional Psychology: Research and Practice, 36*, 355–361. http://dx.doi.org/10.1037/0735-7028.36.4.355

Rodolfa, E., Bent, R., Eisman, E., Nelson, P., Rehm, L., & Ritchie, P. (2005). A cube model for competency development: Implications for psychology educators and regulators. *Professional Psychology: Research and Practice, 36,* 347–354. http://dx.doi.org/10.1037/0735-7028.36.4.347

Rubin, N. J., Bebeau, M., Leigh, I. W., Lichtenberg, J. W., Nelson, P. D., Portnoy, S., . . . Kaslow, N. J. (2007). The competency movement within psychology: An historical perspective. *Professional Psychology: Research and Practice, 38,* 452–462. http://dx.doi.org/10.1037/0735-7028.38.5.452

Scott, D. A., Royal, C. W., & Kissinger, D. B. (2015). *Counselor as consultant.* Thousand Oaks, CA: Sage.

Sears, R., Rudisill, J., & Mason-Sears, C. (2006). *Consultation skills for mental health professionals.* Hoboken, NJ: Wiley.

# 3

# Ethical, Legal, and Professional Issues in Consultation for Psychologists

Jeffrey E. Barnett

Health service psychologists strive to provide the highest possible quality of professional services. The same is true for health service psychologists-in-training, who provide clinical services under supervision to clients while simultaneously developing their competence as clinicians and consultants. Competence involves possessing the knowledge, skills, attitudes, and values necessary to provide effective clinical services and being able to apply these attributes effectively in light of each client's unique characteristics and situation (Falender & Shafranske, 2004; Haas & Malouf, 2005). Similar to other professional practices, such is the case in providing consultation.

Although one typically obtains knowledge primarily through academic course work, the clinical skills and attitudes and values associated with being a health service psychologist typically are obtained and developed through clinical supervision during practicum, internship, and postdoctoral training, and development of expertise continues through the psychologist's career. Consultation complements supervision and significantly contributes to training and to lifelong professional development. It provides an important resource to the practicing clinician by offering assistance and expertise to augment the psychologist's competence and professional practices. This chapter examines perspectives drawn from ethics, law, and professionalism that are integral to consultation as well as discusses the means to instill these principles during graduate and postdoctoral training.

http://dx.doi.org/10.1037/0000153-004
*Consultation in Psychology: A Competency-Based Approach*, C. A. Falender and E. P. Shafranske (Editors)

## SUPERVISION AND CONSULTATION

Although supervision and consultation are similar in a number of ways that this chapter addresses, they have key differences in their role, scope, and responsibilities. Both supervision and consultation are used to develop and enhance the clinician's competence and they each have the goal of ensuring that clients receive the best care possible. By definition, supervisors are licensed professionals who accept responsibility for the professional services provided to clients by their supervisees. In addition, supervisors have evaluative and gatekeeping responsibilities for their supervisees (Falender & Shafranske, 2004, 2017; Thomas, 2010). Supervisors supervise supervisees as they also gain competence in consultation.

Although the American Psychological Association, Commission on Accreditation (APA, 2018) accreditation requirements specify training in consultation, how this training is implemented varies widely across training programs (e.g., Barrett, Hazel, & Newman, 2017), and more specific training may occur during internship or postdoctoral years. Attention to the legal and ethical parameters is essential but appears to not be a consistent component of consultation training—with the exception of a focus on competence.

Postlicensure, when consultation occurs between two independently licensed professionals, the consultant does not bear responsibility or legal liability for the decisions made or services provided by the consultee, and the consultee is not required to follow the suggestions or advice provided by the consultant (Goodyear, Falender, & Rousmaniere, 2017). However, during the course of training, the supervisor of the supervisee who is learning consultation *is* responsible for the supervisee's consultation provided. Consultation is less hierarchical than supervision; it generally occurs between peers or colleagues. Similar to supervision, which typically involves an ongoing professional relationship, consultation frequently occurs on a time limited or as needed basis, although psychologists are increasingly participating in peer consultation groups to enhance competence and perspective throughout their careers (Paulson, Casile, & Jones, 2015; Thomas, 2010). Thus, although consultation and supervision may have a number of goals in common (e.g., promoting the provision of ethical and effective clinical practice), they are distinct entities, and it is essential to distinguish the two. It is important that consultants, supervisors, and supervisees be clear about these distinctions. Therefore, consultants need be mindful about being explicit about their role when working with graduate students, interns, or postdoctoral fellows.

Sears, Rudisill, and Mason-Sears (2006) described consultation as a relationship between colleagues in which the consultant assists the consultee "to work more effectively with their clients" (p. 13). They further explained that this collegial assistance and support may be provided in the areas of knowledge, skill, confidence, and objectivity. Thus, consultants may play a valuable role in assisting mental health professionals to provide ethical and effective services to their clients. Although the consultant does not interact directly with the client, he or she definitely may have a significant impact on the client through his or her work with the clinician who is seeking the consultation. Furthermore, consultants provide a valuable service to their colleagues by assisting them to provide more effective professional services to current and future clients.

## CONSULTATION AS AN AREA OF PROFESSIONAL COMPETENCE

Consultation is one of the "profession-wide competencies" included in the APA (2018) *Standards of Accreditation for Health Service Psychology* doctoral programs (p. 12). Thus, students in all APA-accredited doctoral programs in health service psychology should receive education and training to enable them to ethically and effectively serve in the role of consultant as part of their roles as both students and practicing professionals. The inclusion of consultation in these accreditation requirements for academic programs, internships, and fellowships signifies that serving as a consultant is an essential competency for health service psychologists as well as the ethical mandate to be competent in the role of consultant (Falender & Shafranske, 2004).

The competencies involved in being an effective and ethical consultant are multifaceted. At the most basic level, one must possess two types of competence to be an effective consultant. First, one must be competent in the practice area about which one is consulting. Thus, for example, to provide consultation to an athletic director about best practices in performance enhancement, including the management of performance anxiety, one must first be an experienced expert in these aspects of sport psychology. Second, one must also be skilled in the art and science of consultation and possess competence in serving in the consultant role. For example, competence in consultation includes the ability to establish the consultation relationship, maintain rapport and elicit needed information from the consultee to sufficiently understand the situation at hand, effectively understand the questions being asked and formulate a helpful response, effectively provide the consultee with needed feedback, and effectively and appropriately terminate the consultation relationship (Block, 2000; Caplan & Caplan, 1993). Consultants also need to ensure that they apply each of these competencies ethically, paying particular attention to issues such as informed consent, confidentiality, individual differences, boundaries, multiple relationships, conflicts of interest, and documentation.

To provide ethical and effective consultation, consultants must also possess an understanding of the consultee's work setting, profession, and professional culture. Consultants may provide consultation to members of other professions or to colleagues who work in other work settings. Understanding the culture of the colleague's profession and work setting is helpful to the consultant so that he or she can provide guidance that not only is good in theory but that he or she can implement effectively in the consultee's real-world setting and given the consultee's circumstances. Thus, consultants need to be familiar with, for example, the athletic environment and team culture for a sport psychology consultation, with the legal environment and culture for a consultation request from an attorney, and with the corporate environment and culture for a business consultation request.

When facilitating the development of consultation competence, supervisors need to be skilled in the teaching and supervision of consultation skills. Supervisees benefit from education and supervised experience in each of these areas as they develop the competencies needed to be an effective supervisor of consultation practice. Supervisors may use a range of teaching and supervisory methods to instill these skills; however, direct observation of the supervisee's ability to apply consultation skills effectively are be important for ensuring the development of these needed competencies. It is hoped that supervisors will provide the amount and type of supervision necessary to ensure effective consultation practice and that the intensity of supervision will decrease over time as the supervisee's skills develop. Doing so is consistent with Standard 2.05, Delegation of Work to Others, in the *Ethical Principles of Psychologists and Code of Conduct* (APA Ethics Code; APA, 2017), which requires that when delegating tasks and activities to others, psychologists ensure that these individuals possess the needed education, training, and experience to perform these tasks effectively, and psychologists ensure that they provide sufficient oversight and supervision based on the individual's level of competence.

In addition to maintaining the highest possible standards of competence in all our professional activities in general, developing and maintaining the competence needed to be an effective consultant, in particular, are important professional obligations for all health service psychologists (Falender & Shafranske, 2014)—and the APA (2017) Ethics Code requires such. Standard 2.01, Boundaries of Competence, dictates that psychologists only provide professional services "within the boundaries of their competence, based on their education, training, supervised experience, consultation, study, or professional experience" (APA, 2017, p. 4) and that "psychologists undertake ongoing efforts to develop and maintain their competence" (Standard 2.03, Maintaining Competence; APA, 2017, p. 5). Furthermore, in Standard 2.04, Bases for Scientific and Professional Judgments, the APA Ethics Code requires that "psychologists' work is based upon established scientific and professional knowledge of the discipline" (p. 5), thus requiring that health service psychologists remain current with developments in their specific areas of expertise as well as with developments in the field of consultation. This focus on developing and maintaining professional competence is consistent with the APA Ethics Code's aspirational ideals of beneficence (helping others) and nonmaleficence (avoiding harm to others) and with Standard 3.04, Avoiding Harm.

Thus, health service psychologists must take the necessary steps to develop needed competence in their role as consultants and to then continue the important work of maintaining and enhancing this competence over time. Also, when providing supervision in the practice of consultation, supervisors must ensure that they have the requisite competencies to supervise and ensure supervisee development of competence in consultation. This approach is consistent with the widely accepted pursuit of lifelong learning and ongoing professional development (Wise et al., 2010) that is so essential to ensuring compliance with ethics standards and the provision of high-quality professional services.

## WHEN TO SEEK CONSULTATION

Each health service psychologist needs to seek input, guidance, a second opinion, and assistance from colleagues throughout the course of his or her career. A health service psychologist cannot go through his or her entire career knowing the answer to every question, knowing how to handle each situation, and knowing the best course of action with every dilemma the psychologist experiences. Furthermore, individuals benefit from consultation from different disciplines or subspecialties to ensure appropriate clinical actions. Thus, supervisees are trained to be consultants to physicians, medical personnel, allied health professionals, attorneys, schools, police departments, sports teams, businesses, and other professionals and organizations. Psychologists working in interprofessional practice in multidisciplinary settings find that seeking consultation from expert colleagues is an integral component of their service delivery and training models. Other professionals seek consultation from psychologists and supervisees who are in training in these settings to use their expertise and unique perspectives to assist and support the other professionals' treatment of their patients. In addition, at various times throughout our careers, we must each consult with knowledgeable, skilled, and experienced colleagues whose judgement we trust. We each face a wide range of challenging situations, dilemmas, and questions that we cannot adequately address on our own. And others may seek out our consultation as well.

With regard to the need to seek out consultation to achieve the ethics ideals of the profession, Standard 2.01, Boundaries of Competence, in the APA (2017) Ethics Code is of relevance in stating that psychologists only provide those services they are competent to provide "based on their education, training, supervised experience, *consultation* [italics added], study, or professional experience" (p. 4). Similarly, this standard also states that psychologists planning to provide services "involving populations, areas, techniques, or technologies new to them undertake relevant education, training, supervised experience, *consultation* [italics added], or study" (APA, 2017, p. 5). This standard also addresses the provision of clinical services outside of one's competence but when appropriately trained professionals are not available; it states that in these situations, psychologists need to work to develop the needed competence "by using relevant research, training, *consultation* [italics added], or study" (APA, 2017, p. 5). As Knapp, VandeCreek, and Fingerhut (2017) pointed out, to ensure that the client's best interests are served, Standard 10.01a, Terminating

Therapy, requires that psychologists either consult or refer when clients are not benefiting from treatment or do not appear likely to benefit from treatment.

Thus, the connection between using consultation and maintaining the highest possible standards of competence should be clear. Each health service psychologist should consider consultation to be an accepted practice that supports our efforts to provide each client with ethical and effective care. To seek consultation should not be seen as indicating a weakness or deficiency on the health service psychologist's part; rather, it acknowledges that no one individual can have the answer to every question and that each of us can benefit from input from experienced colleagues.

Throughout their careers and in numerous situations, health service psychologists may find the use of consultation with a knowledgeable colleague to be of value. Representative examples include

- when faced with ethical dilemmas and challenges;

- when clients are not benefiting from treatment, and alternative viewpoints may be helpful in conceptualizing the client's needs and treatment;

- when another subspecialty, discipline, or perspective is important in diagnosis or treatment planning;

- to enhance our clinical decision making and judgment;

- when expanding our practices into new areas, for example, when providing psychological services (other than health services) to individuals, groups, and institutions, such as police departments, religious congregations, and community-based nonprofit organizations;

- because we are not accurate in our self-assessments of our competence and to help us determine what additional education, training, and experience are needed;

- to minimize the effects of professional isolation and to expand the range of perspectives we consider in our clinical roles;

- for emotional support during challenging times, and thus, as a component of our ongoing self-care and the promotion of our wellness; and

- as a risk management strategy and to ensure practice within accepted professional standards. (Barnett, 2008)

It is recommended that each health service psychologist ensure that he or she is a member of a *competence constellation*, a group of colleagues who provide each other with consultation, honest feedback, and support (Johnson, Barnett, Elman, Forrest, & Kaslow, 2012). Although self-awareness and self-reflection are important for the promotion of competence, health professionals are generally found to be quite poor at self-assessing their competence (thus the need for consultation) and that the greater the difficulties with our competence, the more inaccurate our self-assessments tend to be (Dunning, Heath, & Suls, 2004; Kruger & Dunning, 1999). We may at times seek out consultation from colleagues of our own volition; however, there will be times when it is helpful to rely on one's competence constellation for ongoing consultation, feedback, and suggestions. Such active and ongoing participation in a competence constellation is an example of aspiring to achieve the highest ethical ideals of our profession.

## CONSULTATION AND ETHICAL PRACTICE

Health service psychologists regularly face ethical dilemmas, situations in which no immediately appropriate course of action is evident. A wide range of ethical decision-making models are available to assist professionals in making the best possible decisions in these situations (compare with Cottone & Claus, 2000). For example, in Knapp, VandeCreek, and Fingerhut's (2017) five-step ethical decision-making model, Step 2 is to develop alternatives or hypothesize solutions. As these authors stated, "Psychologists can improve the quality of their options through consultation with others" (Knapp, VandeCreek, & Fingerhut, 2017, p. 44); this statement emphasizes the important role consultation plays in this ethical decision-making model. Similarly, Barnett and Johnson (2008) developed a more detailed nine-step ethical decision-making model. In their model, Step 6 is to consult with trusted colleagues to aid in the process of formulating alternative courses of action and to offer alternative viewpoints and perspectives.

In addition to general ethical decision-making models such as the ones just described, other models exist for addressing dilemmas in more specific situations. For example, Barnett and Johnson (2011) developed a nine-step model for decision making with religious clients and religious problems in psychotherapy. Step 6 is to consult with experts in the area of religion and psychotherapy. Because issues relevant to addressing religion and spirituality in psychotherapy with clients may be challenging for psychologists, Barnett and Johnson (2011) recommended seeking out experienced colleagues with expertise in these issues. They also recommended that, when appropriate, psychologists consult with religious leaders to better understand a client's religion or faith tradition and its practices. Because psychologists may experience reactions to clients' religious beliefs and practices, Barnett and Johnson (2011) recommended the use of consultation to address countertransference reactions psychologists may be experiencing (see Chapter 12, this volume). Another example of a specific ethical decision-making model is Younggren and Gottlieb's (2004) model for managing risk when contemplating multiple relationships. In addressing if the psychologist can evaluate the relevant issues objectively, they recommended that "when the answers to questions about personal objectivity are unclear, one should discuss and process them with other individuals to ensure that the answers maximize thoughtful, objective consideration" (Younggren & Gottlieb, 2004, p. 257).

## CONSULTATION AND RISK MANAGEMENT

*Risk management* is the practice of reducing the risk of adverse consequences in clinical practice. It involves effectively managing high-risk clients and situations to both provide the highest possible quality of care and minimize the risk to the psychologist of ethics and licensing board complaints and of the occurrence of malpractice lawsuits. A range of factors exist that contribute to risk for health service psychologists: client factors, such as diagnosis, personality characteristics, and being litigious in nature; contextual risk factors, such as treatment setting and the type of services being provided; and health service psychologist risk factors, such as level of competence, emotional blind spots, professional isolation, level of stress, and decision-making abilities (Knapp, Bennett, & VandeCreek, 2012). Three key strategies comprise effective risk management, each of which is intended to promote ethical and effective treatment: informed consent, documentation, and consultation (Knapp, Younggren, VandeCreek, Harris, & Martin, 2013).

Because of their relevance to consultation, informed consent and documentation are addressed in more detail later in this chapter. But, as risk management strategies, they are essential components of each health service psychologist's practices. *Informed consent* involves sharing adequate information with clients so that they can make an informed decision about participation in the professional services being offered. A timely and thorough informed consent process helps ensure a shared decision-making process, it promotes a collaborative working relationship, and it minimizes the risk of exploitation of or harm to the client (Snyder & Barnett, 2006). *Documentation* provides the tangible record of the health service psychologist's reasonable and good faith efforts to meet the standards of care of the profession. These efforts include documenting the treatment provided, options considered, the rationale for decisions made, the client's role and level of involvement in treatment decisions, and the client's level of participation in treatment and compliance with treatment recommendations. Documentation also should include copies of all treatment agreements and other documents relevant to the client's treatment. Each of these strategies is important from a risk management perspective as well as for promoting and providing quality mental health services.

As a risk management strategy, consultation demonstrates that the clinician knows the limits of his or her competence, understands the need for other perspectives when facing challenging and complex clinical and ethical situations, is aware of clinical complexities when facing high-risk situations, and understands that personal factors may impact decision making and clinical effectiveness. When clients are not improving from the treatment being provided, when an impasse is experienced, and when high-risk behaviors are present, consultation with an expert colleague may prove a valuable risk management strategy (Knapp et al., 2013). The input of expert colleagues may prove invaluable in responding to such challenging situations.

If one's clinical decisions and actions are ever questioned, having consulted with colleagues will help demonstrate a thoughtful process and approach to making treatment decisions. Even when providing optimal treatment to clients, it is possible that treatment outcomes may, at times, be negative. Yet, it is essential that we demonstrate our reasonable and good faith efforts to meet (and exceed) the standards of our profession. Seeking consultation from a knowledgeable and experienced colleague and thoughtfully considering how one might integrate the consultant's feedback and recommendations into our work (and documenting them), help to clearly demonstrate these efforts. It is our documentation that will be looked to for evidence of our efforts to meet the profession's standards of care—including seeking and effectively using consultation. Thus, timely and detailed documentation of consultations sought and of our decision-making process for how to integrate the feedback and suggestions provided by the consultant into our clinical work is an essential part of a comprehensive risk management strategy.

## USE OF INFORMED CONSENT TO ESTABLISH THE CONSULTATION RELATIONSHIP

It is important that from the outset health service psychologists clarify expectations of all professional relationships. The APA (2017) Ethics Code specifically includes consultation among the professional services for which informed consent of the recipient is required before providing the service (Standard 3.10, Informed Consent). This standard also requires that psychologists "appropriately document" all informed consent agreements (p. 6) and that psychologists must obtain informed consent "as early as is feasible" in the professional relationship (p. 9). The requirement to engage in the informed consent process "as early as is feasible" implies that it occurs before the professional services are provided but acknowledges that, at times, circumstances may necessitate delaying this process. But, informed consent should be seen as an ongoing process rather than a one-time event. Psychologists should address any substantive changes anticipated or planned in the consultative relationship through this ongoing process so that the initial informed consent agreement may be updated.

For informed consent to be considered valid, the recipient must give it voluntarily, the recipient must be competent to give this consent (both having the legal right to give consent and having the cognitive and emotional capacity to make thoughtful and reasoned decisions), we must actively ensure the recipient's understanding of what he or she is agreeing to, and the informed consent must be documented (Haas & Malouf, 2005). A wide range of issues may appropriately be addressed in the informed consent to supervision. These include

- clarifying the nature, focus, and goals of the consultation, specifically that consultation is being provided, not supervision, and that the consultee maintains responsibility for all his or her decisions and professional services provided to his or her clients;

- a review of the consultant's and consultee's roles and responsibilities, which includes the consultee's giving the consultant adequate information so that a helpful consultation may be provided while ensuring understanding that the consultee will make his or her own treatment decisions;

- the anticipated length of the consultation (e.g., a single brief consultation about a particular client's treatment or an ongoing consultative relationship, such as when expanding one's skills into a new area of practice);

- any fees to be charged for specific services and tasks such as the time spent providing the consultation and a review of records, if relevant, financial policies, and how and when payment is to be made;

- confidentiality and any limits or exceptions to include any mandatory reporting requirements based on the laws and regulations in one's jurisdiction;

- scheduling, availability, and appropriate expectations for responsiveness to questions and requests for information;

- policies regarding the use of any technologies, including telephone, email, text messaging, and video conferencing, both for the conduct of consultation sessions and for contact and communication between sessions (with appropriate attention being given to the protection of confidential information);

- expectations and practices for documentation of the consultation provided (to include the informed consent agreement); and

- information on the consultant's professional background, expertise, and approach to providing consultation.

It may seem cumbersome to engage in an informed consent process before engaging in a consultative relationship, especially when the consultation being requested is brief or informal, such as when a colleague in one's work setting stops by your office and asks for a quick consultation. Experience demonstrates that what may initially sound like a simple request may turn out to be a much more complicated matter. Furthermore, issues and expectations not clarified up front may later prove to be problematic. Engaging in the informed consent process should be seen as a preventive strategy that promotes optimal outcomes. Clarity of role and expectations ensures that the consultation gets off to a good start as and enhances the working alliance between the consultant and the consultee.

A consultation contract or agreement may be prepared that addresses the key issues and expectations in the relationship, such as the ones detailed earlier (Falender & Shafranske, 2004; Thomas, 2010). This contract or agreement may be especially helpful when considering an ongoing consultative relationship; when issues to be addressed may be complex or require after-hours consultation; and when the referral for consultation comes from a third party, such as a licensing board or an employer. When a brief, time-limited, or uncomplicated consultation is anticipated, authors such as Knapp, Gottlieb, and Handelsman (2017) have recommended a brief letter of agreement that the consultant prepares and sends to the consultee. The letter includes mention of the aforementioned key informed consent issues listed. But, even for the briefest and most straightforward appearing consultation requests, a brief discussion of these issues is recommended, especially because what may initially appear to be simple or straightforward may prove to be more complex as information is shared.

## CONFIDENTIALITY ISSUES IN CONSULTATION

Confidentially is a hallmark of an effective consultation. Confidentiality and any limits or exceptions that can reasonably be anticipated should be addressed during the informed consent process. It may naturally be assumed that consultants will maintain the confidentiality of all information shared by the consultee, but misunderstandings do occur, so clarifying and agreeing on all expectations from the outset are important.

For health service psychologists who are seeking consultation, the issue of how they address and manage their clients' confidentiality is important. The APA (2017) Ethics Code makes it clear in Standard 4.01, Maintaining Confidentiality, that "psychologists have a primary obligation and take reasonable precautions to protect confidential information" (p. 7). Yet, the Ethics Code makes it clear that psychologists should consult with colleagues to assist them to provide the highest quality services possible. In doing so, psychologists will need to share information about their client and the treatment being provided to the consultant. Psychologists may obtain their clients' consent to share their information with a consultant, yet the Ethics Code allows psychologists to disclose confidential client information without the client's consent "to obtain appropriate professional consultations" with the disclosure's being "limited to the minimum that is necessary to achieve the purpose" (p. 7). With regard to the need to share the minimum information necessary, Ethics Code Standard 4.06, Consultations, requires that when seeking consultation, psychologists "do not disclose confidential information that reasonably could lead to the identification of the client/patient" (p. 7), unless the client has given permission to share his or her identifying information.

Thus, health service psychologists may seek consultation with a colleague without needing to share the client's identifying information. One does not need to share the client's name, address, date of birth or exact age, employer, or details of the client's history that are so specific that it might be possible for the consultant to determine the client's identity. Rather, it is recommended that the consultee share more general information about the client. Examples include sharing an age range, such as middle-aged, young adult, or adolescent;

saying that a client is a successful professional rather than sharing that she is a partner in a law firm; or stating that the client lives in a suburban area rather than disclosing the name of the town where the client resides. The goal is to share information sufficient for the consultant to be able to provide a helpful consultation but not so much detailed information that the client's identity and privacy are not protected.

This guidance remains true regardless of the context of the consultation, such as an individual consultation or when seeking consultation from a peer consultation group. However, the more individuals who have access to client information, the greater the risks to privacy. Thus, care should be taken when seeking consultation. It may prove helpful to think through ahead of time what information to disclose to the consultant(s), write out notes in advance of the consultation that include the information to be shared, and then stick with this plan. Such confidentiality and privacy risks are even greater when using professional email LISTSERVs and other group electronic media for consultation. Caution is recommended when consulting via these media because there is no identified consultant with whom to engage in the informed consent process at the beginning of the consultative process. Thus, it is not possible to know what other email management group members' expectations are regarding treating information shared as confidential and the extent to which those members may have access to the information posted. Therefore, it is recommended that only the most general consultations be done using these media. As Goodyear et al. (2017) emphasized, "It should be assumed that a [LISTSERV] is not a confidential forum" (p. 452). To ensure meeting expectations for professionalism and ethical conduct, regardless of the forum or medium used, when seeking consultation, psychologists and supervisees should make all reasonably available actions to protect each client's confidential information.

Confidentiality remains important for health service psychologists serving in the role of consultant as well as for those seeking consultation. Consultants should understand that confidential information is being shared and take all reasonably available precautions to protect this information. In addition, consultees often want it kept confidential that consultation is being sought, so consultants will need to be discrete that consultation has occurred. At all times, professionalism dictates treating the consultation role with care and respect, keeping in mind the sensitive nature of consultations for many who seek them. Furthermore, in unique situations or when the client's identity will be difficult or impossible to disguise, the consultee may ask for informed consent from the client to seek consultation.

## DOCUMENTATION AND RECORD-KEEPING IN CONSULTATION

As with the provision of all other professional services, there are multiple reasons why health service psychologists—whether the consultant or the consultee—should document the process of consultation. Documentation of professional services provided can help us to provide better services. It is impossible to remember everything we recommend or that is recommended to us; it can be helpful to review notes of consultations after the fact to refresh our memory and to further think through the advice given or received. Moreover, the documentation of consultations by both parties can help reduce misunderstandings or miscommunications when what is documented is shared with each other.

Documentation is also an important risk management strategy. The documentation of professional services provides a record of what has transpired that can be helpful to have if questions are raised about these services. From the consultee's perspective, if a client ever files a complaint, it can be helpful to be able to demonstrate that the psychologist or supervisee understood the complexities of the case, sought out expert consultation, thoughtfully considered the consultant's input, and then proceeded in a manner that met or exceeded prevailing professional standards. It is therefore important to document not just what was discussed with the consultant and what the consultant recommended but also options and alternatives considered as well as one's thought process that resulted in the decisions made and actions taken.

These practices are supported by the requirements of the APA (2017) Ethics Code in Standard 6.01, Documentation of Professional and Scientific Work and Maintenance of Records, which requires psychologists to document their professional work. Additional guidance can be found in the APA "Record Keeping Guidelines" (APA, 2007), which provide information on the recommended content, structure, and maintenance of records. Psychologists also are directed to their state licensing laws and regulations for documentation, record retention, and disposal requirements. Many state licensing laws and their associated regulations are similar to the APA Ethics Code in that they require the timely and thorough documentation by psychologists (and those they supervise) of all professional services provided, thus requiring the documentation of consultation services provided and received.

## MULTIPLE RELATIONSHIPS, CONFLICTS OF INTEREST, AND PROFESSIONALISM

It is essential that consultants are able to provide feedback and guidance to consultees that are unencumbered by conflicts of interest or multiple relationships that might adversely impact their objectivity and judgment or their ability to provide honest feedback to the consultee. Health service psychologists who take on the role of consultant are doing so to be of assistance to the consultee and their clients. To be able to be effective in this role of consultant, the health service psychologist must be able to provide clear and honest feedback that could be difficult to provide when a preexisting relationship exists.

Each consultant must carefully consider if the presence of a conflict of interest would limit his or her effectiveness as a consultant and, if so, to refer the consultee to another colleague for consultation. The APA (2017) Ethics Code provides guidance on this matter in Standard 3.06, Conflict of Interest, and advises psychologists not to take on new professional roles "when personal, scientific, professional, legal, financial, or other interests or relationships could reasonably be expected to" result in exploitation of or harm to the other individual or impair the psychologist's objectivity and judgment (p. 6). For example, a health service psychologist might decide it would be inappropriate to serve in a consultant role with his or her business partner, spouse, or child, even when possessing the needed clinical expertise. The ability to provide direct and honest feedback may be limited as a result of these preexisting relationships.

The APA (2017) Ethics Code provides additional guidance in Standard 3.05, Multiple Relationships, in advising that psychologists avoid those multiple relationships that bring with them a reasonably anticipated potential to cause impaired objectivity or judgment or to be exploitative or harmful to others. *Multiple relationships* are described as accepting into consultation an individual with whom the consultant has a preexisting other relationship or entering into another relationship with a current consultee. In each case, one should examine the nature of the secondary relationship and consider the potential for exploitation and harm as well as for impaired objectivity and judgment. Doing so requires honesty with oneself and insight into one's motivations for considering the provision of consultation to this individual. Additional factors to consider when making such decisions include the availability of options and alternatives. For example, am I the only child custody expert my business partner may consult with about a challenging case? Are there respected colleagues to whom I can refer my business partner for this consultation? Can I be objective in my analysis of the appropriateness to offer the consultation myself or to whom I refer, given considerations of professional standing, affiliation, and monetary self-interest?

Deciding whether one should serve as a consultant to an individual with whom one has a preexisting other relationship can be complex and challenging. One may feel pressure not to disappoint or let down the other individual. One may also have a need or desire to please or receive approval from that person. Yet, our professional responsibilities include avoiding harm, not participating in conflict of interest situations, or not engaging in potentially harmful or exploitative multiple relationships. Agreeing to serve as a consultant in these situations may please the consultee initially but may prove to not be helpful to the consultee in the long run when you are unable to provide the honest and direct feedback needed—especially when the consultation centers around the consultee's emotional responses to clients to include sexual feelings, anger, and the like.

When faced with such difficult decisions regarding whether one should agree to serve in a consultation role with an individual with whom one has a preexisting relationship, which includes a close colleague or friend, the best advice is to use an ethical decision-making model like the ones described earlier to assist in the process of logically and rationally thinking through the relevant issues so one can make the best possible decision. And, as highlighted, the use of consultation with a trusted and expert colleague should be included as an important step in every decision-making process. Each of these multiple relationship situations falls on a continuum, and each may be different in the risk to objectivity and impartiality. There is no one rule to follow that applies to all such relationships and consultation requests. One needs to consider the nuances of each relationship and consultation request, including reasonably available options and alternatives, and have the ability to provide honest, impartial, and objective feedback and consultation. It is essential that health service psychologists are comfortable declining requests for consultation if they are unable to provide it in an objective and impartial manner. In these situations, they should tactfully explain such concerns and, if possible, make recommendations for more appropriate colleagues to consider as consultants.

## LEGAL ISSUES IN CONSULTATION

Because consultees are licensed professionals, they retain responsibility for all professional services they provide. Although a complaint could possibly be filed against a consultant, Knapp, Gottlieb, and Handelsman (2017) stated that there are no known cases in which a consultant was found legally liable for the actions (or inaction) of a consultee. Consultants are considered experts in their field, and their professional opinions may be given significant weight by consultees; however, as licensed professionals, consultees retain full responsibility over their decisions and actions.

This does not free consultants from all ethics requirements and legal responsibilities. Health service psychologists who are obligated to follow the APA (2017) Ethics Code should understand that the enforceable standards in the Ethics Code apply to all professional services they provide, including consultation (see the Introduction and Applicability section in the Ethics Code). Similarly, health service psychologists who are serving as consultants are still functioning under their professional license. Therefore, all applicable licensing laws and regulations are relevant to their work as a consultant. Before serving as a consultant, health service psychologists are guided to review these laws and regulations and pay particular attention to enforceable standards relevant to this role. Representative issues already addressed that are regulated in licensing laws and regulations include informed consent, fees and financial arrangements, confidentiality and its limits, documentation and record-keeping, and multiple relationships.

At times, licensing boards may mandate that a psychologist participate in ongoing consultation that includes oversight of the psychologist's work as a way of maintaining the psychologist's license to practice following a board action. In these situations, the consultant should be clear at the outset about the licensing board's expectations. Because the psychologist is the recipient of a licensing board action, before agreeing to serve as a mandated consultant, it is important to obtain copies of all documents relevant to the licensing board's action to ensure an understanding of the relevant issues, challenges, and concerns that may be a focus of the consultation.

Issues to clarify and to include in a written agreement with the consultee include the nature and scope of the consultation to be provided, fees and financial arrangements, limits to confidentiality to include the requirement to provide the licensing board with periodic written reports on the consultee's level of participation and progress, how concerns about the consultee's progress will be addressed, and how the decision to end the consultative relationship will be made. Again, because this type of consultation arrangement is a legal requirement for the consultee, it is important to ensure that all parties are clear from the outset on the goals, objectives, and requirements.

## SUMMARY AND RECOMMENDATIONS

Consultation is an essential role for health service psychologists. Throughout our careers, we each face dilemmas, challenges, and complex situations that exceed our comfort zone or competence. Consultation with trusted, expert colleagues can prove invaluable to assist us to obtain a different perspective, receive feedback, learn new skills, be referred to helpful resources, and provide guidance on how best to assist our clients. It is an ethical imperative that health service psychologists use colleagues for consultation when needed and not rely only on our own knowledge, skills, and judgment when clients are not benefiting from treatment, when a conflict or impasse is experienced, or when we reasonably could be expected to know that our objectivity or judgment is impaired. Consultants can provide us with an important service that can include making recommendations for how to best proceed with a client's treatment; options and alternatives to consider to include referral to another professional; and further attention to our own personal issues and needs, when indicated.

Those health service psychologists who serve as consultants have an obligation to do so ethically and within the limits of their professional competence. We should pay particular attention to conflict of interest situations and multiple relationships that could negatively impact our ability to serve effectively in the consultant role. When unsure if engaging in a particular consultation is appropriate, we can consult with colleagues who have the ability to be more objective in these situations and to provide us with honest feedback and suggestions that serve the consultee's best interests.

## REFERENCES

American Psychological Association. (2007). Record keeping guidelines. *American Psychologist, 62*, 993–1004. http://dx.doi.org/10.1037/0003-066X.62.9.993

American Psychological Association. (2017). *Ethical principles of psychologists and code of conduct* (2002, Amended June 1, 2010, and January 1, 2017). Retrieved from http://www.apa.org/ethics/code/index.aspx

American Psychological Association, Commission on Accreditation. (2018). *Standards of accreditation for health service psychology.* Retrieved from https://www.apa.org/ed/accreditation/about/policies/standards-of-accreditation.pdf

Barnett, J. E. (2008). Impaired professionals: Distress, professional impairment, self-care, and psychological wellness. In M. Herson & A. M. Gross (Eds.), *Handbook of clinical psychology* (Vol. 1, pp. 857–884). New York, NY: Wiley.

Barnett, J. E., & Johnson, W. B. (2008). *Ethics desk reference for psychologists.* Washington, DC: American Psychological Association.

Barnett, J. E., & Johnson, W. B. (2011). Integrating spirituality and religion into psychotherapy: Persistent dilemmas, ethical issues, and a proposed decision-making process. *Ethics & Behavior, 21,* 147–164. http://dx.doi.org/10.1080/10508422.2011.551471

Barrett, C. A., Hazel, C. E., & Newman, D. S. (2017). Training confident school-based consultants: The role of course content, process, and supervision. *Training and Education in Professional Psychology, 11,* 41–48. http://dx.doi.org/10.1037/tep0000128

Block, P. (2000). *Flawless consulting: A guide to getting your expertise used* (2nd ed.). San Francisco, CA: Jossey-Bass.

Caplan, G., & Caplan, R. B. (1993). *Mental health consultation and collaboration.* San Francisco, CA: Jossey-Bass.

Cottone, R. R., & Claus, R. E. (2000). Ethical decision-making models: A review of the literature. *Journal of Counseling & Development, 78,* 275–283. http://dx.doi.org/10.1002/j.1556-6676.2000.tb01908.x

Dunning, D., Heath, C., & Suls, J. M. (2004). Flawed self-assessment: Implications for health, education, and the workplace. *Psychological Science in the Public Interest, 5,* 69–106. http://dx.doi.org/10.1111/j.1529-1006.2004.00018.x

Falender, C. A., & Shafranske, E. P. (2004). *Clinical supervision: A competency-based approach.* Washington, DC: American Psychological Association. http://dx.doi.org/10.1037/10806-000

Falender, C. A., & Shafranske, E. P. (2014). Clinical supervision: The state of the art. *Journal of Clinical Psychology, 70,* 1030–1041. http://dx.doi.org/10.1002/jclp.22124

Falender, C. A., & Shafranske, E. P. (2017). *Supervision essentials for the practice of competency-based supervision* (pp. 17–46). Washington, DC: American Psychological Association. http://dx.doi.org/10.1037/15962-002

Goodyear, R. K., Falender, C. A., & Rousmaniere, T. (2017). Ethics issues regarding supervision and consultation in private practice. In S. Walfish, J. E. Barnett, & J. Zimmerman (Eds.), *Handbook of private practice* (pp. 443–458). New York, NY: Oxford University Press.

Haas, L. J., & Malouf, J. L. (2005). *Keeping up the good work: A practitioner's guide to mental health ethics* (4th ed.). Sarasota, FL: Professional Resources Press.

Johnson, W. B., Barnett, J. E., Elman, N. S., Forrest, L., & Kaslow, N. J. (2012). The competent community: Toward a vital reformulation of professional ethics. *American Psychologist, 67,* 557–569. http://dx.doi.org/10.1037/a0027206

Knapp, S. J., Bennett, B. E., & VandeCreek, L. D. (2012). Risk management for psychologists. In S. J. Knapp, M. C. Gottlieb, M. M. Handelsman, & L. D. VandeCreek (Eds.), *APA handbook of ethics in psychology: Vol. 1. Moral foundations and common themes* (pp. 483–518). Washington, DC: American Psychological Association. http://dx.doi.org/10.1037/13271-019

Knapp, S. J., Gottlieb, M. C., & Handelsman, M. M. (2017). Some ethical considerations in paid peer consultations in health care. *Journal of Health Service Psychology, 43,* 20–25.

Knapp, S. J., VandeCreek, L. D., & Fingerhut, R. (2017). *Practical ethics for psychologists: A positive approach* (3rd ed.). Washington, DC: American Psychological Association. http://dx.doi.org/10.1037/0000036-000

Knapp, S. J., Younggren, J. N., VandeCreek, L. D., Harris, E., & Martin, J. N. (2013). *Assessing and managing risk in psychological practice: An individualized approach* (2nd ed.). Rockville, MD: The Trust.

Kruger, J., & Dunning, D. (1999). Unskilled and unaware of it: How difficulties in recognizing one's own incompetence lead to inflated self-assessments. *Journal of Personality and Social Psychology, 77*, 1121–1134. http://dx.doi.org/10.1037/0022-3514.77.6.1121

Paulson, L. R., Casile, W. J., & Jones, D. (2015). Tech it out: Implementing an online peer consultation network for rural mental health professionals. *Journal of Rural Mental Health, 39*, 125–136. http://dx.doi.org/10.1037/rmh0000034

Sears, R. W., Rudisill, J. R., & Mason-Sears, C. (2006). *Consultation skills for mental health professionals*. Hoboken, NJ: Wiley.

Snyder, T. A., & Barnett, J. E. (2006). Informed consent and the process of psychotherapy. *Psychotherapy Bulletin, 41*, 37–42.

Thomas, J. T. (2010). *The ethics of supervision and consultation: Practical guidance for mental health professionals*. Washington, DC: American Psychological Association. http://dx.doi.org/10.1037/12078-000

Wise, E. H., Sturm, C. A., Nutt, R. L., Rodolfa, E., Schaffer, J. B., & Webb, C. (2010). Life-long learning for psychologists: Current status and a vision for the future. *Professional Psychology: Research and Practice, 41*, 288–297. http://dx.doi.org/10.1037/a0020424

Younggren, J. N., & Gottlieb, M. C. (2004). Managing risk when contemplating multiple relationships. *Professional Psychology: Research and Practice, 35*, 255–260. http://dx.doi.org/10.1037/0735-7028.35.3.255

# 4

# Consultation in Health Service Psychology

## The Present and the Future

David J. Martin

Consultation has long been recognized as an important part of the practice of psychology. Professional practice has expanded across a range of contexts and services, including traditional mental health, and has been applied in other practice niches, as illustrated in this volume. Psychologists providing consultation may be trained in different specialties and training models (e.g., scientist–practitioner, practitioner–scholar) usually with an applied clinical focus. This chapter discusses consultation in the context of health service psychology (HSP), thus reflecting the recently adopted nomenclature for specialties, such as clinical, counseling, and school psychology. Because health service psychologists practice in a range of settings, including mental health, health care, and public health, effective communication and consultation in these cross-disciplinary settings are essential skills. Knowledge of consultation practice in HSP is necessary to understand the competencies required and that such practice is distinct from consulting psychology (see Chapters 1 and 10, this volume). This chapter also provides information on the definition of HSP, scope of HSP practice, and range of activities in which health service psychologists engage (including assessment, intervention, and liaison). It outlines health service psychologist competencies, discusses how they are established and maintained, and summarizes education and training implications. The last section addresses how psychologists can prepare for future challenges and opportunities in HSP.

http://dx.doi.org/10.1037/0000153-005
*Consultation in Psychology: A Competency-Based Approach*, C. A. Falender and
E. P. Shafranske (Editors)

The term *health service psychologist* was adopted out of recognition that psychology has transitioned from a focus on mental health to a more general health profession in which mental health is an important subset (Belar, 2014; Health Service Psychology Education Collaborative [HSPEC], 2013). As the HSPEC (2013) noted in its report, an increased understanding of health and disease processes points to a need to provide psychology education and training that focus broadly on biological, psychological, social, and cultural aspects of health and behavior—a biopsychosocial focus. *Health service psychology* was previously defined by American Psychological Association (APA) policy in 1996 (APA, n.d.-b) and reaffirmed in the 2011 revision of the APA "Model Act for State Licensure of Psychologists" (APA, 2011):

> Psychologists are certified as health service providers if they are duly trained and experienced in the delivery of preventive, assessment, diagnostic, therapeutic intervention and management services relative to the psychological and physical health of consumers based on: (1) having completed scientific and professional training resulting in a doctoral degree in psychology; (2) having completed an internship and supervised experience in health care settings; and (3) having been licensed as psychologists at the independent practice level. ("B. Definitions," para. 5a)

Health service psychology is narrower than professional psychology (which may include other specialties, e.g., industrial-organizational or community psychology) and includes clinical, counseling, and school psychology (cf. APA, 2014). The description by the APA, Commission on Accreditation (2018), further clarifies that HSP is not restricted to the provision of mental health services but, rather, includes the provision of a range of health and mental health services:

> Health service psychology is . . . the integration of psychological science and practice in order to facilitate human development and functioning. [It] includes the generation and provision of knowledge and practices that encompass a wide range of professional activities relevant to health promotion, prevention, consultation, assessment, and treatment for psychological and other health-related disorders. (p. 2)

Health service psychologists provide an array of services for many health conditions at different stages of illness or wellness and across different settings (Brown et al., 2002). Brown et al. (2002) outlined a framework for examining psychologists' roles in health care that can be conceptualized as a matrix with dimensions that correspond to the range of disease states with which psychologists work, the services they provide, and the timing of their contributions to health care. In this framework, psychiatric or mental health disorders are health conditions of the same importance as other disease categories; psychologists have provided services not only in mental health but in an array of health conditions. The timing of services is described as along the lines of primary, secondary, and tertiary prevention. Traditional psychology has typically centered on tertiary prevention in which a disease or illness is treated to reduce suffering and other problems related to the illness or health condition (e.g., pain management, active coping). However, health service psychologists have also contributed to primary prevention and health promotion efforts (e.g., programs to prevent or delay disease onset, e.g., HIV and sexually transmitted disease risk reduction, health promotion to prevent obesity) and to secondary prevention to reduce the impact of a disease or injury that has already occurred through early detection and treatment (e.g., medication adherence intervention for hypertensive patients to prevent future complications).

Health service psychology activities may be broadly characterized as assessment, intervention, and liaison. Health service psychologists provide evaluation or assessment of factors related to health and mental health; factors contributing to disease processes; psychological factors affecting manifestation of symptoms; coping styles; and psychological adaptation to, and consequences of, disease. Assessment activities can take place at any point in the disease or health condition progression. Psychologists may target intervention at behaviors that place an individual at risk for a disease or health condition (primary prevention, e.g., HIV risk reduction), and they may design interventions to ameliorate risk of future illness episodes in patients already diagnosed with a disease process (secondary prevention) or to facilitate coping with an illness (tertiary prevention).

As behavioral medicine has emerged and grown, health service psychologists have collaborated with other health care disciplines, which has necessitated increased communication with other providers on the health care team. Liaison activities help to address this need and may involve educating other professionals regarding psychological issues associated with health and the services that psychologists may provide.

In addition to these patient care activities, possessing a background in research design and methodology provides a basis for health service psychologists to conduct research in health care (cf. Baker, McFall, & Shoham, 2008) and for cross-disciplinary (or transdisciplinary; compare with Choi & Pak, 2006) research collaboration with other health professionals (Brown et al., 2002). Program evaluation skills represent an extension of research skills more typical of academic psychologists. Program evaluation generally occurs at a systemic level and may be characterized as having parallel activities (e.g., needs assessment, intervention or implementation, evaluation or reporting) to those delineated by Brown et al. (2002).

## HEALTH SERVICE PSYCHOLOGISTS' KNOWLEDGE BASE AND COMPETENCIES

The health service psychologists' knowledge base and competencies are not easily separated; considerable overlap between the two constructs exists. One way of conceptualizing the distinction between the two may be the difference between simply having the knowledge or skill and being qualified and capable of undertaking certain activities. Competency generally implies some public verification that the practice is undertaken consistent with standards and guidelines of peer review, ethical principles, and values of the profession, especially those that protect and otherwise benefit the public (Rodolfa et al., 2005).

In 2010, the HSPEC, consisting of members from APA, the Council of Graduate Departments of Psychology, and the Council of Chairs of Training Councils, was formed to address increasing concerns related to education and training for the professional practice of psychology (HSPEC, 2013). The HSPEC drafted a blueprint to outline steps to achieve changes in psychology graduate education and to "strengthen the core preparation and identity of health service psychologists" (p. 416). In addition to these recommended steps, the HSPEC articulated specific competencies critical to the practice of HSP in the domains of science, professionalism, relational (i.e., interpersonal skills and communication), applications, education, and supervision and systems (listed in the appendix of the HSPEC document). These broad competency domains are grounded in the reliance on a biopsychosocial model that emphasizes the need for education and training focused on biological, psychological, social, and cultural aspects of health and behavior in both traditional mental health and other areas of health.

Competency in *science* requires an understanding of scientific knowledge and methods, including basic knowledge from other disciplines. This broader base of knowledge is needed to enable psychologists to treat the whole person in collaboration with other health professionals. Competence in science also includes skills in research, evaluation, or both; health service psychologists must be able to conduct their own research (basic or practice-based) and be consumers of research.

*Professionalism* as a competency includes adherence to a core set of professional values and attitudes (including integrity, accountability, lifelong learning, concern for others' welfare). Competent health service psychologists also value individual and cultural diversity: They are aware of differences across different patient populations in addition to differences among providers with whom they work (e.g., health beliefs, attitudes). Professionalism also entails adherence to ethical and legal standards and policy: Competent health service psychologists abide by the current version of the *Ethical Principles of Psychologists and Code of Conduct* (APA, 2017) and to local, state, and federal laws governing health care practice. They also engage in reflective practice, self-assessment, and self-care.

*Relational competency* entails interpersonal and communication skills to enable effective therapeutic and working relationships with patients, colleagues, and communities in different health care settings.

*Competency in psychological applications* includes evidence-based practice, assessment, intervention, and consultation. Evidence-based practice is "the integration of the best available research with clinical expertise in the context of patient characteristics, culture, and preferences" (APA, 2005). Assessment undertaken by health service psychologists includes psychological measures (i.e., cognitive, behavioral, affective, and interpersonal function) and health problems (e.g., substance abuse, mental health disorders, acute and chronic disease, psychological conditions that manifest somatically, organic conditions that manifest psychologically, behavioral risk factors for illness, psychological adjustment to health conditions, psychological effects of medications). Health service psychologists should understand the relevance of common health care measures (e.g., blood pressure, laboratory assays, radiological studies) and know how to quickly access information about other health assessments. They should be able to tailor their findings to the health care settings and patients served. Health service psychologists should be competent in the most commonly used evidence-based psychological approaches; they should know when to seek consultation and understand how the services they provide may be affected by other health care interventions. Health care psychologists also provide consultation to other providers to help them manage psychological and behavioral elements of presenting problems.

*Competency in education* includes teaching and supervision, including psychology trainees and other health care professionals. It also includes knowledge of professional credentials, licensure, and standards across different health care professions.

*Competency in supervision* includes knowledge, collaborative skills, and attitudes.

*Competency in systems* includes an understanding of interdisciplinary and interprofessional systems, professional leadership development, and advocacy. Understanding interdisciplinary and interprofessional systems includes knowledge of the skills needed for teamwork and effective interdisciplinary functioning. The *Core Competencies for Interprofessional Collaborative Practice* (Interprofessional Education Collaborative Expert Panel, 2011; see also Interprofessional Education Collaborative, 2016) delineate broad and specific competencies recommended for individuals across all disciplines represented in a multidisciplinary team; the HSPEC noted that in addition to these competencies, health service psychologists should be aware of differences that exist across different settings and service delivery types.

Rodolfa et al. (2005) proposed a similar set of competencies that they suggested could be characterized as separate domains: *foundational competencies*— the knowledge, skills, attitudes, and values that are the foundation for the practice of psychology (e.g., reflective practice–self-assessment, scientific knowledge–methods, relationships, ethical–legal standards–policy, interdisciplinary systems)—and *functional competencies*—the major functions that psychologists serve (e.g., assessment–diagnostic–case conceptualization, intervention, consultation, research or evaluation, management–administration). Foundational and functional competencies are both conceptualized to develop or mature over the stages of the psychologist's professional development.

## ESTABLISHMENT AND MAINTENANCE OF COMPETENCIES

In its blueprint for education and training of health service psychologists, the HSPEC (2013) outlined several recommendations related to the establishment and maintenance of competencies. These recommendations included clearly articulated competencies understood by faculty, students, regulators, and the public; guidelines for minimal qualifications for entry into doctoral programs that prepare health service psychologists; articulation and evaluation of the competencies at each level of education and training; increased focus on competency assessment; increased implementation of evidence-based procedures, scientific mindedness, and (basic and applied) research capabilities; self-regulation for education and training through the adoption of a national standard of accreditation; and additional research relevant to the preparation and roles of health service psychologists and ongoing, comprehensive workforce analysis.

The APA *Standards of Accreditation for Health Service Psychology* (APA, Commission on Accreditation, 2018), implemented in 2017, reflect these priorities. The standards require that students or trainees demonstrate competence in research; ethical and legal standards; individual and cultural diversity; professional values, attitudes, and behaviors; communication and interpersonal skills; assessment; intervention; supervision; consultation; and interprofessional or interdisciplinary skills.

## IMPLICATIONS FOR EDUCATION AND TRAINING

The developments in the definition of HSP and increased specification of competencies required for its practice have implications for all levels of psychology training and education from undergraduate to continuing education (i.e., lifelong learning).

### Undergraduate Education

Baker et al. (2008) argued that students entering doctoral programs in clinical psychology should have appropriate grounding in science and mathematics to demonstrate interest in and aptitude for graduate science training and have evidence of academic achievement that would predict likelihood of successful graduate training. The HSPEC (2013) was more prescriptive; it specified that students entering graduate programs in HSP should demonstrate familiarity with psychology's "major concepts, theoretical perspectives, empirical findings, and historical trends" (p. 416); knowledge in human biology; experience in using basic research methods; critical thinking capability; oral and written communication skills; an ability to act ethically, work well with others, self-regulate, and reflect on their own and others' views, behavior, and mental processes; an appreciation and understanding of diversity; and a willingness to examine their personal values and to use relevant knowledge and skills regardless of their beliefs, attitudes, and values. Although Baker et al. argued in support of a new accrediting body for clinical psychologists (i.e., Psychological Clinical Science Accreditation System), whereas the HSPEC's recommendations were outlined in support of changes to existing educational guidelines, both arguments suggest that undergraduate students contemplating application for doctoral education in HSP should carefully evaluate their undergraduate educational objectives to ensure that they are in line with these application requirements. The *Standards of Accreditation for Health Service Psychology* (APA, Commission on Accreditation, 2018) have largely codified the recommendations of the HSPEC, and the Psychological Clinical Science Accreditation System requires applicants for accreditation to demonstrate that entrants into HSP programs meet criteria consistent with those delineated by Baker et al. (2008).

## Graduate Education

The *Standards of Accreditation for Health Service Psychology* (APA, Commission on Accreditation, 2018) distinguish between discipline-specific knowledge and professionwide competencies. *Discipline-specific knowledge* is recognized as the foundation for the formation of health services psychology identity; students in APA-accredited programs are expected to develop a general knowledge base in psychology as a foundation for further training. APA's *Implementing Regulations* (APA, Commission on Accreditation, n.d.) specify that this knowledge base needs to include familiarity with history and systems of psychology; basic content areas in scientific psychology, including affective, biological, cognitive, developmental, and social aspects of behavior; advanced integrative knowledge in scientific psychology; and research methods, statistical analysis, and psychometrics.

*Professionwide competencies* build on discipline-specific knowledge. Consistent with the recommendations of the HSPEC (2013), students in APA-accredited health services psychology doctoral programs are required to demonstrate competence in research; ethical and legal standards; individual and cultural diversity; professional values, attitudes, and behaviors; communication and interpersonal skills; assessment; intervention; supervision; and consultation and interprofessional or interdisciplinary skills. The *Standards of Accreditation for Health Service Psychology* (APA, Commission on Accreditation, 2018) acknowledge the distinction between PhD and PsyD doctoral programs: In general, PhD programs place a greater emphasis on research, whereas PsyD programs generally emphasize clinical practice. However, all accredited doctoral programs are expected to ensure that their students gain knowledge and competency in all of the areas enumerated. Specifically, with the greater current emphasis on scientific training and reliance on evidence-based approaches to treatment as well as the recognition that science and practice should inform and be informed by each other, students whose professional goals are focused on practice must nevertheless be informed in scientific psychology and attain research competencies, and students planning more academic or scientific careers must become competent in the clinical practice aspects of HSP.

## Internship and Postdoctoral Education

At the internship and postdoctoral levels, the emphasis is on continued development of professionwide competencies. The competencies that interns and postdoctoral residents are required to demonstrate do not differ from those articulated for graduate-level training; consistent with the requirement that training in psychology be "sequential, cumulative, graded in complexity, and designed to prepare [trainees] for practice or further organized training" (APA, Commission on Accreditation, 2018), interns and postdoctoral residents are expected to demonstrate increasing levels of competence as their training continues. For example, with regard to research competency, doctoral students are required to

> demonstrate the substantially independent ability to formulate research or other scholarly activities (e.g., critical literature reviews, dissertation, efficacy studies, clinical case studies, theoretical papers, program evaluation projects, program development projects) that are of sufficient quality and rigor to have the potential to contribute to the scientific, psychological, or professional knowledge base, . . . conduct research or other scholarly activities, . . . [and] critically evaluate and disseminate research or other scholarly activity via professional publication and presentation at the local (including the host institution), regional, or national level. (APA, Commission on Accreditation, n.d., C-9 P. Profession-Wide Competencies, I. Research)

Interns are expected to demonstrate "the substantially independent ability to critically evaluate and disseminate research or other scholarly activities (e.g., case conference, presentation, publications) at the local (including the host institution), regional, or national level" (APA, Commission on Accreditation, n.d.). Postdoctoral residents are expected to demonstrate "the integration of science and practice" (APA, Commission on Accreditation, n.d.).

## Lifelong Learning and Continuing Education

Lifelong learning is part of competency in professionalism (HSPEC, 2013). On their completion of training in HSP, psychologists are expected to be competent in self-assessment and lifelong learning; these elements of professionalism should prepare psychologists to work in any health care setting and to maintain currency in evolving and emerging models of health care. Because health service delivery is constantly developing, health service psychologists should be willing to engage in continuing education that aids them in ongoing development and maturing of their professional competencies, some of which may not seem central to their primary interests. For example, psychologists whose interests are primarily in practice may need to attend refresher courses in statistics or research methodology—or overview courses in emerging approaches to statistical analysis and research design—to help them remain competent consumers of research findings. Such activities could be encouraged by offering continuing education credits for attendance at such courses or classes; criteria for continuing education credit may require adjustment to accommodate this shift in continuing education activities.

## PREPARATION FOR THE FUTURE

APA has conducted two surveys of health service psychologists in the past decade (APA Center for Workforce Studies, 2016; Michalski, Mulvey, & Kohout, 2010). The two surveys' similar (but not identical) methodology suggests trends in health service psychologists' employment and employment settings. Inspection of the kinds of work that health service psychologists do and the settings in which they work suggests a wide range of both. Independent practice has remained the single largest employment category.

Health service provision is changing rapidly, and health service psychologists need to be prepared to adapt to these changes. Advances in science and health and mental health care will provide new opportunities for health service psychologists, provided they remain abreast of changes and advances that occur. Areas that may represent opportunities for health service psychologists may include services to new populations, technological advances, increased roles in administration, and advances in targeting psychological interventions in established populations. This section provides an overview of a few directions in which HSP may go in the future.

### Team Science and Interdisciplinary Care

In 2015, the National Institute of Mental Health (NIMH, 2015) released its strategic plan for research. The plan has four major research objectives—Define the Mechanisms of Complex Behaviors; Chart Mental Illness Trajectories to Determine When, Where, and How to Intervene; Strive for Prevention and Cures; Strengthen the Public Health Impact of NIMH-Supported Research—with supportive research strategies for each. It seeks to link advances in biological research (e.g., genomics, neuroscience) to research on environmental factors (e.g., stress, social determinants) that influence mental disorders. The intent of this approach is to improve detection and diagnosis specificity and to pave the way to improved interventions. This increased focus on cross-disciplinary research requires greater use of team approaches to research. Although APA has expressed concern over the relative lack of emphasis on behavioral and social factors in the plan, opportunities remain in behavioral and social research within the framework of the plan.

The plan references research undertaken by Helen Mayberg and her colleagues (Holtzheimer & Mayberg, 2011; McGrath et al., 2013) as an example of this approach of linking biomedical research to behavioral research. McGrath and her colleagues conducted a series of studies of brain structure and function in people with major depression. McGrath et al. (2013) used positron-emission tomography scan measurement of brain glucose metabolism to assess the association of pretreatment brain activity patterns with differential response to antidepressant medication and cognitive behavior therapy. Right anterior insula hypometabolism was associated with remission in response to cognitive behavior therapy and poor response to escitalopram oxalate

(Lexapro™), whereas insula hypermetabolism was associated with remission in response to escitalopram oxalate and poor response to cognitive behavior therapy.

Another example of the role psychology can play in team research may be seen in Martha Farah's research on the effects of poverty on child brain development (Farah et al., 2006; Lawson, Duda, Avants, Wu, & Farah, 2014; Noble, Norman, & Farah, 2005; Rao et al., 2010). After documenting the impact of poverty on language, memory, working memory, and cognitive control among children (Farah et al., 2006), she and her associates demonstrated socioeconomic status association with children's prefrontal cortical thickness (Lawson et al., 2014); moreover, they demonstrated that parental nurturance when the child was 4 years old predicted volume of the left hippocampus in adolescence: Better nurturance predicted smaller hippocampal volume (Rao et al., 2010).

Although neither of these examples points to current assessment or treatment implications, they both represent important directions of research and the importance of team research. They also demonstrate important roles of psychology participation in such research: Both included psychologists in important roles (W. Edward Craighead in Helen Mayberg's research; Martha Farah, Gwedolyn M. Lawson, and Laura M. Betancourt in Farah's research).

The NIMH (2015) strategic plan for research and the advocacy of psychology as a science, technology, engineering, and math discipline (APA, n.d.-a) suggest several implications for health service psychologists. Those involved in health and mental health research are increasingly likely to be involved in multi-disciplinary team research in which psychology is one of several disciplines represented on the team. The NIMH strategic plan for research suggests that current and future mental health care may entail new service delivery models outside of traditional health care systems (e.g., in schools, community settings, workplaces, online) and with integrated care. Health service psychologists need to be prepared to practice in these settings in ways that do not necessarily reflect traditional office practice and that entail coordination with other team members. In turn, these new approaches need to engender new ethical questions (e.g., confidentiality, privacy concerns). Education for psychology students and trainees needs to include training outside the scope of traditional office-based therapy, including behavioral assessment and research (Belar, 1998).

## Technological Advances and Health Service Psychology

Use of electronic reminder strategies, such as primarily pagers, to enhance treatment adherence has a history dating back to at least the mid-1990s (e.g., Heidenreich, Ruggerio, & Massie, 1999; Milch, Ziv, Evans, & Hillebrand, 1996) and has been extensively evaluated in the context of HIV (e.g., Dunbar et al., 2003; Simoni et al., 2009). More recent technological advances have made possible the use of smartphone applications to help clients adhere to treatment; the development and evaluation of these and other applications (e.g., Holloway et al., 2014) represent potential future roles for health service psychologists in multidisciplinary settings.

### Increased Demand for Service and "Psychologist Extenders"

The demand for health and mental health services has greatly expanded in the past 3 decades, and further increased demand is expected (Baker et al., 2008; Petterson et al., 2012; Robiner, 2006). To address the increased need for health care, *physician extenders*—nurse practitioners and physician assistants— have been employed to increase service provision and to decrease the cost of service delivery (Bodenheimer & Pham, 2010; Hooker & Everett, 2012). Quality of care does not appear to have diminished as a result of this approach (compare with Wilson et al., 2005). Health service psychology as a profession may need to assess the feasibility of training and employing psychologist extenders using a similar approach. These psychologist extenders would receive training in a limited number of evidence-based practices for treatment of non-complicated health and mental health problems confronted by psychologists' patients. Licensed psychologists would supervise or oversee the provision of these psychological services.

For example, exposure-based treatment for panic disorder has been demonstrated to be more effective than placebo and as effective as and more durable than treatments using antidepressants (Craske & Barlow, 2014). Barlow and Craske have developed detailed manuals for the treatment of panic disorder (Barlow & Craske, 2006; Craske & Barlow, 2006). Psychologist extenders could be trained in manual-based interventions to provide treatment to relatively uncomplicated patients (e.g., patients not diagnosed with a co-occurring personality disorder; cf. Grant et al., 2008) under the supervision of a licensed psychologist. Health service psychology already has a corollary paradigm in its model for training that could be modified for use with terminal master's level practitioners. Indeed, both doctoral students and licensed psychologists provided the treatment of panic disorder and agoraphobia under supervision in the studies reported by Barlow and Craske (2006; Craske & Barlow, 2006).

### Administration and Program Evaluation

The competencies expected of health service psychologists provide a foundation for additional roles in administration. For example, program evaluation is a crucial part of successful administration. Health service psychologists' background in research provides a basis for additional knowledge and skill development to undertake program evaluation. Program evaluation will become increasingly crucial and have an ongoing emphasis on the importance of evidence-based practice in the provision of health and mental health services. Much of what has been offered as evidence-based practice is grounded in efficacy studies, whereas effectiveness studies are more limited.

Efficacy and effectiveness have their corollaries in internal and external validity. *Internal validity* refers to whether an intervention makes a difference under well-defined and well-controlled experimental conditions. *External validity* refers to the generalizability of an experimental effect to different populations, settings, or treatment and measurement variables. Campbell and Stanley (1967) found an inverse relationship between the two: As internal validity increases, external validity decreases.

Whereas Campbell and Stanley (1967) argued for and sought to identify ways to increase internal validity in research in uncontrolled environments, Chen (2010) argued that program evaluation should focus on external *integrative validity*, which requires that an intervention be scientifically credible as well as relevant to and useful in the community or setting in which the intervention is introduced. Integrative validity adds viable validity to internal and external validity; it refers to the degree to which an intervention works in the real world: It seeks to determine whether it meets community-identified need, whether it is acceptable to the community, whether it can be implemented by ordinary practitioners, whether it is affordable, and whether it is helpful. Chen argued for the involvement of the targeted community in identifying the problem, undertaking the needs assessment, developing the intervention, and designing the evaluation strategy (to assess effectiveness)—a bottom-up approach to program evaluation.

In evaluating a new evidence-based treatment in a health or mental health system, for example, a program evaluation strategy may need to ask the following questions (among others): Does this treatment address a need identified by the community of providers? Does it address a need identified by the community of consumers? Is it acceptable to providers? Is it acceptable to consumers? If it is not acceptable, are there ways to increase its acceptability? Is it successful in addressing the identified problem?

Undertaking such a program evaluation strategy requires a mixed-methods approach that includes qualitative and quantitative approaches. Qualitative research is relatively new to psychology, and health service psychologists may need to acquaint themselves with the different methodological approaches used in qualitative research to inform the more qualitative aspects of their program evaluations. In implementing evidence-based practice in applied settings, program evaluation will be essential in determining their effectiveness in new and diverse populations and communities.

These possibilities represent a small sample of the potential directions that HSP could go. Health and mental health service provision will continue to evolve in ways that are not obvious today. The changes that come will result in new challenges and opportunities for health service psychologists.

## REFERENCES

American Psychological Association. (n.d.-a). Advocacy for psychology as a STEM discipline [Chapter XI of Council of Representatives policy manual]. Retrieved from http://www.apa.org/about/policy/stem-advocacy.aspx

American Psychological Association. (n.d.-b). Chapter X. Professional affairs (Part 1): 1996: Recognition of health service providers [Council of Representatives policy manual]. Retrieved from http://www.apa.org/about/policy/chapter-10.aspx

American Psychological Association. (2005). *Report of the 2005 Presidential Task Force on Evidence-Based Practice*. Retrieved from https://www.apa.org/practice/resources/evidence/evidence-based-report.pdf

American Psychological Association. (2011). Model act for state licensure of psychologists. *American Psychologist, 66*, 214–226. http://dx.doi.org/10.1037/a0022655

American Psychological Association. (2014). *APA guidelines for clinical supervision in health service psychology*. Retrieved from https://www.apa.org/about/policy/guidelines-supervision.pdf

American Psychological Association. (2017). *Ethical principles of psychologists and code of conduct* (2002, Amended June 1, 2010 and January 1, 2017). Retrieved from http://www.apa.org/ethics/code/index.aspx

American Psychological Association, Center for Workforce Studies. (2016). *2015 APA survey of psychology health service providers*. Retrieved from https://www.apa.org/workforce/publications/15-health-service-providers/report.pdf

American Psychological Association, Commission on Accreditation. (n.d.). Implementing regulations: Section C: IRs related to the *Guidelines and principles* for doctoral graduate programs, for internship programs, for postdoctoral residency programs. Retrieved from https://www.apa.org/ed/accreditation/about/policies/implementing-guidelines.pdf

American Psychological Association, Commission on Accreditation. (2018). *Standards of accreditation for health service psychology*. Retrieved from https://www.apa.org/ed/accreditation/about/policies/standards-of-accreditation.pdf

Baker, T. B., McFall, R. M., & Shoham, V. (2008). Current status and future prospects of clinical psychology: Toward a scientifically principled approach to mental and behavioral health care. *Psychological Science in the Public Interest, 9*, 67–103. http://dx.doi.org/10.1111/j.1539-6053.2009.01036.x

Barlow, D. H., & Craske, M. G. (2006). *Mastery of your anxiety and panic: Workbook*. New York, NY: Oxford University Press.

Belar, C. D. (1998). Graduate education in clinical psychology. "We're not in Kansas anymore." *American Psychologist, 53*, 456–464. http://dx.doi.org/10.1037/0003-066X.53.4.456

Belar, C. D. (2014). Reflections on the Health Service Psychology Education Collaborative blueprint. *Training and Education in Professional Psychology, 8*, 3–11. http://dx.doi.org/10.1037/tep0000027

Bodenheimer, T., & Pham, H. H. (2010). Primary care: Current problems and proposed solutions. *Health Affairs, 29*, 799–805. http://dx.doi.org/10.1377/hlthaff.2010.0026

Brown, R. T., Freeman, W. S., Brown, R. A., Belar, C., Hersch, L., Hornyak, L., . . . Reed, G. (2002). The role of psychology in health care delivery. *Professional Psychology: Research and Practice, 33*, 536–545. http://dx.doi.org/10.1037/0735-7028.33.6.536

Campbell, D. T., & Stanley, J. C. (1967). *Experimental and quasi-experimental design for research: Handbook of research on teaching*. Boston, MA: Houghton Mifflin.

Chen, H. T. (2010). The bottom-up approach to integrative validity: A new perspective for program evaluation. *Evaluation and Program Planning, 33*, 205–214. http://dx.doi.org/10.1016/j.evalprogplan.2009.10.002

Choi, B. C., & Pak, A. W. (2006). Multidisciplinarity, interdisciplinarity and transdisciplinarity in health research, services, education and policy: 1. Definitions, objectives, and evidence of effectiveness. *Clinical and Investigative Medicine, 29*, 351–364.

Craske, M. G., & Barlow, D. H. (2006). *Mastery of your anxiety and worry: Therapist guide* (2nd ed.). New York, NY: Oxford University Press.

Craske, M. G., & Barlow, D. H. (2014). Panic disorder and agoraphobia. In D. H. Barlow (Ed.), *Clinical handbook of psychological disorders: A step-by-step treatment manual* (5th ed., pp. 1–61). New York, NY: Guilford Press.

Dunbar, P. J., Madigan, D., Grohskopf, L. A., Revere, D., Woodward, J., Minstrell, J., . . . Hooton, T. M. (2003). A two-way messaging system to enhance antiretroviral adherence. *Journal of the American Medical Informatics Association, 10,* 11–15. http://dx.doi.org/10.1197/jamia.M1047

Farah, M. J., Shera, D. M., Savage, J. H., Betancourt, L., Giannetta, J. M., Brodsky, N. L., . . . Hurt, H. (2006). Childhood poverty: Specific associations with neuro-cognitive development. *Brain Research, 1110,* 166–174. http://dx.doi.org/10.1016/j.brainres.2006.06.072

Grant, B. F., Chou, S. P., Goldstein, R. B., Huang, B., Stinson, F. S., Saha, T. D., . . . Ruan, W. J. (2008). Prevalence, correlates, disability, and comorbidity of *DSM–IV* borderline personality disorder: Results from the Wave 2 National Epidemiologic Survey on Alcohol and Related Conditions. *Journal of Clinical Psychiatry, 69,* 533–545. http://dx.doi.org/10.4088/JCP.v69n0404

Health Service Psychology Education Collaborative. (2013). Professional psychology in health care services: A blueprint for education and training. *American Psychologist, 68,* 411–426. http://dx.doi.org/10.1037/a0033265

Heidenreich, P. A., Ruggerio, C. M., & Massie, B. M. (1999). Effect of a home monitoring system on hospitalization and resource use for patients with heart failure. *American Heart Journal, 138,* 633–640. http://dx.doi.org/10.1016/S0002-8703(99)70176-6

Holloway, I. W., Rice, E., Gibbs, J., Winetrobe, H., Dunlap, S., & Rhoades, H. (2014). Acceptability of smartphone application-based HIV prevention among young men who have sex with men. *AIDS and Behavior, 18,* 285–296. http://dx.doi.org/10.1007/s10461-013-0671-1

Holtzheimer, P. E., & Mayberg, H. S. (2011). Stuck in a rut: Rethinking depression and its treatment. *Trends in Neurosciences, 34,* 1–9. http://dx.doi.org/10.1016/j.tins.2010.10.004

Hooker, R. S., & Everett, C. M. (2012). The contributions of physician assistants in primary care systems. *Health and Social Care in the Community, 20,* 20–31. http://dx.doi.org/10.1111/j.1365-2524.2011.01021.x

Interprofessional Education Collaborative. (2016). *Core competencies for interprofessional collaborative practice: 2016 update.* Retrieved from https://nebula.wsimg.com/2f68a39520b03336b41038c370497473?AccessKeyId=DC06780E69ED19E2B3A5&disposition=0&alloworigin=1

Interprofessional Education Collaborative Expert Panel. (2011). *Core competencies for interprofessional collaborative practice: Report of an expert panel.* Retrieved from https://nebula.wsimg.com/3ee8a4b5b5f7ab794c742b14601d5f23?AccessKeyId=DC06780E69ED19E2B3A5&disposition=0&alloworigin=1

Lawson, G. M., Duda, J. T., Avants, B. B., Wu, J., & Farah, M. J. (2014). Associations between children's socioeconomic status and prefrontal cortical thickness [Special issue]. *Developmental Science, 16,* 641–652. http://dx.doi.org/10.1111/desc.12096

McGrath, C. L., Kelley, M. E., Holtzheimer, P. E., Dunlop, B. W., Craighead, W. E., Franco, A. R., . . . Mayberg, H. S. (2013). Toward a neuroimaging treatment selection biomarker for major depressive disorder. *JAMA Psychiatry, 70,* 821–829. http://dx.doi.org/10.1001/jamapsychiatry.2013.143

Michalski, D., Mulvey, T., & Kohout, J. (2010). *2008 APA survey of psychology health service providers.* Retrieved from https://www.apa.org/workforce/publications/08-hsp/report.pdf

Milch, R. A., Ziv, L., Evans, V., & Hillebrand, M. (1996). The effect of an alpha-numeric paging system on patient compliance with medicinal regimens. *American Journal of Hospice and Palliative Medicine, 13,* 46–48. http://dx.doi.org/10.1177/104990919601300314

National Institute of Mental Health. (2015). *Strategic plan for research* (Publication No. 15-6368). Retrieved from https://www.nimh.nih.gov/about/strategic-planning-reports/nimh_strategicplanforresearch_508compliant_corrected_final_149979.pdf

Noble, K. G., Norman, M. F., & Farah, M. J. (2005). Neurocognitive correlates of socioeconomic status in kindergarten children. *Developmental Science, 8,* 74–87. http://dx.doi.org/10.1111/j.1467-7687.2005.00394.x

Petterson, S. M., Liaw, W. R., Phillips, R. L., Jr., Rabin, D. L., Meyers, D. S., & Bazemore, A. W. (2012). Projecting US primary care physician workforce needs: 2010–2025. *Annals of Family Medicine, 10,* 503–509. http://dx.doi.org/10.1370/afm.1431

Rao, H., Betancourt, L., Giannetta, J. M., Brodsky, N. L., Korczykowski, M., Avants, B. B., . . . Farah, M. J. (2010). Early parental care is important for hippocampal maturation: Evidence from brain morphology in humans. *NeuroImage, 49,* 1144–1150. http://dx.doi.org/10.1016/j.neuroimage.2009.07.003

Robiner, W. N. (2006). The mental health professions: Workforce supply and demand, issues, and challenges. *Clinical Psychology Review, 26,* 600–625. http://dx.doi.org/10.1016/j.cpr.2006.05.002

Rodolfa, E., Bent, R., Eisman, E., Nelson, P., Rehm, L., & Ritchie, P. (2005). A cube model for competency development: Implications for psychology educators and regulators. *Professional Psychology: Research and Practice, 36,* 347–354. http://dx.doi.org/10.1037/0735-7028.36.4.347

Simoni, J. M., Huh, D., Frick, P. A., Pearson, C. R., Andrasik, M. P., Dunbar, P. J., & Hooton, T. M. (2009). Peer support and pager messaging to promote anti-retroviral modifying therapy in Seattle: A randomized controlled trial. *Journal of Acquired Immune Deficiency Syndromes, 52,* 465–473. http://dx.doi.org/10.1097/QAI.0b013e3181b9300c

Wilson, I. B., Landon, B. E., Hirschhorn, L. R., McInnes, K., Ding, L., Marsden, P. V., & Cleary, P. D. (2005). Quality of HIV care provided by nurse practitioners, physician assistants, and physicians. *Annals of Internal Medicine, 143,* 729–736. http://dx.doi.org/10.7326/0003-4819-143-10-200511150-00010

# 5

# Consultation in Interprofessional Practice and Collaboration

Patricia Arredondo

Interprofessional practice is the overarching framework for consultation and collaboration in a wide range of organizations having a cross section of individuals, psychologists, professionals, and laypersons. Interprofessional collaboration has long been recognized as a domain in professional psychology because of its historic practice by psychologists across specialty areas and disciplines, such as nursing and social work (Johnson, Stewart, Brabeck, Huber, & Rubin, 2004). Consultation and collaboration are metaprocesses within interprofessional practice involving individuals and systems to address particular priorities or goals. Fundamental to effective interprofessional practice is cultural competency development (Arredondo et al., 1996; Sue, Arredondo, & McDavis, 1992) and knowledge about intersecting systems that affect human and organizational behaviors. The American Psychological Association's (APA, 2017) *Multicultural Guidelines: An Ecological Approach to Context, Identity, and Intersectionality, 2017,* is a relevant backdrop to interprofessional practice because the guidelines use Bronfenbrenner's (1979) ecological, interdependent systems model to inform education, clinical practice, research, and consultation with different populations. Interprofessional practice provides engagement at interpersonal, group, and systems levels with diverse individuals and in varying contexts to address issues through collaboration and consultation and on teams.

Interprofessional practice also advances change through a social justice focus, as may be seen in societal movements. For example, the first APA

http://dx.doi.org/10.1037/0000153-006
*Consultation in Psychology: A Competency-Based Approach*, C. A. Falender and E. P. Shafranske (Editors)

#Blacklivesmatter march took place at the Denver, Colorado, conference. It was a systems approach to a social issue—the killing of unarmed Black men—that brought together students, professionals from psychology, local Denver groups, and APA leadership. Also evident in this interprofessional practice example was the collaboration and participation of individuals from diverse and intersecting identities to protest unjust behaviors toward other individuals. In short, the cause or purpose of #Blacklivesmatter was the unifying forum for interprofessional practice.

Relevant to the focus on interprofessional practice for social justice advocacy are the "Multicultural and Social Justice Competencies" (Ratts et al., 2015). The document emphasizes action steps for developing cultural awareness and knowledge and for engaging in public policy and advocacy. This competency document also recognizes the force of societal structures that affect the well-being of individuals and families, especially those from historically marginalized groups. The multicultural and social justice competencies are particularly relevant to interprofessional, culturally responsive health care collaborations because the population of interest generally experiences multiple public health disparities (e.g., diabetes, obesity, nutritional deprivation). Moreover, the populations are also affected by structural forces that affect their access to care and other basic needs (Bronfenbrenner, 1979). Experiences of sociopolitical oppression in the forms of classism, racism, sexism, and discrimination are also prevalent and long standing. In effect, interprofessional practice can be a form of social justice advocacy.

In the APA Multicultural Guidelines (APA, 2003), attention is paid to the psychologist's role as an organizational change agent. Guideline 6 states, "Professionals are encouraged to use organizational change processes to support culturally informed organizational (policy) development and practices" (Fouad & Arredondo, 2007, p. 95). Similarly, "interprofessional collaboration refers to education, training, scholarship, practice, and other activities that prepare (and engage) psychologists to work" (Arredondo et al., 2004, p. 789) with individuals from other disciplines, professions, and organizations as well as stakeholders with particular issues that need solutions. For example, a community-based organization was about to lose its Head Start funding; that loss would affect nearly 500 families. Respectful interprofessional collaboration was required and brought together agency leaders and board members, political representatives, and parent representatives to determine how to avoid the crisis. Because the possible loss of funding was known 4 months in advance, it was possible to engage the systems and power brokers to avert that loss.

Similar examples are interwoven into this chapter to illustrate the application of interprofessional practice, consultation, and collaboration in different contexts and engagement in different systems. To further frame premises about interprofessional practice, the chapter discusses culture in organizations, an intersectionality model that describes social identities and the possible effects on interpersonal relationships in practice, culture-centered psychologists, culture-centered leadership, and a model for interprofessional research teams.

## CULTURAL PARADIGMS IN ORGANIZATIONS

Before moving to a description of culture-centered organizations and culture-centered leadership, a review is offered of the definitions of *culture*, broadly speaking, and their relevance for organizations, leadership, and interprofessional practice. Definitions most often emanate from the work of anthropologists and social psychologists. The language and terminology of these definitions inform the interdisciplinary content of multicultural counseling guidelines. A few examples are as follows:

> The set of attitudes, values, beliefs, and behaviors shared by a group of people, but different for each individual, communicated from one generation to the next. (Matsumoto, 1996, p. 16)

> Culture consists of patterns, explicit and implicit, of and for behaviour acquired and transmitted by symbols, constituting the distinctive achievements of human groups, including their embodiment in artifacts; the essential core of culture consists of traditional (i.e., historically derived and selected) ideas and especially their attached values; culture systems may, on the one hand, be considered as products of action, on the other, as conditional elements of future action. (Kroeber & Kluckhohn, 1952, p. 181)

> Culture is a fuzzy set of basic assumptions and values, orientations to life, beliefs, policies, procedures and behavioural conventions that are shared by a group of people, and that influence (but do not determine) each member's behaviour and his/her interpretations of the "meaning" of other people's behaviour. (Spencer-Oatey, 2012, p. 3)

These definitions provide common denominators and varying perspectives about how to recognize and consider the conscious and unconscious application of culture in organizations and how to understand cultural conflicts when they are pointed to as factors that affect harmony, respect, and acceptance of others and their viewpoints in interprofessional practice. Given that the embodiment of culture is a lived and socialized experience, it informs our cognitive processes, emotions, and behavior. As Hofstede (1991) stated, "Culture is the collective programming of the mind which distinguishes the members of one group or category from another" (p. 5). Hofstede's definition and those cited in this chapter are relevant to consultation. This is the case in organizations in which individual members of one unit, for instance, information technology, bring their personal and professional mind-sets to work encounters. They see the task perhaps with a problem-solving, pragmatic approach, whereas a human resources specialist may want to understand the effects of a technological change on employees' productivity, absenteeism, and so forth. Per Hofstede, all humans possess *software of the mind*—cognitive programming influenced by one's national values (country of origin), socialization experiences in schools and religion, expectations based on gender socialization, discipline-specific norms, and organizational influence. Culture and cultural biases are neither static nor neutral, and thus need to be recognized for how they affect consultation and interprofessional collaborations.

## CULTURE AND VALUES-DRIVEN ORGANIZATIONS

### National Values to Organizational Values

The preceding definitions of culture mention value orientations, beliefs, symbols, and policies that are transmitted by culture but, in practice, by people. Seminal research on values and how values socialize individuals are derived from Hofstede's (1980) study in the 1960s on national values in 55 countries. He found four value sets or dimensions that influence a society, institutions, and individuals: individualism versus collectivism, femininity versus masculinity, a high and low orientation to power distance, and a high and low orientation to uncertainty. He also examined his findings with respect to gender; as might be expected, he found differences in how expectations for women in organizations mirrored the societal values for femininity and masculinity, for example. Nearly 50 years later, Hofstede's (1980) research continues to be referenced because of how his four dimensions bring culture and values into understanding workplace values and behavior. Accordingly, workplaces establish goals and priorities informed by these values. Specific to the United States, a heteropatriarchy culture, masculine behavior has been admired, encouraged, and rewarded in organizations and occurs in the military; Fortune 500 corporations, in which 96% of chief executive officers are men (Zarya, 2016); and in political circles. Men are said to be strong, smart, nonemotional for decision making, willing to assume power, and decisive. These attributes are often contrasted with those of women, in general. The data about women in political, corporate, and higher education leadership roles indicate a continuing bias and value for the masculine versus feminine. When introducing intersectionality into these discussions, differences about preferences and privileges for men and women begin to vary by age, ethnicity, sexual orientation, and disability status. Ultimately, it is still the masculine, individualistic value set that is most visible in organizations, thus representing a microcosm of society.

Referring again to the definitions of culture, Arredondo (1996) posited that "all organizations and institutions have a culture" (p. 8). Contributing to a given organization's unique cultural paradigm is its history, founders, mission, and purpose in addition to values, norms and traditions, and organizational structure (Arredondo, 1996). Context, geographic location, the historical era for the founding, and the time in which an organization is looking at inter-professional collaborations and consultation all matter. For example, if a historically Black college and university is approached by a predominantly White institution to identify a pipeline of talented students to admit, all may go well initially because of the intention for the collaboration, but the planning process may have impasses if the predominantly White institution takes a colonization, dominant approach. Historically Black colleges and universities have a long legacy of educating African Americans before enactment of the Civil Rights legislation and do not see themselves beholden to predominantly White institutions. Both are culture-centered organizations and the historically

Black college and university is likely to resist another university's imposition of values and practices.

## Psychologists on Culture-Centered Organizations

Scholarly discussions about the presence, force, and dynamics of culture in organizations have been led by organizational psychologists (Arredondo, 1996; Cox, 1993; Hofstede, 1980, 1991; Lowman, 2013, 2014; Morgan, 2006) and others promoting consultation from psychological perspectives (Dougherty, 2013; Gallessich, 1985). In addressing multicultural and international issues in organizational change and development and consultation processes, Lowman (2014) pointed out that globalization has introduced other cross-cultural dynamics. Multinational companies have come to recognize that business done in Beijing, China, Mexico City, Mexico, and London, England, will vary from "traditional" U.S. practices, particularly at the management level. In addition, Hofstede (1991) stated that organizational change processes related to career planning, promotion, and other personnel matters need to be considered through culturally relevant lenses. The role of national values and the previously cited software of the mind construct are relevant to an explanation of such differences.

Because this chapter is dedicated to consultation and interprofessional practice involving psychologists, other frameworks to consider come from the APA (2017) Multicultural Guidelines, Morgan (2006) in *Images of Organizations*, Arredondo (1996) in *Successful Diversity Management Initiatives: A Blueprint for Planning and Implementation*, and Cox (1993) in *Cultural Diversity in Organizations* (1993). Although they are not necessarily new publications, they continue to be emblematic of how to approach interprofessional practice and consultation that is culture centered and demonstrates collaborations that lead to shared processes of change through diverse, developmental, and systems-based lenses.

Offering metaphors about organizations, Morgan (2006) highlighted how an individual's mind-set, demeanor, and behavior may be affected and even be changed by the organization's prevailing culture. If one enters as a free spirit and an initiator who is willing to take risks, these characteristics may be stifled in an organization that operates like a "psychic prison." In such a cultural milieu, employees are expected to assimilate to the prevailing norms and behaviors; there, Morgan (1997) posited, favored ways of thinking may lead to groupthink. Contextually, organizations may operate as dominators: This type of organization is controlling and even exploitative and socializes employees in one way of thinking and behaving. These examples can come from health care and academic settings, not just corporate workplaces. A culture-centered consultant is able to recognize a health care administrators' rigidity and unwillingness to adapt to new ideas introduced, say, by a community health care leader or researcher. In interprofessional practice, working with representatives of a hospital that fosters a psychic prison or dominator culture is a challenge.

Cox (1993) and Fouad and Arredondo (2007) affirmed the presence of cultural dimensions in all organizations and how these dimensions are often minimized because *culture* frequently is code for looking at issues for people of color. They also pointed out that overly focusing on affirmative action in organizations persists, thereby continuing to create assumptions about individuals' capabilities and underestimating their potential contributions because they are not seen as members of the mainstream. In interprofessional practice, these mind-sets could derail initiatives designed to address depression and substance abuse for immigrant adults, for example. Cognitive psychologists or researchers may prefer to look only at behavior and not the context influencing the behavior. A culture-centered consultant, on the other hand, would remind researchers about the fallacy of objectivity and homogeneity (Davis, Nakayama, & Martin, 2000) and the need to consider the sociocultural influences on behavior of immigrants (Arredondo, Gallardo-Cooper, Delgado-Romero, & Zapata, 2014).

The APA (2017) Multicultural Guidelines introduce an ecological approach that positions context, identity, and intersectionality as essential dimensions to consider in all change-related initiatives. This model, which involves the five Bronfenbrenner (1979) systems and three dynamics of intersectionality, tension, and fluidity in domestic and international settings, highlights the power of an interprofessional framework to create solutions at micro- and macrolevels. The mind-set of interprofessional practices is pervasive in all examples of change for individuals, communities, and systems.

## Acculturation Versus Assimilation in Organizations

Before becoming an employee, individuals have already experienced various cycles of socialization (Harro, 2008), both in their family upbringing during which they learn values and traditions and in schools, where they are introduced to other values and relational dynamics. However, schools are cultural entities informed by national values (Hofstede, 1991) that foster practices favoring brighter and perhaps mainstream identity students as well as boys versus girls, rather than those from marginalized social identities. The same is true for the workplace.

Hiring practices and orientation programs are examples of acculturation and perpetuation of the organization's sameness. According to Schneider (1987), the model for attracting and selecting new hires is consciously or unconsciously based on the tendency to attract and select individuals who look more like those already in place. If individuals cannot adapt or acculturate to the prevailing values and norms regarding socializing, staying late, or making sexist jokes, they will likely leave or otherwise be evaluated as not being team players.

The assimilationist model expects individuals or identity groups to adapt and become more like the majority group. In terms of interprofessional collaboration, consider the health care domain in which there are global or international engagements to understand the cultural worldview about how to best deliver health care services. For example, there may be agreement about a disease and its potential harm; however, varying cultural and health care perspectives on how to treat the disease are likely to be apparent. Quite often, beliefs grounded in spirituality, folk medicine, and religion may come into play, and Western health care professionals are generally new to these practices and beliefs. Although this scenario is presented as an international situation, similar scenarios may be present in U.S. settings with culture-specific dominant communities. Dynamics among coconsultants may become fraught when there are multiple perspectives and individuals who believe in "my way." If physicians as researchers expect other team members to subscribe to their scientific premises (an assimilationist approach) based on a sense of authority, hierarchy, and egocentrism, the likelihood is that the collaboration will falter or end.

## Identity Factors and Intersectionality in Organizations

A framework and practices for interprofessional collaboration, practice, and consultation that recognize and respect identity factors, intersectionality, and dynamics of power and privilege are outlined in the APA (2017) Multicultural Guidelines. Essentially, the guidelines state that consultants and collaborators need to understand that all organizations are cultural and multicultural entities influenced by the identities introduced by their employees, the communities in which they reside, business partners, consumers, and the prevailing organizational culture. As psychologists, we have been trained in culture-bound models that have neglected cultural factors (Bronstein & Quina, 1988) for fear of stereotyping; overlooking environmental conditions and context; and believing in egalitarianism, although not necessarily practicing it. However, the APA (2003) Multicultural Guidelines, dimensions of personal identity model (Arredondo et al., 1996), and research on intersectionality (Crenshaw, 2005) and colorism (Chávez-Dueñas, Adames, & Organista, 2014) point out visible and invisible dimensions of identity that are inherent in all organizations. Furthermore, intersectionality also means reconsidering how we think about identity attributions, equality, and power sharing. Underestimating a team member because of his or her disability and age may mean overlooking potential contributions.

The dimensions of personal identity model (Arredondo et al., 1996) is one paradigm (see Figure 5.1) that describes intersecting identities grounded in historic, geographic, political, and sociocultural conditions ("C" dimension), many of which may not be in an individual's control and that often affect inclusion in contemporary education and work settings. The "A" dimensions are ones often described as immutable and protected categories by legislation. Among the immutable dimensions are ethnicity, race, age, and sexual orientation—all are interdependent and are commonly visible in interprofessional collaborations. The "B" dimensions describe less visible characteristics

**FIGURE 5.1. Dimensions of Personal Identity and Intersectionality**

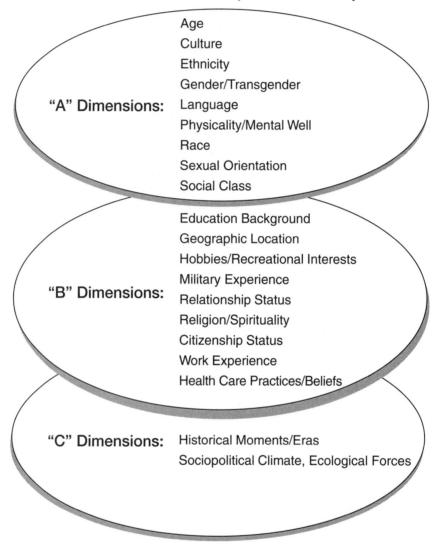

"A" Dimensions:
Age
Culture
Ethnicity
Gender/Transgender
Language
Physicality/Mental Well
Race
Sexual Orientation
Social Class

"B" Dimensions:
Education Background
Geographic Location
Hobbies/Recreational Interests
Military Experience
Relationship Status
Religion/Spirituality
Citizenship Status
Work Experience
Health Care Practices/Beliefs

"C" Dimensions:
Historical Moments/Eras
Sociopolitical Climate, Ecological Forces

of the individuals, such as educational background, work experience, religion, and geographical location. Ironically, these B dimensions of identity for team members may be more sources of contention because they refer to educational preparation, disciplinary identity, and positionality. Regardless, all dimensions interact and also intersect with the A and C dimensions. In short, each person has a unique and holistic identity, and it is this constellation of identity dimensions that individuals bring to interprofessional practice. Colorism cannot be overlooked as another factor present in collaborations. Often, individuals will say they do not see color, but this is a statement that needs to be addressed for successful and culturally competent collaborations.

Intersectionality is present in all organizations. In interprofessional consulting situations, a consultant must be culturally aware of all parties involved, the context or environment, and the purpose of the consultation. Here is a scenario: A bank in Boston, Massachusetts, wanted to establish a relationship with a Chinese community center and provide bilingual services for neighborhood residents. A consultant—experienced in working with culturally diverse communities—was called to mediate a few months after the working arrangement had begun. In the initial interview with the team, a misunderstanding based on cultural differences emerged immediately. The consultant pointed out that both the bank and the Chinese community center shared the same goal for serving Chinese residents, but their strong cultural identities and mind-sets about how to carry out the project were contributing to misunderstandings and impasses. The bank was accustomed to communicating via the Internet, brochures, and goodwill packages to new clients. The goodwill packages generally were food items, such as chocolate candy, power bars, macaroni, and olive oil. The bank was in Chinatown, which has an abundance of fresh fish, chicken, and vegetables that are common to the diet of the Chinese residents. Although the bank had bilingual tellers and customer service personnel who spoke Cantonese, the community agency leaders said potential customers were still uneasy. Banking was a new experience for many of the immigrant adults and their families. A trust issue existed despite having the agency serve as a cultural broker. In this scenario, the challenges to an interprofessional collaboration appear to have been affected by differing worldviews about the processes to attract new Chinese customers. Both culture-centered organizations wanted to serve the community but preferred culturally dissimilar practices. In speaking to residents, ideas emerged that led to "best" ways to engage them in using bank services that were easy, friendly, and linguistically and culturally responsive.

Accordingly, for many psychologist–consultants, it may not be in our DNA to consider the presence of culture and cultural perspectives in the consultation process. Interprofessional encounters may be even more complex because of differences in values, ways to approach an issue, power dynamics, and tensions that may converge. However, as the aforementioned bank scenario demonstrates, accomplishing outcomes is but one part of a collaboration. Multicultural collaborations and interprofessional engagements are complex, and parties cannot declare they are color blind (Neville, Gallardo, & Sue, 2016) or that cultural differences do not matter. We have to remember that unconscious biases are unavoidable and will affect relationships despite good intentions.

## INCLUSIVE INTERPROFESSIONAL CONSULTATION SCENARIOS

In 2002, several APA divisions came together for The Competencies Conference: Future Directions in Education and Credentialing in Professional Psychology. The Consultation and Interdisciplinary Relationships Workgroup was charged with examining how to create a paradigm for consultation inclusive of multiple relationships, competency guidelines, cultural competencies, and new approaches to teaching and practice about consultation. In their report, the workgroup identified key themes and attributes embedded in interprofessional practice (Anderson-Levitt, 2002; Johnson et al., 2004). These themes or attributes indicate that interprofessional collaboration moves away from discipline-specific centrism in which one's discipline has the "final word" to an approach that views the complementarity of varying perspectives or viewpoints in pursuit of shared goals (Arredondo, Shealy, Neale, & Winfrey, 2004). Another theme is that interprofessional collaboration is a best practice on multiple levels and in varying contexts (Arredondo et al., 2004; Johnson et al., 2004). Several issues leading to collaborations were highlighted. For example, funding opportunities or reduction in funding dilemmas increasingly are requiring more than one disciplinary approach. Sometimes technology can drive innovative projects through interprofessional collaborations, although the parties are not tech savvy. University researchers often find that they need community agencies and their boards to conduct research. The scenarios that follow demonstrate how complementarity of multiple perspectives benefits outcomes of research for community health projects through interprofessional practice.

## Scenarios: Interdisciplinary Research and Health Care Services

Federally funded research led by a clinical psychologist with a specialty in health psychology inspired interdisciplinary collaborations to support Latinx families in Chicago, Illinois. For the past 7 to 8 years, Dr. Lisa Sánchez-Johnsen has brought together community partners, researchers, health care providers, and educators on multiple research initiatives. In her intervention study *¡Viva la Salud!* (To good health!), the team knew it had to translate recruitment announcements and workshop materials for the program. Thus, one of the goals before implementing the intervention was to use accurate translations to conduct the research. Rather than take the typical pathway of translating English measures and then engaging in back-translation processes, the team decided on a translation process informed by Latinx culture, intersectionality, and the Spanish language. In the midst of their work, team members also determined that Spanish terms are not always relatable from one Latinx heritage group or another. One example is the word for orange. For persons of Puerto Rican heritage, the term *china* refers to an orange; for Mexican women, it is *naranja*.

Key findings from the team's culturally informed process for translation of the materials were (a) research must rely on instruments developed in Spanish for validation and reliability; (b) development of materials in Spanish first likely increases the cultural appropriateness of the instruments; (c) recognition of the demographics of community groups in a study is key to culturally competent research; and (d) determination of the linguistic fluency of research team members who purport to be bilingual also must be undertaken. Dr. Sánchez-Johnsen affirmed that the input and perspectives of the community partners, educators, and university researchers were all considered, thus creating a sense of *una familia* (a family) among the team (Sánchez-Johnsen, Escamilla, Rodriguez, Vega, & Bolaños, 2015).

An additional example from Dr. Sánchez-Johnsen's interprofessional collaboration involved the use of community boards to affirm that research or training interventions were "good" and relevant for a particular group the board represented. In this collaboration, Dr. Sánchez-Johnsen led a team to examine obesity and weight issues for Latinx men. To address this important public health issue, the community board from a cross-section of organizations, the primary community partner, and the university and hospital researchers formed a collaboration (Sánchez-Johnsen et al., 2017). The community board was instrumental in several respects. First, board members were of the community as were the men who would be invited to the obesity study. Other members of the board could comment on the potential challenges of bringing men to a study on weight. Although the potential subjects were concerned about their weight and went to doctors for solutions, this was much more acceptable culturally. Convincing these men to participate in a study with no guarantees that they would lose weight meant that outreach efforts had to be more personal and persuasive. However, it was not an all-or-nothing approach. In addition to live recruitment at the agencies where the men frequented, fliers were shared by physicians and health care professionals and at street fairs. The board also recommended mutually convenient locations for meeting the potential study participants.

Dr. Sánchez-Johnsen grounded the preparation for research training of her team in the *Guidelines on Multicultural Education, Training, Research, Practice, and Organizational Change for Psychologists* (APA, 2003); these guidelines emphasize the awareness, knowledge, and skills needed to conduct culturally competent research. The training was conducted with project staff and included an overview of culturally competent research practices and a discussion of methods for increasing participation and cultural competence in all aspects of the study. A takeaway from this scenario is Dr. Sánchez-Johnsen's culture-centered leadership and her approach to creating inclusivity among the team through the use of the APA (2003) guidelines.

## Graduate Classes to Prepare for Interprofessional Collaboration and Consultation

Graduate programs are initiating students toward innovative community-based interprofessional consultation and research endeavors. In the scenarios that follow, the goals are ones that primarily promote consumer well-being and efficacy and have collaborations among university researchers and educators, community organizations, and graduate students. These undertakings provide developmental, culture-centered opportunities for the students, clients, and community leaders. Teams form with rich learning about how families, particularly immigrants, manage their lives in the midst of adversity. Along the way, students learn social justice principles and advocacy, how to be culturally intentional, the need to consider context and its complexity, and the importance of paradigms of intersectionality. No longer is it sufficient to be unidimensional with respect to a group's visible identity, nor it is it acceptable to engage in interprofessional practice without recognizing the multidimensionality of all parties and the larger sociocultural context.

## Scenario: Interprofessional Engagement and Giving Back to the Community

Dr. Ed Delgado-Romero wanted his students to recognize that immigrants were growing up in the shadows of the university and that as much as their graduate program spoke about the values of multiculturalism and social justice, it was primarily theoretical. He had first-generation students in the doctoral program, most who had come from predominantly Latinx communities in California, Texas, and Florida. A university in Georgia was different, however: It was primarily White. An immigrant himself, Dr. Delgado-Romero recognized the stressors for immigrant families and noticed the lack of culturally informed counseling services in different city agencies. To this end, he focused his plans on preparing students in interprofessional collaboration with a Latinx agency to address issues for Spanish-speaking clients. A bilingual clinic within the agency was born and was staffed by doctoral students Dr. Delgado-Romero supervised. The agency staff, students, and Dr. Delgado-Romero became cocollaborators, advocating and supporting the Spanish-speaking clients. The system was changed, and Dr. Delgado-Romero pointed out that the benefit for clients was to be able to speak about their experiences, particularly the trauma of the immigrant journey, in their own words, without an intermediary, and with someone who could attend fully. An essential aspect of the supervision was unpacking the students' own feelings about the clients' experiences. Dr. Delgado-Romero relied on the multicultural counseling competencies (Arredondo et al., 1996) to guide his supervision of the students' clinical work.

The bilingual clinic became the hub for additional partnerships to benefit the immigrants. Dr. Delgado-Romero invited colleagues from the local hospital to provide wellness evaluations and special developmental examinations for children. The immigrants willingly agreed because they had the assistance of the bilingual students. This effort was complemented by informational workshops for parents to demystify the examination process with predominantly White professionals. There were many nonclinical needs including housing, legal resources, and how to open a bank account. As word of the bilingual clinic got out, university professors from the law school and the schools of dentistry and pharmacy offered to become part of Dr. Delgado-Romero's team. Through the interprofessional collaborations, communities began to form around the clinic's agenda for the immigrant clients.

Specific to research, Dr. Delgado-Romero and his team of students wanted to inquire about the benefits to parents and children who received clinical services, participated, or both, in psychoeducational programs. Were the participants reporting an improved sense of well-being, self-efficacy, access to basic needs, and a reduction in symptoms of depression? Preliminary findings indicated improvement in the areas examined (Kao, 2017).

### Scenarios: Model for Interprofessional Research Teams

Another example of university-driven interprofessional practice involves a community-based engagement with a Habitat for Humanity community conducted by a team of doctoral students, their advisor, housing consultants, and the board of the housing community overseen by the author (Arredondo). A road map to engage in a research project was planned in collaboration with the housing board of directors to build trust and demonstrate that their input mattered. Similar to the previous scenarios, members of the board advised on the best strategies to involve families in the study, questions that the researchers could ask that would also be beneficial to the community, and the best approaches to gain access to families. For example, they wanted to compile an updated directory of residents, particularly the children, and skills or resources that could be made available within the community. The community-centered approach prioritized the families, thus empowering them to tell their stories. Synergy between the team of students, board, and community director had to be in place before the team proceeded. This real-world collaboration also served as a reminder that nonprofessionals need to be seen as authorities on their priorities and lives (APA, 2017).

The graduate students gathered the relevant data for their respective theses and dissertation studies, but there was a sense of a real partnership and reciprocity among all parties. Additional team members were from the department of architecture and design. A doctoral student who is bilingual and a Mexican national and his advisor wanted to consult with the residents about how they had designed their homes. They were curious about the layout, the use of space, and other culture-specific house designs, particularly the interior. They learned that the parents wanted to re-create, as much as possible, homes that looked like the ones they knew in Mexico. The academics gained information about culturally influenced new designs that they could share in the university classroom.

The following scenario involves a course that engages students in consultation education informed by the multicultural competencies (Arredondo et al., 1996). Dr. Marie-Christine Goodworth teaches the yearlong consultation course Consultation, Education, and Program Evaluation to doctoral students in Portland, Oregon. The syllabus specifies learning outcomes that prepare students for real-world consultation experiences. They are taught skills, such as developing effective consultation questions, developing questionnaires in the appropriate language of the participants, conducting qualitative data analyses, and writing health service psychology reports. To operationalize these objectives, students engage in group consultation projects principally with hospitals, behavioral health organizations, social services agencies, and sometimes units at the university. One example follows from consultation with a large teaching hospital in the Northwest, particularly in the affiliated Federally Qualified Health Center. The projects the students undertook were to (a) evaluate the "no show" rate and make recommendations to the clinic, (b) help the clinic create a survey for the well-child visit using sound survey development skills, (c) evaluate if gender plays a role in who is referred to the behavioral health clinic, and (d) evaluate if gender of provider influences the rate of referral to the behavioral health clinic. Going from classroom theories to real-life consultations with professionals empowered the students about the relevance of their clinical skills and classroom learning to interprofessional practice.

### Culture-Centered Leadership

Studies on culture and leadership indicated that a cultural factor exists in all organizations and that culture and leadership are inextricably intertwined (Groysberg, Lee, Price, & Cheng, 2018). For organizational consultants, these findings mean taking into account the science that can inform their work. The researchers also found four cultural attributes or types of organizational cultures: shared, pervasive, enduring, and implicit. In addition, they found two common denominators across organizations regardless of size, type, geography, or industry: people interactions and response to change (Groysberg et al., 2018). In effect, these two dimensions are ones that can also contribute to effective interprofessional practice. When individuals from different types of organizational cultures come together for a shared undertaking, they also arrive with the mind-set of their specific workplace values, norms, and behaviors. Attending to the people dynamics, cultural worldviews, and the flexibility and adaptability of individuals facilitates the more effective engagement for interprofessional effectiveness.

In what is known as the GLOBE study, researchers examined the cultural universals (*etic*) and cultural specifics (*emic*) through cross-cultural leadership practices in 62 different societies (House, Hanges, Javidan, Dorfman, & Gupta, 2004). They examined leadership styles and found prevailing differences informed by Hofstede's (1980) construct of national values. Findings supported the premise that all leadership is culture bound and influenced by the national values infused into the organization. Examples of cultural divergence (i.e., emic) versus cultural convergence (i.e., etic) are provided to illustrate what leaders need to consider about national values and cultural mind-set in interprofessional practice. *Cultural divergence* suggests that groups favor their known ways of working and may not "play nice" when other practices are introduced in the workplace and may occur in global settings in which team members come from different countries and cultures. Accommodating "foreign" practices for workplace performance may not always be acceptable. *Convergence* refers to behaviors that become more aligned or homogenous; thus, teams have more cohesion. The examples are as follows:

- Participation (speaking up and giving ideas) by employees is more common in the United States and other Western countries but is less practiced in collectivistic societies (e.g., China). Inviting feedback would not be common in said societies and organizations. A leader needs to anticipate consideration of team members' relationship orientation and their experiences on a team. Although the collectivistic orientation may suggest adaptability to teamwork, prevailing values influence how people perform in groups based on gender, status, and disciplinary background.

- In many countries, men primarily assume the leadership. Paternalistic leadership is pervasive in Asian countries with implications of which gender is more highly valued. Although a team member may be U.S. born, family socialization for Chinese girls may continue to be the prevailing worldview in the workplace for some women.

- Communication is also used differently. In China, individuals are given indirect praise, whereas in the United States, one calls our or celebrates publicly the individual who is being commended. With respect to listening, this skill is widely touted in the United States; in academic institutions, it is often emphasized as a desirable practice.

- Non-Western countries emphasize collectivistic leadership. Chief executive officers in the United States tend to be viewed as highly individualistic males, which can be a source of conflict among interprofessional teams.

- In the study cited (House et al., 2004), there is little attention to gender issues or those of underrepresented groups; in short, that study is primarily about men as leaders.

Thus, the GLOBE study and other leadership studies underscore the tendency for cultural convergence with respect to management practices. House et al. (2004) concluded that change in fundamental values is slow and resistant to cultural convergence; divergence persists. For interprofessional teams, these are important cautions.

## The Cultural Factor for Interprofessional Practice

Culture-centered leadership is of relevance to interprofessional practice for numerous reasons. All organizations or disciplinary entities have their socialized ways to demonstrate or exert leadershiplike behavior. For example, in a university department, the program director may be the leader but because it is academic, generally more participation and processes are required to arrive at consensus or agreements. In community agencies, depending on the purpose, size, and nature of services delivered, more of a business leadership model may be applied. The director or chief executive officer may still invite feedback and ideas, but he or she generally reports to a board of directors. In hospital settings, there is a hierarchy: Medical doctors generally have the last word, and others on the team or unit follow his or her lead. Other considerations about expressing leadership in interprofessional collaborations are shared: (a) Generally, there are different disciplinary perspectives, processes for working, and ways of communicating; (b) when there are majority–minority collaborators, there may be biases to how to accomplish a project, which leaves out the views of the "minority" collaborators; (c) individuals arrive with their own experiences as leaders and may want to take over, although it is meant to be a collaboration; (d) perceived status by an entity—the funding entity, for example—may inadvertently suppress the participation of the agency that is hoping to gain funds for an initiative; and (e) visible cultural and linguistic differences cannot be ignored. Ultimately culture-centered leadership is about being an agent of change who is fully aware that culture counts in all collaborations internally and externally. A leader knows his or her audience and leverages that knowledge to engage effectively with different constituencies.

## BLUEPRINT FOR CULTURE-CENTERED INTERPROFESSIONAL CONSULTATION

Throughout this chapter, culture-related concepts are identified, culture and cultural values in organizations as well as culture-centered leadership are discussed, and scenarios describe the implementation of interprofessional practice. Those scenarios involved partners from different disciplinary backgrounds and work settings, and all were committed to effective change for a target population in a culture-specific community. This section introduces and discusses a blueprint for interprofessional collaboration. Rubrics are outlined to guide cultural competency practices (see Appendices 5.1 and 5.2), and, in particular, communication practices among team members to demonstrate inclusion and collaboration.

### About the Blueprint

The "Blueprint for Interprofessional Collaboration" (Arredondo, 2018) was adapted from the original blueprint for the successful diversity management initiatives model (Arredondo, 1996). The interprofessional collaboration blueprint is a developmental, culture-centered, stage-based process model that can guide the collaboration from the beginning. The following is a description of the seven stages and recommended actions for each stage as they relate to interprofessional practice:

1. Preparing for a collaboration. This is likely the most important stage because it sets the groundwork for interpersonal relationships, cultural intentionality as core to the project, agreement to the terms of the collaboration, determinations about leadership-sharing, and other considerations about cultural inclusivity.

2. Articulating a shared intention for the project. A facilitated discussion by an outside consultant may be useful to ensure that all participants share their intentions and desires. Discipline-specific priorities may come into play that go beyond the scope of funding and time to complete the project. In addition, with community partners on the team, it is necessary to respect their priorities and capacity to support the work. Often community agencies are understaffed, and if bilingual professionals are required to complete the project, there will likely be a need for negotiations about how to compensate workload and still cover the day-to-day agency tasks.

3. Providing cultural-competency education to the team. All team members come to an initiative with a different understanding and different education in cultural competency. For guidance on how to create a shared understanding, the team can refer to the 2003 APA Multicultural Guidelines (APA, 2003; Fouad & Arredondo, 2007) that outline fundamental competencies or behaviors for culturally self-aware consultants and interprofessional collaborators. These competencies or behaviors were also outlined in the report of the Consultation and Interprofessional Collaboration Workgroup (Arredondo et al., 2004). Proposed guidelines from that report (Arredondo et al., 2004) have been updated to denote that consultants and collaborators are expected to

   • have awareness of their beliefs, values, unconscious biases, and influences of their personal history on consultation and interprofessional collaboration (Guideline 1);

   • recognize specific biases and assumptions toward other disciplinary groups or community agencies with whom they collaborate (Guideline 2);

   • recognize the populations, contexts, different settings, sociopolitical climate, and other external factors that may affect the consultation process (Guidelines 2 and 6); and

   • identify biases as researchers, educators, or both that may affect their interprofessional practice as outlined in the APA (2017) Multicultural Guidelines (Guideline 4).

   Structured sessions by an outside facilitator are in order. For example, team members can be introduced to the implicit association task (Greenwald, Nosek, & Banaji, 2003), an exercise about their priority dimensions of personal identity (Arredondo et al., 1996), and a cultural competency inventory. There are many inventories available in the public domain.

4. Clarifying desired outcomes. Process consultation (Schein, 1978) typically occurs in interprofessional collaborations and lead to clarification of desired outcomes for a shared project and perhaps even a resetting of goals. It is important to not slide into the doctor–patient or "expert" process model because doing so can upset the intention for equity and inclusion among a diverse team.

5. Developing the workplan. Presumably, the participants on the team bring their expertise and resources. Therefore, open and transparent discussions are necessary to affirm that skill sets, language ability, and other strengths are leveraged.

6. Implementation. The scenarios previously discussed provide examples of the complexity of culture-centered collaborations as well as the benefits that accrue to team members and to the target population for research or an intervention. Implementation is a nuanced stage with multiple moving parts. In climate studies I conducted with a range of organizations from corporate to behavioral health and hospitals, the smoothness of the implementation phase depended on how well the previous stages were accomplished (Arredondo, 1996).

7. Measuring for impact. There are several levels to measure impact that are embedded in the goals for the project. In addition, it is recommended that evaluations be conducted to determine the efficacy of the interprofessional collaboration. Intermittent process assessments are useful to gauge how well team members feel engaged, listened to, respected, and supported. Cultural competency is an important area of inquiry throughout and at the end. Possible questions are: How has your cultural awareness and knowledge been expanded through this collaboration? Were your dimensions of personal identity acknowledged and respected throughout? What were the benefits of this interprofessional collaboration for you?

## CONCLUSION

The premises underlying interprofessional culture-centered consultation are that it (a) is a process of change management; (b) follows a developmental process that has short- and long-term milestones; (c) is grounded in cultural competencies and consultation competencies and ethics; (d) introduces uncomfortable issues from the workplace; (e) is designed to improve inter-personal relations, particularly respect for differences and greater perspective-taking; and (f) involves systems change for multiple stakeholders that represents the project focus, desired outcomes, and relevant constituencies.

---

## APPENDIX 5.1
## RUBRIC: OBSERVING/SCREENING
## FOR DIVERSITY AND REPRESENTATION

1. Who participates in the initial meeting (s)? Are all potential collaborators present?
2. Who is the organizational leader where the meeting is hosted?
3. Who are the senior leaders?
4. What is the ambiance of the setting?

5. Who are other employees in the space?
6. What is the location of the agency (e.g., in a culturally diverse neighborhood)?
7. If there are clients in the agency when you are there, what do you observe?
8. How do you use the data from the observations during your initial visit to prepare your intervention plan for the organization leaders?

---

## APPENDIX 5.2
## RUBRIC: COMMUNICATION PRACTICES AMONG INTERPROFESSIONAL COLLABORATORS

1. Does everyone from academic or health care settings or funders use titles?
2. Are individuals who represent community partners addressed formally?
3. If there are individuals who speak English as a second language, do facilitators check for understanding respectfully?
4. Are acronyms explained?
5. Are there communication guidelines for meetings to ensure efficiency and inclusion?
6. How is respect communicated across collaborators representing different organizations and constituencies?

### REFERENCES

American Psychological Association. (2003). Guidelines on multicultural education, training, research, practice, and organizational change for psychologists. *American Psychologist, 58*, 377–402. http://dx.doi.org/10.1037/0003-066X.58.5.377

American Psychological Association. (2017). *Multicultural guidelines: An ecological approach to context, identity, and intersectionality*. Retrieved from http://www.apa.org/about/policy/multicultural-guidelines.pdf

Anderson-Levitt, K. M. (2002). Teaching culture as national and transnational: A response to teachers' work. *Educational Researcher, 31*(3), 19–21. http://dx.doi.org/10.3102/0013189X031003019

Arredondo, P. (1996). *Successful diversity management initiatives: A blueprint for planning and implementation*. Thousand Oaks, CA: Sage.

Arredondo, P. (2018). *Blueprint for interprofessional collaboration* [PowerPoint presentation]. Archives of the Arredondo Advisory Group, Phoenix, AZ.

Arredondo, P., Gallardo-Cooper, M., Delgado-Romero, E. A., & Zapata, A. L. (2014). *Culturally responsive counseling with Latinas/os*. Alexandria, VA: American Counseling Association.

Arredondo, P., Shealy, C., Neale, M., & Winfrey, L. L. (2004). Consultation and interprofessional collaboration: Modeling for the future. *Journal of Clinical Psychology, 60*, 787–800. http://dx.doi.org/10.1002/jclp.20015

Arredondo, P., Toporek, R., Brown, S. P., Jones, J., Locke, D. C., Sanchez, J., & Stadler, H. (1996). Operationalization of the multicultural counseling competencies. *Journal of Multicultural Counseling and Development, 24*, 42–78. http://dx.doi.org/10.1002/j.2161-1912.1996.tb00288.x

Bronfenbrenner, U. (1979). *The ecology of human development: Experiments by nature and design* (1st ed.). Cambridge, MA: Harvard University Press.

Bronstein, P. A., & Quina, K. E. (1988). *Teaching a psychology of people*. Washington, DC: American Psychological Association.

Chávez-Dueñas, N. Y., Adames, H. Y., & Organista, K. C. (2014). Skin-color prejudice and within group racial discrimination: Historical and current impact on Latino/a populations. *Hispanic Journal of Behavioral Sciences, 36*, 3–26. http://dx.doi.org/10.1177/0739986313511306

Cox, T. H., Jr. (1993). *Cultural diversity in organizations.* San Francisco, CA: Berrett-Koehler.

Crenshaw, K. (2005). Mapping the margins: Intersectionality, identity politics, and violence against women of color (1994). In R. K. Bergen, J. L. Edleson, & C. M. Renzetti (Eds.), *Violence against women: Classic papers* (pp. 282–313). Auckland, New Zealand: Pearson Education New Zealand.

Davis, O. I., Nakayama, T. K., & Martin, J. N. (2000). Current and future directions in ethnicity and methodology. *International Journal of Intercultural Relations, 24*, 525–539. http://dx.doi.org/10.1016/S0147-1767(00)00026-2

Dougherty, A. M. (2013). *Psychological consultation and collaboration in school and community settings.* Belmont, CA: Brooks/Cole.

Fouad, N., & Arredondo, P. (2007). *Becoming culturally oriented: A practical guide for psychologists.* Washington, DC: American Psychological Association. http://dx.doi.org/10.1037/11483-000

Gallessich, J. (1985). Toward a meta-theory of consultation. *Counseling Psychologist, 13*, 336–354. http://dx.doi.org/10.1177/0011000085133002

Greenwald, A. G., Nosek, B. A., & Banaji, M. R. (2003). Understanding and using the implicit association test: I. An improved scoring algorithm. *Journal of Personality and Social Psychology, 85*, 197–216. http://dx.doi.org/10.1037/0022-3514.85.2.197

Groysberg, B., Lee, J., Price, J., & Cheng, J. Y.-J. (2018, January). The leader's guide to corporate culture. *Harvard Business Review.* Retrieved from https://hbr.org/2018/01/the-culture-factor

Harro, B. (2008). Updated version of the cycle of socialization (2000). *Readings for Diversity and Social Justice*, 45–52.

Hofstede, G. (1980). *Culture's consequences: International differences in work-related values.* Beverly Hills, CA: Sage.

Hofstede, G. (1991). *Cultures and organizations: Software of the mind.* London, England: McGraw-Hill.

House, R. J., Hanges, P. J., Javidan, M., Dorfman, P. W., & Gupta, V. (Eds.). (2004). *Culture, leadership, and organizations: The GLOBE study of 62 societies.* Thousand Oaks, CA: Sage.

Johnson, C. E., Stewart, A. L., Brabeck, M. M., Huber, V. S., & Rubin, H. (2004). Interprofessional collaboration: Implications for combined-integrated doctoral training in professional psychology. *Journal of Clinical Psychology, 60*, 995–1010. http://dx.doi.org/10.1002/jclp.20031

Kao, K. (2017, October 31). Counseling psychology professor focuses on giving back to the community. *Columns.* Retrieved from https://news.uga.edu/counseling-psychology-professor-gives-back-community/

Kroeber, A. L., & Kluckhohn, C. (1952). *Culture: A critical review of concepts and definitions.* New York, NY: Vintage.

Lowman, R. L. (Ed.). (2013). *Internationalizing multiculturalism: Expanding professional competencies in a globalized world.* Washington, DC: American Psychological Association. http://dx.doi.org/10.1037/14044-000

Lowman, R. L. (2014). Multicultural and international issues in organizational change and development. In F. T. L. Leong, L. Comas-Díaz, G. C. Nagayama Hall, V. C. McLoyd, & J. E. Trimble (Eds.), *APA handbook of multicultural psychology: Vol. 2. Applications and training* (pp. 627–639). Washington, DC: American Psychological Association. http://dx.doi.org/10.1037/14187-035

Matsumoto, D. R. (1996). *Culture and psychology.* Pacific Grove, CA: Brooks/Cole.

Morgan, G. (1997). *Images of organization* (2nd ed.). Thousand Oaks, CA: Sage.

Morgan, G. (2006). *Images of organizations* (Updated ed.). Thousand Oaks, CA: Sage.

Neville, H. A., Gallardo, M. E., & Sue, D. W. E. (Eds.). (2016). *The myth of racial color blindness: Manifestations, dynamics, and impact.* Washington, DC: American Psychological Association. http://dx.doi.org/10.1037/14754-000

Ratts, M. J., Singh, A. A., Nassar-McMillan, S., Butler, S. K., McCullough, J. R., & Hipolito-Delgado, C. (2015). *Multicultural and social justice counseling competencies.* [Report for American Counseling Association]. Retrieved from https://www.counseling.org/docs/default-source/competencies/multicultural-and-social-justice-counseling-competencies.pdf?sfvrsn=14

Sánchez-Johnsen, L., Craven, M., Nava, M., Alonso, A., Dykema-Engblade, A., Rademaker, A., & Xie, H. (2017). Cultural variables underlying obesity in Latino men: Design, rationale and participant characteristics from the Latino Men's Health Initiative. *Journal of Community Health, 42,* 826–838. http://dx.doi.org/10.1007/s10900-017-0324-9

Sánchez-Johnsen, L., Escamilla, J., Rodriguez, E. M., Vega, S., & Bolaños, L. (2015). Latino community-based participatory research studies: A model for conducting bilingual translations. *Hispanic Health Care International, 13,* 8–18. http://dx.doi.org/10.1891/1540-4153.13.1.8

Schein, E. H. (1978). The role of the consultant: Content expert or process facilitator? *Journal of Counseling and Development, 56,* 339–343.

Schneider, B. (1987). The people make the place. *Personnel Psychology, 40,* 437–453. http://dx.doi.org/10.1111/j.1744-6570.1987.tb00609.x

Spencer-Oatey, H. (2012). What is culture? A compilation of quotations. *GlobalPAD Core Concepts.* Retrieved from http://citeseerx.ist.psu.edu/viewdoc/download?doi=10.1.1.401.3386&rep=rep1&type=pdf

Sue, D. W., Arredondo, P., & McDavis, R. (1992). Multicultural competencies and standards: A call to the profession. *Journal of Multicultural Counseling and Development, 70,* 477–486. http://dx.doi.org/10.1002/j.1556-6676.1992.tb01642.x

Zarya, V. (2016, June 6). The percentage of female CEOs in the Fortune 500 drops to 4%. Retrieved from http://fortune.com/2016/06/06/women-ceos-fortune-500-2016/

# 6

# Can You See Me Now?

## Understanding Culture and Multicultural Phenomena as Essential to the Process of Consultation

William D. Parham

Culture represents a shared set of integrated beliefs, behaviors, conventions, customs, goals, moral codes, and social practices that collectively results in creating designs for living, road maps for negotiating life's challenges, and ways of transferring these protective blueprints to future generations (Haviland & Prins, 2016; Heine, 2016). Culture, in short, provides a conceptual lens through which an individual can see, make sense of, and navigate, both intrapersonally and interpersonally, in relation to their families, communities, and the world around them. Culture also provides persons outside of a particular cultural group ways of using their culture to channel, organize, experience, untangle, and otherwise interpret the attitudes, dispositions, inclinations, and propensities of other cultures relative to how they interact with and respond to their environments.

Culture is juxtaposed onto the larger landscape of social, political, and economic environmental realities of day-to-day living and each individual's multiple identities and their intersections. These identities include age, gender, gender identity, race, ethnicity, culture, national origin, sexual orientation, disability, language, socioeconomic status, intellectual functioning, educational level, political affiliation and beliefs, religion and spirituality, and disability. Culture is what individuals bring to their work settings and what organizations, therefore, are tasked with incorporating into their existing culture (Giorgi, Lockwood, & Glynn, 2015). Organizations can view culture as a potential source of strength if recognized as a value-added dimension of

http://dx.doi.org/10.1037/0000153-007
*Consultation in Psychology: A Competency-Based Approach*, C. A. Falender and
E. P. Shafranske (Editors)

personal identity. The multifaceted internalizations of culture involve the lived and historical experiences of power, privilege, oppression, acceptance, and identity and as such are integral to understanding and initiating the process of consultation and planning. In addition, there are issues of culture of the organization and that of the individual, including potential clashes or misunderstandings. This chapter explores culture and multicultural phenomena as essential throughout all forms of consultation practice.

## CULTURAL FRAMEWORKS

Familiarity with Bronfenbrenner's ecological systems theory (Bronfenbrenner, 1979; Bronfenbrenner & Ceci, 1994) and his later formulation, bioecological theory (Bronfenbrenner, 2005), serve a role regarding awareness of intersecting relational forces chiefly, but not limited to parents, family, neighborhood communities, school systems, faith-based practices, and the media in all of its manifestations (e.g., auditory, visual, written). Such understanding is key to understanding individual "whole person" components that fuel organizational and systems dynamics. This framework not only serves our understanding of consultation but was also instrumental in the conceptualization of the *Multicultural Guidelines: An Ecological Approach to Context, Identity, and Intersectionality* (American Psychological Association [APA], 2017). What one sees and does not see and acknowledge regarding social realities inseparably impact how people think, feel, and behave, and may collude with the forces of inequity and oppression that frame the lived realities of many of America's citizenry (Parham, 2019). To not appreciate another's (or a group's) unique cultural heritage forecloses acceptance and understanding and delimits the effectiveness of consultation.

Consultation represents a diverse set of activities deployed in response to requests from individuals, groups, or organizations for information or guidance that could lead to change. These activities vary widely depending on a multitude of factors, including who, what, when, where, why, and how questions. Essential to all consultation is consideration of multiple levels of culture and multicultural phenomena. Framing considerations include in what environment (e.g., medical, psychiatric, nursing, psychological, legal, corporate, economic policy development, government regulation, school-based, fitness and training, military, forensics, law enforcement, religious) will the consultation be conducted? Who within the environment is making the request (considering role, power, and perspective)? How does the request relate to the culture of the setting? What problems or challenges need to be resolved? When and under what circumstances or contexts did the problems or challenges emerge? What attempts have been made to address or resolve them? Why now, versus earlier, is there a desire for intervention? When will the intervention begin? In what manner will the consultations be carried out? How will all phases of the consultation process be evaluated? How will the consultant approach the situation, problem, or both? It is recommended that a perspective of self-awareness and self-critique be used to address imbalances. In addition, developing nonpaternalistic, reflective consultation relationships with the consultee merits consideration (derived from Tervalon & Murray-García, 1998). Desired accomplishments include assessing the setting or problem; framing of the cultural components, including introducing those as important aspects of the process; assisting with incremental or transformational changes; helping with incorporating tools and techniques for adapting to changes as they are instituted; paying attention to improvements in efficiency, effectiveness, quality, and production; and measuring and monitoring alignment with strategic goals (Burke, 2017; Lowman, 2002).

There is no shortage of consultation models and approaches used as templates for responding to organizational or setting requests for change (Arredondo, Shealy, Neale, & Winfrey, 2004; Burke, 2017; Cameron & Quinn, 2011; Konopaske, Ivancevich, & Matteson, 2018; Lowman, 2002; Sabatino, 2014). Organizational consultation models differ detectably, and each model was spawned from real or perceived needs to fill discipline-related gaps in theory, conceptual underpinnings, multicultural aspects, methodological procedures and processes, and evaluative mechanisms. All models boast strengths as well as limits, and successful implementation of either of the above-referenced models depends on the symmetry of client and consultant expectations. These expectations may manifest in each other's collaborative involvement in the process, anticipations about the process as it unfolds, motivations to surrender to believed-to-be objective examinations of facts and data, and agreements regarding hoped for outcomes (Cameron & Quinn, 2011; Kotter, 2012). The expertise, talents, and experiences of the consultant, as well as the goodness of fit between the consultant and the specific needs of the organization requesting services, also come into play.

Offered for consideration is an observation that consultation models vary in the degree to which they integrate cultural factors, broadly defined. This variability is noteworthy given that such key explanatory variables could help clarify (a) why organizational problems emerge, (b) what fuels their nagging persistence, and (c) the difficulty some organizations experience relative to implementing change. A second observation relative to the formative years of the consultation profession invites query. Given that culture and the larger environmental contexts (e.g., social, political, economic) shape personal beliefs, perspectives, values, and important decisions made by "founding father and founding mother" pioneer consultants, why was acknowledgment of the inextricable role of culture never emphasized?

This omission seems especially noteworthy given that early and formative years of the consultation profession in America occurred amid tremendous social and political unrest (Burke, 2017; Schein, 2015). Those turbulent times marked by ever present structurally supported and socially sanctioned systems of inequities and oppression provided ample grist for the mill relative to defining organizational consultation as a discipline, conceptualizing discipline-related scholarship, and crafting consultation practice activities that would serve subsequently as the profession's building blocks—building blocks that would have infused culture as essential to professional practice. Reasons for this omission of important multiple and critical contexts are be shared later in this chapter.

Essential to the process of consultation includes identifying (a) the client's degree of problem ownership and investment in achieving desired changes, (b) obvious and not-so-obvious variables (including multicultural factors or nuance) contributing to emergence and maintenance of identified problems or challenges, (c) covert and overt impediments to problem or challenge resolution, and (d) multiple ways of evaluating consultation effectiveness. Consultants must keep in mind that the effectiveness of a consultation depends on what an individual, setting, or organization desires to accomplish—that being its goals and outcomes. Guidelines present a framework for cultural and contextual understanding and perspectives as evident in the following three documents, all of which come with invitations to apply multicultural (broadly defined) principles to systems and organizational consultations.

- *Multicultural Guidelines: An Ecological Approach to Context, Identity, and Intersectionality* (APA, 2017) represents a response to a call within the professional psychology and other mental health communities to enrich the earlier version, the APA (2003) *Guidelines on Multicultural Education, Training, Research, Practice, and Organizational Change for Psychologists*, which had framed culture solely within the contexts of African Americans, Asian Americans, Latinx, and American Indian populations. This considerably updated and enhanced document, rooted in the significant growth in research and theory regarding multicultural context that emerged since the original guidelines, illuminates the concept of intersectionality and complex personal identities tied to relational systems of power and privilege that are inseparably interlocked with socially sanctioned systems of inequity, oppression, and marginalization. Thus,

  > intersectionality captures the vast within-group differences in identities found among members of marginalized and dominant groups. Intersectionality theory argues that focusing solely on the effect of one or two reference group identities (e.g., interaction of race and age studied through covariate analyses) on overall identity fails to consider the multiple social and cultural identities that intersect within an individual's life. (APA, 2017, p. 20)

- The original APA (2003) "guidelines" represented a response to a call largely, although not exclusively, from ethnic minority psychologists to acknowledge and affirm cultural understanding as critical contextual criteria for educating and training of professionals who go on to serve in careers as researchers, educators, clinicians, and consultants. At the time, the original guidelines offered a richer understanding of diversity and added substantively to the national discourse within and across professional psychological communities on race and class in America.

- "Multicultural and Social Justice Counseling Competencies: Guidelines for the Counseling Profession" (Ratts, Singh, Nassar-McMillan, Butler, & McCullough, 2016), a revision to the "Multicultural Competencies and

Standards: A Call to the Profession" (Sue, Arredondo, & McDavis, 1992), represents a document of the Association of Multicultural Counseling and Development, a division of the American Counseling Association, that aimed to achieve two goals. The first goal came in the form of suggesting ways to integrate social justice and multicultural competencies into research, theories, and practice. The second goal was to illuminate a developmental path believed to lead to multicultural and social justice competencies.

## THE PRACTICE OF INTEGRATING A MULTICULTURAL PERSPECTIVE IN CONSULTATION

Consultation models vary in the degree to which they integrate multicultural factors. The variance may be attributed, at least partially, to the different and multilayered definitions of culture as it pertains to individuals versus systems versus organizations. Each formulation is complex in nuanced ways and evidences both strengths and weakness. When viewed through either lens of individuality, systems, or organizations, culture can serve as an organizing factor, a way to better understand consultation questions and processes. Relatedly, a cultural lens provides a way to understand larger environmental contexts that influence the issue or problem to be addressed in consultation and, importantly, how decisions are being culturally apprehended by the consultee. On the other hand, when not carefully defined, culture can lead to faulty assessments of problem-seeking resolutions, relational misunderstandings, and prolonged conflicts.

Culture is a central factor regarding the training of clinicians. As applied to consultation, cultural influences affect willingness to work in natural, challenging settings, being attuned to multiple sources of oppression, learning to collaborate and empower consultees, and deemphasizing psychopathology and stigmatization in assessment and consultation conceptualization. Furthermore, there are issues of hierarchical versus nonhierarchical consultation and notions of empowerment. Also included are attention to sociopolitical environmental factors or divisions, systemic structures that might sanction inequity or oppression, and multicultural factors that are implicitly unequal (e.g., gender or racial inequity).

All of these factors in multicultural training and consultation models occur within a frame of historical inequities, oppression, and hierarchical structures. Multicultural competence is inextricably bound to the role of the consultant. For example, Lowman (2007) described the concepts of role of perception of culture-specific concepts and the relationship of trust as essential to building consultation relationships.

Remarkably, multicultural competence has not necessarily been included in consultation training. For example, for school psychology (Ingraham, 2017), it frequently is not included, and consultants may feel uncomfortable talking about race (Newell, Newell, & Looser, 2013). In a review of school consultation training literature published from 1970 to 2012, Newell and Newman (2014) found only three studies on multicultural consultation. These and other research findings suggest that cultural differences are likely inadequately infused into consultation research (Meyers, 2002; Ortiz, 2006). Hoffman et al. (2006) described a model of consultation and decried historical failure to address multicultural issues in the training of consultants. In their model, they defined a nonhierarchical structure in contrast to generally hierarchical consultation models. Through consideration of extrapersonal and external forces, a culturally responsive and empowering process, the role of the consultant is envisioned as an agent of change and an advocate for the consultee and the system while attending to the consultation process itself. Essential is consideration of the existing culture of the organization. including its rules, norms, and power structures. Collaboration occurs through empowerment of the individuals in the setting or organization, so consultants learn from consultees.

## Context Is Everything

Implicit—and essential—in every consultation is consideration of the multiple identities of the individuals who compose the organization or setting and those who requested the consultation (e.g., school, police, forensic question) as well as the contextual factors, organizational culture, demand characteristics, and history. Implicit in consultation is the necessity to identify the potential sources of strength in the individuals or available workforce to (a) render accurate assessments of the presenting problem(s), (b) conceptualize and plan multiple possible alternatives for interventions, (c) implement viable interventions that best address the presenting concern(s) and that are culturally syntonic, and (d) evaluate the impact of chosen consultation interventions.

These observations are important for several reasons. First, providing organizational assessments leading to change for the better with less than a complete picture of the potential sources of strength available in the existing workforce sets the stage for camouflage or failure. Operating with a-believed-to-be-but-not-real organizational profile raises the possibility that suggested interventions actually represent a reshuffling of the deck of dysfunctional variables that lead, initially, to the necessity for a change agent to be considered. Failure to tap into the most complete picture of organizational or situational challenges fosters an illusion that assessments, interventions, and postintervention evaluations are working and that promised changes are forthcoming. But these evaluations may mask cultural incongruities and underlying cultural dynamics that are critical to the consultation process to understand and address. Conversely, the ability to recognize and integrate cultural contexts, including individuals, groups, organizations, and environmental settings, into consultation experiences enhances the conceptual and process dimension of the experience and the interpretive value of the consultation.

## Multiculturalism Consultation Training Models

A number of training models have been introduced that promote social justice and multicultural competencies into consultation. Flores et al. (2014) described a model social justice practice in consultation that is built on social justice competencies (Ratts et al., 2016). The role of the consultant, thus, is to enhance an organization's ability to recognize diversity and to adapt or maintain practices that facilitate equal access and opportunities (from Flores et al., 2014). Flores et al. designed a social justice consultation project implemented within a prison setting as part of experiential learning to be a multiculturally competent psychologist.

The program was elaborated from Goodman et al.'s (2004) principles that frame social justice consultation practice. These principles included engaging in ongoing self-awareness (including biases, stereotypes, and privilege) of consultant and individuals in a consultation setting, valuing contributions of each, raising consciousness regarding historical and system inequities, focusing on interpersonal functioning, embracing and adapting to cultural styles, fostering equity, addressing institutional and other forms of oppression, sharing power, giving voice, and sharing tools. The principles of sharing power and engaging in self-examination includes understanding and sharing societal power. The principles of giving voice, sharing tools, and raising consciousness all instill the socially privileged practitioner with the responsibility of exploring and inciting action within the client (individual or community).

Ingraham (2017) described a model that incorporates a focus on social justice, privilege, and power in school consultation and is applicable more generally. In this model, training in social justice draws on feminist and multicultural principles and includes focus on (a) ongoing self-examination and self-assessment; (b) an introduction to sharing power; (c) the empowerment of individuals and the giving of voice; (d) the facilitation of social consciousness-raising; (e) the building on strengths of individuals, institutions, and settings; and (f) the provision of tools to consultees that empower them and their work toward social change (Goodman et al., 2004). The consultation process also involves applying a multicultural and ecosystemic framework for constructing meaning with individuals in the setting (Falicov, 2014).

The importance of training models directly addressing social justice and multiculturalism in consultation was highlighted by research by Newell (2010) in an investigation of consultant multicultural judgments within four settings. She found that both African American and European American consultants demonstrated limited use of ecological approaches and a general lack of cultural responsiveness—which, when they varied their approaches, had race as a defining classification. With African American clients, she identified more of a deficit orientation than with European American students. She suggested that consultants in school settings need to develop more comfort with discussions of race and the impact of multicultural factors, including race, in their practices. This discussion included a need for relationship development in the context of multicultural identities. Newell et al. (2013) reported that consultants may have knowledge of cultural factors, but such knowledge was not demonstrated in their consultation activities.

However, as Lowman (2014) noted, addressing social justice is not typically included in clinical or industrial–organizational psychology training programs, so consultants may not be prepared to address nuances that are involved. He described that, by nature of their work, consultants are required to serve the clients' best interests—and the client may be a system or organization, not individuals. Challenges are identifying, reconciling, and addressing the contrasting worldviews driven by productivity and effective process with those of social justice—and the designated role of the consultant.

## An Inclusive Move Forward

A clear and present need is to incorporate multicultural guidelines and conceptual frames in consultation practice as applied to corporate organizations, school systems, law enforcement agencies, and a myriad of other settings. For example, in a review of school consultation training literature published 1970–2012, Newell and Newman (2014) found only three studies on multicultural consultation. These research findings suggest that cultural differences are not yet routinely infused into consultation research (Meyers, 2002; Ortiz, 2006). Three critical questions are: How could multicultural contexts be used as frames for understanding and appreciating the challenges in the consultation settings? What value is attached to cultural contexts as a mechanism for future sustained progress, growth, and understanding? Are cultural contexts minimized or discounted, and how can consultation address this issue?

Clearly, cultural contexts are essential and indispensable factors framing consultation success. How can consultants concretely and measurably model observing and honoring culture as essential contexts for problem-resolution and growth? And how can this understanding and appreciation of culture as context serve as catalysts for creating an organizational and setting culture that sustains and maximizes individual and workforce strengths and talent while simultaneously enhances the setting?

## Learn From Past Mistakes

Why have corporate, law enforcement, forensic, medical, school, and other systems not included multicultural guidelines as key to understanding their respective environments? Returning to an observation shared earlier in this chapter, America through the 1950s and 1960s witnessed the growth of organizations that, arguably, paid virtually no attention to personal stories, cultural traditions, and generational legacies of employees with whom they were in relationship. The past focus on establishing and fortifying structural foundations for future growth, branding and marketing organizational images to lure customers, and maximizing organization profitability were all necessary and simultaneously insufficient pursuits. The longtime downplay of the importance of life realities as contextual variables (Francis, 2014; Janken, 2015; Levine, 2000) that influence organizational performance represents missed opportunities for generating broader-based perspectives and clarity about employees as persons and as productive contributors to organization vitality and profits.

In contrast, the zeitgeist of the 1960s through the 1970s, for example, provided ample context from which organizational leaders could draw information about how to function with greater inclusivity without sacrifice to profitably. The civil rights movement and national dialogues on race, class, sexism, and social power (Francis, 2014; Levine, 2000; Williams & Bond, 2002/2013)—signature events of the 2 decades—painfully unmasked America's system of oppression, exclusion, and White privilege (McIntosh, 1989). The 1960s and 1970s decades were characterized in part by the determination of traditionally marginalized populations to assertively reclaim stolen personal, cultural, ethnic, gender, age, sexual, political, and other identities. During those years of considerable political and social turbulence and violence and confusion, blanket adherence to the status quo called into question America's proclamation to its citizenry that "all men are created equal" (*Thomas Jefferson, et al., July 4, Copy of Declaration of Independence*, 1776). The reticence of American organizations to portray the ugliness of systemic social inequities versus listen to the voices of those screaming their presence as value-added contributors to organizational growth and sustainability was tantamount to acts of collusion with the status quo to keep the have-and-have-not systems of exploitation, oppression, and marginalization operative.

The reclamation of personal identities characteristic of the 1950s through the 1970s civil rights movement also awakened the voices of the New Right (Andrews, Cockett, Hooper, & Williams, 1999; Gottfried & Fleming, 1988; Lowndes, 2009; McGirr, 2002; Viguerie, 1981). The ascendance of this ultra-conservative political movement during the 1960s was fueled initially by the perceived need among White American conservatives to reclaim perceived loss of political, social, and economic authority and control (Gottfried & Fleming, 1988; McGirr, 2002; Viguerie, 1981). The sustaining energy of the New Right, evidenced in the brazen expressions of White supremacy by the visible and vocal alt-right (alternative right) movement, that was promoted as an alternative to American conservatism was reignited, in part, by the 2009 election of the first African American and 44th president of the United States, Barack Hussein Obama. Race and its divisiveness have not receded as the signature conversation in America. America's racial divide continues to be a seminal challenge that eludes reconciliation and redemption (Dyson, 2017).

The feminist movement was part of this national rebellion and generated abundant feminist-informed scholarship (Bloom & Breines, 2011; Deslippe, 2000; Rosen, 2006) from which American organizations during their early and formative years could draw. Fighting against oppression and exploitation, working to dismantle and replace socially constructed hegemonic beliefs about "a woman's place," and declaring with crystal clarity stances that asserted the mantra "politics is personal" collectively represent responses that have defined women's calls for fairness and equity through the decades.

## Taking Stock

Why should these historical events matter, and why are they included in this chapter? There is absolutely no way for the aforementioned historical events to not have influenced the quest of America's organizations to be at their best as competitors and to be profitable as well as for individuals to strive to be effective and of value to the larger societal context. Also, invited for consideration is the observation that fruitful and productive conversations and new and fresh ways of thinking emerge when subjects of investigative inquiries are viewed from different, even sometimes conflicting, perspectives. The best perspectives are often the ones you have yet to entertain. Thus, if theories, hypotheses, and practices that framed America's organizations were examined through additive conceptual and theoretical lenses of social, political, and economic movements, then other templates of interactional possibilities for studying person-in-environment organizational relationships might have materialized. And in that vein, transformations of individuals' professional lives would also have been enhanced.

As important, if additive lenses were viewed through cultural, political, economic, ethical, and historical frames of reference, two additional outcomes might have been possible. First, ideological premises and assertions that provide systemic structure and interpretive flexibility favoring inequity to America's social systems might have been examined more critically. Second, a teeming cornucopia of characteristics and qualities about being human and about actual lived experiences of individuals and the realities they navigate might have been brought to light.

Believing that the organizational or consultation setting bottom line will not be sacrificed but likely enhanced strengthens the resolve to address these previously omitted environmental data sets. A deliberate and intentional shift in focus is essential. The shift in focus is away from identifying isolated variables presumed to increase or enhance performance to insisting that culture will operate from a more inclusive and authentic perspective evidenced in leadership that equips and thus enables its workforce to cocreate productive and enriched work environments. Such efforts might be seen as essential to consultation committed to fully integrating and respecting culture.

## The More Things Change, the More They Stay the Same

A move forward by consultants to organizations, schools, forensic, legal, medical, and pediatric settings, will increase competence—knowledge, skills, and attitudes that are reflective of the multiculturally diverse workforce and contexts. Advances in consultation must be predicated on the belief that multiple social, political, and economic forces influence the lives of the organizations and settings as well as the consultants. Monitoring and accountability are essential to ensure that consultation practice is culturally competent, sound, relevant, and respectful of the multiple entities impacted.

## Multiculturalism in Consultation

Multiple multicultural aspects exist in consultation processes. The consultant needs to be self-aware of cultural assumptions and identities with which he or she approaches the consultation task as well as one's personal cultural intersecting identities and the diversity of identities at the consultation site (Liebowitz & Blattner, 2015), all of which may serve as resources when approached with attitudes of respect, valuing, appreciating, and utilizing.

Critical to consider are the role of the consultant's perceptions and how those perceptions can be influenced by contexts that are culture specific, including emotion and expression of emotion as a culturally laden context. For example, the complexity of face-saving in non-Western cultures is such that smiling or giving positive feedback may not be affirmatory or have a positive valence as they are generally perceived by Westerners. Trust in the relationship, which is essential for successful consultation, may also entail cultural aspects that cannot simply be inferred. Lowman (2007) urged consideration of whether culture is context in the consultation task at hand or whether it is a significant determinant of behavior. Consultants require competence in understanding relational dynamic forces, including implicit bias, stereotype threat, and a need for cultural safety, that influence every consultation experience and every consultation setting. Examination of the processes and practices of how consultants are taught, what they are taught, and the contexts within which their lessons are framed merits closer scrutiny.

## Critical Pedagogy

*Critical pedagogy* is the questioning of important and pressing responses to traditional principles and practices of teaching and learning, empowerment, and the addressing of systemic structures of oppression and inequity under the guise of apolitical neutrality (Giroux & McLaren, 1986; McLaren, 1989). Scholars of critical pedagogy take a penetrating look at the relationship between humans, the societies in which they reside, and the system of education from which they emerged (Darder, Baltodano, & Torres, 2003; Rasmussen, 1996). Scholars of critical pedagogy pay close attention to intellectual traditional ways of conveying information through teaching and ways of knowing (learning) using multiple perspectives (e.g., cultural, political, economic, ethical, historical) to frame their analyses, critiques, discourse, and strategies for change.

Multiple theorists (Darder, 2002; Dewey, 1916/2013; Giroux, 2003; Green, 2003, McLaren, 2003) have proposed reexamination and revived analyses of ideologies that inform consultation viewpoints and practices. Authors of critical pedagogy advocate strongly for a reexamination of who, what, why, and how graduate students are taught, and this reexamination is represented in consultation practice: addressing the emphasis on sustaining the status quo and embracing asymmetrical power dynamics that may foster racialized and gender-influenced disparities (Darder et al., 2003).

Failure to examine these relational phenomena through the lens of critical pedagogy positions the practice of consultation to express potential shortcomings. Consultants may fail to examine relational dynamics that lead to biases regarding experiences of and consequences for those they serve. Second, failure to use critical pedagogy as a tool for learning about different human relational phenomena all but ensures the perpetual reenactment of business-as-usual beliefs and practices, effectively maintaining status quo operations. Third, failure to use critical pedagogy as an exploratory tool for understanding and appreciating human relational phenomena precludes discovery of ideologies and practice that may be rooted deeply in historical inequities that continue to support current socially constructed and structurally supported systems of inequity. The ramification is a failure to identify and use lessons from the past. This failure may result in assessments that do not address power imbalances.

## Implicit Bias

*Implicit bias* refers to how attitudes, stereotypes, and prejudices unconsciously yet unequivocally affect our understanding of persons, situations, and circumstances; decisions that are made as a result of this understanding; and actions that are taken as a result of those decisions (Beattie, 2013; Dasgupta, 2013; Dovidio, Kawakami, & Gaertner, 2002; Greenwald et al., 2002; Greenwald & Krieger, 2006; Kawakami & Dovidio, 2001; Sevo & Chubin, 2008; Staats, Capatosto, Wright, & Jackson, 2016). Scholars of implicit bias research (Dasgupta, 2013; Rutland, Cameron, Milne, & McGeorge, 2005) describe that implicit bias represents phenomena to which all people, irrespective of culture, race, ethnicity, gender, age, sexual identity, ability status, religion, or other dimensions of personal identity, are susceptible—and that little that can be done to prevent implicit bias from impacting the ways humans understand, decide, and act. The implicit associations we make subconsciously about persons relative to their culture, race, ethnicity, gender, age, ability status, religion, sexuality, and physical appearance (e.g., height, weight, complexion) originate during the earliest ages of life and remain constant throughout.

Implicit bias is measured by response times to given stimuli (response latency) that are believed to provide clues to the strength of connection between two concepts (Greenwald, Poehlman, Uhlmann, & Banaji, 2009; Hofmann, Gawronski, Gschwendner, Le, & Schmitt, 2005; Kang & Lane, 2010). Implicit bias has important implications for all consulting settings and individuals in them. It can affect organizational decision making, hiring practices, employee retention, employee satisfaction, employee evaluations, and policy development (Baker, Cobley, Schorer, & Wattie, 2017; Blau, Brinton, & Grusky, 2006; UNC Executive Development, 2015).

Implicit associations are so deeply ingrained, there may be a misalignment between our explicitly declared beliefs and endorsements and our implicit associations (Reskin, 2000, 2005). Thus, attempts to fully understand and appreciate setting and consultant performance absent awareness of these relational dynamics are problematic.

## Stereotype Threat

Complementing implicit bias is the concept of stereotype threat (Désert, Préaux, & Jund, 2009; Maass, D'Ettole, & Cadinu, 2008). *Stereotype threat* represents a performance-related evaluative experience in which a person is in a position to feel at risk for confirming stereotypes about his or her own or other groups (e.g., cultural, ethnic, social, political, economic, athletic, religious). Thus, individuals fear being viewed through the lens of a negative stereotype or fear that they may be conforming to a stereotyped expectation (Steele, Spencer, & Aronson, 2002). For example, a female employee may discount an opportunity to move up in organization, knowing that women typically do not advance to senior-level responsibilities. The added pressures in her perceived need to work even harder is related to her feeling that she now needs not only to prove herself as capable but also counteract the perceived stereotypes of women's leadership abilities that may exist in male-dominated organization leadership. Stereotypes are present for individuals of color, with disabilities, LGBTQ identified, religious minorities, and other traditionally marginalized groups in combination with stereotype threat (Kray & Shirako, 2012). Knowledge of implicit bias and critical pedagogy are also essential to consultation.

## Development of Foundational and Functional Competencies

It is essential for consultants to develop and maintain both foundational as well as functional competencies relative to multicultural awareness and to the aforementioned relational dynamics. Foundational competencies, according to Rodolfa et al. (2005), include attitudes, beliefs, knowledge, and skills that are essential for constructing the base on which functional competencies rest. In short, foundational competencies represent cornerstone areas of consultation that all consultants should possess irrespective of the specific day-to-day activities in which they might engage. Having solid grounding in law and ethics within a framework of organization and systems consultation as well as in the history of organizational and systems consultation represent agreed on, common, and across-the-board foundational consultation competencies. Offered for consideration is a recommendation that knowledge and appreciation of ethnic, gender, faith-based, sexual identity, and other traditionally marginalized populations; the impact that implicit bias and stereotype threat experiences have on organizational behaviors and decision making and employee performances and the active practice of cultural humility; a reflective process; and respect and an attitude of not knowing but being respectfully curious represents additional examples of critical foundational consultation competencies.

Functional competencies consist of the actual duties and responsibilities a professional is expected to perform on a day-to-day basis (Fouad et al., 2009; Rodolfa et al., 2005). Competence implies the daily habitual and judicious practice (Epstein & Hundert, 2002) of a package of skill sets used to serve others. Kaslow (2004) and Kaslow et al. (2004) defined *competencies* as components of competence that compose specific knowledge, skills, and attitudes. Essential functional consultation competencies with a multicultural framework include (a) conducting thorough assessments using established research-based measures while recognizing their cautious application to ethnic, gender, faith-based, and traditionally marginalized communities; (b) designing data-gathering strategies that take cultural, ethnic, racial, and other diversity into account; (c) using appropriate and relevant multiculturally sensitive tools for evaluating outcomes; and (d) providing client feedback that captures and capitalizes on their strengths as a diversity-rich organization and system.

## CONCLUSION AND FUTURE DIRECTIONS

Three recommendations are offered for consideration. The first recommendation invites learning from past mistakes (Lewis & D'Orso, 1998), including resisting the urge to overlook or otherwise justify abundant source material found within the framework of current and past social, political, and economic environments as important and relevant factors that frame the lived experiences of their culturally rich workforce. American organizations and systems have been reticent to examine these deeper and arguably richer areas of exploration (Kray & Shirako, 2012). Perhaps the hesitancy comes in knowing that honest self-reflection might result in surfacing previously buried organizational truths. Surrendering to the resolute practice of self-reflection, including understanding the historical context of race relations in America and related legacies of hate and condemnation, has the potential to surface within American organizations long-held attitudes, beliefs, dispositions, perceptions, and prejudices that evidence collusion with the maintenance of socially sanctioned systemic inequities relative to the education and training of discipline aspirants (Dyson, 2017; Zinn, 2003). Embracing a quest for enriched perspectives and insights about being human and about navigating social, political, economic, and historic systems that reward and punish differently based on markers of identity (e.g., culture, race, ethnicity, gender, sexual identity, ability status, religion) is a good place to continue. Furthermore, infusion of this bigger picture awareness positions organizations and systems to leverage and likely enhance organization and systems results and bottom line (Cascio, 2012).

A second recommendation invites consideration of the importance of infusing the aforementioned rich data sets into organization and systems awareness of the impact that critical pedagogy, implicit bias, and stereotype threat experiences have on organization and system functioning. Infusing these ingredients strengthens the move ahead.

Recommendation number three invites consideration that graduate education is a place to more intentionally focus on the preparation of aspirants who are pursuing careers as organization and systems consultants and change agents. Insisting on the use of accountability measures in education and training programs and internships as well as in continuing education courses for professionals represents an important decision in American organization's move toward excellence. Coursework or experiences in the intersectionality, implicit bias, stereotype threat, critical pedagogy, or other topics, or both, subsumed under the multicultural umbrella as an integral component of a traditional organizational consultation and systems curriculum, are essential in the preparation of would-be organizational and systems consultants.

In the final analysis, self-reflection represents a portal through which American consultants and consultees can pass en route to developing and appreciating approaches to consultation practice that feel more inclusive and better capture the nuanced lived experiences of the people and communities. American organizations and consultation settings purport to serve. Changing habitual ways of thinking about and behaving toward persons whose individual and collective personal identities are different from one's own identities represents a wise investment in moving the needle of real change.

Opportunities for ongoing self-examination and behavior change that bring promised revelations and light-bulb-moment insights are available if one chooses to see what is right in front of them hiding in plain sight! Viewing the expansion of theory, research, and practice within America's organizations and settings from this point forward through lenses of critical pedagogy, implicit bias, and stereotype threat positions America's organizations to reap the benefits of a more inclusive and engaged workforce.

## REFERENCES

American Psychological Association. (2003). Guidelines on multicultural education, training, research, practice, and organizational change for psychologists. *American Psychologist, 58,* 377–402. http://dx.doi.org/10.1037/0003-066X.58.5.377

American Psychological Association. (2017). *Multicultural guidelines: An ecological approach to context, identity, and intersectionality.* Retrieved from http://www.apa.org/about/policy/multicultural-guidelines.pdf

Andrews, G., Cockett, R., Hooper, A., & Williams, M. (Eds.). (1999). *New left, new right and beyond: Taking the sixties seriously.* Basingstoke, England: Macmillan.

Arredondo, P., Shealy, C., Neale, M., & Winfrey, L. L. (2004). Consultation and interprofessional collaboration: Modeling for the future. *Journal of Clinical Psychology, 60,* 787–800. http://dx.doi.org/10.1002/jclp.20015

Baker, J., Cobley, S., Schorer, J., & Wattie, N. (Eds.). (2017). *Routledge handbook of talent identification and development in sport.* New York, NY: Routledge.

Beattie, G. (2013). *Our racist heart: An exploration of unconscious prejudice in everyday life.* London, England: Routledge. http://dx.doi.org/10.4324/9780203100912

Blau, F. D., Brinton, M. C., & Grusky, D. B. (Eds.). (2006). *The declining significance of gender?* New York, NY: Russell Sage Foundation.

Bloom, A., & Breines, W. (2011). *Takin' it to the streets: A sixties reader* (3rd ed.). New York, NY: Oxford University Press.

Bronfenbrenner, U. (1979). Contexts of child rearing: Problems and prospects. *American Psychologist, 34,* 844–850. http://dx.doi.org/10.1037/0003-066X.34.10.844

Bronfenbrenner, U. (Ed.). (2005). *Making human beings human: Bioecological perspectives on human development.* Thousand Oaks, CA: Sage.

Bronfenbrenner, U., & Ceci, S. J. (1994). Nature–nurture reconceptualized in developmental perspective: A bioecological model. *Psychological Review, 101,* 568–586. http://dx.doi.org/10.1037/0033-295X.101.4.568

Burke, W. W. (2017). *Organization changes: Theory and practice* (5th ed.). Thousand Oaks, CA: Sage.

Cameron, K. S., & Quinn, R. E. (2011). *Diagnosing and changing organizational culture.* San Francisco, CA: Jossey-Bass.

Cascio, W. F. (2012). *Managing human resources: Productivity, quality of work life, profits* (9th ed.). New York, NY: McGraw-Hill.

Darder, A. (2002). *Reinventing Paulo Freire: A pedagogy of love.* Boulder, CO: Westview.

Darder, A., Baltodano, M., & Torres, R. D. (2003). *The critical pedagogy reader.* New York, NY: Routledge.

Dasgupta, N. (2013). Implicit attitudes and beliefs adapt to situations: A decade of research on the malleability of implicit prejudice, stereotypes and the self-concept. *Advances in Experimental Social Psychology, 47,* 233–279. http://dx.doi.org/10.1016/B978-0-12-407236-7.00005-X

Désert, M., Préaux, M., & Jund, R. (2009). So young and already victims of stereotype threat: Socio-economic status and performance of 6 to 9 years old children on Raven's progressive matrices. *European Journal of Psychology of Education, 24,* 207–218. http://dx.doi.org/10.1007/BF03173012

Deslippe, D. A. (2000). *Rights, not roses: Unions and the rise of working-class feminism, 1945–80.* Champaign: University of Illinois Press.

Dewey, J. (2013). *Democracy and education: An introduction to the philosophy of education.* New York, NY: Macmillan. (Original work published 1916)

Dovidio, J. F., Kawakami, K., & Gaertner, S. L. (2002). Implicit and explicit prejudice and interracial interaction. *Journal of Personality and Social Psychology, 82,* 62–68. http://dx.doi.org/10.1037/0022-3514.82.1.62

Dyson, M. E. (2017). *Tears we cannot stop: A sermon to White America.* New York, NY: St. Martin's Press.

Epstein, R. M., & Hundert, E. M. (2002). Defining and assessing professional competence. *JAMA, 287,* 226–235. http://dx.doi.org/10.1001/jama.287.2.226

Falicov, C. J. (2014). Psychotherapy and supervision as cultural encounters: The MECA framework. In C. A. Falender, E. P. Shafranske, & C. J. Falicov (Eds.), *Multiculturalism and diversity in clinical supervision: A competency-based approach* (pp. 29–58). Washington, DC: American Psychological Association. http://dx.doi.org/10.1037/14370-002

Flores, M. P., De La Rue, L., Neville, H. A., Santiago, S., ben Rakemayahu, K., Garite, R., . . . Ginsburg, R. (2014). Developing social justice competencies: A consultation training approach. *Counseling Psychologist, 42,* 998–1020. http://dx.doi.org/10.1177/0011000014548900

Fouad, N. A., Grus, C. L., Hatcher, R. L., Kaslow, N. J., Hutchings, P. S., Madson, M. B., . . . Crossman, R. E. (2009). Competency benchmarks: A model for understanding and measuring competence in professional psychology across training levels. *Training and Education in Professional Psychology, 3*(4, Suppl.), S5–S26. http://dx.doi.org/10.1037/a0015832

Francis, M. M. (2014). *Civil rights and the making of the modern state.* Cambridge, MA: Cambridge University Press.

Giorgi, S., Lockwood, C., & Glynn, M. A. (2015). The many faces of culture: Making sense of 30 years of research on culture in organization studies. *Academy of Management Annals, 9,* 1–54. http://dx.doi.org/10.5465/19416520.2015.1007645

Giroux, H. A. (2003). Critical theory and educational practice. In A. Darder, M. Baltodano, & R. D. Torres (Eds.), *The critical pedagogy reader* (pp. 27–56). New York, NY: RoutledgeFalmer.

Giroux, H. A., & McLaren, P. (1986). Teacher education and the politics of engagement: The case for democratic schooling. *Harvard Educational Review, 56,* 213–239. http://dx.doi.org/10.17763/haer.56.3.trr1473235232320

Goodman, L. A., Liang, B., Helms, J. E., Latta, R. E., Sparks, E., & Weintraub, S. R. (2004). Training counseling psychologists as social justice agents: Feminist and multicultural principles in action. *Counseling Psychologist, 32,* 793–836. http://dx.doi.org/10.1177/0011000004268802

Gottfried, P., & Fleming, T. J. (1988). *The conservative movement.* Boston, MA: Twayne.

Green, M. (2003). In search of a critical pedagogy. In A. Darder, M. Baltodano, & R. D. Torres (Eds.), *The critical pedagogy reader* (pp. 97–112). New York, NY: RoutledgeFalmer.

Greenwald, A. G., Banaji, M. R., Rudman, L. A., Farnham, S. D., Nosek, B. A., & Mellott, D. S. (2002). A unified theory of implicit attitudes, stereotypes, self-esteem, and self-concept. *Psychological Review, 109*, 3–25. http://dx.doi.org/10.1037/0033-295X.109.1.3

Greenwald, A. G., & Krieger, L. H. (2006). Implicit bias: Scientific foundations. *California Law Review, 94*, 945–967. http://dx.doi.org/10.2307/20439056

Greenwald, A. G., Poehlman, T. A., Uhlmann, E. L., & Banaji, M. R. (2009). Understanding and using the Implicit Association Test: III. Meta-analysis of predictive validity. *Journal of Personality and Social Psychology, 97*, 17–41. http://dx.doi.org/10.1037/a0015575

Haviland, W. A., & Prins, H. E. L. (2016). *Cultural anthropology: The human challenge* (15th ed.). Boston, MA: Cengage Learning.

Heine, S. J. (2016). *Cultural psychology* (3rd ed.). New York, NY: Norton.

Hoffman, M. A., Phillips, E. L., Noumair, D. A., Shullman, S., Geisler, C., Gray, J., . . . Ziegler, D. (2006). Toward a feminist and multicultural model of consultation and advocacy. *Journal of Multicultural Counseling and Development, 34*, 116–128. http://dx.doi.org/10.1002/j.2161-1912.2006.tb00032.x

Hofmann, W., Gawronski, B., Gschwendner, T., Le, H., & Schmitt, M. (2005). A meta-analysis on the correlation between the implicit association test and explicit self-report measures. *Personality and Social Psychology Bulletin, 31*, 1369–1385. http://dx.doi.org/10.1177/0146167205275613

Ingraham, C. L. (2017). Educating consultants for multicultural practice of consultee-centered consultation. *Journal of Educational & Psychological Consultation, 27*, 72–95. http://dx.doi.org/10.1080/10474412.2016.1174936

Janken, K. R. (2015). *The Wilmington ten: Violence, injustice, and the rise of Black politics in the 1970s*. Chapel Hill: University of North Carolina Press.

Kang, J., & Lane, K. (2010). Seeing through colorblindness: Implicit bias and the law. *UCLA Law Review, 58*, 465–520.

Kaslow, N. J. (2004). Competencies in professional psychology. *American Psychologist, 59*, 774–781. http://dx.doi.org/10.1037/0003-066X.59.8.774

Kaslow, N. J., Borden, K. A., Collins, F. L., Jr., Forrest, L., Illfelder-Kaye, J., Nelson, P. D., . . . Willmuth, M. E. (2004). Competencies Conference: Future Directions in Education and Credentialing in Professional Psychology. *Journal of Clinical Psychology, 60*, 699–712. http://dx.doi.org/10.1002/jclp.20016

Kawakami, K., & Dovidio, J. F. (2001). The reality of implicit stereotyping. *Personality and Social Psychology Bulletin, 27*, 212–225. http://dx.doi.org/10.1177/0146167201272007

Konopaske, R., Ivancevich, J. M., & Matteson, M. T. (2018). *Organizational behavior and management* (11th ed.). New York, NY: McGraw-Hill.

Kotter, J. P. (2012). *Leading change*. Boston, MA: Harvard Business Review Press.

Kray, L. J., & Shirako, A. (2012). Stereotype threat in organizations: An examination of its scope, triggers and possible interventions. In M. Inzlicht & T. Schmader (Eds.), *Stereotype threat: Theory, process, and application* (pp. 173–187). New York, NY: Oxford University Press.

Levine, E. S. (2000). *Freedom's children: Young civil rights activists tell their own story*. New York, NY: Puffin Books.

Lewis, J., & D'Orso, M. (1998). *Walking with the wind: A memoir of the movement*. New York, NY: Simon & Schuster.

Liebowitz, B., & Blattner, J. (2015). On becoming a consultant: The transition for a clinical psychologist. *Consulting Psychology Journal: Practice and Research, 67*, 144–161. http://dx.doi.org/10.1037/cpb0000037

Lowman, R. L. (Ed.). (2002). *Handbook of organizational consulting psychology: A comprehensive guide to theory, skills, and techniques*. San Francisco, CA: Jossey-Bass.

Lowman, R. L. (2007). Coaching and consulting in multicultural contexts: Integrating themes and issues. *Consulting Psychology Journal: Practice and Research, 59*, 296–303. http://dx.doi.org/10.1037/1065-9293.59.4.296

Lowman, R. L. (2014). Social justice and industrial-organizational and consulting psychology. In J. Diaz, Z. Franco, & B. K. Nastasi (Eds.), *The Praeger handbook of social justice and psychology: Vol. 3. Youth and disciplines in psychology* (pp. 165–182). Santa Barbara, CA: Praeger.

Lowndes, J. E. (2009). *From the New Deal to the New Right: Race and the southern origins of modern conservatism*. New Haven, CT: Yale University Press.

Maass, A., D'Ettole, C., & Cadinu, M. (2008). Checkmate? The role of gender stereotypes in the ultimate intellectual sport. *European Journal of Social Psychology, 38*, 231–245. http://dx.doi.org/10.1002/ejsp.440

McGirr, L. (2002). *Suburban warriors: The origins of the New American Right*. Princeton, NJ: Princeton University Press.

McIntosh, P. (1989, July/August). Unpacking the invisible knapsack. *Peace and Freedom Magazine*, pp. 10–12.

McLaren, P. (1989). *Life in schools: An introduction to critical pedagogy and the foundations of education*. New York, NY: Longman.

McLaren, P. (2003). Critical pedagogy: A look at the major concepts. In A. Darder, M. Baltodano, & R. D. Torres (Eds.), *The critical pedagogy reader* (pp. 69–96). New York, NY: RoutledgeFalmer.

Meyers, J. (2002). A 30 year perspective on best practices for consultation training. *Journal of Educational and Psychological Consultation, 13*, 35–54. http://dx.doi.org/10.1080/10474412.2002.9669452

Newell, M. (2010). The implementation of problem-solving consultation: An analysis of problem conceptualization in a multiracial context. *Journal of Educational and Psychological Consultation, 20*, 83–105. http://dx.doi.org/10.1080/10474411003785529

Newell, M. L., Newell, T. S., & Looser, J. (2013). A competency-based assessment of school-based consultants' implementation of consultation. *Training and Education in Professional Psychology, 7*, 235–245. http://dx.doi.org/10.1037/a0033067

Newell, M., & Newman, D. (2014). Assessing the state of evidence in consultation training: A review and call to the field. In W. P. Erchul, & S. M. Sheridan (Eds.), *Handbook of research in school consultation* (2nd ed.; pp. 421–449). New York, NY: Routledge.

Ortiz, S. O. (2006). Multicultural issues in school psychology practice. *Journal of Applied School Psychology, 22*, 151–167. http://dx.doi.org/10.1300/J370v22n02_08

Parham, W. D. (2019). Hiding in plain sight: Discovering the promises of multicultural sport psychology. In M. H. Anshel (Ed.), *APA handbook of sport and exercise psychology* (Vol. 1, pp. 489–508). Washington, DC: American Psychological Association.

Rasmussen, D. M. (1996). *The handbook of critical theory*. Oxford, England: Blackwell.

Ratts, M. J., Singh, A. A., Nassar-McMillan, S., Butler, S. K., & McCullough, J. R. (2016). Multicultural and social justice counseling competencies: Guidelines for the counseling profession. *Journal of Multicultural Counseling and Development, 44*, 28–48. http://dx.doi.org/10.1002/jmcd.12035

Reskin, B. F. (2000). Getting it right: Sex and race inequality in work organizations. *Annual Review of Sociology, 26*, 707–709. http://dx.doi.org/10.1146/annurev.soc.26.1.707

Reskin, B. F. (2005). Unconsciousness raising: The pernicious effects of unconscious bias. *Regional Review, 14*, 32–37.

Rodolfa, E., Bent, R., Eisman, E., Nelson, P., Rehm, L., & Ritchie, P. (2005). A cube model for competency development: Implications for psychology educators and regulators. *Professional Psychology: Research and Practice, 36*, 347–354. http://dx.doi.org/10.1037/0735-7028.36.4.347

Rosen, R. (2006). *The world split open: How the modern women's movement changed America* (2nd ed.). New York, NY: Penguin Books.

Rutland, A., Cameron, L., Milne, A., & McGeorge, P. (2005). Social norms and self-presentation: Children's implicit and explicit intergroup attitudes. *Child Development, 76*, 451–466. http://dx.doi.org/10.1111/j.1467-8624.2005.00856.x

Sabatino, C. A. (2014). *Consultation theory and practice: A handbook for school social workers.* New York, NY: Oxford University Press. http://dx.doi.org/10.1093/acprof:oso/9780199934621.001.0001

Schein, E. H. (2015). Organizational psychology then and now: Some observations. *Annual Review of Organizational Psychology and Organizational Behavior, 2,* 1–19. http://dx.doi.org/10.1146/annurev-orgpsych-032414-111449

Sevo, R., & Chubin, D. E. (2008). *Bias literacy: A review of concepts in research on discrimination.* Retrieved from https://www.napequity.org/nape-content/uploads/8-BiasLiteracy.pdf

Staats, C., Capatosto, K., Wright, R. A., & Jackson, V. W. (2016). *State of the science: Implicit bias review.* Retrieved from http://kirwaninstitute.osu.edu/wp-content/uploads/2016/07/implicit-bias-2016.pdf

Steele, C. M., Spencer, S. J., & Aronson, J. (2002). Contending with group image: The psychology of stereotype and social identity threat. *Advances in Experimental Social Psychology, 34,* 379–440. http://dx.doi.org/10.1016/S0065-2601(02)80009-0

Sue, D. W., Arredondo, P., & McDavis, R. (1992). Multicultural competencies and standards: A call to the profession. *Journal of Counseling & Development, 70,* 477–486. http://dx.doi.org/10.1002/j.1556-6676.1992.tb01642.x

Tervalon, M., & Murray-García, J. (1998). Cultural humility versus cultural competence: A critical distinction in defining physician training outcomes in multicultural education. *Journal of Health Care for the Poor and Underserved, 9,* 117–125. http://dx.doi.org/10.1353/hpu.2010.0233

*Thomas Jefferson, et al., July 4, Copy of Declaration of Independence.* (1776, July 4). [Manuscript/mixed material]. Retrieved from the Library of Congress, https://www.loc.gov/item/mtjbib000159/

UNC Executive Development. (2015, October 8). The real effects of unconscious bias in the workplace [Blog post]. Retrieved from http://execdev.kenan-flagler.unc.edu/blog/the-real-effects-of-unconscious-bias-in-the-workplace-0

Viguerie, R. A. (1981). *The New Right: We're ready to lead.* Falls Church, VA: Viguerie.

Williams, J., & Bond, J. (2013). *The eyes on the prize: America's civil rights years, 1954–1965.* New York, NY: Penguin Books. (Original work published 2002)

Zinn, H. (2003). *A people's history of the United States: 1492–present.* New York, NY: HarperCollins.

# EXEMPLARS AND APPROACHES

# 7

# Pediatric Consultation

Michael C. Roberts, Rebecca J. Johnson, and Christina M. Amaro

Pediatric and clinical child psychologists have long provided consultation to pediatricians, nurses, social workers, and allied health professionals in children's hospitals and pediatric medicine clinics, as well as to parents and caregivers of children with health problems. Indeed, an early American psychologist, Lightner Witmer, in 1897 provided consultation through his psychological clinic with parents, caregivers, and physicians on issues related to children's educational and educational concerns. Over time, multiple clinical collaborations developed between psychologist and pediatricians. When Logan Wright (1967) articulated the developing field of pediatric psychology, he included a distinctive focus for psychologists to be consultants to physicians and parents.

The subsequent history of pediatric psychology presents a rich array of activities, roles, and functions most often involving the integration of science and practice (see Drotar, 1995; Roberts, Aylward, & Wu, 2014; Roberts & Steele, 2017; Wu, Aylward, & Roberts, 2014). In early and now current conceptualizations of the field, the pediatric psychologist is seen as potentially providing a variety of services, which inherently involve consultation (Roberts et al., 2014): (a) psychological assessment and treatment of behavioral and emotional problems that appear in medical units (e.g., disruptive behaviors resulting from painful medical procedures); (b) psychological services to children and their families regarding pediatric health conditions (e.g., adjustment to and coping with disease, quality of life, adherence to medical regimens; dealing with pain

http://dx.doi.org/10.1037/0000153-008
*Consultation in Psychology: A Competency-Based Approach*, C. A. Falender and
E. P. Shafranske (Editors)

and painful medical procedures; traumatic medical stress); (c) interventions for behavioral and emotional problems presenting in pediatric offices that may not be associated with a pediatric health problem but are referred to a frontline medical practitioner; and (d) assistance in creating policies, practices, and routinized procedures in medical settings that support children and families in developmentally appropriate, patient-centered, and humane ways. Thus, the psychologist's interventions in pediatric settings are not just illness related or only patient directed but address behavioral problems and medical personnel as well. In providing this range of services, pediatric psychologists frequently provide direct services to children, adolescents, and their families, but also provide consultation to the full complement of other health and educational service providers, including pediatricians, nurses, social workers, speech and language specialists, child life specialists, and teachers and principals, among others. This role of a pediatric consultant as one part of the health service psychology (HSP) roles is the focus of this chapter in outlining models of consultation.

## MODELS OF PEDIATRIC PSYCHOLOGY CONSULTATION

Roberts and Wright (1982) presented three models in an early formulation of pediatric psychology consultation that were built off general writings in consultation and descriptions of pediatric psychology roles and functions. In the *independent functions model,* the psychologist functions as an independent specialist and primarily communicates with the pediatrician before and after the referral and provides direct services to a child and family. This model takes a relatively noncollaborative role with the pediatrician. In the *indirect psychological consultation model,* the psychologist indirectly provides care by working primarily with the pediatrician. The psychologist, who has limited to no contact with the patient, consults with the pediatrician by providing information and advice. The physician then implements the intervention. In the *collaborative team model,* the psychologist and pediatrician collaborate on a case in which they both share responsibility and take part in the decision-making process to develop a treatment plan and implement it (Roberts & Wright, 1982). Subsequently, Mullins, Gillman, and Harbeck (1992) added a fourth model to pediatric consultation: the *systems-oriented model.* This model uses a systems approach in which interventions are developed with various higher levels in mind. These consultative interventions might involve multiple professionals in developing and implementing, such as establishing child-oriented policies and procedures in a hospital unit or developing consensus-based standards of care for children with acute and chronic illnesses. Drotar (1995) later emphasized the collaborative aspects of professional work with pediatricians while delineating multiple ways of implementing consultative relationships. These early articulations of models apply to today's pediatric consultation roles and functions; more recent frameworks providing specific applications are discussed later in this chapter (compare with Carter et al., 2017; Carter, Thompson, & Thompson, 2014).

## EDUCATION AND TRAINING IN PEDIATRIC CONSULTATION LEADING TO CONSULTATION COMPETENCIES

Over the years, several efforts have been made to develop and define competencies specific to pediatric psychologists and to describe appropriate training sequences for the field (e.g., La Greca, Stone, Drotar, & Maddux, 1988; Palermo et al., 2014; Spirito et al., 2003; Tuma, 1980). Education and training of pediatric psychologists are built on the core competencies in HSP coupled with the competencies in clinical child psychology but with an additional emphasis in child and adolescent health and illness in order to work in medical settings. With respect to core competencies in clinical child psychology, Jackson, Wu, Aylward, and Roberts (2012) described the more general competencies, which indicated that competencies in consultation are built on an understanding of developmental principles and family-centered principles. In particular, they outlined specific consultation knowledge base and application-based competencies as involving a knowledge-base of

A. Understanding of the role of other service providers to children (i.e., pediatricians, teachers) and the interplay between agencies serving children and understanding the literature as it relates to the role of consultants to child mental health care; B. Awareness of the mission of systems of care, agencies and professionals present in settings that service children (i.e., hospitals, schools); C. Awareness of the role of culture in systems of care and in the child's life as methods are best identified for meeting the child's needs; D. Understanding of other specialty fields as they apply to clinical child psychology (i.e., school psychology, developmental psychology). (Jackson et al., 2012, Table 3)

The application-based competency for consultation includes

A. Understands the referral question and conceptualizes the needs of the child based on developmental level and environmental demands; B. Appropriately discusses mental health findings to systems and nonpsychological professionals to meet the child's mental health needs; C. Shares with relevant stakeholders, incorporates relevant research in forming consultation advice, identifies diverse methods and levels of analysis that are best suited to responding to the referral question, and communicates these findings effectively; D. Ethically manages issues that may arise in consultation; E. Applies and communicates about clinical intervention to meet the needs of non-clinical referral questions. (Jackson et al., 2012, Table 3)

These points serve as the clinical child psychology basis for professional functioning in pediatric psychology and for subsequent competencies in pediatric consultation.

Within the more focused field of pediatric psychology, three task forces have outlined sequential recommendations for training and competencies for pediatric psychologists and reference consultation practices in the field. Each of the recommendations has become more detailed in identifying knowledge, attitudes, and skills necessary for pediatric consultation. Reporting for a task force commissioned by the Society of Pediatric Psychology (SPP), La Greca et al. (1988) provided rather general suggestions for obtaining adequate training and experiences while indicating that multiple pathways to the field have been observed. In a report of a second SPP task force, Spirito et al. (2003) discussed the multiple domains of pediatric psychology training to indicate the breadth of topics to cover in training and functioning in the field, including lifespan developmental psychology; lifespan developmental psychopathology; child, adolescent, and family assessment; intervention strategies; research methods and systems evaluations; professional, ethical, and legal issues; diversity; role of multiple disciplines in service delivery systems; prevention, family support, and health promotion; social issues affecting children, adolescents, and families; consultation and liaison roles; and disease process and medical management. Spirito et al. (2003) delineated the consultation and liaison roles and the rising professionals' preparation with several "shoulds" as to what trainees should experience, including opportunities to observe supervisors in the process of consulting, serve on specialty teams consulting on clinical cases and on research activities, participate in seminars on consultation-liaison (C-L) models that have topics on the function of a health care professional and patient–physician communication, and receive supervised clinical experiences consulting about patients and assessment and intervention with their presenting problems.

More recently, the report of the Palermo et al. (2014) training task force for SPP expanded on these points by providing recommendations for core competencies within pediatric psychology, including science, professionalism, interpersonal functioning, application (including consultation), education, systems, and crosscutting knowledge competencies. In particular, the report indicated that

> consultation is a core pediatric psychology clinical activity directed toward improving health and behavior. It involves effectively working with health-care professionals across disciplines (e.g., pediatrics, nursing) as well as systems (e.g., health care, school, family, and social welfare) to improve the provision of services to identified patients, typically through responding to specific referral questions. The pediatric psychologist as consultant fulfills a variety of roles, including translating and communicating relevant clinical findings in response to a wide range of C-L questions that emerge in the course of child, family, and health-care team response to illness and coping. (Palermo et al., 2014, p. 975)

With greater specificity than earlier reports, Palermo et al. defined the consultation competencies in application as "5.1.D. Provides consultative/liaison services to health-care professionals across disciplines and systems related to health and behavior; 5.2.D. Translates and communicates relevant clinical findings as they bear on health-care consultation/liaison questions" (Palermo et al., 2014, Table V, Cluster Application, p. 976). This report then provided behavioral anchors that described sequential readiness for trainee clinical practicum, internship, and practice, namely:

> [*Practicum:*] Demonstrates exposure level awareness of the pediatric psychologist's consultant's role, including features distinguished from other professional roles in a health-care setting;

> [*Internship:*] Demonstrates knowledge of the pediatric psychologist consultant's role and its unique features as distinguished from other professional roles (such as therapist, supervisor, teacher); Informs consultee of assessment findings in health-care settings with moderate supervision;

[*Practice:*] Applies knowledge to provide effective consultee feedback and to articulate appropriate recommendations in health-care settings. (Palermo et al., 2014,
Table V, p. 976)

These pediatric consultation competencies relate to the competencies sets
developed over time for professional psychology more generally (e.g., Fouad
et al., 2009; Grus, Falender, Fouad, & Lavelle, 2016; Hatcher, Fouad, Campbell,
et al., 2013; Hatcher, Fouad, Grus, et al., 2013; Kaslow et al., 2009).

On a general level of preparation for HSP roles, the Health Service Psychology Education Collaborative (HSPEC; 2013) developed a blueprint to inform
changes in graduate training through recommendations for training in HSP and
also developed a list of competencies in the following areas within which consultation was included: science (scientific knowledge and methods, research or
evaluation); professionalism (professional values and attitudes, individual and
cultural diversity, ethical and legal standards and policy, reflective practice or
self-assessment or self-care); relational: interpersonal skills and communication
and applications (evidence-based practice, assessment, intervention, consultation); education (teaching, supervision); and systems (interdisciplinary or
interprofessional leadership development, advocacy; HSPEC, 2013). In terms
of competency within consultation, the HSPEC blueprint stated that health
service psychologists "provide consultative psychological services to patients
and their families, other health care professionals, and systems related to health
and behavior" (HSPEC, 2013, p. 425). Specifically, the blueprint indicated that
psychologists should have an understanding of evidence-based consultation
and develop competency in this area. Furthermore, the report noted that consultation requires several interprofessional skills, including communication and
management of multiple relationships. In addition, skills required for working
with interdisciplinary or interprofessional systems are noted within the blueprint's "systems" domain. For example, health service psychologists should be
able to "use health informatics, including electronic health records, to communicate with other health professionals and patients as appropriate" (HSPEC,
2013, p. 426). These competencies are correspondingly translated into the
training goals with measurable outcomes for doctoral training programs in HSP.

## THE ROLE OF PSYCHOLOGISTS IN PEDIATRICS
## AND COMMON AREAS OF CONSULTATION

Pediatric psychologists working in C-L roles or as hospitalist psychologists provide a range of consultation services. Access to professionals who can address
the behavioral health needs of pediatric populations is recognized as an important service for children and their families (Drotar, 2013). In a recent practice
model for C-L psychology, Carter et al. (2014) defined common practice areas
addressed by consultants as the *5 Cs:* crisis, coping, adherence (compliance),
communication, and collaboration. Carter et al. (2017) later proposed a sixth *C*—
changing systems—to capture the work that psychologists do to influence

health care policy and planning, research, and design; to advocate for health care delivery that integrates physical and behavioral health at the population level; and to promote effective prevention and intervention at all levels of the environment. As these six types of consultation suggest, C-L psychologists perform many roles in multiple settings and have the potential to influence health care at all levels. A discussion of these Cs follows.

## Crisis

In the pediatric setting, psychologists often serve as consultants to medical providers and to children and their families during situations that involve crises. Crises may include new onset illness, a significant decline in a child's medical condition, a traumatic event or injury, or self-harm behavior (Carter et al., 2014). The experience of social and medical crises and the heightened emotions that typically accompany these situations affect child and family coping, functioning, and decision making (Drotar & Zagorski, 2001). Providing timely, appropriate psychosocial interventions is important for promoting child and family adjustment (Ernst, Piazza-Waggoner, & Ciesielski, 2015).

Some of the roles of the consultant include assisting families with managing emotional distress, including targeted interventions; coordinating care among allied health professionals, such as chaplaincy, child life, and social work; and identifying which patients or caregivers may be at risk for posttraumatic stress disorder or depression and providing referrals for ongoing evidence-based intervention or care. When children or adolescents have engaged in self-harm or are at risk for self-harm, services may also include consultation with the referring provider and staff regarding safety measures that need to be in place while the patient is stabilized (e.g., one-to-one supervision), placement determinations (i.e., discharge home or admission to an inpatient psychiatric unit), coordination with social work to arrange appropriate outpatient services, and family consultation regarding means restriction and safety planning.

## Coping

Although psychological intervention may focus on stabilization and management of emotional distress during acute situations, when patients have extended or chronic health conditions, the focus turns to coping with the stressors associated with having a chronic condition (Rodrigue, Gonzalez-Peralta, & Langham, 2004) and long-term or ongoing adjustment. Chronic health conditions, such as diabetes, cystic fibrosis, cancer, sickle cell disease, inflammatory bowel disease, and solid organ transplant, are associated with a multitude of stressors, including complex and time-consuming treatments; invasive procedures; appointments and admissions that interrupt daily routines; exacerbations, flare-ups, or complications from the disease that necessitate additional treatment or care; and changes to appearance, either from the disease process or treatments or from the placement of devices, such as gastrostomy tubes or implantable venous access systems. For caregivers, additional stressors include coordinating medical appointments with other family activities or employment; attending to siblings; managing equipment, supplies, and refills of medications; and communicating with medical systems and insurance organizations.

Psychological consultation can assist patients and families in identifying ways to develop or enhance coping, including maintaining normative activities and having a consistent daily routine, planning school reentry, identifying coping styles or strategies to match the stressor, finding opportunities for personal control, and increasing acceptance (Ernst et al., 2014). Much of this work can and does use a strengths-based focus in that it recognizes that families are resilient and have significant capacities for coping (Drotar, 2013). Behavioral health consultation can improve outcomes; for example, early intervention may reduce length of admission (Kishi, Meller, Kathol, & Swigart, 2004), and targeting parent responses and coping can facilitate children's coping during invasive medical procedures (Campbell, DiLorenzo, Atkinson, & Pillai Riddell, 2017).

## Adherence (Compliance)

The World Health Organization (2003) defined *adherence* as "the extent to which a person's behaviour—taking medication, following a diet, and/or executing lifestyle changes[—]corresponds with agreed recommendations from a health care provider" (p. 3). Taking into account the complexities of families, illness, treatments, and health care systems, agreement among caregivers, the patient, and medical providers on a treatment plan can be challenging. Psychological consultants use their expertise to clarify expectations and facilitate communication. Even if a treatment plan is agreed on, nonadherence is common (approximately one third of patients do not finish treatment for an acute illness, and for chronic conditions, average adherence is estimated at 50% to 55%; Rapoff, 2011). Nonadherence affects patients' health and quality of life, affects clinical decision making, increases unnecessary health care use and costs, and impacts clinical trials (Drotar, 2000; Rapoff, 2011). Thus, psychological consultants have important opportunities to improve children's health and quality of life through consultations to improve adherence.

A number of potential barriers to adherence may be a focus of the consultant. These barriers include family psychosocial complexity, patient or caregiver skills deficits, poor communication or misunderstanding between the family and providers, or fear or anxiety on the part of the family (Carter et al., 2003; Rapoff, 2011). In addition, some families engage in volitional, or intentional, nonadherence, for a number of reasons: so aversive side effects will be reduced; because the drug or treatment is not having the desired result; family and provider treatment goals are not aligned; or due to a desire for reduced treatment burden (R. J. Johnson, 2017; Schurman, Cushing, Carpenter, & Christenson, 2011). The consultant may work with both the family and the referring provider or team to clarify or revise goals. As adherence goals are identified, pediatric psychologists use a variety of educational, organizational, or behavioral interventions to improve adherence (Rapoff, 2011).

## Communication

Within the context of complex chronic health conditions and during crises when emotional and cognitive resources of patients and caregivers may be over-whelmed, good communication is crucial for optimal care. Health care systems present many opportunities for miscommunication or misunderstandings, and poor communication can negatively impact care (Carter et al., 2014; Drotar, 2013). Psychologists are often asked to consult on cases in which communication is not optimal, is complicated, or has been compromised. Carter et al. (2014) described psychology consultants as integral to diffusing conflict by reframing behaviors and clarifying goals to improve understanding and communication among patients, caregivers, and providers. Identifying sources of mutual misunderstanding can improve communication and promote shared decision making, and of the many skills that psychologists bring to consultation, key strengths are facilitating empathy and understanding and building relationships.

## Collaboration

Collaboration is a key part of psychological consultation in the pediatric health care setting. Psychologists work with physicians, surgeons, nurses, social workers, coordinators, chaplains, child life specialists, pharmacists, dieticians, and a host of other providers and staff. Successful, effective collaboration benefits the other Cs: Patients are more likely to cope effectively when the appropriate resources have been mobilized, collaboration between psychologists and providers can inform interventions to improve adherence, collaboration among providers improves communication, and communication errors are a frequent source of patient dissatisfaction with care.

## Changing Systems

Pediatric psychologists possess skill sets and knowledge needed to modify systems and improve policies that impact children's care and physical and behavioral health outcomes. Psychologists are in a unique position to do this work in that they have knowledge of and experience with complex hospital systems and can research, design, and advocate for health delivery systems that improve the care of children and families (Carter et al., 2014, 2017). Psychologists can also work to improve health care by using empirically supported communication and problem-solving techniques (e.g., clinical coaching; Greco & Pitel, 2016).

## Consultation Vignette

Mark, a 20-year-old kidney transplant patient, was admitted to a medical inpatient unit for renal biopsy and subsequent treatment of graft rejection.[1] He had been employed since graduating from high school, lived alone, and had little instrumental or social support from his family. He was referred to psychology following some angry outbursts at staff and refusal to follow the treatment plan

---

[1]All clinical case material has been altered to protect client confidentiality.

(i.e., demanding to be discharged before completion of treatment). Psychology was consulted to assess the patient's concerns and understanding of the need for treatment. Interview revealed a number of patient concerns, including fear he would lose his job, which would increase financial stressors; frustration with treatment delays and uncertain length of admission; history of mood dysregulation and problems managing anger; and nonadherence to his posttransplant medication regimen. He reported treatment fatigue in that he could no longer motivate himself to take numerous immunosuppressant and transplant-related medications on time, twice a day. He also endorsed acute distress related to his diagnosis of graft rejection and feelings of hopelessness regarding his future. Through discussion with the medical team and the patient, goals of consultation were identified: (a) clarify the patient's understanding of diagnosis, treatment, and prognosis, and provide education as appropriate; (b) assist him with managing acute distress; (c) identify ways to improve communication between the patient and staff; and (d) assess the patient's readiness for and motivation to improve his adherence postdischarge. Interventions included working with the patient to articulate questions he had about his treatment and requesting that a member of the medical team address these questions at bedside. One of the results of this intervention was to lessen the patient's distress in that the provider was able to reiterate that although graft rejection was serious, it was also potentially treatable. The consultant then worked with the patient to identify those aspects of his care over which he had control, those that required collaboration with the medical team to modify, and those that were fixed. A key area of focus was helping the patient see that he did have choices and control over many factors, which lessened his distress and feelings of helplessness. The patient was asked to identify active coping strategies that he found helpful, and he was also taught self-regulation strategies, such as taking slow, deep breaths. Social work was consulted to assist the patient with documentation for his employer and identification of available resources to reduce financial stress. The patient agreed to remain admitted for treatment.

Once the more acute concerns were addressed, the consultant did a more thorough assessment of the patient's adherence over the past several weeks and months, including facilitators of and barrier to adherence. This assessment included both a paper-and-pencil measure on medication barriers and an interview style that was matter-of-fact, free of reprimands or judgment, focused on specific time frames, and involved asking specific questions about adherence and his medication routine (Rapoff, 2011). The assessment revealed that a number of factors were affecting adherence, including changes in routine, chronic nausea (and, relatedly, lack of food in the home), and depressogenic thinking about his disease and its treatment. The patient was open to outpatient therapy to address these barriers and also to an appointment with psychiatry to assess the appropriateness of, and patient's desire for, psychotropic medication to manage long-standing mood concerns.

An important function of the consultant is to communicate back to the referring provider and the medical team the goals and interventions identified, any progress toward those goals, and recommendations for future intervention.

Throughout the consultation, the psychologist had frequent communication with the medical team regarding progress and the mobilization of allied services, such as social work and a financial counselor. What could and could not be shared with the medical team was negotiated with the patient, who was agreeable to sharing the key aspects of the consultation with the referring provider and the medical team. This consultation addressed five of the six Cs, namely, crisis, coping, adherence (compliance), communication, and collaboration.

## PEDIATRIC PRIMARY CARE

Pediatric primary care (PPC) typically serves as a child or adolescent's medical home. It is the outpatient setting in which the majority of youths receive health care services, which are coordinated by a primary care provider (PCP) who is typically a pediatrician, nurse practitioner, physician assistant, or family medicine physician (Stancin & Perrin, 2014). Youths commonly present with behavioral, developmental, and emotional issues in the PPC that psychologists are well suited to address. For example, presenting concerns may include toileting issues (e.g., enuresis, encopresis), sleep difficulties, developmental delays, behavioral problems (e.g., noncompliance), and academic concerns (Drotar, 1995). Several advantages accrue for providing mental and behavioral health services in the PPC setting. Regular well-child visits provide the opportunity to conduct frequent screenings for mental and behavioral health concerns, which may permit early identification and intervention, particularly when concerns may be less severe (Stancin, Sturm, & Ramirez, 2014). In addition, psychological services offered in PPC may overcome some barriers to treatment, such that families may view this setting as less stigmatizing and may be more likely to seek services offered in PPC as opposed to pursuing outside referrals (Kolko, Campo, Kilbourne, & Kelleher, 2012; Stancin et al., 2014).

In pediatric psychology, there has been a long-standing history of consultation and practice within PPC. Most notably, Carolyn Schroeder established an integrated practice in 1973 that provided a variety of psychosocial services, including evening parent groups, developmental screening, call-in and walk-in hours during which parents could ask questions and discuss presenting concerns, and prevention programs (e.g., Schroeder, 1979, 2004). Over the years, other psychologists have provided encouragement for the expansion of mental and behavioral services offered in PPC (e.g., Brown & Roberts, 2000; Christophersen, 1982; Routh, Schroeder, & Koocher, 1983); however, the number of pediatric psychologists providing services in PPC has remained relatively limited compared with numbers in hospital-based consultation.

### Collaborative and Integrated Practice in Primary Pediatric Care

In establishing consultation services and practice in PPC, it is important for a psychologist to consider the level of collaboration and integration in this setting. Both collaborative and integrated practices foster coordinated care of patients and interprofessional work involving psychologists and PCPs as well as other members of the health care team (Stancin et al., 2014); however, the level of collaboration or integrated practice in PPC can vary. At a basic level of collaboration in PPC, pediatric psychologists may be colocated in the primary care office, such that all of the providers are in the same suite or building. In colocation, the PCP may regularly communicate with the psychologist about specific patients who have been referred for psychological services. Although colocation enables all providers to be in close proximity, the psychologist may not function as a member of the primary care office and may act as a separate provider with a completely independent practice (Stancin et al., 2014). For example, a psychologist may rent office space in the same building as the PPC office and see patients for psychoeducational evaluations. Although the psychologist may receive some referrals from the PCP, the psychologist's practice has its own scheduling, billing, and medical records that are separate from the primary care office.

In an integrated practice, on the other hand, psychologists function as a member of the PPC team, providing mental health and behavioral services as needed for any patient seen in the primary care office. In integrated primary care settings, psychologists also participate in staff meetings, may conduct joint appointments with the PCP, document progress notes in the same medical chart as do other PPC providers, and bill for services through the PPC office (Stancin & Perrin, 2014; Stancin et al., 2014).

## Roles and Training in Primary Pediatric Care

Competencies specific to psychologists' various roles in primary care have been developed. For instance, McDaniel et al. (2014) described competencies and sample behavioral anchors for psychologists who practice in primary care. In addition, descriptions of behavioral anchors have been developed for pediatric psychologists who practice in integrated primary care (Hoffses et al., 2016). In primary care settings, psychologists provide direct consultation services to youths and families as well as members of the primary care team. As such, psychologists initially work with the primary care team to establish ways to incorporate psychological services, including consultation, within the practice. They may discuss what situations would be appropriate for consulting with the psychologist or what potential automatic triggers are for consultation. Within this setting, psychologists may also maintain several other roles, including involvement with screening, direct clinical services, research, training, supervision, and advocacy (Stancin, Sturm, Tynan, & Ramirez, 2017).

With regard to training psychologists to work in primary care, McDaniel, Belar, Schroeder, Hargrove, and Freeman (2002) proposed a curriculum comprising 12 core areas of knowledge and skills for primary care psychology as a supplement to standard graduate training in psychology. At the graduate level, there may also be opportunities for students to gain exposure to primary care through practicum sites. Internship and postdoctoral training also provide opportunities for trainees to gain additional experience with primary care psychology. For example, internship training in integrated primary care is emphasized at MetroHealth Medical Center in Cleveland, Ohio (Nielsen, 2014), and integrated behavioral health tracks are offered at some internship sites, such as Nemours/Alfred I. duPont Hospital for Children in Wilmington, Delaware (Novotney, 2014), and the Nebraska Internship Consortium in Professional Psychology at Munroe-Meyer Institute, University of Nebraska Medical Center in Omaha (see Grus & Cope, 2016, for a directory of internship programs with training opportunities in primary care). Furthermore, Talmi et al. (2015) described an integrated behavioral health services program, Project Consultation Liaison in Mental Health and Behavior, which provides postdoctoral fellows training in primary care psychology.

## COMMON CHALLENGES TO CONSULTATION

### Ethical Challenges

Awareness and understanding of how to navigate ethical issues in pediatric psychology consultation are important aspects of training for pediatric psychologists (Palermo et al., 2014; Spirito et al., 2003), and resources and case examples exist to guide supervisors and prepare trainees for some of the ethical issues encountered in the setting of consultation (Cousino & Mednick, 2016; Fehr, Hazen, & Nielsen, 2017; Kelly, Morris, Mee, Brosig, & Self, 2016). Frequently addressed are issues of autonomy, consent, confidentiality, and complex medical or end-of-life decision making (Rae, Brunnquell, & Sullivan, 2017). Obtaining informed consent in the consultation setting involves obtaining parental permission and child assent or consent from the patient if he or she is 18 years of age or older, informing the family of the reason for the consult, and discussing with whom information will be shared. To protect confidentiality and the therapeutic relationship, consultants are careful to share the minimally necessary information with the referring provider and other health care professionals. Confidentiality should be discussed during the consent process, including the limits of confidentiality, expectations for the confidentiality of older children and adolescents, who on the health care team will have access to information, and what information will be shared (Rae et al., 2017). Consultants should understand the different expectations for confidentiality that institutions, referring providers, parents, and patients might have and be prepared to navigate discrepant expectations and clarify confidentiality expectations for those involved (Rae et al., 2017). Pediatric psychologists have less ambivalence about when to break confidentiality for safety concerns, such as suicidal or homicidal ideation, but more ambivalence when it comes to a child or adolescent's risky behaviors (Rae, Sullivan, Razo, George, & Ramirez, 2002). Most C-L psychologists use an electronic health record and must also consider issues of confidentiality with regard to documentation (Nielsen, 2015).

When ethical issues do arise, the majority of children's hospitals have ethics committees that evaluate and mediate challenging situations (Kesselheim,

Johnson, & Joffe, 2010). Psychologists often participate in this process or serve on ethics committees and should have knowledge regarding relevant ethics codes and laws, institutional policies, and end-of-life decision making (Cardona, 2017; Ernst et al., 2015). Medical decision making has been identified as an issue commonly referred to ethics committees in pediatric settings (L. M. Johnson, Church, Metzger, & Baker, 2015). When medical decision making involves withdrawing, withholding, or refusing care, psychologists help families ask questions, clarify options and complex medical information, and identify the family's values. Rae et al. (2017) described the psychological consultant as someone who can assist the patient and family to "integrate their value systems into the fact situation" (p. 19) and translate the family's perspectives for the health care team. Children and adolescents should be involved in decisions about their own care to the extent that they have the capacity to participate, and psychologists often play a role in assessing patients' abilities to participate in and contribute to the decision-making process (Miller, Drotar, & Kodish, 2004; Rae et al., 2017), including developmental and clinical issues that impact level of involvement (McCabe, 1996). As treatment innovations and medical technology advance, psychologists navigate new ethical issues, such as those related to risk notification and disclosure in genetic testing and neuroethics.

## Communication Challenges

In addition to communication among patients, caregivers, and the health care team, psychology consultants may also address communication challenges among providers of multiple subspecialties caring for children with complex or chronic conditions to coordinate an effective response to their complex medical needs (Drotar, 2013). Consultation-liaison psychologists may initiate care conferences attended by multiple providers to share information and delineate a clear treatment plan; they also may provide staff education to promote communication and increase awareness of the psychosocial aspects of caring for children and their families (Carter et al., 2017).

## Challenges Related to the Referral Question and Goals

A particular professional challenge encountered by C-L psychologists is identifying the consultation question, the goals of consultation, or both (Carter et al., 2017; Kullgren et al., 2015). Sometimes the referral question is unclear or cannot be answered by the consultant (e.g., the question is not appropriate for the inpatient setting; the patient is not medically stable enough for interview; the medical workup is incomplete). When an appropriate referral question is identified, the consultant may need to clarify the goals for the consultation with the referring provider or the health care team. Agreement with regard to the goals of consultation is associated with positive ratings by referring providers and also provider, patient, and caregiver satisfaction with consultation services (Carter et al., 2003).

## Divided Responsibilities or Competing Demands

Productivity in the inpatient setting can be unpredictable, and, thus, many C-L psychologists have clinical productivity expectations in the outpatient setting as well (Carter et al., 2017). In addition to these responsibilities, C-L psychologists often perform work that involves research, teaching and training, participation in professional activities, quality improvement work, and program development. The challenges associated with multiple roles can lead to stress, job dissatisfaction, and burnout, particularly when the time and resources for activities outside of clinical work are limited.

## Burnout

*Burnout* is defined as a prolonged response to chronic job-related emotional and interpersonal stressors, and includes exhaustion, cynicism, and inefficacy (Maslach, Schaufeli, & Leiter, 2001). The nature of C-L work (i.e., routine exposure to families in crisis or under extreme stress; unpredictable work demands; navigation of competing goals and interests among providers, patients, and families; and frequent handling of communication problems) may increase risk of burnout. Kullgren et al. (2015) reported that although the majority (82%) of C-L psychologists endorse having job satisfaction and adequate resources to perform their jobs, about a third reported feeling burnout some of the time, and 5% reported it most or all of the time. Faculty were more likely to report burnout than trainees, who may enjoy more protections and have fewer competing demands. Working in a larger hospital (i.e., more beds) was associated with having more resources for research, teaching, and other activities. Although information on burnout in pediatric psychology is limited, information on physician burnout has been more frequently disseminated (for information on pediatricians, see Starmer, Frintner, & Freed, 2016, and for physicians more generally, see Shanafelt et al., 2015).

## Funding Challenges

Carter et al. (2017) discussed some of the challenges of funding inpatient C-L services, including emergent services that require tight time frames, lack of insurance preauthorization for services, services that must be provided regardless of insurance coverage, higher proportion of insurance denials, and nonbillable activities that are necessary for completion of consultation activities (e.g., time spent coordinating care, attendance at team meetings, documentation demands). Kullgren et al. (2015) found that, on average, C-L psychologists spend 62% of their time directly with patients, and other studies have found almost a third of time spent in nonreimbursable activities (Bierenbaum, Katsikas, Furr, & Carter, 2013). Thus, funding C-L services can be a challenge, and because clinical collections typically account for less than half of the service's financial support (Bierenbaum et al., 2013; Kullgren et al., 2015; Piazza-Waggoner, Roddenberry, Yeomans-Maldonado, Noll, & Ernst, 2013), most C-L services depend on more than one funding source. Health and behavior codes, which were developed for use in pediatric settings, do not require preauthorization, and there is growing evidence that they can be used successfully to obtain reimbursement (Brosig & Zahrt, 2006; Piazza-Waggoner et al., 2013).

## PEDIATRIC CONSULTATION IN OTHER DOMAINS

Most of this chapter addressed consultation in clinical service roles. In addition, because of the strong research skills and empirical science orientation of psychologists, pediatric consultation frequently involves research consultation with health care professionals and administrators, such as evaluating programs and improving quality in addition to conducting clinical trials to investigate the effects of psychosocial- and health-enhancing interventions. Pediatric psychologists have developed sophisticated scientific and professional scholarship, including investigating specialized assessment and measurement approaches and developing evidence-based treatments for a wide range of clinical problems. The field has developed specialized research methodologies and longitudinal studies that involve advanced statistical methods and often multisite studies to enhance sample size for generalizability. Thus, the pediatric psychologist often serves as a scientist–practitioner in consulting and conducting clinical research with other professionals in the health care field.

Included in the skill development outlined in publications on competencies (e.g., McDaniel et al., 2014; Palermo et al., 2014; Spirito et al., 2003) are consulting activities to educate the public and other health care professionals about the psychosocial aspects of children's safety, illness, and health. Also, within the competencies of pediatric psychologists are consultation activities involving the development of public and institutional policies, such as how to provide developmentally appropriate, family-centered care for children in hospitals and medical settings as well supporting laws on and recommendations for improving child health and safety.

## REFERENCES

Bierenbaum, M. L., Katsikas, S., Furr, A., & Carter, B. D. (2013). Factors associated with non-reimbursable activity on an inpatient pediatric consultation-liaison service. *Journal of Clinical Psychology in Medical Settings, 20,* 464–472. http://dx.doi.org/10.1007/s10880-013-9371-2

Brosig, C. L., & Zahrt, D. M. (2006). Evolution of an inpatient pediatric psychology consultation service: Issues related to reimbursement and the use of health and behavior codes. *Journal of Clinical Psychology in Medical Settings, 13,* 420–424. http://dx.doi.org/10.1007/s10880-006-9047-2

Brown, K. J., & Roberts, M. C. (2000). Future issues in pediatric psychology: Delphic survey. *Journal of Clinical Psychology in Medical Settings, 7,* 5–15. http://dx.doi.org/10.1023/A:1009589101926

Campbell, L., DiLorenzo, M., Atkinson, N., & Pillai Riddell, R. (2017). Systematic review: A systematic review of the interrelationships among children's coping responses, children's coping outcomes, and parent cognitive–affective, behavioral, and contextual variables in the needle-related procedures context. *Journal of Pediatric Psychology, 42,* 611–621. http://dx.doi.org/10.1093/jpepsy/jsx054

Cardona, L. (2017). Ethical considerations in the care of children with life-limiting conditions: A case illustration of the role of a pediatric psychologist on a hospital ethics committee. *Clinical Practice in Pediatric Psychology, 5,* 287–293. http://dx.doi.org/10.1037/cpp0000205

Carter, B. D., Kronenberger, W. G., Baker, J., Grimes, L. M., Crabtree, V. M., Smith, C., & McGraw, K. (2003). Inpatient pediatric consultation-liaison: A case-controlled study. *Journal of Pediatric Psychology, 28,* 423–432. http://dx.doi.org/10.1093/jpepsy/jsg032

Carter, B. D., Kronenberger, W. G., Scott, E. L., Kullgren, K. A., Piazza-Waggoner, C., & Brady, C. E. (2017). Inpatient pediatric consultation-liaison. In M. C. Roberts & R. G. Steele (Eds.), *Handbook of pediatric psychology* (5th ed., pp. 105–118). New York, NY: Guilford Press.

Carter, B. D., Thompson, S. M., & Thompson, A. N. (2014). Pediatric consultation-liaison. In M. C. Roberts, B. Aylward, & Y. P. Wu (Eds.), *Clinical practice of pediatric psychology* (pp. 63–77). New York, NY: Guilford Press.

Christophersen, E. R. (1982). Incorporating behavioral pediatrics into primary care. *Pediatric Clinics of North America, 29,* 261–296. http://dx.doi.org/10.1016/S0031-3955(16)34141-4

Cousino, M. K., & Mednick, L. (2016). Should a teen with nonadherence be listed for kidney transplant? Ethical issues and clinical decision-making. *Clinical Practice in Pediatric Psychology, 4,* 98–103. http://dx.doi.org/10.1037/cpp0000137

Drotar, D. (1995). *Consulting with pediatricians: Psychological perspectives.* New York, NY: Plenum Press.

Drotar, D. (2000). *Promoting adherence to medical treatment in childhood chronic illness: Concepts, methods, and interventions.* Mahwah, NJ: Erlbaum. http://dx.doi.org/10.4324/9781410605108

Drotar, D. (2013). Reflections on clinical practice in pediatric psychology and implications for the field. *Clinical Practice in Pediatric Psychology, 1,* 95–105. http://dx.doi.org/10.1037/cpp0000017

Drotar, D., & Zagorski, L. (2001). Providing psychological services in pediatric settings in an era of managed care. In J. N. Hughes, A. La Greca, & S. C. Conoley (Eds.), *Handbook of psychological services for children and adolescents* (pp. 89–104). New York, NY: Oxford University Press. http://dx.doi.org/10.1093/med:psych/9780195125238.003.0005

Ernst, M. M., Piazza-Waggoner, C., Chabon, B., Murphy, M. K., Carey, J., & Roddenberry, A. (2014). The hospital-based consultation and liaison service. In C. M. Hunter, C. L. Hunter, & R. Kessler (Eds.), *Handbook of clinical psychology in medical settings: Evidence-based assessment and intervention* (pp. 369–416). New York, NY: Springer.

Ernst, M. M., Piazza-Waggoner, C., & Ciesielski, H. (2015). The role of pediatric psychologists in facilitating medical decision making in the care of critically ill young children. *Clinical Practice in Pediatric Psychology, 3,* 120–130. http://dx.doi.org/10.1037/cpp0000091

Fehr, K. K., Hazen, R. A., & Nielsen, B. A. (2017). Ethical decision-making for psychology trainees in the clinical pediatric setting: Case examples and practical solutions for trainees and supervisors. *Clinical Practice in Pediatric Psychology, 5,* 123–136. http://dx.doi.org/10.1037/cpp0000162

Fouad, N. A., Grus, C. L., Hatcher, R. L., Kaslow, N. J., Hutchings, P. S., Madson, M. B., . . . Crossman, R. E. (2009). Competency benchmarks: A model for understanding and measuring competence in professional psychology across training levels. *Training and Education in Professional Psychology, 3*(Suppl.), S5–S26. http://dx.doi.org/10.1037/a0015832

Greco, P., & Pitel, P. (2016). Utilizing the strengths of the pediatric psychologist in health care improvement efforts. *Clinical Practice in Pediatric Psychology, 4,* 84–89. http://dx.doi.org/10.1037/cpp0000133

Grus, C., & Cope, C. (2016). *Directory of internship programs with training opportunities in primary care psychology.* Retrieved from https://www.apa.org/ed/graduate/internship-directory.pdf

Grus, C. L., Falender, C., Fouad, N. A., & Lavelle, A. K. (2016). A culture of competence: A survey of implementation of competency-based education and assessment. *Training and Education in Professional Psychology, 10,* 198–205. http://dx.doi.org/10.1037/tep0000126

Hatcher, R. L., Fouad, N. A., Campbell, L. F., McCutcheon, S. R., Grus, C. L., & Leahy, K. L. (2013). Competency-based education for professional psychology: Moving from concept to practice. *Training and Education in Professional Psychology, 7,* 225–234. http://dx.doi.org/10.1037/a0033765

Hatcher, R. L., Fouad, N. A., Grus, C. L., Campbell, L. F., McCutcheon, S. R., & Leahy, K. L. (2013). Competency benchmarks: Practical steps toward a culture of competence. *Training and Education in Professional Psychology, 7,* 84–91. http://dx.doi.org/10.1037/a0029401

Health Service Psychology Education Collaborative. (2013). Professional psychology in health care services: A blueprint for education and training. *American Psychologist, 68,* 411–426. http://dx.doi.org/10.1037/a0033265

Hoffses, K. W., Ramirez, L. Y., Berdan, L., Tunick, R., Honaker, S. M., Meadows, T. J., . . . Stancin, T. (2016). Topical review: Building competency: Professional skills for pediatric psychologists in integrated primary care settings. *Journal of Pediatric Psychology, 41,* 1144–1160. http://dx.doi.org/10.1093/jpepsy/jsw066

Jackson, Y., Wu, Y. P., Aylward, B. S., & Roberts, M. C. (2012). Application of the competency cube model to clinical child psychology. *Professional Psychology: Research and Practice, 43,* 432–441. http://dx.doi.org/10.1037/a0030007

Johnson, L. M., Church, C. L., Metzger, M., & Baker, J. N. (2015). Ethics consultation in pediatrics: Long-term experience from a pediatric oncology center. *American Journal of Bioethics, 15,* 3–17. http://dx.doi.org/10.1080/15265161.2015.1021965

Johnson, R. J. (2017). Nonadherence. In B. A. Warady, F. Schafer, & S. R. Alexander (Eds.), *Pediatric dialysis case studies: A practical guide to patient care* (pp. 231–238). Cham, Switzerland: Springer. http://dx.doi.org/10.1007/978-3-319-55147-0_31

Kaslow, N. J., Grus, C. L., Campbell, L. F., Fouad, N. A., Hatcher, R. L., & Rodolfa, E. R. (2009). Competency assessment toolkit for professional psychology. *Training and Education in Professional Psychology, 3*(4, Suppl.), S27–S45. http://dx.doi.org/10.1037/a0015833

Kelly, S. L., Morris, N., Mee, L., Brosig, C., & Self, M. M. (2016). The role of pediatric psychologists in solid organ transplant candidacy decisions: Ethical considerations. *Clinical Practice in Pediatric Psychology, 4,* 417–422. http://dx.doi.org/10.1037/cpp0000155

Kesselheim, J. C., Johnson, J., & Joffe, S. (2010). Ethics consultation in children's hospitals: Results from a survey of pediatric clinical ethicists. *Pediatrics, 125,* 742–746. http://dx.doi.org/10.1542/peds.2009-1813

Kishi, Y., Meller, W. H., Kathol, R. G., & Swigart, S. E. (2004). Factors affecting the relationship between the timing of psychiatric consultation and general hospital length of stay. *Psychosomatics, 45,* 470–476. http://dx.doi.org/10.1176/appi.psy.45.6.470

Kolko, D. J., Campo, J. V., Kilbourne, A. M., & Kelleher, K. (2012). Doctor–office collaborative care for pediatric behavioral problems: A preliminary clinical trial. *Archives of Pediatrics & Adolescent Medicine, 166,* 224–231. http://dx.doi.org/10.1001/archpediatrics.2011.201

Kullgren, K. A., Tsang, K. K., Ernst, M. M., Carter, B. D., Scott, E. L., & Sullivan, S. K. (2015). Inpatient pediatric psychology consultation-liaison practice survey: Corrected version. *Clinical Practice in Pediatric Psychology, 3,* 340–351. http://dx.doi.org/10.1037/cpp0000114

La Greca, A. M., Stone, W. L., Drotar, D., & Maddux, J. E. (1988). Training in pediatric psychology: Survey results and recommendations. *Journal of Pediatric Psychology, 13,* 121–140. http://dx.doi.org/10.1093/jpepsy/13.1.121

Maslach, C., Schaufeli, W. B., & Leiter, M. P. (2001). Job burnout. *Annual Review of Psychology, 52,* 397–422. http://dx.doi.org/10.1146/annurev.psych.52.1.397

McCabe, M. A. (1996). Involving children and adolescents in medical decision making: Developmental and clinical considerations. *Journal of Pediatric Psychology, 21,* 505–516. http://dx.doi.org/10.1093/jpepsy/21.4.505

McDaniel, S. H., Belar, C. D., Schroeder, C., Hargrove, D. S., & Freeman, E. L. (2002). A training curriculum for professional psychologists in primary care. *Professional Psychology: Research and Practice, 33,* 65–72. http://dx.doi.org/10.1037/0735-7028.33.1.65

McDaniel, S. H., Grus, C. L., Cubic, B. A., Hunter, C. L., Kearney, L. K., Schuman, C. C., . . . Johnson, S. B. (2014). Competencies for psychology practice in primary care. *American Psychologist, 69,* 409–429. http://dx.doi.org/10.1037/a0036072

Miller, V. A., Drotar, D., & Kodish, E. (2004). Children's competence for assent and consent: A review of empirical findings. *Ethics & Behavior, 14,* 255–295. http://dx.doi.org/10.1207/s15327019eb1403_3

Mullins, L. L., Gillman, J., & Harbeck, C. (1992). Multiple-level interventions in pediatric psychology settings: A behavioral-systems perspective. In A. M. La Greca, L. J. Siegel, J. L. Wallander, & C. E. Walker (Eds.), *Stress and coping in child health* (pp. 377–399). New York, NY: Guilford Press.

Nielsen, B. (2014, Fall). *How to start an internship in less than a year.* Retrieved from https://ahcpsychologists.org/wp-content/uploads/2018/05/Grandrounds.11.2014.pdf

Nielsen, B. (2015). Confidentiality and electronic health records: Keeping up with advances in technology and expectations for access. *Clinical Practice in Pediatric Psychology, 3,* 175–178. http://dx.doi.org/10.1037/cpp0000096

Novotney, A. (2014). Leading the charge. *Monitor on Psychology, 45*(10), 43–45.

Palermo, T. M., Janicke, D. M., McQuaid, E. L., Mullins, L. L., Robins, P. M., & Wu, Y. P. (2014). Recommendations for training in pediatric psychology: Defining core competencies across training levels. *Journal of Pediatric Psychology, 39,* 965–984. http://dx.doi.org/10.1093/jpepsy/jsu015

Piazza-Waggoner, C., Roddenberry, A., Yeomans-Maldonado, G., Noll, J., & Ernst, M. M. (2013). Inpatient pediatric psychology consultation-liaison program development: 5-year practice patterns and implication for trends in health care. *Clinical Practice in Pediatric Psychology, 1,* 28–41. http://dx.doi.org/10.1037/cpp0000008

Rae, W. A., Brunnquell, D., & Sullivan, J. R. (2017). Ethical and legal issues in pediatric psychology. In M. C. Roberts & R. G. Steele (Eds.), *Handbook of pediatric psychology* (5th ed., pp. 14–25). New York, NY: Guilford Press.

Rae, W. A., Sullivan, J. R., Razo, N. P., George, C. A., & Ramirez, E. (2002). Adolescent health risk behavior: When do pediatric psychologists break confidentiality? *Journal of Pediatric Psychology, 27,* 541–549. http://dx.doi.org/10.1093/jpepsy/27.6.541

Rapoff, M. A. (2011). *Adherence to pediatric medical regimens* (2nd ed.). New York, NY: Springer.

Roberts, M. C., Aylward, B. S., & Wu, Y. P. (2014). Overview of the field of pediatric psychology. In M. C. Roberts, B. Aylward, & Y. P. Wu (Eds.), *Clinical practice of pediatric psychology* (pp. 63–77). New York, NY: Guilford Press.

Roberts, M. C., & Steele, R. G. (Eds.). (2017). *Handbook of pediatric psychology* (5th ed.). New York, NY: Guilford Press.

Roberts, M. C., & Wright, L. (1982). The role of the pediatric psychologist as consultant to pediatricians. In J. M. Tuma (Ed.), *Handbook for the practice of pediatric psychology* (pp. 251–289). New York, NY: Wiley.

Rodrigue, J. R., Gonzalez-Peralta, R. P., & Langham, M. R., Jr. (2004). Solid organ transplantation. In R. T. Brown (Ed.), *Handbook of pediatric psychology in school settings* (pp. 679–699). Mahwah, NJ: Erlbaum.

Routh, D. K., Schroeder, C. S., & Koocher, G. P. (1983). Psychology and primary health care for children. *American Psychologist, 38,* 95–98. http://dx.doi.org/10.1037/0003-066X.38.1.95

Schroeder, C. S. (1979). Psychologists in a private pediatric practice. *Journal of Pediatric Psychology, 4,* 5–18. http://dx.doi.org/10.1093/jpepsy/4.1.5

Schroeder, C. S. (2004). A collaborative practice in primary care. In B. G. Wildman & T. Stancin (Eds.), *Treating children's psychosocial problems in primary care* (pp. 1–34). Greenwich, CT: Information Age.

Schurman, J. V., Cushing, C. C., Carpenter, E., & Christenson, K. (2011). Volitional and accidental nonadherence to pediatric inflammatory bowel disease treatment plans: Initial investigation of associations with quality of life and disease activity. *Journal of Pediatric Psychology, 36,* 116–125. http://dx.doi.org/10.1093/jpepsy/jsq046

Shanafelt, T. D., Hasan, O., Dyrbye, L. N., Sinsky, C., Satele, D., Sloan, J., & West, C. P. (2015). Changes in burnout and satisfaction with work-life balance in physicians and the general US working population between 2011 and 2014. *Mayo Clinic Proceedings, 90,* 1600–1613. http://dx.doi.org/10.1016/j.mayocp.2015.08.023 (Erratum published 2016, *Mayo Clinic Proceedings, 91,* p. 276. http://dx.doi.org/10.1016/j.mayocp.2016.01.001)

Spirito, A., Brown, R. T., D'Angelo, E., Delamater, A., Rodrigue, J., & Siegel, L. (2003). Society of pediatric psychology task force report: Recommendations for the training of pediatric psychologists. *Journal of Pediatric Psychology, 28,* 85–98. http://dx.doi.org/10.1093/jpepsy/28.2.85

Stancin, T., & Perrin, E. C. (2014). Psychologists and pediatricians: Opportunities for collaboration in primary care. *American Psychologist, 69,* 332–343. http://dx.doi.org/10.1037/a0036046

Stancin, T., Sturm, L., & Ramirez, L. Y. (2014). Pediatric psychology practice in primary care settings. In M. C. Roberts, B. S. Aylward, & Y. P. Wu (Eds.), *Clinical practice in pediatric psychology* (pp. 78–92). New York, NY: Guilford Press.

Stancin, T., Sturm, L. A., Tynan, W. D., & Ramirez, L. (2017). Pediatric psychology and primary care. In M. C. Roberts & R. G. Steele (Eds.), *Handbook of pediatric psychology* (5th ed., pp. 550–565). New York: Guilford Press.

Starmer, A. J., Frintner, M. P., & Freed, G. L. (2016). Work–life balance, burnout, and satisfaction of early career pediatricians. *Pediatrics, 137,* e20153183. http://dx.doi.org/10.1542/peds.2015-3183

Talmi, A., Lovell, J. L., Herbst, R. B., Margolis, K. L., Muther, E. F., & Buchholz, M. (2015). Postdoctoral fellows' developmental trajectories in becoming pediatric primary care psychologists. *Clinical Practice in Pediatric Psychology, 3,* 233–240. http://dx.doi.org/10.1037/cpp0000100

Tuma, J. M. (1980). Training in pediatric psychology: A concern of the 1980s. *Journal of Pediatric Psychology, 5,* 229–243. http://dx.doi.org/10.1093/jpepsy/5.3.229

Witmer, L. (1897). The organization of practical work in psychology. *Psychological Review, 4,* 116–117.

World Health Organization. (2003). *Adherence to long-term therapies: Evidence for action.* Geneva, Switzerland: Author. Retrieved from https://apps.who.int/iris/bitstream/handle/10665/42682/9241545992.pdf;jsessionid=7E1EA6E4A24798CFDAAFA0693C55343E?sequence=1

Wright, L. (1967). The pediatric psychologist: A role model. *American Psychologist, 22,* 323–325. http://dx.doi.org/10.1037/h0037666

Wu, Y. P., Aylward, B. S., & Roberts, M. C. (2014). Cross-cutting issues in pediatric psychology. In M. C. Roberts, B. S. Aylward, & Y. P. Wu (Eds.), *Clinical practice of pediatric psychology* (pp. 63–77). New York, NY: Guilford Press.

# 8

# Consultation in Medical Settings

Barbara Cubic

Psychological consultations within medical settings provide expert psychological guidance to patients and their families and includes other health care professionals and health care systems. Provision of a well-conducted psychological consultation can also be important for patient satisfaction, adherence to treatment, and recovery from illness. The most successful consultations incorporate building rapport with the consultee, gathering information relevant to the reason for referral, understanding the patient's perspective, sharing information with the patient as needed, reaching agreement on the problems to address and actions to take to do so, and communicating effectively with the patient and the patient's health care team to ensure effective and comprehensive care of the patient (Makoul, 2001).

When conducting a consultation in a medical setting, a psychologist often serves in the role of a provider for other health care providers. The psychologist may be offering the consultation to establish diagnostic accuracy, provide other health care providers skills to improve their patients' adherence to medical regimens (e.g., asthma, diabetes), support health care providers in dealing with the emotional issues that their patients experience, or improve relationship challenges in the provider–patient relationship. In addition, the psychologist can assist medical providers in understanding their patients' motivations and concerns as well as the barriers to health that they are experiencing. Psychologists in health care settings are also commonly asked to help medical practitioners cope with their own difficulties in providing care, especially to patients who

http://dx.doi.org/10.1037/0000153-009
*Consultation in Psychology: A Competency-Based Approach*, C. A. Falender and
E. P. Shafranske (Editors)

are quite challenging. To be helpful, a psychologist must learn basic medical terminology; understand the pace and culture of the medical settings where they are providing consultations; and be able to provide direct, practical advice. The overarching goal of the consultation is to gather current, symptom-relevant information in the briefest time possible to allow for the development of a solution-focused health care intervention plan for the patient.

This chapter focuses on the unique contextual features of psychology practice in a medical setting, the competencies required to work and to consult in a medical environment, and best practices within medical settings.

## COMPETENCIES NEEDED TO PERFORM PSYCHOLOGICAL CONSULTATIONS IN MEDICAL SETTINGS

Working in a medical environment is different from working in a traditional mental health setting. Although psychologists can be in a unique position to provide beneficial consultations to medical patients and health care teams, the number of psychology health service providers who identify as clinical health psychologists is low—estimated at 7% for primary focus and only 12% as secondary focus (American Psychological Association [APA] Center for Workforce Studies, 2016). Subsequently, many general clinical psychologists are asked to see medical patients or provide services in medical settings. Without specific training experiences in medical facilities with health care teams, psychologists often fail to recognize the perspectives of medical patients and other health care team members. Furthermore, they may be unclear as to what is needed in a consultation and must seek additional training to make significant contributions to the prevention of medical conditions and treatment of medical patients (Bluestein & Cubic, 2009).

Because of key differences in context, unique competencies are required to thrive in medical environments. Fortunately, several frameworks for the types of competencies needed by psychologists have been developed for clinical health psychology (Larkin & Klonoff, 2014) and in primary care psychology (Hoge, Morris, Laraia, Pomerantz, & Farley, 2014; Kinman, Gilchrist, Payne-Murphy, & Miller, 2015; McDaniel et al., 2014). These competencies build on the general profession-wide competencies required in accredited psychology doctoral training programs (see APA's, 2018, *Standards of Accreditation for Health Service Psychology*) and can be developed at any point across the training continuum from practicum to postdoctoral level or beyond.

### Areas of Knowledge

In medical settings, a biopsychosocial integrative approach is more beneficial to patients and their families than a singular focus only on biomedical or psychosocial aspects of care. The biopsychosocial model states that biological (including genetic, physical, and medical), psychological (including emotions, thoughts, and behaviors), and social (including socioeconomic, environmental, and cultural) factors all contribute to human functioning and dysfunction (both health and mental health related; Engel, 1977). The model emphasizes functional improvement and measurable outcomes.

General areas of knowledge needed to effectively provide psychological consultations in medical settings are outlined in Exhibit 8.1. In addition, providers must have

- basic clinical skills (e.g., clinical interviewing, assessment, intervention),

- an understanding of the health care system's rules and regulations,

- an ability to access and record in electronic health records,

- an awareness of infection control procedures,

- an understanding of the importance of immediacy of feedback from the consultation, and

- an ability to be flexible about the logistics about when (e.g., coordinating with other health care providers and medical testing and procedures) and where (e.g., bedside, examination room, private office) to do the consultation.

Consultations in medical settings also often requires specific and detailed knowledge about a specific medical condition (e.g., cancer, diabetes, cardiac illness)

---

**EXHIBIT 8.1**

**Common Areas of Knowledge Needed to Provide Psychological Consultations in Medical Settings**

- Health promotion strategies and services
- Medical terminology
- Behavioral risk factors for disease, injury, or disability
- Common biomedical assessments used in health care
- Common medical, dental, and allied health treatments and their sequelae
- Psychological conditions secondary to illness
- Psychophysiological disorders and somatic presentations of psychological dysfunction
- Psychological presentations of organic problems
- Psychological assessment approaches across biological, psychological, social, lifespan, and cultural components of health
- Evidence-based psychological interventions in the prevention, treatment, and rehabilitation of common health and mental health problems
- Strategies for prevention of physical and psychological complications from medical procedures
- Physical symptoms responsive to behavioral interventions
- Challenges faced by health care providers and health care systems
- Cost-effectiveness of psychological treatments in a particular clinical context
- Professional and legal standards associated with health care practice
- Health care policies impacting health care systems and the delivery of services

or medical procedure (e.g., bariatric surgery, spinal cord stimulator) or type of setting. Table 8.1 provides a sample of the types of competencies a psychologist needs for clinical consultation in primary care settings. Because the competencies needed may vary, a psychologist must reflect to determine whether his or her general knowledge of the biological, cognitive–affective, and social bases of health, disease, and behavior is sufficient to provide the psychological

**TABLE 8.1  Sample of Competencies for Clinical Consultation in a Primary Care Setting**

| Essential component(s) | Sample behavioral anchors |
| --- | --- |
| Assists in the development of standardized and reliable processes for consultative services for PC psychology | Assists the PC team regarding when and how to incorporate a PC psychologist into the process of care |
| | Uses empirical literature to develop parameters for when PC psychology consultations (which may be referred to as "consults") should be triggered (e.g., diagnosis of a chronic pain triggers an evaluation for pain management) |
| Clarifies, focuses on, and responds to consultation question raised in an efficient manner | Conducts a thorough health record review of the referred patient |
| | Includes other PC team members in response to consultation question |
| Helps PC team conceptualize challenging patients in a manner that enhances patient care | Collaborates with other PC team members to ensure the entire health care team interacts more effectively and efficiently with patients and their support systems |
| | Is readily available to PC team to discuss ways to interact effectively with patients with challenging interpersonal styles (e.g., patients with personality disorders) and complicated cases (e.g., significant comorbidities, family dysfunction, limited intellect, low health literacy) |
| Tailors recommendations to PC work pace and environment | Gives PC providers actionable recommendations that are brief, concrete, and evidence based |
| | Provides immediate (e.g., same day), brief feedback to the consulting PC provider while avoiding psychological jargon |
| Follows up with other PC clinicians as indicated | Uses oral and or written communication effectively |
| | Conveys and receives both urgent and routine clinical information to PC team members using appropriate infrastructure or clinic procedures (e.g., face-to-face, e-mail communication, assignment of tasks in electronic health record, consults, chart notes) |
| Ensures integrity of the consultation process when algorithm-based automated triggers for consultation occur | Effectively explains to a patient the rationale for the consultation that has been automatically triggered |
| | Completes feedback loop with PC provider following consultation |

*Note.* PC = primary care. Adapted from "Competencies for Psychology Practice in Primary Care," by S. H. McDaniel, C. L. Grus, B. A. Cubic, C. L. Hunter, L. K. Kearney, C. C. Schuman, . . . S. B. Johnson, 2014, *American Psychologist, 69,* pp. 422–423. Copyright 2014 by the American Psychological Association.

consultation or whether an individual with more expertise in the field is needed. Belar et al. (2001) suggested questions to ask oneself to assess readiness to provide consultation in a medical setting:

- Am I knowledgeable about the
  - developmental or individual bases of health, disease, and behavior regarding this problem?
  - interactions between this problem and the patient and his or her environment (including family, health care system, and sociocultural environment)?
  - empirically supported assessment methods for this problem?
  - empirically supported interventions relevant to this problem?
  - impact of the planned psychological intervention on physiology and vice versa?
  - roles and functions of other health care professionals involved?

- Do I have the skills to
  - provide the empirically supported assessment methods needed for this problem?
  - deliver the empirically supported interventions relevant to this problem?
  - communicate and collaborate with other health care team members?

- Do I understand the
  - sociopolitical features of the health care delivery system that impact this problem?
  - health policy issues relevant to this problem?

- Am I aware of the ethical, legal, and special professional issues related to this problem?

These questions are useful to the psychologist when preparing to provide consultation in a medical setting and support the process of metacompetence.

## Interdisciplinary Systems

The core competencies for interprofessional practice (Interprofessional Education Collaborative, 2016; Interprofessional Education Collaborative Expert Panel, 2011) described in Chapter 5, this volume, are highly relevant for the psychologist who will be offering consultations in inpatient and outpatient medical settings. Because health care teams require collaborative practice, one must remain cognizant of the values and ethics associated with interprofessional practice, the roles and responsibilities or other health care team members, ways to engage in interprofessional communication, and how to function effectively as a health care team member. It is also crucial to remain knowledgeable about the outcomes literature associated with the delivery of services by health care teams.

Given the transition of the health care field to electronic health records, the psychologist must be prepared to use health informatics, including electronic health records, to coordinate care and communicate with other health professionals and patients as appropriate. All medical environments are different, so the provider must be familiar with various types of health care systems and service delivery models and their implications for practice and understand where the setting that the consultation occurs (e.g., inpatient, residential, outpatient) falls on the continuum of systems and models. Some settings require immediate feedback following the consultation, whereas others allow more time to create recommendations and write a report. Some settings allow for a more in-depth consultation, including the opportunity for elaborate psychological assessment, and others need brief assessments and interventions to be recommended and used.

## COMMON TYPES OF CONSULTATIONS

A competency-based approach to consultation outlines the knowledge (information), skills (behaviors), and attitudes (values-based dispositions) that a psychologist needs. Training in health care settings can provide a psychologist with the knowledge needed for the medical environment. However, an attitudinal change is also needed for the psychologist to embrace the use of brief assessment and intervention methods, recognize the time-sensitive nature of medical consultations, be flexible in providing consultations on the spot by accepting warm handoffs, stay in tune with the goals of a patient-centered medical home, and avoid psychological jargon.

The types of consultations a psychologist might provide in a medical setting for a patient and the patient's family span lifespan development, preventative practices, and subclinical and clinical presentations. The consultation may take place in an outpatient facility that offers primary care services, a specialty care setting (e.g., endocrinology clinic), or a medical hospital. Patient-centered consultation requires that the referral question(s) be thoroughly understood, and the focus should be on what the referring provider needs to know in the present to provide the best patient care. Recommendations need to be tailored to the medical environment and focus on providing information that is succinct and clear. The psychologist must choose consultation methods that are time efficient, targeted, and focused on the referral question and that provide intervention recommendations that are narrow in scope and likely much briefer than in traditional mental health settings. In doing so, the psychologist needs to add value to the health care team by conveying information the health care team really needs while also adding information the team would not typically seek if that information is relevant to improving the patient's outcome. The availability of the psychologist to complete the consultation in a timely fashion is critical.

A psychologist's consultation skills can be quite valuable as applied to consulting with the health care team about team systems and processes. Consultations focused on team systems and processes need to be provided in a manner that feels team focused, collaborative, and actionable and that promotes the most optimal delivery of patient care services. The typical structure of a consultation in a medical setting is provided in Exhibit 8.2, which lays out the sequential steps.

### Diagnostic Dilemmas

Health care teams are expected to provide accurate diagnoses to offer their patients ideal treatment protocols. Unfortunately, many physical and mental health conditions are difficult to identify and can overlap. Ensuring an accurate diagnosis can be a time-consuming process. Therefore, one of the most common reasons for a psychological consultation in a medical setting is aimed at assisting a health care team in diagnosis and treatment planning (Sethre, 2018). Typical referral questions focus on whether the patient has a mental health condition (e.g., depression, anxiety) or substance abuse issue; whether the patient is experiencing cognitive difficulties or dementia; whether somatization is primary; and on the types of behavioral factors that might interfere with adherence to medical recommendations.

### Decisional Capacity

Patient autonomy is a goal for health care. However, many times, a patient's ability to make decisions in his or her own best interest may not be present; thus, a psychological consultation may be necessary to determine whether the patient has capacity. Capacity is different from *competency,* which is a global assessment of an individual's ability to make any decisions on his or her own behalf and requires that a legal determination be made by a judge in court.

---

**EXHIBIT 8.2**

**Typical Structure of a Consultation in a Medical Setting**

1. Ask questions about the referral question as needed to ensure a thorough understanding of the goals of the consultation.
2. Review the electronic health record.
3. Introduce yourself to the patient, health care team, or both.
4. Discuss the rationale for the consultation.
5. If the consultation is patient centered, obtain a snapshot of the patient's current concerns to add to information received from the treatment team.
6. Provide feedback to the patient, health care team, or both about impressions, when warranted.
7. Discuss possible intervention strategies and what seems doable right now.
8. Develop a plan.
9. Discuss possible outcomes of the encounter for the patient (e.g., change in medical regimen, no follow-up, follow-up at given intervals or at the next medical appointment, referral out) or for the health care team (e.g., process changes, meet more frequently, attend certain activities for skill development).

---

*Capacity* refers to conducting a functional assessment to make a clinical determination about a patient's ability to make a specific decision and is determined by a health care clinician (Dastidar & Odden, 2011). Most commonly, consultations related to capacity are completed in inpatient settings. Common issues that evoke a consultation about capacity generally are related to whether a patient can accept or decline a medical intervention, such as medication protocol, amputation, or life support. Special care must be exerted in these types of consultations because revoking an individual's decision-making rights can have significant ramifications.

The primary method for determining capacity is the clinical interview in which the focus is on the patient's ability to show adequate comprehension of his or her medical condition and treatment options despite any issues that may be creating impairment. The patient must be able to articulate an understanding of the advantages and disadvantages of moving forward with the interventions recommended (or not) and the alternatives available. When warranted, a brief measure of cognitive functioning, for example, the Mini-Mental State Examination (Folstein, Folstein, & McHugh, 1975) or the Montreal Cognitive Assessment (Nasreddine et al., 2005), might be used to supplement the interview. On rare occasions, a more detail cognitive assessment, for example, such as the Repeatable Battery for the Assessment of Neuropsychological Status (Randolph, 1998), might be used. Additional measures such as the MacArthur Competence Assessment Tool for Treatment (Grisso & Appelbaum, 1998) can also be helpful. The *Assessment of Older Adults With Diminished Capacity: A Handbook for Psychologists* published by the American Bar Association Commission on Law and Aging jointly with APA (2008) can be a helpful resource in understanding how to conduct capacity evaluations.

## Risk

Health care providers often report that they feel ill equipped to conduct an assessment for suicidal or homicidal risk because the amount of training in mental health issues they receive is limited (National Action Alliance for Suicide Prevention Clinical Workforce Preparedness Task Force, 2014). However, many health care providers are in medical settings, notably, emergency rooms, where they must assess risk. Therefore, psychologists are often be consulted to determine whether a patient should be hospitalized, remain hospitalized, or can return home safely. By conducting these types of consultations, the psychologist not only ensures that the patient remains safe and receives the level of care needed but also takes a burden off of other health care providers who are less trained to complete the type of evaluation warranted. The Joint Commission (2016) provides resources for use in medical settings to assess and treat suicidal ideation.

## High Health Care Utilizers

The highest utilizers of health care resources are typically those with both significant physical health and mental health conditions. Data show that 5% of the American population accounts for close to half of the nation's health care costs (Cohen, 2015) because of their complex medical needs. In addition, research has consistently shown that when an individual has a physical illness comorbid with depression, that person's annual health care costs are much greater than an individual with the same physical illness absent depression (Katon, 2011). Psychological consultations for these complex presentations can guide the health care team to better understand and, therefore, empathize with these challenging patients who present with family conflict and dysfunction, limited intellect, low health literacy, characterological personality styles, or other types of barriers to ideal health care.

## Pain Management

Acute and chronic pain are commonplace, and using a simplistic medical model to diagnose, treat, and eliminate the cause(s) of pain often is too limited an approach. A biopsychosocial framework of pain can take into account the continuum of potential causes for pain, the impact of interventions offered, and the patient's expectations and experiences. And although treatments for minimizing or eliminating the pain individuals experience have become more sophisticated, for many, there are still no truly effective interventions (Institute of Medicine, Committee on Advancing Pain Research, Care, and Education, 2011). In addition, many of the medications available to treat pain are addictive; currently, the United States is in an opioid crisis because many individuals die using the medication prescribed to them (Rudd, Seth, David, & Scholl, 2016). Therefore, it is not uncommon for psychologists to receive consultations to provide individuals with severe, chronic pain with comprehensive, integrated, and evidence-based assessment and treatment.

Psychologists also guide the health care team to empathize with the patient with pain and teach the patient strategies that facilitate self-management of the pain. Most notably, the psychologist may be able to obtain information about the type of pain experienced, the patient's life history and personality traits, and the family and social environments of the patient that affect the patient's ability to cope with pain. Creating a compassionate and trusting relationship for patients with their health care providers can also help the individual with pain develop a change in their emotions, beliefs, and behaviors related to their experience of pain.

## Medication and Health Care Regimen Adherence

The National Health Council (2014) defined a *chronic disease* (e.g., diabetes, hypertension, asthma) as a medical condition that persists for 3 months or longer. Chronic diseases can be diagnosed at any age but are more likely to be diagnosed as a person ages. Most medical interventions for a chronic disease are designed for symptom management because cures are generally unavailable, thus requiring patient adherence to ongoing medication protocols and health chronic diseases exist, an individual's lifestyle choices often serve as a buffer from a disease or increase the likelihood of developing the disease. For example, individuals who eat poorly and are inactive are more likely to develop a chronic disease. Unfortunately, current estimates are that more than half of the American population has one or more chronic diseases (Centers for Disease Control and Prevention, n.d.). The presence of multiple chronic diseases means that managing the health care of that patient becomes even more complex and often involves an interdisciplinary approach that integrates a behavioral health component.

Because lifestyle choices (e.g., inadequate nutrition, limited exercise, tobacco and substance use) and poor adherence to medical regimens have a major impact on chronic disease development and outcome trajectories, psychologists are often consulted to provide guidance to patients with chronic diseases. Although poor adherence to medical regimens occurs across the lifespan, it happens more often in older adults due to the high number of comorbid conditions they experience and the subsequent polypharmacy and complexity of lifestyle requirements (Costa et al., 2015). The most helpful psychological consultations focus on identifying barriers to healthier choices and adherence and problem-solving about how to overcome identified obstacles in a manner that empowers the patient to be more active in his or her management of the chronic disease. Psychological interventions recommended from the consultation can be vital in facilitating healthy lifestyles germane to prevention and management of chronic diseases.

## Transplant Evaluations and Determinations of Surgical Preparedness

Before most transplant surgeries and numerous other surgical procedures (e.g., bariatric surgery, gender affirming surgery, left ventricular assistance device implantation, spinal cord stimulator implantation), a psychological evaluation is recommended to ensure that the patient is ready for the procedure and all of its ramifications and lifestyle changes. These evaluations are often in-depth assessments of the patient's knowledge of his or her medical condition, the procedure under consideration, the risks of the procedure, and the lifestyle changes required of the patient to be successful. Family members often are included in these types of consultations. During these types of evaluations, the psychologist must be sure to weigh the psychological indications and contraindications against the medical risk imposed if the procedure is not performed. Guidelines for these types of evaluations frequently are available to assist the psychologist's decision making. For example, for psychological consultations of bariatric surgery candidates, the psychologist could refer to Applegate and Friedman (2014).

## Multicultural Issues

"Health disparities" refer to adversely impacted "groups of people who have systematically experienced greater obstacles to health based on their racial or ethnic group; religion; socioeconomic status; gender; age; mental health; cognitive, sensory, or physical disability; sexual orientation or gender identity; or geographic location" (Office of Disease Prevention and Health Promotion, n.d.). Part of overcoming health disparities is cultural competence on the part of health care providers because cultural competence is necessary to create a health care system that is effective at delivering high-quality care to every patient regardless of race, ethnicity, culture, or language or other factors. Therefore, psychologists must understand how social stressors and cultural norms distract from adherence to medical regimens and how cultural differences between patients and providers may pose additional barriers, especially in the care of complex medical scenarios. As consultants, psychologists can collaborate with health care providers to break down social barriers; unify fractionalized care; discover creative solutions; and reduce annoyance, burnout, and compassion fatigue (Holleman, Bray, Davis, & Holleman, 2004).

### Health Care Team Dysfunction

When health care teams are not working effectively, a number of communication failures, miscommunications, and interpersonal conflicts can occur; these conflicts can become impediments to collaborations that optimize patient care (Horwitz, Horwitz, & Barshes, 2011). Although there is a proliferation of research on the role of effective teamwork to accomplish complex tasks, most of the research has been applied to business organizations and not to medical settings. Oftentimes, a psychologist who is not currently part of the health care team dysfunction may be asked to provide a consultation to offer recommendations for improved collaboration and communication.

### Skill Development for the Medical Providers

In medical settings, a psychologist can provide in-services or one-on-one consultations to other medical providers on topics like mental health conditions; symptom management; ways to encourage adherence to medications, nutritional changes, or exercise; or motivational interviewing approaches to encourage substance use reduction or abstinence.

### Development of Standardized and Reliable Processes for Psychology Consultative Services

An important role for a psychologist in a medical setting is to assist the other health care providers regarding when and how to use a psychologist in care. To do so, the psychologist should use empirical data to develop parameters for when psychology consultations should be triggered (e.g., diagnosis of chronic pain triggers psychological consultation for pain management) and in situations in which psychological consultation is required (e.g., all patients seeking bariatric surgery are provided a psychological consultation once evaluated by the bariatric surgeon and provided psychoeducation and nutritional information about required nutritional changes).

To be an effective consultant in a medical setting, the psychologist must be comfortable with assessing and advising on a wide range of issues and should have a toolbox of resources (e.g., assessment measures, app information, treatment tools, referral resources) readily available to provide to the patient and the patient's health care team. Efficiency, accuracy, and succinctness are vital when sharing information from a psychological consultation in a medical environment. The referral question should provide the focus for the psychologist's assessment of the patient, and the use of empirically based, reliable assessment approaches is vital. To provide consultations on complicated patients (e.g., suicidal patients, patients with multiple comorbidities) or to address transplant or surgical preparedness, the consultant needs more time with the patient (e.g., 2–4 hours) so must plan accordingly. In addition to the written note in the electronic health record, when possible, the consultant should provide succinct oral feedback to the medical provider.

The best consultations are provided in a manner in which the recommendations made show an understanding of the consultee's circumstances as well as the health care context; recognize how to differentiate roles of the health care team members; and translate the psychological findings to the medical practice and context in a manner that is attainable, optimally leading to enhanced collaborations among the patient, the patient's family, and the health care team members.

## Cultural Considerations

Practice guidelines such as APA's (2017b) *Multicultural Guidelines: An Ecological Approach to Context, Identity, and Intersectionality* underscore the importance of psychologists' exhibiting an awareness, sensitivity, and skills to work with diverse populations. Cultural competence is crucial in medical settings, and this type of competence must ensure both an awareness of individual differences as well as an understanding of the unique nature of the medical culture.

For example, it is abundantly clear within the medical world that *health disparities,* that is, differences in the incidence and prevalence of health conditions and health status between groups, commonly occur. Simultaneously, health care providers strive for *health equity*, that is, a society in which everyone has the opportunity to attain his or her full health potential and no one is disadvantaged from achieving this potential because of that person's social position or other socially determined circumstance (Brennan Ramirez, Baker, & Metzler, 2008). Therefore, psychological consultations provided must be respectful of and responsive to individual cultural health beliefs and practices, preferred languages, health literacy levels, and communication needs. The psychologist must also be knowledgeable about the literature on health disparities and use that knowledge when applying their psychological consultation skills and making their recommendations. Psychologists should encourage all members of the health care organization(s) in which they provide services to strive to eliminate health disparities and provide patients with an experience that respects them as individuals.

## Ethical Considerations

In all activities, psychologists are tasked with abiding by the APA (2017a) *Ethical Principles of Psychologists and Code of Conduct* and must engage in ethical decision making in collaboration with others. Medical settings can pose some challenges because each medical profession has its own ethical code, and sometimes the codes of one profession are at odds with the codes of another profession (Kanzler, Goodie, Hunter, Glotfelter, & Bodart, 2013). Basic questions that can be relevant to the provision of psychological consultations and create an ethical challenge within medical settings include

- Who has responsibility for the physical and mental health of the patient? This question is especially relevant when multiple providers are involved in complex cases.

- Who is the ultimate decision maker about which aspects of the patient care?

- Can the psychologist take action on his or her own recommendations, or does the psychologist need to do so in accordance with the attending physician's plan for the patient?

- How should confidentiality and informed consent be dealt with?
  - Does the patient understand the role of psychology in his or her health care?
  - Has the patient been fully informed about the purpose of the consultation and how the information from the consultation will be used?
  - Where should details about the interaction with the patient be located in the electronic health record? Open access to all health care team members? Limited access?
  - How much information should be detailed in the electronic health record from the psychological consultation?
  - What does the health care team need to do to avoid diffusion of responsibility?
  - How will the health care team work together to deal with issues of diversity within the health care team? Within the patient population?

### Informed Consent

*Informed consent* is "the process of providing information to the patient prior to treatment concerning patient rights and the provision of treatment information necessary to make informed decisions" (Hudgins, Rose, Fifield, & Arnault, 2013, p. 11). Before the psychological consultation, it is the patient's right (and the right of the patient's families, if applicable) to have full disclosure about what information the psychologist will or will not share with the patient's health care team and the implications of sharing or not sharing information. In medical settings, sharing of information is commonplace, and restricting information sharing can create dilemmas (Serrano, 2014). However, patients have the right to confidentiality, which requires that the psychologist be savvy in differentiating between what needs to be shared versus what should remain private. The rule of thumb is to only share the information relevant to the reason for the psychological consultation and to use written consents as a safeguard if needed.

Psychologists should identify themselves to patients as psychologists but describe their role rather than overemphasize their profession (e.g., "I'm Dr. Cubic, a clinical psychologist, working with Dr. Bluestein, and I'm here to discuss strategies with you for coping with your headaches"). Identifying the profession avoids any possible misrepresentation of the provider as a physician and emphasizes the purpose of the visit, which may decrease the likelihood of the patient's feeling stigmatized.

## Documentation

Following a consultation that is patient related in a medical setting, the psychologist needs to document the encounter in the electronic health record. The psychologist should carefully choose the language used in the documentation to provide an honest accounting of the findings from the consultation while minimizing the chance that any of the psychological information could be misinterpreted or taken out of appropriate context (Reitz, Common, Fifield, & Stiasny, 2012). It is important to recognize that any diagnoses given will remain in the patient's historical record and can impact future medical appointments or hospitalizations. For example, if no medical evidence supports the validity of the patient's symptoms and a psychologist documents the possibility of a somatization disorder, health care providers who are not savvy about mental health conditions may believe the patient is fabricating his or her symptoms or may quickly dismiss future physical complaints without thorough medical evaluation of them. If the consultation note is written in a manner in which it could be readily shared with the patient and the patient's family, it will help the psychologist be more mindful of the language used. The focus of the written documentation should be on final conclusions and recommendations that are provided as succinctly as possible.

The psychologist should also be aware that, depending on the setting, he or she may be documenting in an electronic health record that allows open access, whereas in other settings, he or she may have the ability to protect the note to allow limited access. The psychologist should word sensitive matters carefully and only included that information in the note if relevant to the consultation's purpose (e.g., discussions about a marital affair could be worded as "discussed interpersonal stressor").

## Disagreements Among Providers About Appropriate Care Methods

Consultations are usually requested when the current providers are unsure about how to proceed and, therefore, the health care team will be receptive to the recommendations offered. However, it is possible that the psychologist's recommendations will not be in line with the health care team's goals or the patient's circumstances may change in a manner that do not allow the recommendations to be implemented.

## SUMMARY AND CONCLUSION

The provision of psychological consultations in medical settings gives psychologists an opportunity to use their unique skills in assessment and intervention. Several keys to success as a consultant in medical environments are to be interpersonally savvy, culturally sensitive and respectful with other health care providers and medical patients, and knowledgeable about the medical conditions and procedures related to the consultations offered. Provide the consultations and feedback concisely and promptly. Avoid psychological jargon in discussions and documentation about the consultation. Provide the information that is most relevant to the referral question. And avoid disclosing any unnecessary revealed patient information while providing specific recommendations or plans for follow-up.

## REFERENCES

American Bar Association Commission on Law and Aging jointly with the American Psychological Association. (2008). *Assessment of older adults with diminished capacity: A handbook for psychologists*. Retrieved from https://www.apa.org/images/capacity-psychologist-handbook_tcm7-78003.pdf

American Psychological Association. (2017a). *Ethical principles of psychologists and code of conduct* (2002, Amended June 1, 2010 and January 1, 2017). Retrieved from http://www.apa.org/ethics/code/index.aspx

American Psychological Association. (2017b). *Multicultural guidelines: An ecological approach to context, identity, and intersectionality*. Retrieved from http://www.apa.org/about/policy/multicultural-guidelines.pdf

American Psychological Association, Center for Workforce Studies. (2016). *2015 survey of psychology health service providers*. Retrieved at http://www.apa.org/workforce/publications/15-health-service-providers/index.aspx

American Psychological Association, Commission on Accreditation. (2018). *Standards of accreditation for health service psychology*. Retrieved from http://www.apa.org/ed/accreditation/about/policies/standards-of-accreditation.pdf

Applegate, K. L., & Friedman, K. E. (2014). Introduction to psychological consultations for bariatric surgery patients. In C. D. Still, D. B. Sarwer, & J. Blankenship (Eds.), *The ASMBS textbook of bariatric surgery: Vol. 2. Integrated health* (pp. 33–42). New York, NY: Springer-Verlag. http://dx.doi.org/10.1007/978-1-4939-1197-4

Belar, C., Brown, R. A., Hersch, L. E., Hornyak, L. M., Rozensky, R. H., Sheridan, E. P., . . . Reed, G. W. (2001). Self-assessment in clinical health psychology: A model for ethical expansion of practice. *Professional Psychology: Research and Practice, 32*, 135–141. http://dx.doi.org/10.1037/0735-7028.32.2.135

Bluestein, D., & Cubic, B. A. (2009). Psychologists and primary care physicians: A training model for creating collaborative relationships. *Journal of Clinical Psychology in Medical Settings, 16*, 101–112. http://dx.doi.org/10.1007/s10880-009-9156-9

Brennan Ramirez, L. K., Baker, E. A., & Metzler, M. (2008). *Promoting health equity: A resource to help communities address social determinants of health*. Retrieved from http://www.cdc.gov/nccdphp/dch/programs/healthycommunitiesprogram/tools/pdf/SDOH-workbook.pdf

Centers for Disease Control and Prevention. (n.d.). *Promoting healthy spring: Learn strategies for a health spring.* Retrieved from http://www.cdc.gov/chronicdisease/index.htm

Cohen, S. B. (2015, September). *Differentials in the concentration of health expenditures across population subgroups in the U.S., 2013* (Statistical Brief No. 480). Retrieved from Agency for Health Care Policy and Research website: https://meps.ahrq.gov/data_files/publications/st480/stat480.shtml

Costa, E., Giardini, A., Savin, M., Menditto, E., Lehane, E., Laosa, O., . . . Marengoni, A. (2015). Interventional tools to improve medication adherence: Review of literature. *Patient Preference and Adherence, 9,* 1303–1314. http://dx.doi.org/10.2147/PPA.S87551

Dastidar, J. G., & Odden, A. (2011, August). How do I determine if my patient has decision-making capacity? *The Hospitalist.* Retrieved from https://www.the-hospitalist.org/hospitalist/article/124731/how-do-i-determine-if-my-patient-has-decision-making-capacity

Engel, G. L. (1977). The need for a new medical model: A challenge for biomedicine. *Science, 196,* 129–136. http://dx.doi.org/10.1126/science.847460

Folstein, M. F., Folstein, S. E., & McHugh, P. R. (1975). "Mini-mental state": A practical method for grading the cognitive state of patients for the clinician. *Journal of Psychiatric Research, 12,* 189–198. http://dx.doi.org/10.1016/0022-3956(75)90026-6

Grisso, T., & Appelbaum, P. S. (1998). *MacArthur Competence Assessment Tool for Treatment (MacCAT-T).* Sarasota, FL: Professional Resource Press/Professional Resource Exchange.

Hoge, M. A., Morris, J. A., Laraia, M., Pomerantz, A., & Farley, T. (2014). *Core competencies for integrated behavioral health and primary care.* Washington, DC: SAMHSA–HRSA Center for Integrated Health Solutions.

Holleman, W. L., Bray, J. H., Davis, L., & Holleman, M. C. (2004). Innovative ways to address the mental health and medical needs of marginalized patients: Collaborations between family physicians, family therapists, and family psychologists. *American Journal of Orthopsychiatry, 74,* 242–252. http://dx.doi.org/10.1037/0002-9432.74.3.242

Horwitz, S. K., Horwitz, I. B., & Barshes, N. R. (2011). Addressing dysfunctional relations among health care teams: Improving team cooperation through applied organizational theories. *Advances in Health Care Management, 10,* 173–197. http://dx.doi.org/10.1108/S1474-8231(2011)0000010017

Hudgins, C., Rose, S., Fifield, P. Y., & Arnault, S. (2013). Navigating the legal and ethical foundations of informed consent and confidentiality in integrated primary care. *Families, Systems & Health, 31,* 9–19. http://dx.doi.org/10.1037/a0031974

Institute of Medicine, Committee on Advancing Pain Research, Care, and Education. (2011). 3. Care of people with pain. In *Relieving pain in America: A blueprint for transforming prevention, care, education, and research.* Washington, DC: National Academies Press. Retrieved from National Center for Biotechnology Information website: https://www.ncbi.nlm.nih.gov/books/NBK92517/

Interprofessional Education Collaborative. (2016). *Core competencies for interprofessional collaborative practice: 2016 update.* Retrieved from https://nebula.wsimg.com/2f68a39520b03336b41038c370497473?AccessKeyId=DC06780E69ED19E2B3A5&disposition=0&alloworigin=1

Interprofessional Education Collaborative Expert Panel. (2011). *Core competencies for interprofessional collaborative practice: Report of an expert panel.* Retrieved from https://nebula.wsimg.com/3ee8a4b5b5f7ab794c742b14601d5f23?AccessKeyId=DC06780E69ED19E2B3A5&disposition=0&alloworigin=1

The Joint Commission. (2016, February 24). Detecting and treating suicide ideation in all settings. *Sentinel Event Alert.* Retrieved from https://www.jointcommission.org/assets/1/18/SEA_56_Suicide.pdf

Kanzler, K. E., Goodie, J. L., Hunter, C. L., Glotfelter, M. A., & Bodart, J. J. (2013). From colleague to patient: Ethical challenges in integrated primary care. *Families, Systems & Health, 31,* 41–48. http://dx.doi.org/10.1037/a0031853

Katon, W. J. (2011). Epidemiology and treatment of depression in patients with chronic medical illness. *Dialogues in Clinical Neuroscience, 13*, 7–23.

Kinman, C. R., Gilchrist, E. C., Payne-Murphy, J. C., & Miller, B. F. (2015). *Provider- and practice-level competencies for integrated behavioral health in primary care: A literature review* (AHRQ Publication No. 14-0073-EF). Rockville, MD: Agency for Healthcare Research and Quality.

Larkin, K. T., & Klonoff, E. A. (2014). *Specialty competencies in clinical health psychology.* New York, NY: Oxford University Press.

Makoul, G. (2001). Essential elements of communication in medical encounters: The Kalamazoo consensus statement. *Academic Medicine, 76*, 390–393. http://dx.doi.org/10.1097/00001888-200104000-00021

McDaniel, S. H., Grus, C. L., Cubic, B. A., Hunter, C. L., Kearney, L. K., Schuman, C. C., . . . Johnson, S. B. (2014). Competencies for psychology practice in primary care. *American Psychologist, 69*, 409–429. http://dx.doi.org/10.1037/a0036072

Nasreddine, Z. S., Phillips, N. A., Bédirian, V., Charbonneau, S., Whitehead, V., Collin, I., . . . Chertkow, H. (2005). The Montreal Cognitive Assessment, MoCA: A brief screening tool for mild cognitive impairment. *Journal of the American Geriatrics Society, 53*, 695–699. http://dx.doi.org/10.1111/j.1532-5415.2005.53221.x

National Action Alliance for Suicide Prevention Clinical Workforce Preparedness Task Force. (2014). *Suicide prevention and the clinical workforce: Guidelines for training.* Washington, DC: Author.

National Health Council. (2014, July 29). *About chronic diseases.* Retrieved from http://www.nationalhealthcouncil.org/sites/default/files/NHC_Files/Pdf_Files/AboutChronicDisease.pdf

Office of Disease Prevention and Health Promotion, U.S. Department of Health and Human Services. (n.d.). *Disparities.* Retrieved from https://www.healthypeople.gov/2020/about/foundation-health-measures/Disparities

Randolph, C. (1998). *Repeatable Battery for the Assessment of Neuropsychological Status* [RBANS manual]. San Antonio, TX: Psychological Corporation.

Reitz, R., Common, K., Fifield, P., & Stiasny, E. (2012). Collaboration in the presence of an electronic health record. *Families, Systems & Health, 30*, 72–80. http://dx.doi.org/10.1037/a0027016

Rudd, R. A., Seth, P., David, F., & Scholl, L. (2016). Increases in drug and opioid-involved overdose deaths—United States, 2010–2015. *Morbidity and Mortality Weekly Report, 65*, 1445–1452. http://dx.doi.org/10.15585/mmwr.mm655051e1

Serrano, N. (Ed.). (2014). *The implementer's guide to primary care behavioral health.* Retrieved from https://itunes.apple.com/us/book/implementers-guide-to-primary/id833906873?mt=11

Sethre, R. (2018, March 8). Consulting in medical settings expands practice. *National Psychologist.* Retrieved from https://nationalpsychologist.com/2018/03/consulting-in-medical-settings-expands-practice/104316.html

# Consultation in Leadership

Jennifer Wootten and Nadine J. Kaslow

There has been a long-standing debate about the extent to which leadership is a core competency in health service psychology (HSP). It was not deemed a foundational or functional competency at the 2002 Competencies Conference (Kaslow et al., 2004; Rodolfa et al., 2005), nor is it a required competency in the recent *Standards of Accreditation for Health Service Psychology* (American Psychological Association, 2018). However, it is included in the operational definition of the HSP management-administration competency (Fouad et al., 2009; Hatcher et al., 2013). Similarly, leadership is not a core competency within other health professions (Swing, 2002). The lack of active attention to the leadership competency is problematic given that health professionals increasingly are called on to assume leadership roles. In addition, it is concerning that even though consultation related to leadership development has become increasingly popular (Kaiser & Curphy, 2013), there is a dearth of focus on the consultation competency as applied to leadership for health service psychologists. We concur with recent calls for health service psychologists to become scientist–practitioner–advocate–leaders who act to create a socially just environment (Shullman, 2017) and advocate for a competency- and capability-based approach to leadership consultation in HSP.

Because interest in leadership development is at its peak, a growing need for consultative efforts is aimed at expanding the capacity of institutional and organizational members to engage competently in leadership roles and processes.

http://dx.doi.org/10.1037/0000153-010
*Consultation in Psychology: A Competency-Based Approach*, C. A. Falender and
E. P. Shafranske (Editors)

This chapter aims to advance the nascent literature on consultation for leadership in HSP. To set the stage, we present background information about the leadership competency and approaches to leadership consultation that build on the dominant models for leadership. Next, we describe best practices for consultation that focus on leadership development programs and leadership coaching. We offer a case example about a leadership consultation within an HSP training program and conclude with reflections about the consultation competency as applied to leadership moving forward.

## LEADERSHIP COMPETENCY

### Competency Definition

*Leadership* is difficult to define and, as a result, has a variety of definitions (Guthey & Jackson, 2011). Recently, it has been depicted as a process of social influence that maximizes the efforts of others toward the achievement of a goal. It involves exercising high-level conceptual skills and decisiveness, analyzing the internal and external environment, developing a shared vision and mission, designing and implementing strategies for solving problems, inspiring people, satisfying followers' needs, and changing culture (Thompson, Peteraf, Gamble, & Strickland, 2013). It entails displaying courage-related knowledge and moral, creative, and biological characteristics (Şen, Kabak, & Yanginlar, 2013). Leadership success typically reflects a combination of the styles and qualities of the leaders and the followers and the interaction between leaders' personal attributes and environmental contexts (Daft, 2014; Hackman & Wageman, 2007). The qualities associated with successful leaders include intelligence, emotional intelligence, wisdom, curiosity, courage, tenacity, creativity, passion, flexibility, compassion, collaboration, fairness, risk tolerance, and ethicality (Şen et al., 2013; Shullman, 2017; Sternberg, 2007). Good followers who support effective leaders display knowledge, skills, dedication, participation, strong work ethic, cooperation, and independence (Şen et al., 2013).

### Leadership Versus Management and Administration

Although related to management and administration, leadership differs from these competencies in underlying philosophy, function, and outcomes (Algahtani, 2014; Toor & Ofori, 2008; VanVactor, 2012). Vision and mission based and people focused, leadership is about coping with and advocating for change. Leaders establish direction; align people; and inspire, empower, and persuade team members to assume key roles aimed at mission attainment. Leaders tend to use a transformational approach in which they inspire others to work toward a shared vision and promise intrinsic rewards for vision attainment. They focus their energy on big impact decisions, strategic initiatives, and policy formulation.

In contrast, management is task and work based, and managers are expected to ensure smooth organizational functioning and the attainment of expected outcomes, advocate for stability, and cope with complexity. Managers plan, build, and direct systems to accomplish missions and goals. Administration is focused on the efficient accomplishment of goals. Administrators are appointed to plan, organize, lead, and control. Managers and administrators tend to use an authoritarian and transactional style in which they tell subordinates what to do and reward them for reaching the goals set for them. They are concerned with shaping existing organizational structures and processes to ensure that desired results are attained, make many decisions, and involve themselves in the day-to-day operations.

Despite these differences, effective leaders, managers, and administrators are all involved in decision making, work with people to accomplish a goal, hold people accountable for goal attainment, and are action oriented. Thus, it is not surprising that leadership has been identified as an essential component of the management-administration competency (Fouad et al., 2009), deemed a functional competency (Kaslow et al., 2004; Rodolfa et al., 2005) and later placed under the systems rubric in the streamlined competency framework (Hatcher et al., 2013).

## APPROACHES TO LEADERSHIP CONSULTATION

Leadership consultation aims to build people's competence in leadership. Little attention has been paid to conceptual models for leadership consultation despite the abundance of literature on models of leadership (Fassinger & Shullman, 2017). This section applies the current models of leadership to the process of leadership consultation. Effective leadership consultants blend elements of the behavioral patterns associated with these models, are developmentally informed based on consultees' levels of leadership training and experience, and are attuned to the ecological contexts in which leadership is occurring (Fassinger & Good, 2017).

### Transactional Approach

Transactional leadership consultants encourage consultees to function like managers and attend to controlling, organizing, and engaging in short-term planning (Bass, 1998). They tend to recommend that their consultees be directive and action oriented as leaders and motivate their followers by appealing to their self-interests. They suggest that as leaders, their consultees set clearly defined goals and targets for meeting the goals, create clear structures, communicate what is expected of their followers, reward contingently effort and good performance, and initiate actions to prevent mistakes and ensure compliance within their organization. Transactional leadership consultants are effective in situations in which efficiency is key and organizational problems are simple and clearly defined.

## Transformational Approaches

Multiple approaches to leadership consultation are guided by transformational theory: transformational, inclusive, collaborative, authentic, servant, and values based. Transformational leadership consultants attend to leader–follower relationships and the contributions of the followers (Bass, 1998). In promoting leadership strategies and solutions for their consultees, they encourage them to facilitate individual, group, or organizational performance by forming strong emotional connections with their followers; provide their followers the confidence to exceed performance expectations; and inspire their followers to be proactive and creative to realize their full potential (Piccolo et al., 2012).

Consultants who espouse an inclusive approach encourage their consultees to facilitate belongingness and appreciate uniqueness, which results in team members' feeling more identified with the group and empowered. This approach enables their consultees to be more creative as leaders, have better job performance, and remain on the team for a longer duration (Randel et al., 2018). These consultants serve as models for their consultees with regard to the value of soliciting different perspectives, encourage their consultees to invite and acknowledge others' contributions, and provide their consultees with the requisite knowledge and skill to involve others in decision-making efforts that incorporate multiple perspectives (Nembhard & Edmondson, 2006).

Consultants who use a collaborative leadership framework emphasize to their consultees the necessity of building relationships within and across organizations, ensuring the effectiveness of heterogeneous teams in accomplishing mutually agreed on goals, balancing between leading enterprises and nurturing development, and inspiring and modeling learning while simultaneously ensuring that the goals of various stakeholders are achieved (DeWitt, 2017). These consultants underscore the need for leaders to manage in a constructive and professional manner the tensions that emerge when working with people with diverse perspectives and to share control with others to attain desired outcomes (Archer & Cameron, 2013).

Consultants who draw on a model of authentic leadership promote self-awareness, balanced information processing, relational transparency, and an internalized moral perspective (Walumbwa, Avolio, Gardner, Wernsing, & Peterson, 2008). They emphasize the multicultural limitations of communal leadership models and highlight to consultees the importance of attending to the dynamic relationships among leaders, followers, and the cultural contexts in which the leadership is embedded (Avolio, 2007). In their consultations, they capitalize on the findings that authentic leadership is associated with positive workplace outcomes (Olaniyan & Hystad, 2016) and that followers prefer authentic leaders (Romager, Hughes, & Trimble, 2017).

Consultants whose value is servant leadership capitalize on consultees' inclination to go beyond their self-interests to serve others (Greenleaf, 1998). They encourage their consultees to function as servant-leaders by empowering and developing others, being humble and authentic, accepting and understanding others, providing direction, and modeling stewardship and service engagement (van Dierendonck, 2011). They highlight to their consultees that effective servant leadership promotes positive leader–follower relationships, trust, and fairness, which are associated with self-actualization, work satisfaction, improved performance, and sustainable and socially responsible organizations (van Dierendonck, 2011).

Although all leadership consultations should be guided by the moral foundation that informs decisions and actions (Ahn, Ettner, & Loupin, 2011), values-based consultants underscore to their consultees that a clear, compelling vision within a values-based culture is needed for organizational sustainability and success. They highlight the need for leaders and the organizations they lead to be guided by integrity, justice or fairness, and good judgment so that trusting relationships form between leaders and those they lead. They model humility and leading by example in terms of their actions, decisions, and deportment.

### Learning Leadership Approaches

In recent years, attention has been paid to the ways people can lead strategically in response to rapidly changing societal and global demands and environmental situations characterized by volatility, uncertainty, complexity, and ambiguity (VUCA world; Bennett & Lemoine, 2014; T. O. Jacobs, 2002). Leadership consultants aligned with these approaches provide for their consultees strategies to manage individual, group, organizational, and community-level uncertainty and ambiguity. They focus their consultations on facilitating their consultees' efforts to create organizational environments that empower all parties to perform optimally in the face of ongoing change and to lead with antidotes to VUCA (i.e., VUCA Prime: vision, understanding, clarity, and agility to mitigate VUCA world; Fassinger & Shullman, 2017; Horney, Pasmore, & O'Shea, 2010; Kinsinger & Walch, 2012). They stress that VUCA Prime leaders must foster change by shaping the organization's capacity to anticipate factors that influence the conditions, recognizing the impact of issues and actions, understanding the interdependence of various aspects of the organization's functioning, planning for unexpected challenges, and considering and pursuing relevant opportunities.

## BEST PRACTICES FOR LEADERSHIP CONSULTATION

This section reviews the two major consultation practices for facilitating people's acquisition and development of the leadership competence: leadership development programs and leadership coaching. Organizations may benefit most when their leaders participate in a combination of these best practices (Seidle, Fernandez, & Perry, 2016).

## Leadership Development Programs

### Structure and Content

Leadership development programs are one of the most written about and studied practices for leadership consultation. These programs often are informed by theories of leadership development (Hewitt et al., 2017). They usually include both didactic components—often presented in lectures and via case discussions—focused on technical and conceptual knowledge and experiential components, such as opportunities to observe leadership in action, skills training and practice, exercises to increase understanding of oneself as a leader, and individual or group-based leadership development projects (Lucas, Goldman, Scott, & Dandar, 2018; Phillips et al., 2017). The topics most frequently covered include models of leadership; impact of gender, culture, and societal context on leadership; assessment of organizational culture; and effective leadership strategies (e.g., supporting teamwork, inspiring and developing others, managing politics and change; Avolio, Walumbwa, & Weber, 2009; Ayman & Korabik, 2010; Bunker & Wakefield, 2005; Fassinger & Good, 2017; Fassinger & Shullman, 2017; Fassinger, Shullman, & Buki, 2017; Holt & Seki, 2012; McCleskey, 2014; Paustian-Underdahl, Walker, & Woehr, 2014). Given the sociodemographic changes in leaders, growing complexity of the demands encountered, and increasingly interdependence among organizations, these programs are focusing on contemporary cultural models of leadership that prioritize empowering followers to achieve a shared vision, supporting and mentoring followers, and including all parties and perspectives (Eagly & Chin, 2010). They increasingly teach processes for solving leadership challenges in a VUCA world (Fassinger et al., 2017).

### Specific Populations

Given that sociodemographic and professional factors influence leadership development and performance, programs have been created for specific populations, such as women leaders. Compared with general programs, women's leadership development programs tend to be based on an assumption of connected rather than separate knowing, development of relational rather than autonomous self, and relational and identity based rather than agentic and transactional leadership approaches (Sugiyama, Cavanagh, van Esch, Bilimoria, & Brown, 2016). In addition to topics covered in general programs, women's leadership programs attend to unconscious gender bias and its impact on the identity and experience of women leaders and offer gender-relevant leadership strategies related to such topics as negotiation and change management (R. J. Ely, Ibarra, & Kolb, 2011). There is empirical support for the value of such programs: Women have noted that participation is associated with greater leadership competency attainment and career and leadership progression, and their superiors have noted that participation results in more effective leaders who are more prepared for leadership promotions and success (Dannels et al., 2008; Helitzer et al., 2014; McDade, Richman, Jackson, & Morahan, 2004; Morahan, Gleason, Richman, Dannels, & McDade, 2010).

## Assessments

Frequently, these programs require engagement in a multisource or 360-degree feedback process (Day, Fleenor, Atwater, Sturm, & McKee, 2014) in which participants gather ratings of leader-related behaviors and effectiveness from multiple sources (e.g., bosses, peers, subordinates, external stakeholders, self). This process is designed to foster self-awareness, facilitate leadership development, and guide the creation of a leadership development plan. Given that self- and other reports often differ, attention to the breadth of input and the differences in perspective offers comprehensive and meaningful feedback to participants (Solansky, 2010). In many leadership programs, participants complete measures related to personality characteristics and interpersonal styles considered relevant to leadership strengths and areas needing development. The following are some of the commonly used assessment tools. The Myers–Briggs Type Indicator (Myers, 2010) taps four dimensions (introversion–extraversion, sensation–intuition, thinking–feeling, judging–perceiving) to classify respondents into one of 16 personality types. The Fundamental Interpersonal Relations Orientation-Behavior measure assesses interpersonal needs in three domains (inclusion, control, affective) and the extent to which each interpersonal need is desired and expressed by the individual (Schultz, 1958). The Birkman method, which focuses on occupational preferences (interests), effective behaviors (usual behaviors), interpersonal and environmental expectations (needs or expectations), and less-than-effective behaviors (stress behaviors; Birkman, Elizondo, Lee, Wadlington, & Zamzow, 2008), yields four distinct behavioral descriptions that combine to create a unique profile for each individual. They may be asked to complete surveys that tap leadership styles, such as the Servant Leadership Survey (van Dierendonck & Nuijten, 2011) or the Servant Leadership Assessment Instrument (Dennis & Bocarnea, 2005), both of which tap servant leadership qualities or the Turning Point Collaborative Leadership Self-Assessment Questionnaires that focus on behaviors associated with collaborative leadership (https://cdn2.hubspot.net/hubfs/316071/Resources/Article/Collababorative_Leader_self-assessments.pdf). Typically, group- and individual-level results are presented and reviewed; the aim is to assist participants to increase their awareness of their own characteristics and styles and their impact and the advantages and challenges of other traits and styles.

## Leadership Projects

Many programs require individual, group-level, or both, action leadership projects (Frich, Brewster, Cherlin, & Bradley, 2015; Hewitt et al., 2017; Phillips et al., 2017). Such hands-on projects develop people's leadership potential and leadership self-efficacy by affording them the opportunity to engage in activities in which they can practically apply newly learned leadership understanding and tools. Such projects, when done in a group, also afford people the chance to hone their capacity for collaborating with other leaders to achieve a shared vision. If leadership projects are implemented, they may advance an institution or organization. Programs that incorporate multiple learning methods, including leadership projects, have the greatest impact even though they are more resource intensive (Frich et al., 2015).

### Mentors

Programs often provide mentoring leaders who offer advice and expertise to enhance their mentees' leadership skills and assist them in understanding their strengths and areas for growth. Mentoring leaders positively impact their mentees (Phillips et al., 2017), especially if they focus on coaching and communicating in a manner that fosters their mentees' openness and sharing of information (Solansky, 2010). Even when mentoring leaders are not provided, people seek out peer or senior mentors (Doran, Galloway, Ponce, & Kaslow, 2018).

### Outcome Data

Surveys have examined the impact of leadership development programs. People typically are satisfied with these programs and have reported that participation enhanced their understanding of leadership development and leadership skills and expertise, increased their knowledge of self as a leader, bolstered their self-confidence, strengthened their social connections and networks, and led to their attainment of more major leadership roles (Frich et al., 2015; Hewitt et al., 2017; Phillips et al., 2017). Some studies have demonstrated favorable organizational performance (e.g., improved quality indicators) as a result of leaders' participation in these program (Frich et al., 2015). The most effective programs are comprehensive and longitudinal, include an intraprofessional cadre of participants, and require individual or institutional projects (Sonnino, 2016).

### Leadership Coaching

#### Definition and Process

Coaching has become popular as a leadership development training tool throughout the professional life cycle; the past 15 years has witnessed a marked increase in the number of coaches and coaching programs (Carey, Philippon, & Cummings, 2011; K. Ely et al., 2010). Coaching aims to foster coachees' development and provide guidance and strategy related to specific leadership challenges and dilemmas. Although there are many definitions of coaching, key elements include formal one-on-one trusting coach–coachee relationships that facilitate professional and personal growth and behavioral change via learning and self-awareness in a manner that is associated with individual and organizational success. These collaborative and dynamic relationships focus on assessing and understanding coachees' leadership development, attends to ways coachees can make progress toward leadership goals within the constraints of their leadership contexts, and offer vehicles for accountability and further growth (Ting & Hart, 2004). Coaches may be hired from inside (internal coaches) or outside (external coaches) the organization. There is no consensus about the superiority of either approach; rather, the choice depends on coachees' needs and organizational contexts (Carey et al., 2011). Coaching relationships may be short or long term such that coaches shift to becoming trusted leadership advisors (Wasylyshyn, 2015). Coaching offers a safe context for people in leadership roles to improve their self-confidence, learn to manage the change process in an effective and creative fashion, bolster their approach to communication, and develop and sustain productive working relationships with diverse colleagues.

## Components

There are five key elements to effective models for coaching as a component of leadership consultation (Carey et al., 2011). The first pertains to relationship building and the formation of coach–coachee relationships that are supportive, open, and nonjudgmental and successful at enhancing coachees' competence and expertise. Such relationships tend to develop when coaches engage in empathic and respectful ways, encourage and model self-reflection, demonstrate perceptiveness and good judgment, and display the capacity to be diplomatic and manage conflicts with integrity (Athanasopoulou & Dopson, 2018; Joo, 2005; Stein, 2017; Truijen & van Woerkom, 2008). They also emerge when coaches use consultation techniques, such as feedback, dialogue, and reflection, and offer coaching consistent with their coachees' organizational contexts. The second relates to the collaborative defining of problems and setting of goals. The third focuses on problem-solving and the development of action plans related to the aforementioned goals. These action plans often include a variety of tools, strategies, and psychological techniques. The fourth emphasizes the transformation process and the need for shifts in thinking and changes in behavior on the part of coachees in response to action plans and the development of increased self-awareness. The final component relates to the determination of outcomes in response to the coaching process; attention is paid to enhanced personal performance and better organizational functioning.

## Addressing Specific Leadership Challenges

Often leaders use coaching relationships when they experience challenges as leaders and want assistance determining and implementing solutions. When leadership coaching focuses on such challenges, coaches must listen and attend with curiosity to the stories coachees tell about the social contexts in which they are embedded. They must collaboratively engage with coachees to examine problems in detail, review potential solutions, and ascertain the effectiveness of solutions tried or alternatives to be considered. Commonly coaching focuses on contextual, interpersonal, or organizational challenges.

Leaders may desire coaching about difficulties they encounter related to specific context(s) in which they are embedded. Common contextual difficulties relate to limited finances and resources; technological advances; demands for organizational transformation; lack of organizational support (e.g., time, resources, resistance to change) for leadership involvement, development, and success; and systemic oppression within the environment related to social identities that serves as a barrier to leadership development and fulfillment of leadership roles (Carey et al., 2011; Fassinger & Good, 2017; Hewitt et al., 2017). Such oppression often reflects pervasive unconscious biases (i.e., subtle and not-so subtle forms of discrimination that individuals experience related to leadership based on their gender, race or ethnicity, age, sexual orientation, ability status, and so on) within the organization. For example, women encounter a myriad of obstacles related to becoming and succeeding as leaders, which are compounded for individuals with intersecting identities, such as women of color (Sanchez-Hucles & Davis, 2010). Difficulties related to oppression also may be manifestations of institutionalized racism (Hewitt et al., 2017). As another example, gay male leaders are rated less effective than their heterosexual counterparts and often are perceived as most suited for leadership positions associated in a stereotypic fashion with women leaders because they are viewed as interpersonally oriented (Barrantes & Eaton, 2018). Leadership coaching consultations may encourage these leaders to build strong and supportive teams that create and pursue a shared vision and share in the leadership burden, communicate and attend to the vision while simultaneously managing and responding to day-to-day situations, and be proactive and creative in addressing and reacting to organizational challenges. Culturally diverse leaders who can serve as role models and mentors can be powerful antidotes to unconscious biases and oppression (Fassinger & Good, 2017); observing and interacting with such individuals facilitates people's ability to visualize being people from marginalized groups as leaders and are empowering (Hewitt et al., 2017). Coachees should be advised to access support from mentors and sponsors; engage in self-education and self-reflection; and find, create, or both, organizational cultures that value and promote diversity (Pingleton, Jones, Rosolowski, & Zimmerman, 2016).

One stressful challenge for many leaders is problematic interpersonal situations, such as difficulties with teamwork and collaboration; opposition, hostility, or both, from powerful forces; criticism from inside or outside the organization; and oppositional followers. Leaders often have personal and contextual barriers against directly addressing relational problems in the workplace (S. C. Jacobs et al., 2011). Leadership coaches may recommend that coachees participate in "difficult conversations" regarding interpersonal situations and remind them that such conversations are most effective when framed as learning conversations aimed at finding mutual solutions (Stone, Patton, & Heen, 2010). They can speak with coachees about ensuring that all parties are given the opportunity to share their perspectives and feelings, address how the situation impacts them, and feel acknowledged and validated by their leaders (Stone et al., 2010). They may recommend that coachees prepare for such conversations by practicing with a nonthreatening partner and reading pertinent books (Fisher, Ury, & Patton, 2011).

Another challenge focal in leadership coaching is leaders' experience of organizational crises, which typically involve unexpected events that threaten or are perceived to threaten the system's capacity to reach its vision- and mission-driven goals and that leave individuals feeling uncertain. Organizational crises may include organizational traumas, which are collective experiences that overwhelm systems, making them more vulnerable and potentially permanently damaged (Hormann & Vivian, 2013). Such traumas may move a system away from its vision and primary missions, decrease organizational effectiveness, and render people anxious and stressed. When coaching leaders about responding to organizational crises and traumas, coaches may recommend that coachees help a system use a crisis as an opportunity for posttraumatic growth (Tedeschi & Calhoun, 2004), prioritize situational awareness, acknowledge and capitalize on the strengths and adaptive capacity of the system, and be mindful about the system's vulnerabilities and invested in overcoming them (Lee, Vargo, & Seville, 2013; McManus, Seville, Vargo, & Brunsdon, 2008).

### Outcome Data

Some qualitative and quantitative research is being conducted to ascertain the effectiveness of leadership coaching as a best practice in leadership consultation. A recent review demonstrated that participation in coaching is associated with positive outcomes related to personal development, behavioral interactions with others, and work performance among coachees (Athanasopoulou & Dopson, 2018). It is indirectly linked to improved organizational performance. Although the findings are promising, they need to be considered in light of significant methodological limitations (K. Ely et al., 2010; Kaiser & Curphy, 2013).

## CASE EXAMPLE: LEADERSHIP COACHING WITH TRAINING PROGRAMS

In recent years, training programs have sought leadership consultations in response to leadership changes, significant leadership challenges, investment, or all three, in the leadership competency. In the example that follows, the second author (Kaslow) of this chapter was invited to serve as a leadership coach for a training director of an HSP program in which there was limited diversity and a desire for more inclusivity. The leadership coach met with the training director to gather her perspective and determine what guidance she desired. After a series of conversations, the leadership coach determined she needed a more systemic understanding before she could offer valuable input. She suggested to the training director that a comprehensive assessment of and plan to address the leadership challenges could best be attained from gathering data from other parties. The training director consented to this approach, and as a result, the coach conducted separate focus groups with faculty, relevant leaders outside the program, and trainees. The questions addressed attitudes about diversity and inclusiveness, willingness to change the program to enhance its diversity, strategies tried, perceived barriers, and views of leader effectiveness. It became evident in these focus groups that people felt helpless and that although they had tried concrete strategies to increase the program's diversity, they had not prioritized creating a training culture that would be truly welcoming to people from diverse backgrounds.

Building on the focus group data and the literature (Chin, Desormeaux, & Sawyer, 2016), the leadership coach offered the training director strategies for leading the training community's effort to construct and promote a diversity supportive and inclusive environment. Together, they modified the recommendations to create a plan the training director believed she could implement with the coach's guidance based on her leadership style and strengths and her relationships with others in the community. After gaining stakeholder input, the plan was modified as follows:

- Gain acceptance from the training community by collaborating with individuals from diverse backgrounds (e.g., administrators, trainers, trainees, staff) with differing views to build consensus about a vision for diversity and inclusiveness for the training environment and to collectively determine and implement a strategy to advance this vision.

- Place greater emphasis on forging ethically engaged and trusting relationships and attention to power dynamics and diverse perspectives.

- Ensure all parties receive ongoing training so they are culturally competent, humble, and flexible; mindful about the impact of unconscious bias, microaggressions, oppression, and marginalization; and engage in meaningful conversations about these topics.

- Empower all members of the community to be authentic in sharing and capitalizing on their multiple identities because there was more diversity than had previously been revealed and to be respectful of and interested in others' identities.

- Partner with others in the training community to interact with individuals from diverse communities outside the training program and involve these community colleagues in significant ways in the training program.

- Provide cultural mentors for trainers and trainees from diverse backgrounds so they are supported, protected, and empowered and have role models for successful functioning.

- Determine with others in the community benchmarks for progress and an approach and time frame for the evaluation of change.

The leadership consultant worked with the training director to implement and follow through on the aforementioned recommendations. In addition, the training director applied for and was accepted into a leadership development program at her home institution.

## CONCLUSION

There has been a long tradition in HSP to train scientist–practitioners (Belar & Perry, 1992; Raimy, 1950). As the discipline has evolved and psychologists have assumed more diverse roles and responsibilities, this framework has been expanded to an emphasis on training psychologists to be scientist–practitioner–advocates (Mallinckrodt, Miles, & Levy, 2014) and recently scientist–practitioner–advocate–leaders (Shullman, 2017). Including leadership in this model underscores the value of providing competency- and capability-based leadership consultation to graduate students, interns, residents, and psychologists.

A number of principles should guide such leadership consultation practices (Hackman & Wageman, 2007). Given that leadership is a science and an art, leadership consultations must target both elements of this competency (VanVactor, 2012). Leadership consultations, regardless of their format, should encourage consultees to adopt the role of a "learning leader," namely, an individual who perceives himself or herself and is viewed by others as potentially offering leadership in most contexts (Shullman, 2017). Furthermore, the value of lifelong learning must be capitalized on and nurtured, and emphasis should be placed on capitalizing on one's strengths and minimizing one's limitations, including those associated with one's internal mental models of leadership (Sternberg, 2007). These consultation practices also should prioritize encouraging people to recognize the leadership strategies that they use and the appropriateness of these strategies in their various leadership roles and contexts (Vroom & Jago, 2007). Finally, they must focus on effective leadership in the context of crisis (Avolio, 2007).

## REFERENCES

Ahn, M. J., Ettner, L. W., & Loupin, A. (2011). From classical to contemporary leadership challenges. *Journal of Leadership Studies*, *5*, 6–22. http://dx.doi.org/10.1002/jls.20201

Algahtani, A. (2014). Are leadership and management different?: A review. *Journal of Management Policies and Practices*, *2*, 71–82. http://dx.doi.org/10.15640/jmpp.v2n3a4

American Psychological Association. (2018). *Standards of accreditation for health service psychology*. Retrieved from http://apa.org/ed/accreditation/about/policies/standards-of-accreditation.pdf

Archer, D., & Cameron, A. (2013). *Collaborative leadership: Building relationships, handling conflict, and sharing control* (2nd ed.). New York, NY: Routledge. http://dx.doi.org/10.4324/9780203067505

Athanasopoulou, A., & Dopson, S. (2018). A systematic review of executive coaching outcomes: Is it the journey or the destination that matters the most? *Leadership Quarterly*, *29*, 70–88. http://dx.doi.org/10.1016/j.leaqua.2017.11.004

Avolio, B. J. (2007). Promoting more integrative strategies for leadership theory-building. *American Psychologist*, *62*, 25–33. http://dx.doi.org/10.1037/0003-066X.62.1.25

Avolio, B. J., Walumbwa, F. O., & Weber, T. J. (2009). Leadership: Current theories, research, and future directions. *Annual Review of Psychology*, *60*, 421–449. http://dx.doi.org/10.1146/annurev.psych.60.110707.163621

Ayman, R., & Korabik, K. (2010). Leadership: Why gender and culture matter. *American Psychologist, 65*, 157–170. http://dx.doi.org/10.1037/a0018806

Barrantes, R. J., & Eaton, A. A. (2018). Sexual orientation and leadership suitability: How being a gay man affects perceptions of fit in gender-stereotyped positions. *Sex Roles: A Journal of Research, 79*, 549–564. http://dx.doi.org/10.1007/s11199-018-0894-8

Bass, B. M. (1998). *Transformational leadership: Industrial, military, and educational impact.* Mahwah, NJ: Erlbaum.

Belar, C. D., & Perry, N. W. (1992). The National Conference on Scientist–practitioner Education and Training for the Professional Practice of Psychology. *American Psychologist, 47*, 71–75. http://dx.doi.org/10.1037/0003-066X.47.1.71

Bennett, N., & Lemoine, G. J. (2014). What a difference a world makes: Understanding threats to performance in a VUCA world. *Business Horizons, 57*, 311–317. http://dx.doi.org/10.1016/j.bushor.2014.01.001

Birkman, R. W., Elizondo, F., Lee, L. G., Wadlington, P. L., & Zamzow, M. W. (2008). *The Birkman method manual.* Houston, TX: Birkman International.

Bunker, K. A., & Wakefield, M. A. (2005). *Leading with authenticity in times of transition.* Greensboro, NC: Center for Creative Leadership.

Carey, W., Philippon, D. J., & Cummings, G. G. (2011). Coaching models for leadership development: An integrative review. *Journal of Leadership Studies, 5*, 51–69. http://dx.doi.org/10.1002/jls.20204

Chin, J. L., Desormeaux, L., & Sawyer, K. (2016). Making way for paradigms of diversity leadership. *Consulting Psychology Journal: Practice and Research, 68*, 49–71. http://dx.doi.org/10.1037/cpb0000051

Daft, R. L. (2014). *The leadership experience* (6th ed.). Stamford, CT: Cengage Learning.

Dannels, S. A., Yamagata, H., McDade, S. A., Chuang, Y. C., Gleason, K. A., McLaughlin, J. M., . . . Morahan, P. S. (2008). Evaluating a leadership program: A comparative, longitudinal study to assess the impact of the Executive Leadership in Academic Medicine (ELAM) program for women. *Academic Medicine, 83*, 488–495. http://dx.doi.org/10.1097/ACM.0b013e31816be551

Day, D. V., Fleenor, J. W., Atwater, L. E., Sturm, R. E., & McKee, R. A. (2014). Advances in leader and leadership development: A review of 25 years of research and theory. *Leadership Quarterly, 25*, 63–82. http://dx.doi.org/10.1016/j.leaqua.2013.11.004

Dennis, R. S., & Bocarnea, M. (2005). Development of the Servant Leadership Assessment Instrument. *Leadership & Organization Development Journal, 26*, 600–615. http://dx.doi.org/10.1108/01437730510633692

DeWitt, P. M. (2017). *Collaborative leadership: Six influences that matter most.* Thousand Oaks, CA: Sage.

Doran, J. M., Galloway, M. P., Ponce, A. N., & Kaslow, N. J. (2018). Leadership mentoring: A survey of early career psychologist leaders. *Mentoring & Tutoring: Partnership in Learning, 26*, 165–182. http://dx.doi.org/10.1080/13611267.2018.1471339

Eagly, A. H., & Chin, J. L. (2010). Diversity and leadership in a changing world. *American Psychologist, 65*, 216–224. http://dx.doi.org/10.1037/a0018957

Ely, K., Boyce, L. A., Nelson, J. K., Zaccaro, S. J., Hernez-Broome, G., & Whyman, W. (2010). Evaluating leadership coaching: A review and integrated framework. *Leadership Quarterly, 21*, 585–599. http://dx.doi.org/10.1016/j.leaqua.2010.06.003

Ely, R. J., Ibarra, H., & Kolb, D. M. (2011). Taking gender into account: Theory and design for women's leadership development programs. *Academy of Management Learning & Education, 10*, 474–493. http://dx.doi.org/10.5465/amle.2010.0046

Fassinger, R. E., & Good, G. E. (2017). Academic leadership and counseling psychology: Answering the challenge, achieving the promise. *Counseling Psychologist, 45*, 752–780. http://dx.doi.org/10.1177/0011000017723081

Fassinger, R. E., & Shullman, S. L. (2017). Leadership and counseling psychology: What should we know? Where could we go? *Counseling Psychologist, 45*, 927–964. http://dx.doi.org/10.1177/0011000017744253

Fassinger, R. E., Shullman, S. L., & Buki, L. P. (2017). Future shock: Counseling psychology in a VUCA world. *Counseling Psychologist, 45*, 1048–1058. http://dx.doi.org/10.1177/0011000017744645

Fisher, R., Ury, W. L., & Patton, B. (2011). *Getting to yes: Negotiating agreement without giving in* (3rd ed.). New York, NY: Penguin Books.

Fouad, N. A., Grus, C. L., Hatcher, R. L., Kaslow, N. J., Hutchings, P. S., Madson, M. B., . . . Crossman, R. E. (2009). Competency benchmarks: A model for the understanding and measuring competence in professional psychology across training levels. *Training and Education in Professional Psychology, 3*(4, Suppl.), S5–S26. http://dx.doi.org/10.1037/a0015832

Frich, J. C., Brewster, A. L., Cherlin, E. J., & Bradley, E. H. (2015). Leadership development programs for physicians: A systematic review. *Journal of General Internal Medicine, 30*, 656–674. http://dx.doi.org/10.1007/s11606-014-3141-1

Greenleaf, R. K. (1998). *The power of servant-leadership*. San Francisco, CA: Berrett-Koehler.

Guthey, E., & Jackson, B. (2011). Cross-cultural leadership revisited. In A. Bryman, D. Collinson, K. Grint, B. Jackson, & M. Uhl-Bien (Eds.), *The SAGE handbook of leadership* (pp. 165–178). Los Angeles, CA: Sage.

Hackman, J. R., & Wageman, R. (2007). Asking the right questions about leadership: Discussions and conclusions. *American Psychologist, 62*, 43–47. http://dx.doi.org/10.1037/0003-066X.62.1.43

Hatcher, R. L., Fouad, N. A., Grus, C. L., Campbell, L. F., McCutcheon, S. R., & Leahy, K. L. (2013). Competency benchmarks: Practical steps toward a culture of competence. *Training and Education in Professional Psychology, 7*, 84–91. http://dx.doi.org/10.1037/a0029401

Helitzer, D. L., Newbill, S. L., Morahan, P. S., Magrane, D., Cardinali, G., Wu, C.-C., & Chang, S. (2014). Perceptions of skill development of participants in three national career development programs for women faculty in academic medicine. *Academic Medicine, 89*, 896–903. http://dx.doi.org/10.1097/ACM.0000000000000251

Hewitt, A. A., Watson, L. B., DeBlaere, C., Dispenza, F., Guzman, C. E., Cadenas, G., . . . Ferdinand, L. (2017). Leadership development in counseling psychology: Voices of Leadership Academy alumni. *Counseling Psychologist, 45*, 992–1016. http://dx.doi.org/10.1177/0011000017740429

Holt, K., & Seki, K. (2012). Global leadership: A developmental shift for everyone. *Industrial and Organizational Psychology: Perspectives on Science and Practice, 5*, 196–215. http://dx.doi.org/10.1111/j.1754-9434.2012.01431.x

Hormann, S. L., & Vivian, P. (2013). *Organizational trauma and healing*. North Charleston, SC: CreateSpace.

Horney, N., Pasmore, B., & O'Shea, T. (2010). Leadership agility: A business imperative for a VUCA world. *Human Resource Planning, 33*, 32–38.

Jacobs, S. C., Huprich, S. K., Grus, C. L., Cage, E. A., Elman, N. S., Forrest, L., . . . Kaslow, N. J. (2011). Trainees with professional competency problems: Preparing trainers for difficult but necessary conversations. *Training and Education in Professional Psychology, 5*, 175–184. http://dx.doi.org/10.1037/a0024656

Jacobs, T. O. (2002). *Strategic leadership: The competitive edge*. Washington, DC: National Defense University, Industrial College of the Armed Forces.

Joo, B. (2005). Executive coaching: A conceptual framework from an integrative review of practice and research. *Human Resource Development Review, 4*, 462–488. http://dx.doi.org/10.1177/1534484305280866

Kaiser, R. B., & Curphy, G. (2013). Leadership development: The failure of an industry and the opportunity for consulting psychologists. *Consulting Psychology Journal: Practice and Research, 65*, 294–302. http://dx.doi.org/10.1037/a0035460

Kaslow, N. J., Borden, K. A., Collins, F. L., Jr., Forrest, L., Illfelder-Kaye, J., Nelson, P. D., . . . Willmuth, M. E. (2004). Competencies Conference: Future Directions in

Education and Credentialing in Professional Psychology. *Journal of Clinical Psychology*, *60*, 699–712. http://dx.doi.org/10.1002/jclp.20016

Kinsinger, P., & Walch, K. (2012, July 9). *Living and leading in a VUCA world*. Phoenix, AZ: Thunderbird University.

Lee, A. V., Vargo, J., & Seville, E. (2013). Developing a tool to measure and compare organizations' resilience. *Natural Hazards Review*, *14*, 29–41. http://dx.doi.org/10.1061/(ASCE)NH.1527-6996.0000075

Lucas, R., Goldman, E. F., Scott, A. R., & Dandar, V. (2018). Leadership development programs at academic health centers: Results of a national survey. *Academic Medicine*, *93*, 229–236. http://dx.doi.org/10.1097/ACM.0000000000001813

Mallinckrodt, B., Miles, J. R., & Levy, J. J. (2014). The scientist-practitioner-advocate model: Addressing contemporary training needs for social justice advocacy. *Training and Education in Professional Psychology*, *8*, 303–311. http://dx.doi.org/10.1037/tep0000045

McCleskey, J. A. (2014). Situational, transformational, and transactional leadership and leadership development. *Journal of Business Studies Quarterly*, *5*, 117–130.

McDade, S. A., Richman, R. C., Jackson, G. B., & Morahan, P. S. (2004). Effects of participation in the Executive Leadership in Academic Medicine (ELAM) program on women faculty's perceived leadership capabilities. *Academic Medicine*, *79*, 302–309. http://dx.doi.org/10.1097/00001888-200404000-00005

McManus, S. E., Seville, E., Vargo, J., & Brunsdon, D. (2008). Facilitated process for improving organizational resilience. *Natural Hazards Review*, *9*, 81–90. http://dx.doi.org/10.1061/(ASCE)1527-6988(2008)9:2(81)

Morahan, P. S., Gleason, K. A., Richman, R. C., Dannels, S. A., & McDade, S. A. (2010). Advancing women faculty to senior leadership in U.S. academic health centers: Fifteen years of history in the making. *NASPA Journal About Women in Higher Education*, *3*, 140–165. http://dx.doi.org/10.2202/1940-7890.1042

Myers, I. B. (with Myers, P. B.). (2010). *Gifts differing: Understanding personality type*. Mountain View, CA: Davies-Black.

Nembhard, I. M., & Edmondson, A. C. (2006). Making it safe: The effects of leader inclusiveness and professional status on psychological safety and improvement efforts in health care teams. *Journal of Organizational Behavior*, *27*, 941–966. http://dx.doi.org/10.1002/job.413

Olaniyan, O. S., & Hystad, S. W. (2016). Employees' psychological capital, job satisfaction, insecurity, and intentions to quit: The direct and indirect effects of authentic leadership. *Journal of Work and Organizational Psychology*, *32*, 163–171. http://dx.doi.org/10.1016/j.rpto.2016.09.003

Paustian-Underdahl, S. C., Walker, L. S., & Woehr, D. J. (2014). Gender and perceptions of leadership effectiveness: A meta-analysis of contextual moderators. *Journal of Applied Psychology*, *99*, 1129–1145. http://dx.doi.org/10.1037/a0036751

Phillips, J. C., Hargons, C., Chung, Y. B., Forrest, L., Oh, K. H., & Westefeld, J. (2017). Society of Counseling Psychology Leadership Academy: Cultivating leadership competence and community. *Counseling Psychologist*, *45*, 965–991. http://dx.doi.org/10.1177/0011000017736141

Piccolo, R. F., Bono, J. E., Heinitz, J. R., Rowold, J., Duehr, E., & Judge, T. A. (2012). The relative impact of complementary leader behaviors: Which matter most? *Leadership Quarterly*, *23*, 567–581. http://dx.doi.org/10.1016/j.leaqua.2011.12.008

Pingleton, S. K., Jones, E. V. M., Rosolowski, T. A., & Zimmerman, M. K. (2016). Silent bias: Challenges, obstacles, and strategies for leadership development in academic medicine—Lessons from oral histories of women professors at the University of Kansas. *Academic Medicine*, *91*, 1151–1157. http://dx.doi.org/10.1097/ACM.0000000000001125

Raimy, V. C. (Ed.). (1950). *Training in clinical psychology*. New York, NY: Prentice Hall.

Randel, A. E., Galvin, B. M., Shore, L. M., Ehrhart, K. H., Chung, B. G., Dean, M. A., & Kedharnath, U. (2018). Inclusive leadership: Realizing positive outcomes through belongingness and being valued for uniqueness. *Human Resource Management Review, 28,* 190–203. http://dx.doi.org/10.1016/j.hrmr.2017.07.002

Rodolfa, E. R., Bent, R. J., Eisman, E., Nelson, P., Rehm, L., & Ritchie, P. (2005). A cube model for competency development: Implications for psychology educators and regulators. *Professional Psychology: Research and Practice, 36,* 347–354. http://dx.doi.org/10.1037/0735-7028.36.4.347

Romager, J. A., Hughes, K., & Trimble, J. E. (2017). Personality traits as predictors of leadership style preferences: Investigating the relationship between social dominance orientation and attitudes towards authentic leaders. *Social Behavior Research and Practice Open Journal, 3,* 1–9. http://dx.doi.org/10.17140/SBRPOJ-3-110

Sanchez-Hucles, J. V., & Davis, D. D. (2010). Women and women of color in leadership: Complexity, identity, and intersectionality. *American Psychologist, 65,* 171–181. http://dx.doi.org/10.1037/a0017459

Schultz, W. C. (1958). *FIRO: A three-dimensional theory of interpersonal behavior.* New York, NY: Holt, Rinehart & Winston.

Seidle, B., Fernandez, S., & Perry, J. L. (2016). Do leadership training and development make a difference in the public sector? A panel study. *Public Administration Review, 76,* 603–613. http://dx.doi.org/10.1111/puar.12531

Şen, A., Kabak, K. E., & Yanginlar, G. (2013). Courageous leadership for the twenty-first century. *Procedia: Social and Behavioral Sciences, 75,* 91–101. http://dx.doi.org/10.1016/j.sbspro.2013.04.011

Shullman, S. L. (2017). Leadership and counseling psychology: Dilemmas, ambiguities, and possibilities. *Counseling Psychologist, 45,* 910–926. http://dx.doi.org/10.1177/0011000017744644

Solansky, S. T. (2010). The evaluation of two key leadership development program components: Leadership skills assessment and leadership mentoring. *Leadership Quarterly, 21,* 675–681. http://dx.doi.org/10.1016/j.leaqua.2010.06.009

Sonnino, R. E. (2016). Health care leadership development and training: Progress and pitfalls. *Journal of Healthcare Leadership, 8,* 19–29. http://dx.doi.org/10.2147/JHL.S68068

Stein, H. F. (2017). *Listen deeply: An approach to understanding and consulting in organizational culture* (2nd ed.). Columbia: University of Missouri Press.

Sternberg, R. J. (2007). A systems model of leadership: WICS. *American Psychologist, 62,* 34–42. http://dx.doi.org/10.1037/0003-066X.62.1.34

Stone, D., Patton, B., & Heen, S. (2010). *Difficult conversations: How to discuss what matters most (10th-anniversary edition).* New York, NY: Penguin.

Sugiyama, K., Cavanagh, K. V., van Esch, C., Bilimoria, D., & Brown, C. (2016). Inclusive leadership development: Drawing from pedagogies of women's and general leadership development programs. *Journal of Management Education, 40,* 253–292. http://dx.doi.org/10.1177/1052562916632553

Swing, S. R. (2002). Assessing the ACGME general competencies: General considerations and assessment methods. *Academic Emergency Medicine, 9,* 1278–1288. http://dx.doi.org/10.1197/aemj.9.11.1278

Tedeschi, R. G., & Calhoun, L. G. (2004). Posttraumatic growth: Conceptual foundations and empirical evidence. *Psychological Inquiry, 15,* 1–18. http://dx.doi.org/10.1207/s15327965pli1501_01

Thompson, A. A., Peteraf, M. A., Gamble, J. E., & Strickland, A. J., III. (2013). *Crafting & executing strategy: The quest for competitive advantage: Concepts and cases* (19th ed.). New York, NY: McGraw-Hill.

Ting, S. A., & Hart, E. W. (2004). Formal coaching. In C. D. McCauley & E. V. Velsor (Eds.), *The Center for Creative Leadership handbook of leadership development* (pp. 116–150). San Francisco, CA: Wiley.

Toor, S.-U.-R., & Ofori, G. (2008). Leadership versus management: How they are different, and why. *Leadership and Management in Engineering, 8,* 61–71. http://dx.doi.org/10.1061/(ASCE)1532-6748(2008)8:2(61)

Truijen, K. J. P., & van Woerkom, M. (2008). The pitfalls of collegial coaching. *Journal of Workplace Learning, 20,* 316–326. http://dx.doi.org/10.1108/13665620810882923

van Dierendonck, D. (2011). Servant leadership: A review and synthesis. *Journal of Management, 37,* 1228–1261. http://dx.doi.org/10.1177/0149206310380462

van Dierendonck, D., & Nuijten, I. (2011). The Servant Leadership Survey: Development and validation of a multidimensional measure. *Journal of Business and Psychology, 26,* 249–267. http://dx.doi.org/10.1007/s10869-010-9194-1

VanVactor, J. D. (2012). Collaborative leadership model in the management of health care. *Journal of Business Research, 65,* 555–561. http://dx.doi.org/10.1016/j.jbusres.2011.02.021

Vroom, V. H., & Jago, A. G. (2007). The role of the situation in leadership. *American Psychologist, 62,* 17–24. http://dx.doi.org/10.1037/0003-066X.62.1.17

Walumbwa, F. O., Avolio, B. J., Gardner, W. L., Wernsing, T. S., & Peterson, S. J. (2008). Authentic leadership: Development and validation of a theory-based measure. *Journal of Management, 34,* 89–126. http://dx.doi.org/10.1177/0149206307308913

Wasylyshyn, K. M. (2015). The trusted leadership advisor: Another view from the bridge between business and psychology. *Consulting Psychology Journal: Practice and Research, 67,* 279–297. http://dx.doi.org/10.1037/cpb0000050

# 10

# Consultation in Corporations and Organizations

Rodney L. Lowman

Most health care delivery—direct patient service as well as consultation—takes place in the context of organizations, many of which are large and complicated. Add to that the government's extensive direct and indirect involvement in health care delivery and it becomes clear that there is more to functioning effectively in health service psychology (HSP) delivery than just being a competent service provider. Yet, despite increasing involvement of psychologists in consultation (e.g., Cooper, Newman, & Fuqua, 2012), they appear to rarely receive graduate training in team or organizational psychology either before or after receiving their doctoral degrees. Although the *Standards for Accreditation for Health Service Psychology* (American Psychological Association [APA], 2018) requires coverage in social bases of behavior, such course work primarily focuses on social aspects, primarily of individual-level behavior, an important but only partially relevant competency in consultation. The *Standards for Accreditation* (APA, 2018) requires training in consultation; however, consultation is not explicitly defined, so it could include consulting to individual clients on HSP-related issues or, conceivably, also include consulting to the organizations through which HSP services are delivered.

This chapter focuses on organizational consulting in the context of corporations and with a particular focus on health care companies. In addition to delineating the competencies required, I make a plea for health service psychologists to widen their perspectives to better understand—and be able to function effectively and to work within—the context in which their services

http://dx.doi.org/10.1037/0000153-011
*Consultation in Psychology: A Competency-Based Approach*, C. A. Falender and E. P. Shafranske (Editors)

are delivered, which, almost inevitably in today's world, is in and through organizations.

This book itself represents a step forward in the recognition that consulting skills are important in becoming a fully competent health service psychologist. This chapter introduces a unique area of consultation and, as such, aims to delineate some of the territory to be traversed in doing such work. It would be naive to think that a single chapter—or book, for that matter—is a sufficient basis to become a consulting psychologist, much less one who is competent in consulting to corporations. (For a more detailed overview of consulting psychology, see Lowman, 2016b, *An Introduction to Consulting Psychology: Working With Individuals, Groups, and Organizations*; APA, 2017; Cooper et al., 2012; Lowman, 2002).

Judging from their training standards and curricula, health service psychologists spend a lot of time in their professional training programs learning about the role of normal and aberrant human behavior in health, well-being, and dysfunction. By analogy, for those who would consult to corporations and other organizations, the need is to spend time learning about the various components of organizations (for consulting psychologists, the three levels of individuals, groups, and organizations and the many components of each of these levels that provide a useful organizing device by which to map the territory; see Lowman, 2016a, 2016b).

As in the HSP area, much of psychology's contributions to understanding human behavior in organizations and in consulting have been focused on the individual level, for example, What competencies are needed for work performance? What attracts individuals to particular lines of work, jobs, or organizations? What are the best predictors of success on the job? A slimmer but important literature also exists on groups or teams in organizations (e.g., Hackman, 1989) and less still at the organizational level (Katz & Kahn, 1978). Knowledge of organizations is not just about what psychology can contribute to or readily understand about that enterprise. Accounting, finance, marketing, legal, and control systems are also important factors that help determine whether an organization will survive and thrive, and psychologist–consultants need to know enough about those areas to assess when expertise other than theirs is what is called for to address or fix a problem.

## KNOWLEDGE, SKILLS, AND ABILITIES IN CONSULTATION

In the vast literature on personnel selection (mostly created by industrial and organizational [I/O] psychologists; see Farr & Tippins, 2017), most approaches begin with a job analysis. From the list of job duties in the job analysis, knowledge, skills, abilities, and other characteristics (e.g., personality, interests) are identified. The assessment measures that subsequently are identified must be tied to the job dimensions, and there must be some underlying evidence of an empirical or other demonstrable relationship between the predictors and the criteria, or outcome, measures.

It is not surprising, then, that the fields of I/O and consulting psychology emphasize the importance of competencies in their respective educational and training guidelines. Indeed, in its *Guidelines for Education and Training in Industrial-Organizational Psychology*, the Society for Industrial and Organizational Psychology (SIOP, 2016) identified 26 competencies that may be included in the training of I/O psychologists at the master's level, doctoral level, or both. Among these are the following "professional competencies": "Effective consulting encompasses problem-solving and decision-making skills, communicating solutions in layperson's terms, selling products and services, developing and maintaining relationships with clients, and providing high quality customer service" (SIOP, 2016, p. 7).

Clearly in the SIOP (2016) training guidelines, organizational consulting is not a stand-alone competency but builds on a broad and extensive knowledge base and on competencies from the broader field of I/O and consulting psychology. One cannot simply learn a few consulting-specific skills and be able to be professionally competent.

Far more detailed are the APA (2017) training guidelines on consulting psychology, *Guidelines for Education and Training at the Doctoral and Postdoctoral Level in Consulting Psychology (CP)/Organizational Psychology (OCP)*. These guidelines provide a detailed summary of the competencies needed in this work at the individual, group, and organizational levels.

With the understanding, then, that the purpose of this chapter is not to suggest a quick or painless way to retrain professionals from one area of psychology to another, I identify generic knowledge, skills, attitudes, and other characteristics that are important for not only those who consult to corporations but also those who work in organizations.

## FOUNDATIONAL KNOWLEDGE FOR ORGANIZATIONAL CONSULTING PSYCHOLOGISTS

This section provides a brief overview of the fundamental knowledge that is important for consulting psychologists to have. It discusses the role of organizational mission and purpose and the relationship of the organization to its environment.

### The Role of Organizational Mission and Purpose

Fundamental to many aspects of organizations is their mission. Organizations exist to serve a useful purpose that someone in the world—clients or customers—finds of value. That purpose may be complex or simple, but it colors all aspects of the organization and determines, in part, the values likely to predominate. In the case of not-for-profits, emphasis may be more on providing services to those needing health care with a sliding scale that determines fees. A for-profit institution, say, a pharmaceutical manufacturer, may have its primary mission to delivery profits to shareholders, but it still must do that through providing a product of value with respect to health care. Among health care organizations, there are also for-profit organizations, not-for-profit, nongovernmental organizations, and government-run ones. Consultants need to know what the mission of the organization is, just as do employees, and how well it is fulfilling that mission.

## The Relationship of the Organization to Its Environment

Organizations thrive, struggle, or die in the context of an environment. In a classic book on organizations as systems, Katz and Kahn (1978) influenced generations of consultants with their application of systems theory to organizations. Organizations rely on their environment for inputs necessary to fulfill their mission and, in turn, must be able to successfully disperse their products and services into an environment. Therefore, to understand the behavior of organizations and of the people within them, consulting psychologists need also to understand the industry and trends in which the organization exists. They must learn the major players or competitors in that environment, where the organization fits into the broader competitive network, the role of the larger economy and its impact on that type of industry, and the particular environmental stressors organizations in that sector are experiencing.

Country and region also matter. Organizations delivering health services in the United States, for example, must successfully navigate a particularly complex health organization environment (e.g., "ACA Still Plagued by Uncertainty," 2017). Wildly dynamic changes have occurred with the role of government in funding health care; many believe in the importance of having free access to entrepreneurial development with the premise that better health care solutions will come from innovation (e.g., Lehoux, Miller, Daudelin, & Denis, 2017). In other industries, the current market forces may suggest an industry is on the decline (e.g., fossil fuels versus renewable energy), or on a meteoric rise (information technology and apps). Environmental factors influence whether the organization is under the stress of decline, experiencing steep growth, or is relatively quiescent. Knowing the economic forces with which the organization is striving to cope is be helpful in understanding the sources of stress within the organization. And although corporations may seem like hefty behemoths that will be around forever, those perceptions belie a fragility reflected in the finding that, of the Fortune 500 companies from the early 1950s, only 12% are still in business today (Perry, 2016).

As for health care organizations, many aspects of the environment are influential. Whatever their political affiliation, psychologists and psychologists-in-training would be hard pressed in today's world not to be aware of the influence that political realities have on affecting their ability to deliver health services. Shrinking resources to fund service delivery and for research into the causes and cures of health dysfunctions as well as the factors leading to health promotion have real consequences on psychologists' ability to deliver their services. Yet, this is just another way to say that psychological services are influenced by group, organizational, and societal forces.

## FOUNDATIONAL KNOWLEDGE FOR ORGANIZATIONAL CONSULTING PSYCHOLOGY

Organizational consultants need to learn about three major levels: individual, group, and organizational.

### Individual-Level Consulting

In a classic and influential article entitled "The People Make the Place," Schneider (1987) presented a framework noting an attraction-selection-attrition cycle. That cycle derives, he stated, from individuals' being attracted to particular types of work that match their interests and personality. In turn, the character of organizations (and the ease with which change can be made) is significantly influenced by the types of people who end up in the organization. Organizations are not random collections of individuals but rather have characteristics associated with the nature of the work (see Lowman, 2016b). It follows that the structures, values, and functional processes assume particular characteristics.

At the individual level, consulting psychologists need to understand individuals not from the perspective of psychopathology (except when relevant) but rather by using assessment and intervention models that derive from work-related individual difference variables, in particular, occupational interests, abilities (broadly defined), and personality (mostly using models of normal personality; see Lowman, 1991, 1993). They work with individuals to determine match to jobs or organizations and to help them improve themselves in the context of their work.

### The Group Level: Working With and in Teams

Much of the world's work is performed in and through work groups or teams. It follows that consultants to organizations need to be competent in understanding group-level phenomena. These phenomena can be complex and are different than individual dynamics (e.g., Freedman & Leonard, 2002; Wheelan, 2005). Groups can be a target of assessment or intervention, or they can be part of a more complicated project in which the interaction among teams, team leadership, or the intersection of teams and the larger organization is the focus. Alternatively, an organization may be creating a structure in which teams are purposefully being set up to have more decision-making authority. Considerable research is available now on team science and research-based approaches to teams (Salas et al., 2015; Thayer, Rico, Salas, & Marlow, 2014). The work of health care teams has increasingly been shown to affect patient outcome variables (e.g., Averbukh & Southern, 2014). An important part of this work is taking into account multicultural and international team composition (see Lopez & Ensari, 2013; Lowman, 2013, 2014).

### Organizational-Level Consulting

Consulting at the organizational level involves large-scale organizational change efforts; assessments, particularly of the "people aspects" of the organization; consulting with key decision makers in the organization on issues that affect multiple aspects of the organization; and helping to set up organizational systems to measure process or performance-related outcomes. For example, a consulting psychologist might be hired to conduct annual surveys of workplace motivation, morale, and perceptions of management. Through the collection of those data (e.g., Mohrman & Lawler, 2012), they identify patterns needing systemic attention or parts of the organization that are functioning less effectively on the variables of interest. Psychologists may then be part of the process of intervention. In time, they may train managers and internal consultants to create a culture in which data are routinely collected, analyzed, and acted on.

## STRUCTURE, SUBPARTS, AND FOCAL ISSUES OF ORGANIZATIONS

In this section, I note that organizations, however large and complex they may be, also consist of smaller parts that may be the focus of the consultation. Then, I identify some well-studied issues in organizational psychology that are potential challenges for organizations.

### Structure and Subparts

Except for very small organizations, those of any size have structures that divide the day-to-day work into smaller parts. These subparts of organizations also have their specific missions and purposes that are usually subordinate to, but aligned with, the organization's larger mission. It is unlikely that consulting psychologists will work with the entirety of a huge corporation, such as Google, Walmart, or AT&T. Rather, they typically will work with a business unit. Alternatively, they will work with a collection of smaller units, such as all the accounting departments across multiple locations. Issues to be addressed in the smaller units may differ from when consulting to the organization as a whole. Although productivity issues may be relevant, some situations may involve difficulties with the team members' getting along or challenges with a leader whose style is abrasive or mismatched with those of the members.

Organizational psychologists have spent decades studying and working with aspects of work that, if functioning well, are likely to improve performance and productivity or, if problematic, to impair it. Here, I identify a few of these areas to provide the reader with a brief introduction to the types of issues with which organizational consultants are likely to be involved.

## Focal Issues

### Work Motivation

Successful organizations are able to channel employees' knowledge, skills, and abilities into the work needs of the organization. When workers are not well motivated or when they feel underpaid or underappreciated, the work and organizational performance are likely to suffer. Health service psychologists and many others in the health professions are intrinsically motivated to help. However, when they are kept from doing their jobs due to bureaucratic over-control or feel underappreciated by the organization, motivation (and the quality of care provided to patients) can suffer. Psychologists have extensively studied work motivation (e.g., Perreira, Innis, & Berta, 2016), and there is also a literature specific to work motivation in health care organizations and among particular health care professionals (e.g., Toode, Routasalo, & Suominen, 2011).

### Person–Group and Person–Organization Fit

In most cases, the job and the work to be done is a given; the person who does the work is not. The nature of the work is typically reflected in a formal job analysis (e.g., Pearlman & Sanchez, 2017). The degree to which individuals are well suited for the work and position can be a matter for formal assessment and selection using psychological measures of interests, abilities, and personality, or less systematic and less well-validated approaches can be used. Job-relatedness is a critical construct that consultants need to understand and work to assure. When people are unhappy or ineffective in their work roles, one of the first questions to be asked by consultants is, Why? Modally, a poor supervisor is often the source of individual-level unhappiness (e.g., Chen & Wang, 2017; Zenger & Folkman, 2012). Still, many other reasons may include that the person is ill suited to the position by virtue of interests, abilities, or personality. As in HSP, there is a need to assess the problem using psychological expertise and knowledge and to help determine a solution likely to work.

### Leadership

Leaders and managers exert considerable control over what happens in an organization. They also control the purse strings that determine which consultants should be hired and which should not. In addition, when consultants are able to positively influence leaders, those leaders, in turn, can make a difference in how the organization functions and in the well-being of subordinates. For example, helping an overly controlling, angry leader change his or her behavior and relate more positively to his or her employees and peers can influence the work lives of many people besides the focal manager. The leader can make a large difference in whether employees feel positive and wanted or exploited and abused (Skinner & Spurgeon, 2005). Values and behavior matter and, to some extent, are trainable (e.g., Vaux & Gamble, 2014).

### Work Performance

Work outcomes relate to the purposes of the organization. Establishing reliable and valid processes for measuring work and organizational outcomes is a skill of

I/O and consulting psychologists (Borman, Grossman, Bryant, & Dorio, 2017). However, whether consulting psychologists help to create such measures or simply make use of already established ones, they need to be focused on goals that largely are determined by the organization and on which there is consensus. The literature increasingly is showing a connection between individual-level variables (e.g., strain, stress, group and organizational climate, well-being) and team- and organizational-level outcomes (see Albrecht, 2012; Harter, Schmidt, & Keyes, 2003); these outcomes also need to be taken into account.

## Multiculturalism in Corporations

Undoubtedly, American health service psychologists have been well trained in U.S.-centric models of multiculturalism; their training standards require it. However, corporations themselves constitute a different type of multiculturalism. The difference relates to the purpose of the organization that, in turn, attracts people with relevant skills, interests, and abilities. The focus and purpose of the organization create a culture and subcultures. Health care organizations, for example, typically include a combination of helpers; technical expertise; and people with highly specific, evidence-based knowledge (see Lowman, 1991, 1993). In addition, complex organizations usually are international in scope, introducing a new set of diversity issues that blend internationalism and learning about new cultures (see Lowman, 2013, 2014).

## Power and Politics

Power in organizations is differentially exercised; with that process comes organizational politics (see Cairns, 2017). *Politics* is the process of trying to exercise influence and to build alliances and coalitions that, in turn, exercise power and influence. There are those (including many psychologists) who may regard all such efforts as ethically challenged and, well, dirty. Yet, consulting psychologists have to become experts at understanding the power dynamics of organizations—who has power, who had it, who is trying to get it, and the issues and conflicts that those quests create within the organizations. As psychologists, consultants need to be able to seek common ground and to avoid aligning themselves solely with dominant power coalitions. Physicians in hospitals, for example, usually have the most power of the medical providers, but within that group, there are many power differentials. Moreover, physician leaders may have less influence than certain administrators. The consultant's job is not to make power differentials go away; it is to help organizations be more effective at using all of their resources, including the various stakeholder groups.

## TECHNICAL SKILLS AND TOOLS OF THE TRADE

Consulting psychologists need to know how to, or to work with those who know how to, conduct interviews, surveys, focused assessments, individual assessments related to work, coaching, conflict management, and a variety of other skills. Here are a few of them.

## Assessments

Assessments provide an efficient way to ascertain employees' attitudes, work motivation, and engagement. Indeed, one of the most famous surveys—still in use now—of presidential opinion polling was created by psychologist George Gallup. After Gallup's death, his company was bought out by the company, Selection Research, of another psychologist, Donald O. Clifton (see Lowman, 2004). Clifton, who would later be one of the creators of the StrengthsFinder™ (see Buckingham & Clifton, 2005) and an architect of the positive psychology movement, built a large and thriving assessment firm. Consulting psychologists need assessment skills at the individual, group, and organizational levels.

## Interventions

A wide range of interventions is available to organizational and consulting psychologists (e.g., Lowman, 2002). Again, these interventions vary by level but can include, at the individual level, coaching, interventions with groups, and team building; and at the organizational level, board development, survey feedback, organization-wide or systemic interventions, talent management, and strategic planning. These are only representative of many other types of interventions with which consultants may become involved. One important issue is that consultants will often be providing services in for-profit organizations. Many psychologists may be conflicted about working with such organizations; and just as I/O psychologists may be overly identified with business values (versus psychology's values), the reverse may be the case for those whose primary work has been with individual-level mental health and health issues (see Lefkowitz, 2017). Consultation to for-profit organizations may not be the right choice of professional activities for psychologists who cannot respect business values while retaining their values as psychologists.

## PROCESS ASPECTS OF CONSULTATION

I have intentionally saved process aspects of consultation until last because process consultation skills are often in high supply among health service psychologists. Still, those skills should not be considered as a sufficient basis alone on which to consult with corporations.

   As in most forms of consultation, being able to establish and maintain a consulting relationship is a primary competency. The relationship in working with executives is not a therapy relationship, although having and being able to communicate understanding of, and caring about, the organization, including managers and major stakeholders alike, are important. The relationship cannot be established, however, or maintained if the perception of competence in the assessment or intervention is not communicated from the beginning. By and large, corporate consultation is engaged with executives or managers who make their living by being able to evaluate data and people and make decisions, often quickly, about actions to take or not to take. Canned approaches or process approaches (e.g., "Well, what do you think the solution is?"), if that is all that can be offered, are not going to be a solid basis for a relationship. Rather, those making the decisions to contract or hire consultants need—quickly—to be convinced that the consulting psychologist knows what he or she is talking about and is a good fit for the particular organization and players. Consultants can be expected to be tested from the beginning of every engagement as to whether the clients wish to engage with them. Considerable due diligence will likely have gone into the decision even to interview a prospective service provider. Those who are not competent or sufficiently well trained for the work will likely not be chosen to consult or, if later discovered, to continue consultation.

It is not just managers and executives with whom consultants must be able to engage. They must learn how to work effectively with individuals and groups at all levels of the organization, including board members. Learning how to facilitate meetings with first-line supervisors and hourly workers is as important as being able to be taken seriously by those at higher levels of the organization. Senior managers will see the ability to collect data objectively and dispassionately as a value added and something that is often difficult for managers or executives to do. Consulting psychologists are not there to take sides or to be advocates; their dispassion, objectivity, and ability to care about all in the organization help them facilitate the organization's processes. Sometimes that facilitation involves "speaking truth to power"; always it involves excellent listening skills and being able to engage with a variety of people in a variety of positions and at a variety of levels in a fair-minded way.

Consulting psychology (Lowman, 2016b) has long recognized that interpersonal and process consulting skills are an important part of psychologist's set of skills and competencies (see Schein, 2013). It also takes this recognition a step further in suggesting that consulting skills require a paradigm shift from learning how to assess and treat at the individual level to better understand how to affect and influence organizations themselves in which service delivery is embedded. And one does not have to become an organizational consulting psychologist to appreciate that organizations matter in terms of peoples' lives.

Psychologists who consult to organizations—businesses and corporations, not-for-profit organizations, government, and nongovernmental organizations—are not managers. They are not experts in marketing, accounting, or information technology—all of which are important functions in helping an organization to run smoothly.

## SUMMARY AND CONCLUSION

This chapter has provided an introduction, or primer, to some aspects involved in consulting to corporations, especially in the health care arena. Well-trained organizational and consulting psychologists can help organizations be more effective with the human side of enterprise. Health service psychologists with limited knowledge of organizations can, with proper supervision, also provide a limited range of services within their competencies. Psychologists who can move beyond individual conceptualizations and who can work effectively with groups, teams, and organizations have a great opportunity to influence a broad range of stakeholders and organizations to be more effective.

I have not met many health service psychologists who started out to become organizational or corporate consultants. However, I know a number of health service psychologists and mental health psychologists who worked at the individual level for a number of years and became frustrated at the small sphere of influence they were having with one-on-one work. Over time, they became effective, well-regarded organizational consultants. They were able to learn to think at the group and organizational levels and to meld their original training with new training. Either they knew their limits or they retrained to overcome their areas of deficiency.

Health service organizations need psychologists' expertise as never before. For those with passion for the work to be done and the willingness to learn, the opportunities to make meaningful contributions are wide ranging.

## REFERENCES

ACA still plagued by uncertainty. (2017, August 21). *Chain Drug Review, 39*(12), 1–8.

Albrecht, S. L. (2012). The influence of job, team and organizational level resources on employee well-being, engagement, commitment and extra-role performance: Test of a model. *International Journal of Manpower, 33*, 840–853. http://dx.doi.org/10.1108/01437721211268357

American Psychological Association. (2017). *Guidelines for education and training at the doctoral and postdoctoral level in consulting psychology (CP)/organizational psychology (OCP).* Retrieved from https://www.apa.org/about/policy/education-training.pdf

American Psychological Association, Commission on Accreditation. (2018). *Standards of accreditation for health service psychology.* Retrieved from http://www.apa.org/ed/accreditation/about/policies/standards-of-accreditation.pdf

Averbukh, Y., & Southern, W. (2014). A "reverse July effect": Association between timing of admission, medical team workload, and 30-day readmission rate. *Journal of Graduate Medical Education, 6*, 65–70. http://dx.doi.org/10.4300/JGME-D-13-00014.1

Borman, W. C., Grossman, M. R., Bryant, R. H., & Dorio, J. (2017). The measurement of task performance as criteria in selection research. In J. L. Farr & N. T. Tippins (Eds.), *Handbook of employee selection* (2nd ed., pp. 439–462). New York, NY: Routledge.

Buckingham, M., & Clifton, D. O. (2005). *Now, discover your strengths: How to develop your talents and those of the people you manage.* Omaha, NE: Gallup Press.

Cairns, T. D. (2017). Power, politics, and leadership in the workplace. *Employment Relations Today, 43*, 5–11. http://dx.doi.org/10.1002/ert.21598

Chen, Z-x., & Wang, H-y. (2017). Abusive supervision and employees' job performance: A multiple mediation model. *Social Behavior and Personality: An International Journal, 45*, 845–858. http://dx.doi.org/10.2224/sbp.5657

Cooper, S. E., Newman, J. L., & Fuqua, D. R. (2012). Counseling psychologists as consultants. In N. A. Fouad, J. A. Carter, & L. M. Subich (Eds.), *APA handbook of counseling psychology: Vol. 2. Practice, interventions, and applications* (pp. 515–539). Washington, DC: American Psychological Association. http://dx.doi.org/10.1037/13755-021

Farr, J. L., & Tippins, N. T. (Eds.). (2017). *Handbook of employee selection* (2nd ed.). New York, NY: Routledge.

Freedman, A. M., & Leonard, E. S. (2002). Organizational consulting to groups and teams. In R. L. Lowman (Ed.), *Handbook of organizational consulting psychology: A comprehensive guide to theory, skills, and techniques* (pp. 27–53). San Francisco, CA: Jossey-Bass.

Hackman, J. R. (1989). *Groups that work (and those that don't): Creating conditions for effective teamwork.* New York, NY: Wiley.

Harter, J. K., Schmidt, F. L., & Keyes, C. L. M. (2003). Well-being in the workplace and its relationship to business outcomes: A review of the Gallup studies. In C. L. M. Keyes & J. Haidt (Eds.), *Flourishing: Positive psychology and the life well-lived* (pp. 205–224). Washington, DC: American Psychological Association. http://dx.doi.org/10.1037/10594-009

Katz, D., & Kahn, R. L. (1978). *The social psychology of organizations* (2nd ed.). New York, NY: Wiley.

Lefkowitz, J. (2017). *Ethics and values in industrial-organizational psychology* (2nd ed.). New York, NY: Routledge.

Lehoux, P., Miller, F. A., Daudelin, G., & Denis, J.-L. (2017). Providing value to new health technology: The early contribution of entrepreneurs, investors, and regulatory agencies. *International Journal of Health Policy and Management, 6,* 509–518. http://dx.doi.org/10.15171/ijhpm.2017.11

Lopez, P. D., & Ensari, N. (2013). Fostering multiculturally and internationally competent individuals and teams. In R. L. Lowman (Ed.), *Internationalizing multiculturalism: Expanding professional competencies in a globalized world* (pp. 173–198). Washington, DC: American Psychological Association. http://dx.doi.org/10.1037/14044-007

Lowman, R. L. (1991). *The clinical practice of career assessment: Interests, abilities, and personality.* Washington, DC: American Psychological Association.

Lowman, R. L. (1993). The inter-domain model of career assessment and counseling. *Journal of Counseling & Development, 71,* 549–554. http://dx.doi.org/10.1002/j.1556-6676.1993.tb02240.x

Lowman, R. L. (Ed.). (2002). *Handbook of organizational consulting psychology: A comprehensive guide to theory, skills, and techniques.* San Francisco, CA: Jossey-Bass.

Lowman, R. L. (2004). Donald O. Clifton (1924–2003). *American Psychologist, 59,* 180. http://dx.doi.org/10.1037/0003-066X.59.3.180

Lowman, R. L. (Ed.). (2013). *Internationalizing multiculturalism: Expanding professional competencies in a globalized world.* Washington, DC: American Psychological Association. http://dx.doi.org/10.1037/14044-000

Lowman, R. L. (2014). Multicultural and international issues in organizational change and development. In F. T. L. Leong, L. Comas-Diaz, G. C. Nagayama Hall, V. C. McLoyd, & J. E. Trimble (Eds.), *APA handbook of multicultural psychology: Vol. 2. Applications and training* (pp. 627–639). Washington, DC: American Psychological Association. http://dx.doi.org/10.1037/14187-035

Lowman, R. L. (2016a). Business and other organizations. In J. C. Norcross, G. R. VandenBos, & D. K. Freedheim (Eds.), *Handbook of clinical psychology: Vol. 1. Roots and branches* (pp. 477–493). Washington, DC: American Psychological Association.

Lowman, R. L. (2016b). *An introduction to consulting psychology: Working with individuals, groups, and organizations.* Washington, DC: American Psychological Association.

Mohrman, S. A., & Lawler, E. E. (2012). Generating knowledge that drives change. *Academy of Management Perspectives, 26,* 41–51. http://dx.doi.org/10.5465/amp.2011.0141

Pearlman, K., & Sanchez, J. I. (2017). Work analysis. In J. L. Farr, & N. T. Tippins (Eds.), *Handbook of employee selection* (2nd ed., pp. 73–98). New York, NY: Routledge.

Perreira, T. A., Innis, J., & Berta, W. (2016). Work motivation in health care: A scoping literature review. *International Journal of Evidence-Based Healthcare, 14,* 175–182. http://dx.doi.org/10.1097/XEB.0000000000000093

Perry, M. J. (2016, December 13). Fortune 500 firms 1955 v. 2016: Only 12% remain, thanks to the creative destruction that fuels economic prosperity. Retrieved from http://www.aei.org/publication/fortune-500-firms-1955-v-2016-only-12-remain-thanks-to-the-creative-destruction-that-fuels-economic-prosperity/

Salas, E., Benishek, L., Coultas, C., Dietz, A., Grossman, R., Lazzara, E., & Oglesby, J. (2015). *Team training essentials: A research-based guide*. New York, NY: Routledge.

Schein, E. H. (2013). *Humble inquiry: The gentle art of asking instead of telling*. San Francisco, CA: Berrett-Koehler.

Schneider, B. (1987). The people make the place. *Personnel Psychology, 40*, 437–453. http://dx.doi.org/10.1111/j.1744-6570.1987.tb00609.x

Skinner, C., & Spurgeon, P. (2005). Valuing empathy and emotional intelligence in health leadership: A study of empathy, leadership behaviour and outcome effectiveness. *Health Services Management Research, 18*, 1–12. http://dx.doi.org/10.1258/0951484053051924

Society for Industrial and Organizational Psychology. (2016). *Guidelines for education and training in industrial-organizational psychology*. Bowling Green, OH: Author.

Thayer, A. L., Rico, R., Salas, E., & Marlow, S. L. (2014). Teams at work. In M. C. W. Peeters, J. de Jonge, & T. W. Taris (Eds.), *An introduction to contemporary work psychology* (pp. 434–457). New York, NY: Wiley-Blackwell.

Toode, K., Routasalo, P., & Suominen, T. (2011). Work motivation of nurses: A literature review. *International Journal of Nursing Studies, 48*, 246–257. http://dx.doi.org/10.1016/j.ijnurstu.2010.09.013.

Vaux, E., & Gamble, J. (2014). Learning leadership skills in practice through quality improvement. *Clinical Medicine, 14*, 12–15. http://dx.doi.org/10.7861/clinmedicine.14-1-12

Wheelan, S. A. (2005). *Creating effective teams: A guide for members and leaders* (2nd ed.). Thousand Oaks, CA: Sage.

Zenger, J., & Folkman, J. (2012, July 16). How damaging is a bad boss, exactly? *Harvard Business Review*. Retrieved from https://hbr.org/2012/07/how-damaging-is-a-bad-boss-exa

# 11

# School-Based Consultation

Markeda Newell, Carly Tindall, Kelsie Reed, and Scott Zwolski

In reviewing the research literature, it is evident that consultation models rather than consultation competencies have driven the evolution of school-based consultation (Newell & Newman, 2014). That is, much of the research has focused on the creation and evaluation of models of consultation instead of identification of the knowledge, skills, and attitudes needed for psychologists to be effective in school settings. With this imbalance, training in school-based consultation has largely focused on teaching-specific models of consultation rather than competencies, especially with respect to process and multicultural competence (see Hazel, Laviolette, & Lineman, 2010; Newell, Newell, & Looser, 2013a; Newell & Newman, 2014; Newman, Barrett, & Hazel, 2015). Furthermore, training has focused on the transmission of knowledge of models rather than the development of skills to implement the models in practice. The implication is that school-based consultants are tied to specific models of consultation that might limit their ability to solve problems. Thus, there is a need for more attention to identifying the competencies consultants require that can transcend specific models and more comprehensive training that goes beyond the transmission of knowledge to also include attitudes and skills to truly advance consultation to a functional competence for all health service psychologists.

http://dx.doi.org/10.1037/0000153-012

*Consultation in Psychology: A Competency-Based Approach,* C. A. Falender and E. P. Shafranske (Editors)

## DEFINITION OF SCHOOL-BASED CONSULTATION

*School-based consultation* is a systematic process during which school-based consultants collaboratively problem solve with educators (e.g., teachers, administrators), parents, or both, to improve academic, behavioral, and social-emotional outcomes for all students (Erchul & Martens, 2010). Beyond addressing the needs of students, school-based consultation can also function as a form of professional development that helps educators develop skills so that they can intervene on similar problems in the future. With the focus on solving problems and equipping educators with skills, the goals of school-based consultation are to prevent problems from worsening, maintain students in the general education context, and reduce the likelihood that students are referred for special education evaluations (Kratochwill, 2008). Therefore, school-based consultants ideally work with teachers to address problems in the general education classroom before the problems warrant more intensive intervention. To facilitate this process, school-based consultants typically provide consultation in the structure of a consultation triad, which means the consultant works with the educator (consultee) to serve the needs of the student (client; Erchul & Martens, 2010).

Research has shown that school-based consultation can improve academic and behavioral student outcomes, and teachers are oftentimes satisfied with the consultation process (see Erchul & Sheridan, 2014). Despite the demonstrated effectiveness of consultation in improving teacher and student outcomes, consultation is one of the most under-researched areas of school psychological service delivery (Kaslow et al., 2009). As a result, there is limited empirical evidence to inform the identification, development, and evaluation of school-based consultation competence (Newell & Newman, 2014). Nevertheless, it is important to review and synthesize the research that has been conducted to provide a current state of the evidence on the competencies consultants need to effectively consult in schools. Therefore, the purpose of this chapter is to detail a competency-based approach to school-based consultation that can be used not only as a model to prepare health service psychologists for school-based consultation but also as a guide for effective practice.

## COMPETENCIES FOR SCHOOL-BASED CONSULTATION

A competency-based model of consultation in school-based settings is an approach to consultation that is driven by foundational knowledge, skills, and attitudes that transcend specific theoretical models of consultation so that consultants can flexibly adapt the consultation process to meet the wide array of needs that can arise at the individual level, group level, systems level, or all three levels, in a school setting. Not only is this flexibility important to ensure consultants can work with a range of professionals to address different problems, but it is also critical to consulting with a multicultural population that has diverse beliefs, values, perspectives, and behaviors (see Arredondo, Shealy,

Neale, & Winfrey, 2004; Ingraham, 2014). In this section of the chapter, we delineate the foundational knowledge, attitudes, and skills school-based consultants need to engage in competency-based consultation.

Newell (2012) reviewed several key sources to identify the competencies needed to consult in school-based settings. In her analysis, she reviewed the American Psychological Association (APA, 2007) Division 13's *Guidelines for Education and Training at the Doctoral and Postdoctoral Levels in Consulting Psychology/ Organizational Psychology*, National Association of School Psychologists' (2010) standards for the credentialing school psychologists, National Association of School Psychologists' *A Blueprint for Training and Practice III* (Ysseldyke et al., 2006), and APA competency benchmarks (Fouad et al., 2009). For this chapter, the revised APA (2017) Division 13 *Guidelines for Education and Training at the Doctoral and Postdoctoral Level in Consulting Psychology (CP)/Organizational Consulting Psychology (OCP)* were also reviewed. From this analysis, six competencies that are evident across all of these guiding documents and are particularly important for school-based consultants were identified. Thus, school-based consultants need the knowledge, attitudes, and skills to (a) consult with a diverse, multicultural population of consultees and clients; (b) develop coequal, collaborative relationships; (c) use a range of consultation models that can be applied at the individual, team, and system levels; (d) engage consultees in the consultation process; (e) assess academic, behavioral, social-emotional, and mental health problems; and (f) design and evaluate effective, indirect interventions that can be implemented with integrity. Each of these competencies is further elaborated in the sections that follow. Because large bodies of research discuss each of these competencies, the following are brief descriptions of these competencies as they relate to school-based consultation, and readers are referred to additional resources to obtain more details. These competencies are not presented in any particular order because they are all essential to the school-based consultation process.

## Consulting With a Diverse, Multicultural Population

According to the National Center for Education Statistics, 5.2 million children are enrolled in public and private, K–12 schools in the United States (McFarland et al., 2018). Furthermore, based on data in the *Digest of Educational Statistics 2016* (Snyder, de Brey, & Dillow, 2018), the school-aged population became a majority racial or ethnic minority population in 2014 because 50.3% of the population identified as racial or ethnic minorities compared with 49.8% of the population identifying as White. The Hispanic population is the fastest growing population in schools. Relatedly, almost 10% of the population are English language learners. Approximately 19% of students live in poverty, and 25% of students attend high-poverty schools (i.e., schools in which more than 75% of students receive free or reduced lunch). Therefore, the school-aged population is the most racially, ethnically, linguistically, economically, and culturally diverse population in the United States (U.S. Census Bureau, 2018).

Beyond the demographic diversity, students present a range of academic, behavioral, and mental health needs. According to the National Center for Education Statistics (n.d.), only 37% of fourth graders scored at or above the proficient level in reading, whereas 40% of fourth graders scored at or above proficient in math. Based on these data, most students are performing below grade-level expectations in reading and math, and this level of performance is still evident by the eighth grade. About 13% of students have a disability and are receiving special education services (National Center for Education Statistics, n.d.). Furthermore, about 20% (one in five) children have experienced a mental health disorder in a given year (Centers for Disease Control and Prevention, 2013), and most children in the United States receive their only mental health support in schools (Hoagwood, Burns, Kiser, Ringeisen, & Schoenwald, 2001). Taken together, there is a large number of students attending schools, and the academic, behavioral, and mental health needs among this population are high. Although the diversity of the school-aged population is a strength, this diversity also poses challenges for professionals who aim to understand the unique manifestations of needs that can arise.

To serve a diverse population, the field of psychology generally has adopted the Sue, Arredondo, and McDavis (1992) model of multicultural competence. This model essentially has been integrated into the practice of consultation to develop a multicultural approach to consultation (see Ingraham, 2000, for a school-based multicultural consultation model). The development and study of multicultural, school-based consultation is relatively new (Ingraham, 2014), and little research exists on how to develop multicultural, school-based consultation competence (Newell & Newman, 2014). Further complicating this process for school-based consultants is that the Sue et al. (1992) model is based on the delivery of service to adults, but school-based consultants work with children and adults. At this time, there is no existing model of multicultural competence when working with children. Therefore, the multicultural competence model is inherently limited when working in school-based settings (or with children and adolescents). Compounding this issue is that consultation research with racial or ethnic minority students is limited. In a review of research on consultation with racial or ethnic minority students, Newell (2016) found only 11 school-based consultation studies in which the demographics of the sample were described. Although the results of those studies indicated student performance improved, it was impossible to assess the effect on the racial or ethnic minority students in the sample. Therefore, it is unclear how effective school-based consultation is in improving outcomes for racial or ethnic minority students. Even so, researchers have identified essential knowledge, attitudes, and skills to consult with a multicultural, school-aged population (Ingraham, 2014, 2017).

Based on the available evidence base, the most critical area of multicultural school-based consultation competence is accurately identifying the problem. The problem identification stage is the most significant aspect of the consultation process because consultants who accurately identify the problem are more likely to complete the consultation process and have effective outcomes (Bergan & Tombari, 1976). This stage has added significance in a multicultural context because, for decades, school-based psychologists (Newell & Chavez-Korell, 2017) and educators (Valencia, 1997) have embraced a deficit-based approach to serving minority students. The result has been that student problems have been attributed to within-person (oftentimes cultural) deficits. These deficit-based conceptualizations are most likely to manifest during the problem identification stage of consultation, which can then bias the rest of the consultation process and increase the likelihood that the process will be ineffective. For this reason, to use a strengths-based approach to problem identification, a multiculturally competent, school-based consultant must have knowledge of ecological theories of behavior in school contexts (Illback, 2014; Ysseldyke, Lekwa, Klingbeil, & Cormier, 2012) and understand cultural differences in behavior (Ingraham, 2000). Along with this knowledge, school-based consultants must have an *attitude of cultural humility* during problem identification, which is "the ability to maintain an interpersonal stance that is other-oriented (or open to the other) in relation to aspects of cultural identity that are most important to the client . . . and express respect and lack of superiority" (Hook, Davis, Owen, Worthington, & Utsey, 2013, p. 354). With this attitude, consultants can recognize they must learn from the consultee and clients, and they must engage in ongoing self-reflection to ensure they are not inappropriately biasing their consultation as a result of their conceptualization of the problem based on their own beliefs, values, and perspectives. School-based consultants must then translate this knowledge and attitude to skills during the problem identification process.

The core multicultural skills during problem identification include applying a strengths-based, ecological perspective to identify a problem; and inquiring about and discussing cultural topics during the problem identification process. Applying a strengths-based, ecological perspective to identify the problem is important because this approach increases the likelihood that consultants will identify the students' strengths and skills as well as the environmental factors (e.g., instruction, classroom management, curriculum) that are contributing, causing, or both, the problem instead of blaming the problem on a within-child deficit, which disproportionately occurs with minority students (Gravois & Rosenfield, 2006; Ingraham, 2000; Newell, 2010). In addition, school-based consultants need the knowledge, attitudes, and skills to inquire about topics or issues related to diversity. Specifically, Newell (2010, 2012) found that school-based consultants struggled to ask consultees questions about cultural diversity during the consultation process. Specifically, a failure to ask questions related to cultural context provides the consultant with a limited understanding of cultural differences that affect the identification of the problem (Newell, 2012). On being interviewed, the consultants reported feeling uncomfortable asking about culture or that they did not know what to ask. On the other hand, Ingraham (2003) found that regardless of the race of the consultant, those consultants who directly discussed culture were more successful in identifying and addressing cultural hypotheses. Thus, consultants who are able to inquire about diversity and discuss cultural hypotheses are better positioned to address the cultural context of the consultation process and thereby more accurately identifying the problem. School-based consultants need to have multicultural competence because of the diversity of the population they serve. In addition to having this competence, school-based consultants must also develop the competence to consult within the organizational structure of the school.

## Developing Coequal, Collaborative Relationships

Schools are oftentimes described as being *loosely coupled systems*, which means autonomous professionals work together in a system that has multiple forms of leadership (e.g., principal, master teacher), and these professionals largely manage their own work (e.g., teacher is in charge of his or her classroom; Weick, 1976). Understanding this central, organizing feature of schools is important because schools do not have traditional hierarchical structures, nor do school-based consultants have authority over other professionals. Given the lack of authority, participation in consultation frequently is voluntary and thus requires consultants to develop coequal, collaborative relationships (Erchul & Martens, 2010).

Coequal and collaborative are fundamental aspects of school-based consultation. *Coequal* can be misinterpreted to indicate there is no difference in expertise within a consultative relationship (Sheridan, 1992). Rather, *coequal* means "equal in decision-making status, not equal in content or process expertise" (Sheridan, 1992, p. 90). When consultants and consultees accurately understand the coequal nature of school-based consultation, they can form a complementary, interprofessional collaborative relationship. Thus, collaboration is also a fundamental aspect of school-based consultation, in particular, interprofessional collaboration. According to Arredondo et al. (2004), *interprofessional collaboration* calls for health service psychologists to work "with individuals, groups, systems, and organizations that may have diverse values, ethical perspectives, or worldviews, and accountability to different constituencies" (p. 789) in a respectful, integrative manner. Essential to interprofessional collaboration is being a culturally self-aware collaborator, which requires a consultant to reflect on how his or her their own history can impact the process and to know the boundaries of his or her own competence (Arredondo et al., 2004). Hence, consulting in school-based settings requires interprofessional collaboration that respects the autonomy and expertise of consultees in a manner that allows for fluidity in roles and responsibilities that is informed by the demands of the situation. These elements of interprofessional collaboration are well aligned with the loosely coupled organizational structure of schools because school-based consultants must integrate the complementary knowledge, attitudes, and skills of others to serve the individual, group, and system-level needs that arise in schools. For this reason, school-based consultation models are built on a foundation of interprofessional collaboration.

## Flexibly Using Different Consultation Models

Of the several models of school-based consultation, the most prominent ones are behavioral consultation (Kratochwill & Bergan, 1990), conjoint-behavioral consultation (Sheridan, Kratochwill, & Bergan, 1996), instructional consultation (Rosenfield, 2002a), multicultural consultation (Ingraham, 2000), problem-solving consultation (Kratochwill, 2008), and ecobehavioral consultation (Gutkin, 1993). Behavioral consultation has the largest empirical basis of evidence and is the most widely used model of consultation in schools (Erchul & Martens, 2010; Newell & Newman, 2014). According to Martens (1993), behavioral consultation is commonly used in school settings because there is an abundance of behavioral analysis research with which educators are familiar and can draw on when using this model. Thus, behavioral consultation is regarded as the most effective and widely used model of school-based consultation.

Briefly, *behavioral consultation* is a four-stage problem-solving process that embraces a behavioral theory conceptualization of the problem (Kratochwill & Bergan, 1990). The four stages are problem identification, during which the target problem is defined in behavioral terms; problem analysis, during which data are collected to understand the level of the problem and why the problem is occurring; the plan implementation stage, during which the consultee designs and implements the intervention; and plan evaluation, during which the intervention outcome data are assessed. Behavioral consultation can be used to address a range of academic, behavioral, and social-emotional difficulties with students in kindergarten to the high-school level.

That behavioral consultation is the most widely used school-based consultation model is not inherently problematic; rather, the problem arises when school-based consultants are only able to use one model. As Newell (2010) argued, "This theoretical approach [behavioral] to problem solving raises concern about the degree to which the broader context of the problem can be acknowledged" (p. 250). Consequently, "the behavioral approach narrows the focus to a large degree on the behavior itself while leaving out an examination of other contextual variables such as cultural differences" (Newell, 2010, p. 250). Therefore, school-based consultants who largely rely on this model may neglect important factors that may be contributing to or causing the problem. For example, school-based consultants are frequently asked to consult on disruptive behavioral issues in the classroom. Oftentimes, the focus is on one student who might be the most disruptive. If the consultant only focuses on understanding the behavior of that one student through a behavioral theory conceptualization, then that consultant may miss that 50% of the students in the class are just as disruptive, which means the problem is classroom management rather than an individual student-level problem. Taking this same example, this student could be exhibiting disruptive behavior, and the teacher (consultee) believes the student has attention deficit/hyperactivity disorder; however, the student is instead experiencing poverty-related stress (see Wadsworth et al., 2008). A consultant with a behavioral approach is unlikely to ask the questions or collect the data to identify this important factor that is contributing to the student's behavior. To be fair, these limitations are not unique to behavioral consultation; every model has limitations that focus the consultant in one direction over another.

In addition to the limitation of narrowing the examination of contributing factors, problems can arise at the individual level, classwide level, systems level, or all three (Ingraham, 2015), and school-based consultants may have to consult in a team structure (for a review of team-based consultation, see Dowd-Eagle & Eagle, 2014; Rosenfield, Newell, Zwolski, & Benishek, 2018). Therefore, any school-based consultant who is only trained in a specific model will be limited by the boundaries of that model. For this reason, consultants need the knowledge and skills to implement multiple models of school-based consultation so they can select the model that is most appropriate for the client, context, and concern. Moreover, school-based consultants must not only possess the competence to consult in this flexible manner, but they also must able have the competence to educate consultees on the process so that the consultees can address similar problems later without the consultant's support.

## Engaging Consultees in the Consultation Process

Process consultation competence requires consultants to explain the consultation process so that the consultee can understand the problem as well as the decision-making process (APA, 2007). It is this competence that transforms consultation into a form of professional development. That is, by understanding the process, consultees can be equipped with the skills to understand the problem, analyze the problem, and intervene with similar problems in the future. To actualize this competence, school-based consultants need the knowledge of the consultation process—the attitude of "giving away psychology" so that consultees do not need to rely on consultants in the future—and the skill to effectively explain the consultation process to someone who is not a psychologist.

Having knowledge of the consultation process requires consultants to not only understand what they are doing during the consultation process but also why they are doing it. In their study of consultation training in school psychology, Newman et al. (2015) found that only about 37% of respondents had training in process competence. Newell and Newman (2014) also found in their review of school-based consultation research that process consultation was one of the least studied areas of consultation training. Moreover, Newell (2012) and Newell, Newell, and Looser (2013b) found that novice consultants demonstrated low levels of process competence when completing computer-simulated consultation cases; consultants had difficulty explaining the consultation process and including the consultee in the decision making. On the basis of this evidence, school-based consultants may have limited training and, thus, knowledge on understanding the consultation process. This knowledge, however, is only one element of process competence; consultants also need the attitude of giving away psychology.

Miller (1969) famously said, "Our responsibility is less to assume the role of experts and try to apply psychology ourselves than to give it away to the people who really need it—and that includes everyone" (p. 1071). Consultation is the most robust manifestation of this charge because consultants should explain the process to consultees so that consultees can independently problem solve similar issues (Erchul & Martens, 2010). With this attitude, consultants openly discuss each stage of the consultation process with the consultee and explain why they are taking each step. Furthermore, consultants are ensuring that the consultee is collaboratively making the decisions to ensure a full understanding of the process. This collaborative decision-making process is also aligned with interprofessional, collaborative consultation competence described earlier.

To translate this knowledge and attitude to skills, school-based consultants must develop the skill of explaining the consultation process to someone who is not a psychologist (e.g., teachers, administrators, parents). The greatest barrier to the implementation of this skill, though, is time: School-based consultants have reported that lack of time is one of the most significant barriers to consulting in schools (Wilczynski, Mandal, & Fusilier, 2000). It takes more time to explain the process and collaboratively make decisions; therefore, consultants make save time by simply telling the consultant what to do (which is more akin to an expert model). For this reason, consultants must prioritize this skill because it has benefits that can help consultees generalize the skills they learned during the consultation process, thereby making them more effective in their roles when serving children (Riley-Tillman & Eckert, 2001). Giving psychology away in schools is important because it is impossible for one professional to meet the needs of all students in a school, and this approach equips other educators with skills they can use to address student needs on their own.

**Conducting Assessment**

During the problem analysis stage of the consultation process, school-based consultants gather data to understand the current level of the problem, identify the causes of or contributors to the problem, and design and evaluate an evidence-based intervention (Christ & Arañas, 2014). Furthermore, data collected during consultation should be multidimensional (i.e., data using multiple methods from more than one source and setting) as well as self-referent, norm-referent, or both (Christ & Arañas, 2014). The data collected during school-based consultation must meet these criteria because multidimensional data help the consultant to discern whether the problem is situational (remember students go to different classes throughout the day). Self- and norm-referent data are used because the student's performance is typically being compared with their previous performance; moreover, self- and norm-referent data are more sensitive to capturing incremental change (Christ & Arañas, 2014). Using measures that are sensitive to incremental change is essential in consultation because school-based consultation is a time-limited process (typically about 4–6 weeks). Every day in which a student is performing below expectation is a day that the student is falling behind; therefore, school-based consultants must be able to quickly measure change—no matter how incremental—to assess whether a student is improving.

Given these assessment parameters for school-based consultation, school-based consultants need knowledge of self- and norm-referent tools that they can use to assess academic, behavioral, social-emotional, and mental health functioning (e.g., observations; curriculum-based measures; rating scales, e.g., goal attainment scales.). Self-referent, norm-referent, or both, tools may not be available for the specific indicator that needs to be measured. Therefore, school-based consultants must develop an attitude of adaptability or creativity, which will allow them to adapt or modify or develop assessment tools needed during the consultation process. Skills needed for assessment competence are collecting and interpreting the data in an objective manner that is free from confirmation bias. Sandoval (2013) explained that confirmation bias occurs when consultants collect and interpret data to confirm a preexisting belief, and this bias can also occur when the consultant adopts the consultee's conceptualization of the problem. To guard against this bias, school-based consultants should collect multidimensional data and analyze them for divergences and convergences (Sandoval, 2013).

Most school-based consultants are school psychologists, and assessment is a foundational competence for all school psychologists (Ysseldyke et al., 2006); therefore, assessment is an area of strength for most school-based consultants. Newell (2010, 2012) as well as Newell and Newell (2011) found that although assessment was a relative strength for school-based consultants, there were weaknesses. More specifically, Newell (2012) found that novice school-based consultants tended to collect data from only a few sources and to rely on self-referent data analysis. Similarly, in a study including school psychologists across multiple years of practice, Newell and Newell (2011) found that the majority of participants requested few data, and when requesting data, did not seek data from multiple settings and domains. Taken together, assessment is a relative strength for school-based consultants. However, Newman et al. (2015) surveyed school-based consultants and found that about 56% of them reported being trained in assessment during their consultation training; thus, more training on how to conduct assessment within the context of consultation may be needed because this part of the process drives the design of interventions.

## Designing Effective Interventions

A primary reason consultants conduct assessments during consultation is to use the data to design effective interventions (Batsche, Castillo, Dixon, & Forde, 2008). Designing interventions in the context of consultation is unique because consultants must design interventions that another professional can easily implement with integrity. Consultation is defined by the ability of consultants to support consultees in implementing an intervention with integrity; therefore, if the consultee does not implement the intervention, then the process cannot be described as consultation. Given the wide array of concerns students can present, school-based consultants must be able to design academic, behavioral, social-emotional, or mental health interventions, or all of these, at the individual, classwide, and schoolwide levels. To this end, school-based consultants need knowledge of instruction, curriculum, learning, classroom management (Rosenfield, 2008) and theories of human behavior as well as child development and developmental psychopathology (Beauchaine & Hinshaw, 2017). In addition, school-based consultants need knowledge of evidence-based interventions that a consultee can implement in the school-based setting.

Equipped with this knowledge, school-based consultants also should develop a supportive, coaching attitude, which helps facilitate the intervention process because the consultee may need a significant amount of resources and guidance to implement the intervention with integrity. Therefore, school-based consultants may need to explain the intervention, demonstrate the implementation of the intervention, provide material resources for the intervention, and be available to answer questions or provide support during implementation (Sandoval, 2013). With this knowledge and attitude, school-based consultants need skills to adapt or modify evidence-based interventions to address cultural and contextual factors (Morales & Norcross, 2010) and implement strategies to increase treatment integrity, such as performance feedback (Reinke et al., 2014; Sanetti, Chafouleas, Fallon, & Jaffrey, 2014). This combination of knowledge, attitudes, and skills will ensure that school-based consultants can select or design a wide range of evidence-based interventions that consultees can implement with integrity.

## SUMMARY OF SCHOOL-BASED CONSULTATION COMPETENCIES

The aforementioned six core school-based consulting competencies transcend consulting guidelines for health service psychologists. Underlying each of these six competencies are essential knowledge, attitudes, and skills consultants must develop to effectively consult in school-based settings. As explained, all consultants need these competencies, but the knowledge, attitudes, and skills required to carry them out in schools is unique because the context of schools is unique. Although the research on these competencies in school-based settings is limited, the existing research provides promising evidence that school-based consultants who possess these competencies have an increased likelihood of effectively consulting in schools. These competencies provide the flexibility necessary for consultants to address the myriad needs of a diverse, multicultural population at the individual, classwide, and systems levels. Therefore, school-based consultants should be trained to develop these competencies instead of only being trained to implement a specific model of consultation.

## IMPLICATIONS FOR TRAINING

To most fully develop competence, consultant training must focus on all three elements of competence: knowledge, attitudes, and skills. At this time, there is no evidence-based guidance on how to best train health service psychologists to become competent, school-based consultants (Newell & Newman, 2014). In their review of research on school-based consultation training, Newell and Newman (2014) found most of the research to be outdated and based on small sample sizes, and that the research largely used small-$N$ designs (e.g., single-case design). Based on the available evidence in this review, graduate students should first complete content knowledge courses (e.g., assessment and intervention) before taking a consultation course. Furthermore, students may need to take more than one consultation course (e.g., one course focused on theories and models) and a second course focused on skills development and supervised implementation (Newell & Newman, 2014). Research on school-based consultation training to date indicates that most school psychology programs require students to take one consultation course, and that course may or may not include supervised practice experiences. Based on this information, it is unlikely that students are developing the requisite knowledge, attitudes, and skills with supervised practice to adequately develop consulting competence (Rosenfield, 2002b). For this reason, having exposure to exemplar school-based consultation cases is an important aspect of understanding the competencies needed to consult in schools. Thus, in the next section, a classwide behavioral consultation case is presented to illuminate how these competencies are used in school-based consultation.

## COMPETENCY-BASED SCHOOL CONSULTATION: CLASSWIDE BEHAVIORAL CONSULTATION CASE EXAMPLE

### Description of School and Classroom Context

Sunny Middle School is located in a high-poverty urban setting and serves predominantly African American and Latinx students.[1] Of the students, 12% are English language learners and 14% receive special education services. High staff turnover is evident: The principal and most teachers have been at the school less than 3 years. Most teachers are White and female, administrators are White, and most paraprofessionals are racial or ethnic minorities. By district accounting, in the past 5 years, a disproportion number of racial or ethnic minority students have been suspended or expelled.

The consultee is a sixth-grade science teacher, White, middle-aged, and female and has taught for a decade. She sought consultation regarding behavior management in her first period science class. Of the 28 students, most of the students identify as African American or Latino; the majority are performing below grade level. The consultant recognized that the demographics mirror many high-poverty public schools. The teacher is responsible for 42% of the school's disciplinary referrals this year.

---

[1]All clinical case material has been altered to protect client confidentiality.

## Consultation Request and Problem Identification Interview

The teacher described off-task, out-of-seat behavior during lab group time. The consultant scheduled a before-school meeting, validated the difficulty of the situation, and began to formulate the questions with the teacher.

At the meeting, the consultant described the process and roles or responsibilities of the consultant and consultee. Although fearful of extra work, the teacher agreed to the process. Out-of-seat behavior was occurring daily and especially during unstructured lab group time. She had tried redirection to no avail and described this as the worst class she had ever had. The consultant empathized and selected a behavioral consultation approach to set behavioral expectations. The consultant collected quantitative data: number of students leaving their seats, duration, and frequency as well as the current rules and classroom expectations and the teacher's response to both out-of-seat and in-seat student behavior. The teacher reported that she had no classroom rules because the students are in middle school and should know how to behave. When students are out of their seats, she tells them to sit down; if noncompliant, she sends them to the office. At this point, the consultant identified knowledge and skills needed and engaged in rapport building with the teacher. The consultant also elicited the teacher's attribution that the children did not learn to behave at home, although the consultant had not had parental contact. The consultant redirected the teacher to focus on proximal factors in the classroom that she could control. She also noted the teacher's success in other parts of the class when teaching the subject matter. The selected approach was a behavioral management program. By redirecting the teacher from a potentially biased or deficit-based frame, the consultant proposed a positive, active approach and did so in a collaborative manner.

## Operationalized Definition of the Behavior

The first period science class engaged in off-task out-of-seat behavior in lab group time, including leaving their seat or group or talking to students in other groups. Frequency was high, and redirection was ineffective.

*Hypothesis.* The first period science class engages in out-of-seat behavior because of the unstructured nature of the lab room and because of the lack of clear behavioral expectations.

## Problem Analysis

Five systematic observations were completed to learn the function of the out-of-seat behavior and collect baseline data on its frequency. A frequency count data collection method was used for the first three observations and an antecedent-behavior-consequence (ABC) method was used. For comparison, ABC data were collected in both the target class and a math class. The frequency count data identified that students in the target class were typically out of their seats on average 17 times per period.

*Confirmation of Hypothesis.* Results of the ABC observation indicated that the out-of-seat behavior might result in peer attention. Observation of the same student group in math class revealed that these students are capable of remaining in their seats for most of the period in a structured environment.

With these data, the consultant developed a new hypothesis with the teacher: The unstructured nature of the lab may be contributing to the out-of-seat behavior, and this lack of structure is exacerbated by a lack of behavioral expectations in the lab. The main function of the behavior appears to be peer attention. Given the baseline data, the teacher set a goal for the class: Students could only be out of their seats 10 times on average per period by the end of the consultation process. By collaborating with the consultee, the consultant can gain clarity about the problem and hypotheses that impact solving it and provide meaning to the causes and possible solutions. This collaboration guides intervention, implementation, and evaluation. This phase depends highly on the relationship established with the consultee because the data may conflict with previous conceptions. Thus, the process must be reflective and empathic.

## Plan Implementation

It was collaboratively determined that the selected intervention needed to target the classroom's out-of-seat behavior and also needed to target the functions of the behavior: peer attention and lack of behavioral expectations. The consultant and consultee reviewed two potential intervention options and selected *The Good Behavior Game* (Barrish, Saunders, & Wolf, 1969), an evidence-based intervention designed to reduce classroom disruptive behavioral problems. This intervention was selected due to its efficacy in similar population demographics.

For implementation, the teacher introduced the behavioral expectation—in this instance, in-seat behavior. To support implementation, the consultant and the consultee introduced and explained the intervention to the class. The teacher implemented, and the consultant observed. The class was divided into two teams, and a tally was kept on the board of out-of-seat behavior during lab group. At the end of the week, the scores were totaled, and the winning team—that with less out-of-seat behavior—was identified. The game continued for 4 weeks, and the consultant monitored progress. Throughout the intervention implementation period, the consultant attended the consultee's class to collect progress monitoring data and share data and feedback with the consultee. In addition to performance feedback, the consultee was also able to obtain any additional implementation information.

## Plan Evaluation

The consultant monitored student progress one to two times per week using the same method as for the collection of baseline and integrity data. According to the data collected, the classroom students engaged in out-of-seat behavior an average frequency of seven times throughout intervention implementation. Furthermore, the integrity data identified that the teacher adhered to the intervention steps outlined in the protocol on average of 92% of the time. To evaluate the overall effectiveness of the intervention, the percentage of non-overlapping data points between both baseline and intervention was determined by calculating the percentage of data points in Phase B (intervention) that are equal to or lower than the median data point in Phase A (baseline). The median data point in Phase A was 16. During Phase B, all six data points collected were below 16. Therefore, the results of the formula reveal that the percentage of nonoverlapping data points was 100%. Thus, The Good Behavior Game (Barrish et al., 1969) was highly effective in reducing out-of-seat behavior. In addition, the teacher completed an intervention acceptability survey, which assessed her attitudes toward the consultation and intervention implementation process. Overall, the teacher strongly agreed that the intervention was appropriate and effective in addressing the students' behavioral needs. During the final consultation meeting, the consultee stated that she would like to continue using The Good Behavior Game when working with students in the lab.

The consultant must possess the knowledge and skills to recognize when an intervention is ineffective and the competence to know how to move forward. In some instances, the consultant must address the consultee's intervention fidelity. This is a difficult conversation that is much easier to facilitate if the consultant has established rapport with the consultee. Instances may arise during which the consultee is implementing the intervention with fidelity, but the students are not responding to the intervention. What is required is that the consultant take a step backward to revisit the problem analysis phase. The problem-solving consultation method is a fluid process. Thus, as long as the consultant relies on knowledge of the process and the emerging data to make decisions, he or she can expect efficacy.

## CONCLUSION

This chapter delineated six competencies that school-based consultants need to effectively consult in schools: (a) consult with a diverse, multicultural population of consultees and clients; (b) develop coequal, collaborative relationships; (c) use a range of consultation models that can be applied at the individual, team, and system levels; (d) engage consultees in the consultation process; (e) assess academic, behavioral, social-emotional, and mental health problems; and (f) design and evaluate effective, indirect interventions that can be implemented with integrity. Collectively, these competencies help school-based consultants accurately identify problems in the context of multiple (sometimes) conflicting perspectives and conduct robust assessments that produce data that can drive the design of effective interventions. In this process, consultants foster more collaborative relationships with other professionals, and the process equips them with the skills necessary to independently address similar problems in the future. With these competencies, the needs of students and educators can be met.

Although the evidence on the knowledge, attitudes, and skills underlying these competencies is promising, much more research is needed, specifically, research on the relationship between these competencies and consultation outcomes. In addition, research that can inform how to develop these competencies during training is necessary. At this time, there is no evidence-based approach to training school-based consultants (Newell & Newman, 2014); therefore, training programs have disparate approaches to teaching consultation as well as the content included in those courses (Hazel et al., 2010; Newman et al., 2015). To advance consultation in health service psychology, consultation must be given the attention it needs in research, training, and practice.

## REFERENCES

American Psychological Association. (2007). Guidelines for education and training at the doctoral and postdoctoral levels in consulting psychology/organizational consulting psychology. *American Psychologist, 62*, 980–992.

American Psychological Association. (2017). *Guidelines for education and training at the doctoral and postdoctoral level in consulting psychology (CP)/organizational consulting psychology (OCP)*. Retrieved from https://www.apa.org/about/policy/education-training.pdf

Arredondo, P., Shealy, C., Neale, M., & Winfrey, L. L. (2004). Consultation and interprofessional collaboration: Modeling for the future. *Journal of Clinical Psychology, 60*, 787–800. http://dx.doi.org/10.1002/jclp.20015

Barrish, H. H., Saunders, M., & Wolf, M. M. (1969). Good behavior game: Effects of individual contingencies for group consequences on disruptive behavior in a classroom. *Journal of Applied Behavior Analysis, 2*, 119–124. http://dx.doi.org/10.1901/jaba.1969.2-119

Batsche, G. M., Castillo, J. M., Dixon, D. N., & Forde, S. (2008). Best practices in designing, implementing, and evaluating quality interventions. In A. Thomas & J. Grimes (Eds.), *Best practices in school psychology V* (pp. 177–193). Bethesda, MD: National Association of School Psychologists.

Beauchaine, T. P., & Hinshaw, S. P. (Eds.). (2017). *Child and adolescent psychopathology* (3rd ed.). Hoboken, NJ: Wiley.

Bergan, J. R., & Tombari, M. L. (1976). Consultant skill and efficiency and the implementation and outcomes of consultation. *Journal of School Psychology, 14*, 3–14. http://dx.doi.org/10.1016/0022-4405(76)90057-1

Centers for Disease Control and Prevention. (2013, May 17). Mental health surveillance among children—United States, 2005–2011. *Morbidity and Mortality Weekly Report, 62*(Suppl. 2), 1–35. Retrieved from https://www.cdc.gov/mmwr/preview/mmwrhtml/su6202a1.htm?s_cid=su6202a1_w

Christ, T. J., & Arañas, Y. A. (2014). Best practices in problem analysis. In A. Thomas & J. Grimes (Eds.), *Best practices in school psychology VI* (pp. 87–98). Bethesda, MD: National Association of School Psychologists.

Dowd-Eagle, S., & Eagle, J. (2014). Team-based school consultation. In W. P. Erchul & S. M. Sheridan (Eds.), *Handbook of research in school consultation* (2nd ed., pp. 450–472). New York, NY: Routledge.

Erchul, W. P., & Martens, B. K. (2010). *School consultation: Conceptual and empirical bases of practice* (3rd ed.). New York, NY: Springer. http://dx.doi.org/10.1007/978-1-4419-5747-4

Erchul, W. P., & Sheridan, S. M. (Eds.). (2014). *Handbook of research in school consultation* (2nd ed.). New York, NY: Routledge.

Fouad, N. A., Grus, C. L., Hatcher, R. L., Kaslow, N. J., Hutchings, P. S., Madson, M. B., . . . Crossman, R. E. (2009). Competency benchmarks: A model for understanding and measuring competence in professional psychology across training levels. *Training and Education of Professional Psychologists, 3*(Suppl.), S5–S26. http://dx.doi.org/10.1037/a0015832

Gravois, T. A., & Rosenfield, S. A. (2006). Impact of instructional consultation teams on the disproportionate referral and placement of minority students in special education. *Remedial and Special Education, 27,* 42–52. http://dx.doi.org/10.1177/07419325060270010501

Gutkin, T. B. (1993). Moving from behavioral to eco-behavioral consultation: What's in a name? *Journal of Educational & Psychological Consultation, 4,* 95–99. http://dx.doi.org/10.1207/s1532768xjepc0401_6

Hazel, C. E., Laviolette, G. T., & Lineman, J. M. (2010). Training professional psychologists in school-based consultation: What the syllabi suggest. *Training and Education in Professional Psychology, 4,* 235–243. http://dx.doi.org/10.1037/a0020072

Hoagwood, K., Burns, B. J., Kiser, L., Ringeisen, H., & Schoenwald, S. K. (2001). Evidence-based practice in child and adolescent mental health services. *Psychiatric Services, 52,* 1179–1189. http://dx.doi.org/10.1176/appi.ps.52.9.1179

Hook, J. N., Davis, D. E., Owen, J., Worthington, E. L., Jr., & Utsey, S. O. (2013). Cultural humility: Measuring openness to culturally diverse clients. *Journal of Counseling Psychology, 60,* 353–366. http://dx.doi.org/10.1037/a0032595

Illback, R. J. (2014). Organization development and change facilitation in schools: Theoretical and empirical foundations. In W. P. Erchul & S. M. Sheridan (Eds.), *Handbook of research in school consultation* (2nd ed., pp. 276–303). New York, NY: Routledge.

Ingraham, C. L. (2000). Consultation through a multicultural lens: Multicultural and cross-cultural consultation in schools. *School Psychology Review, 29,* 320–343.

Ingraham, C. L. (2003). Multicultural consultee-centered consultation: When novice consultants explore cultural hypotheses with experienced teacher consultees. *Journal of Educational & Psychological Consultation, 14,* 3–4, 329–362. http://dx.doi.org/10.1207/s1532768xjepc143&4_7

Ingraham, C. L. (2014). Studying multicultural aspects of consultation. In W. P. Erchul & S. M. Sheridan (Eds.), *Handbook of research in school consultation* (pp. 323–348). New York, NY: Routledge.

Ingraham, C. (2015). Competencies for systems-level consultants within diverse schools. *Journal of Educational & Psychological Consultation, 25,* 148–159. http://dx.doi.org/10.1080/10474412.2014.963227

Ingraham, C. (2017). Educating consultants for multicultural practice of consultee-centered consultation. *Journal of Educational & Psychological Consultation, 27,* 72–95. http://dx.doi.org/10.1080/10474412.2016.1174936

Kaslow, N. J., Grus, C. L., Campbell, L. F., Fouad, N. A., Hatcher, R. L., & Rodolfa, E. R. (2009). Competency assessment toolkit for professional psychology. *Training and Education in Professional Psychology, 3*(4, Suppl.), S27–S45. http://dx.doi.org/10.1037/a0015833

Kratochwill, T. R. (2008). Best practices in school-based problem-solving consultation: Applications in prevention and intervention systems. In A. Thomas & J. Grimes (Eds.), *Best practices in school psychology V* (pp. 1673–1688). Bethesda, MD: National Association of School Psychologists.

Kratochwill, T. R., & Bergan, J. R. (1990). *Behavioral consultation in applied settings: An individual guide.* New York, NY: Plenum Press.

Martens, B. K. (1993). A behavioral approach to consultation. In J. E. Zins, T. R. Kratochwill, & S. N. Elliott (Eds.), *Handbook of consultation services for children: Applications in educational and clinical settings* (pp. 65–86). San Francisco, CA: Jossey-Bass.

McFarland, J., Hussar, B., Wang, X., Zhang, J., Wang, K., Rathbun, A., . . . Bullock Mann, F. (2018). *The condition of education 2018* (NCES Publication No. 2018-144). Washington, DC: U.S. Department of Education, National Center for Education Statistics. Retrieved from https://nces.ed.gov/pubsearch/pubsinfo.asp?pubid=2018144

Miller, G. A. (1969). Psychology as a means of promoting human welfare. *American Psychologist, 24*, 1063–1075. http://dx.doi.org/10.1037/h0028988

Morales, E., & Norcross, J. C. (2010). Evidence-based practices with ethnic minorities: Strange bedfellows no more. *Journal of Clinical Psychology, 66*, 821–829. http://dx.doi.org/10.1002/jclp.20712

National Association of School Psychologists. (2010). *Standards for graduate preparation of school psychologists.* Retrieved from https://www.nasponline.org/Documents/Standards%20and%20Certification/Standards/1_Graduate_Preparation.pdf

National Center for Education Statistics. (n.d.). *The nation's report card: How did U.S. students perform on the most recent assessments?* Retrieved from https://www.nationsreportcard.gov

Newell, M. L. (2010). The implementation of problem-solving consultation: An analysis of problem conceptualization in a multiracial context. *Journal of Educational & Psychological Consultation, 20*, 83–105. http://dx.doi.org/10.1080/10474411003785529

Newell, M. L. (2012). Transforming knowledge to skill: Evaluating the consultation competence of novice school-based consultants. *Consulting Psychology Journal: Practice and Research, 64*, 8–28. http://dx.doi.org/10.1037/a0027741

Newell, M. (2016). Consultation-based intervention services for racial minority students. In S. L. Graves & J. J. Blake (Eds.), *Psychoeducational assessment and intervention for ethnic minority children: Evidence-based approaches* (pp. 197–211). Washington, DC: American Psychological Association. http://dx.doi.org/10.1037/14855-012

Newell, M. L., & Chavez-Korell, S. (2017). The evolution of multiculturalism: An interdisciplinary perspective. In E. C. Lopez, S. G. Nahari, & S. L. Proctor (Eds.), *Handbook of multicultural school psychology: An interdisciplinary perspective* (pp. 3–17). New York, NY: Routledge. http://dx.doi.org/10.4324/9780203754948-1

Newell, M. L., & Newell, T. S. (2011). Problem analysis: Examining the selection and evaluation of data during problem-solving consultation. *Psychology in the Schools, 48*, 943–957. http://dx.doi.org/10.1002/pits.20606

Newell, M. L., Newell, T. S., & Looser, J. (2013a). A competency-based assessment of school-based consultants' implementation of consultation. *Training and Education in Professional Psychology, 7*, 235–245. http://dx.doi.org/10.1037/a0033067

Newell, M. L., Newell, T. S., & Looser, J. (2013b). Examining how novice consultants address cultural factors during consultation: Illustration of a computer simulated case-study method. *Consulting Psychology Journal: Practice and Research, 65*, 74–86. http://dx.doi.org/10.1037/a0032598

Newell, M., & Newman, D. (2014). Assessing the state of evidence in consultation training: A review and call to the field. In W. P. Erchul & S. M. Sheridan (Eds.), *Handbook of research in school consultation* (2nd ed., pp. 421–449). New York, NY: Routledge.

Newman, D. S., Barrett, C. A., & Hazel, C. (2015). School consultation practice in the early career: Does training matter? *Consulting Psychology Journal: Practice and Research, 67*, 326–347. http://dx.doi.org/10.1037/cpb0000048

Reinke, W. M., Stormont, M., Herman, K. C., Wang, Z., Newcomer, L., & King, K. (2014). Use of coaching and behavior support planning for students with disruptive behavior within a universal classroom management program. *Journal of Emotional and Behavioral Disorders, 22*, 74–82. http://dx.doi.org/10.1177/1063426613519820

Riley-Tillman, T. C., & Eckert, T. L. (2001). Generalization programming and school-based consultation: An examination of consultees' generalization of consultation-related skills. *Journal of Educational & Psychological Consultation, 12*, 217–241. http://dx.doi.org/10.1207/S1532768XJEPC1203_03

Rosenfield, S. (2002a). Best practices in instructional consultation. In A. Thomas & J. Grimes (Eds.), *Best practices in school psychology IV* (pp. 609–623). Washington, DC: National Association of School Psychologists.

Rosenfield, S. (2002b). Developing instructional consultants: From novice to competent to expert. *Journal of Educational & Psychological Consultation, 13*, 97–111. http://dx.doi.org/10.1207/S1532768XJEPC1301&2_08

Rosenfield, S. (2008). Best practice in instructional consultation and instructional consultation teams. In A. Thomas & J. Grimes (Eds.), *Best practices in school psychology V* (pp. 1645–1659). Bethesda, MD: National Association of School Psychologists.

Rosenfield, S., Newell, M., Zwolski, S., Jr., & Benishek, L. E. (2018). Evaluating problem-solving teams in K–12 schools: Do they work? *American Psychologist, 73*, 407–419. http://dx.doi.org/10.1037/amp0000254

Sandoval, J. H. (2013). Consultation and intervention series in school psychology. *An introduction to consultee-centered consultation in the schools: A step-by-step guide to the process and skills.* New York, NY: Routledge. http://dx.doi.org/10.4324/9780203145814

Sanetti, L. M. H., Chafouleas, S. M., Fallon, L. M., & Jaffrey, R. (2014). Increasing teachers' adherence to a classwide intervention through performance feedback provided by a school-based consultant: A case study. *Journal of Educational & Psychological Consultation, 24*, 239–260. http://dx.doi.org/10.1080/10474412.2014.923734

Sheridan, S. M. (1992). What do we mean when we say "collaboration"? *Journal of Educational & Psychological Consultation, 3*, 89–92. http://dx.doi.org/10.1207/s1532768xjepc0301_7

Sheridan, S. M., Kratochwill, T. R., & Bergan, J. R. (1996). *Conjoint behavioral consultation: A procedural manual.* New York, NY: Plenum Press. http://dx.doi.org/10.1007/978-1-4757-2512-4

Snyder, T. D., de Brey, C., & Dillow, S. A. (2018). *Digest of education statistics 2016* (NCES Publication No. 2017-094). Washington, DC: U.S. Department of Education, National Center for Education Statistics.

Sue, D. W., Arredondo, P., & McDavis, R. J. (1992). Multicultural counseling competencies and standards: A call to the profession. *Journal of Multicultural Counseling and Development, 20*, 64–88. http://dx.doi.org/10.1002/j.2161-1912.1992.tb00563.x

U.S. Census Bureau. (2018). American community survey: Data profiles: 2012–2016 ACS 5-year data profiles. Retrieved from https://www.census.gov/acs/www/data/data-tables-and-tools/data-profiles/2016/

Valencia, R. R. (1997). *Dismantling contemporary deficit thinking: Educational thought and practice.* New York, NY: Taylor & Francis.

Wadsworth, M. E., Raviv, T., Reinhard, C., Wolff, B., Santiago, C. D., & Einhorn, L. (2008). An indirect effects model of the association between poverty and child functioning: The role of children's poverty-related stress. *Journal of Loss and Trauma, 13*, 156–185. http://dx.doi.org/10.1080/15325020701742185

Weick, K. E. (1976). Educational organizations as loosely coupled systems. *Administrative Science Quarterly, 21*, 1–19. http://dx.doi.org/10.2307/2391875

Wilczynski, S. M., Mandal, R. L., & Fusilier, I. (2000). Bridges and barriers in behavioral consultation. *Psychology in the Schools, 37*, 495–504. http://dx.doi.org/10.1002/1520-6807(200011)37:6<495::AID-PITS2>3.0.CO;2-J

Ysseldyke, J. E., Burns, M. K., Dawson, M., Kelly, B., Morrison, D., Ortiz, S., & Telzrow, C. (2006). *School psychology: A blueprint for training and practice III.* Bethesda, MD: National Association of School Psychologists.

Ysseldyke, J., Lekwa, A. J., Klingbeil, D. A., & Cormier, D. C. (2012). Assessment of ecological factors as an integral part of academic and mental health consultation. *Journal of Educational & Psychological Consultation, 22*, 21–43. http://dx.doi.org/10.1080/10474412.2011.649641

# 12

# Consultation With Religious Professionals and Institutions

Thomas G. Plante

One of the most untapped opportunities for professional psychological consultation is with religious organizations and institutions. The vast majority of Americans are associated with some religious or spiritual organization and tend to approach clerical professionals, such as priests, nuns, pastors, rabbis, deacons, imams, youth ministers, and others who represent religious organizations, before considering approaching or securing the services from the professional mental health community, such as psychologists (Myers, 2000; Plante, 2009). Furthermore, religious institutions sponsor and run countless religiously affiliated hospitals, clinics, homeless shelters, summer camps, elementary and secondary schools, colleges and universities, and so many other community resources and thus are actively engaged with the educational, medical, spiritual, and community needs of much of the population. Because few psychologists are trained and interested in providing services to these organizations or have not ever seriously considered doing so (Delaney, Miller, & Bisono, 2007), rich opportunities abound for those who are interested in helping with consultation to religious organizations regarding a wide variety of issues and concerns (McMinn & Dominquez, 2005; Plante, 1999, 2013). Those who are well trained, experienced, and can work well with religious professionals and communities are likely to enjoy more work than they can handle because comfortable, collaborative professional relationships between psychologists and clerics are sorely needed.

http://dx.doi.org/10.1037/0000153-013
*Consultation in Psychology: A Competency-Based Approach*, C. A. Falender and
E. P. Shafranske (Editors)

221

There are many important examples of collaboration between the faith and psychological professionals. With too many to highlight in one brief book chapter, I address several in particular that focus on my own clinical, consultative, and research experience with Roman Catholic, Episcopalian, Orthodox Christian (e.g., Russian, Greek, Ukrainian), and Jewish examples. More specifically, I primarily focus on the following four types of collaborative efforts:

1. psychological evaluation screenings by psychologists for those interested in becoming religious clerics (e.g., priests, deacons, pastors, ministers, rabbis; Plante, 1999, 2013);

2. psychological evaluations, psychotherapy, and consultation for clerics struggling with mental health, behavioral, or relational problems (e.g., alcoholism, sex offending, affective disorders, stress management, pornography addiction, personality challenges; Plante, 2003, 2004b; Plante & McChesney, 2011);

3. psychological evaluations, psychotherapy, and consultation for religious congregants referred to psychologists by clerics or religious communities (Plante, 2015a, 2015b, 2016, 2017); and

4. consultation with religious institutions regarding policies and procedures associated with child protection and other behavioral and mental health matters of concern to their organizations, institutions, congregants, and clerics (Plante, 1999, 2004b, 2013, 2014, 2015a; Plante & McChesney, 2011).

In addition, professional psychology and other mental health professionals have potentially rich opportunities for a wider array of consultation services with religious institutions and professionals. Opportunities include team building and leadership training with religious leaders and their staffs, integration of religious and spiritual matters into medical and health care institutions through chaplaincy programs, and complementary and holistic behavioral medicine services among other integrated health care programs. Within religious institutions, these opportunities offer occasions to promote health, such as church-based mental and physical health screenings and interventions; presentations to religious congregations on the psychological and health benefits of forgiveness, gratitude, volunteerism; other positive psychology-associated best practices; groups on how to cope with chronic illness; and programming that addresses chronic psychiatric, medical, or addiction challenges experienced by congregants and their families (McMinn & Dominquez, 2005; Plante, 2013). The list is endless with many opportunities for professional psychology and related fields to closely collaborate with religious organizations and professionals for mutual benefit. This brief chapter highlights just a few of these many opportunities and needs.

Books, journal articles, professional organizations, and other resources have emerged to highlight and provide evidence-based guidelines regarding collaboration and consultation between religious institutions and professional psychology. Although most of these resources come from the psychological community, some are from religious organizations (e.g., Committee on Clergy, Consecrated Life and Vocations, 2015; Congregation for Catholic Education, 2005; United States Conference of Catholic Bishops, 2002). Thankfully, many quality resources are now available to help members of the professional psychological and health care communities to thoughtfully and respectfully collaborate with those professionals from the faith-based religious and spiritual traditions and institutions (see Appendix 12.1 for resource details).

## COMPETENCY-BASED CONSULTATION

Achieving competency in consultation with religious institutions is often challenging because most secular graduate school, internship, and post-doctoral training programs in professional psychology offer little, if any, training, supervision, and experience in this area (e.g., Russell & Yarhouse, 2006). Russell and Yarhouse (2006) reported that two thirds of clinical internship directors did not see any current or future training efforts on religion and spiritual groups or institutions being integrated into their training programs. And although multiculturalism associated with age, race, ethnicity, gender, gender identity, sexual orientation, and so forth has been well integrated into professional ethics and practice guidelines (e.g., American Psychological Association [APA], 2003, 2017a, 2017b), training associated with religion and spirituality is typically lacking.

Some notable exceptions are most often associated with religiously based private graduate and postgraduate training programs (e.g., Fuller Theological Seminary, Regent University, Rosemead School of Psychology at Biola University, George Fox University, Wheaton College, and the Institute for the Psychological Sciences at Divine Mercy University). Because these programs are closely affiliated or sponsored by religious institutions, consultation experiences, training, and supervision are made much more of a priority than in secular universities or freestanding professional school programs and institutions. Thus, these specialized training opportunities that focus on spirituality- and religion-integrated psychological and behavioral health care are rare in the more commonly found traditional and secular public or private university and professional school environments. In addition, few professionals specialize in this area. Although this subspecialty is still emerging, it likely will take many more years to achieve a critical mass of well-trained and competent psychology professionals working in this area to be able to offer the kind of high-quality training, experience, and supervision to help train many students from across the country.

Thus, interested students and professionals need thoughtfully, creatively, and proactively obtain adequate experience, training, and supervision to become competent in this area of professional consultation. Typically, professionals who are actively engaged within their own faith tradition are leading candidates who want to make this type of work and training a priority. Yet, personal experience and interest in religion and spirituality and perhaps even being an active and engaged member of a particular faith or spiritual tradition certainly do not qualify someone as an expert in this area of consultation and professional work (Plante, 2013, 2016). Perhaps personal familiarity may assist, but it also can hamper due to biases, limitations in experience, counter-transference reactions, or a false sense of competency; thus, developing high-level and evidence-based professional skills are necessary to work well in this specialty area. Finding mentors and consultants through organizations such as the Society for the Psychology of Religion and Spirituality (Division 36 of APA), Spirituality and Health special interest group of the Society of Behavioral Medicine, Albert & Jessie Danielsen Institute at Boston University, and Applied Spirituality Institute among other resources (see Appendix 12.1) might be a good first step for interested students and novices in securing helpful direction to this kind of professional work. Fortunately, advances in technology and communications (e.g., Skype, Zoom, e-mail, instant messaging, LISTSERVs) make consultation and mentorship from across the country and globe more easily obtainable.

## Knowledge

To be respectful and effective, professionals wishing to engage in consultation with religious institutions must have adequate knowledge about the religious communities with which they plan to work. Although they do not necessarily need to be experts or have theological degrees, they must know enough about the religious and spiritual tradition, orthodoxy and orthopraxis information, and the general rules of the road within these organizations to work with them. Examples might include rules about who is (and is not) eligible to become clerics in the religious communities of interest (e.g., Roman Catholic, Greek Orthodox, Conservative Jewish congregations, Episcopalian) and how the hierarchy within these traditions work (e.g., Catholic priests, bishops, archbishops, cardinals, the Pope) as well as the expectations for behavior of both clerics (e.g., religious vows), and congregants within these communities.

Those working with religious institutions and communities also must have an understanding and appreciation for the religious community's culture, such as ways of talking and interacting, language usage, biblical or other religious references, styles and rules of interacting with others, attire, and touching (or not touching) each other. Understanding the religious culture and learning to be comfortable working within that culture is critically important for effective consultation. Examples might include working within cloistered monasteries, church rectories, diocesan chancelleries, retreat centers, evangelical traditions, orthodox environments, and kosher communities.

In addition, professionals and trainees who are asked to engage in various professional services, such as psychological testing, psychotherapy, group therapy, or lecture or workshop presentations, with religious institutions must be adequately trained to provide those services. For example, the screening of applicants who wish to become clerics typically means using the Minnesota Multiphasic Personality Inventory—2 (MMPI–2; Butcher, Graham, Tellegen, & Kaemmer, 1989; Hathaway & McKinley, 1989), and so psychologists need to be sure that they are adequately trained in administering, interpreting, and integrating the MMPI–2 in general and with religious applicants in particular. Other commonly administered tests, such as the Millon Clinical Multiaxial Inventory-III (Millon, Millon, Davis, & Grossman, 2008) and the Sixteen Personality Factors Questionnaire (Cattell, Cattell, & Cattell, 2002), also are typically needed for these evaluations, and thus expertise with these testing instruments is necessary for competence in this area.

## Skills

Typically, working with religious communities and institutions requires being able to discuss psychological principles (including those from testing results) in ways that are understandable to people without psychological training. Technical professional language concerning psychological testing, psychotherapy, and psychological theories and principles must be translated in ways that are understandable to nonpsychologists. Doing so frequently is challenging for trainees and seasoned professionals alike because they quickly grow accustomed to talking and consulting with peers and other mental health professionals and often forget that many people have no exposure to or training in psychology. In addition, it is important for professionals to be able to translate and apply psychological results and principles in useful and practical ways to those working in religious communities and institutions. These challenges are not academic or hypothetical but are usually based on concerns and issues requiring immediate and practical solutions. For example, professionals need to be able to speak to how their consultation findings and insights might result in specific changes to religious communities or to those who are part of the religious community (e.g., clerics, congregants).

The consultant needs to highlight and focus on practical implications in easy-to-understand language so that religious communities and institutions can benefit most from the consultation services. In addition, psychology professionals often need to win over sometimes highly skeptical clients who may be reluctant to trust the advice of those from the secular and often perceived "God-less" world of professional psychology and the mental health community. Thus, to be an effective consultant who is viewed as a trusted professional by religious organizations and communities, personal skills and charm need to be included as part of one's competence and communications skills.

## Attitudes

Because religious individuals, communities, and institutions can often be leery of secular professionals, they may be especially sensitive to perceived judgment, criticism, and skepticism. It is critically important for professionals to offer a respectful, accepting, and compassionate attitude and to communicate that attitude in a clear manner to all involved with religious organizations.

Frequently, professional psychology and religious communities have had an ambivalent at best and tumultuous relationship at worst over the years. Sometimes they have merely ignored each other (Delaney et al., 2007; Plante, 2009; Russell & Yarhouse, 2006; Shafranske, 2000). The relationship has been strained by the negative views about religion offered by influential psychologists and other psychiatric leaders, including Sigmund Freud, John Watson, Albert Ellis, and B. F. Skinner (e.g., Ellis, 1971; Freud, 1927/1961; Watson, 1924/1983). Furthermore, negative and harsh views of secular psychology by religious leaders have sometimes created mistrust and discomfort. Conflicts regarding goals, differences in values, expectations for "right" thinking and behavior, liberal versus conservative worldviews, and the criteria for what constitutes "evidence" have added to the long-standing tensions between religion and psychology over many years. Importantly, psychology's emphasis on empirical and evidence-based science has conflicted with ways of knowing within and between religious traditions and institutions. The conflict between general matters of science and faith is clearly manifest when observing the relationship between psychology and religion.

Our professional Ethics Code (APA, 2017a) and multicultural guidelines (APA, 2003, 2017b) speak about religion as a multicultural issue and suggest that psychologists need to be as respectful and informed about religious diversity as we are about gender, racial, ethnic, and other forms of diversity. Religious communities and institutions may hold values and rules that are contrary to those of professional psychology. For example, the role of women and rules about marriage, divorce, homosexuality, abortion, and gender identity and gender equality may conflict with those supported by professional psychology (e.g., Congregation for Catholic Education, 2005). Although it is unnecessary for psychologists to agree with all of the values, rules, and doctrines of the religious communities with which they work, psychologists do need to respect them. Trainees from secular training programs with little experience or training with religious organizations must be hypervigilant in this regard because they may have absorbed the attitudes of their secular mentors who may share the negative views about religion and religious organizations and clerics from famous leaders like Freud, Watson, Ellis, Skinner and from peers and mentors. Gonsiorek, Richards, Pargament, and McMinn (2009) offered several reflection questions that trainees and professionals should ask themselves as they work in this area:

- Do I have the ability to create a spiritually safe and affirming therapeutic environment for my clients?

- Do I have the ability to conduct an effective religious and spiritual assessment of my clients?

- Do I have the ability to use or encourage religious and spiritual interventions, if indicated, in order to help clients access the resources of their faith and spirituality during treatment and recovery?

- Do I have the ability to effectively consult and collaborate with, and when needed, refer to clergy and other pastoral professionals? (p. 389)

## CONSULTATION EXAMPLES

A variety of scenarios are offered in this section to provide examples of how collaboration between professional psychology and religious communities can be conducted while being mindful about the knowledge, skills, and attitudes needed to best provide competency-based consultation.

### Scenario: Psychological Screening and Testing for Applicants to Seminary in Catholic, Episcopal, and Orthodox Churches

Individuals who wish to enter seminary or be ordained as ministers within religious organizations and institutions typically are required to complete a psychological screening evaluation. Standardized measures of psychological and personality functioning, such as the MMPI–2, Millon Clinical Multiaxial Inventory-III, and the Sixteen Personality Factors Questionnaire, are used along with a structured or semistructured clinical interview to provide some understanding of the applicant's psychological and behavioral fitness and to identify risk factors for behavioral or psychiatric problems that are likely to unfold. Standard protocols and advice about these evaluations have been published by psychologists and religious organizations (e.g., Committee on Clergy, Consecrated Life and Vocations, 2015; Plante & Boccaccini, 1998). The role of the evaluator is not to provide advice about who the religious institution should or should not accept or reject but rather to provide the religious authorities (e.g., vocation or seminary director, bishop, religious superior) a more thoughtful and evidence-based picture of the applicant's psychological and personality functioning as well as to identify any potential risk factors so that they and their committees can make informed decisions about who to accept or not into ordained religious ministry.

Evaluators need to be well aware of the nature of seminary and religious life and understand the stressors and challenges that clerics likely will face in ministry. They also need to be aware of the rules for behavior and be able to address how applicants might respond to those religious rules (e.g., vows of obedience, chastity, poverty). Risks of substance abuse, impulse control challenges (e.g., anger management, gambling), and behaviors that might be unseemly for religious clerics representing their spiritual and religious faith traditions must be considered.

## Scenario: Psychotherapy for Referred Clerics Accused of Pornography Use, Alcoholism, Gambling, Personality Clashes, Anxiety, and Depression

Clerics, like anyone else, are not immune to the range of psychological, behavioral, and relational problems that members of the general public face. Addictions associated with alcohol, other legal and illegal substances, pornography, gambling, compulsive overeating, and so forth as well as common psychiatric conditions, such as anxiety, depressive, and personality disorders, are experienced among clerics from all spiritual and religious traditions. Conflicts with congregants and with religious superiors and colleagues can be commonly experienced, too. Clerics may need assessment, consultation, and psychotherapy when these and other psychological, behavioral, and relational issues arise, and psychologists working with clerics need to be attuned to the unique challenges and experiences of these individuals and their religious communities.

In addition, careful attention to confidentiality is needed, especially among clerics who live under vows of obedience to their religious superiors. For example, religious superiors may force clerics under their charge to seek psychotherapy or a psychological evaluation and disclose the contents of their treatment or assessment to their religious superiors. Psychologists therefore must be clear about the terms of engagement with clerics and their religious communities to obtain full and informed consent as well as to avoid potential conflicts and misunderstandings.

## Scenario: Consultation With Religious Superior Who Has Conflicts With Novice in Cloistered Monastery

Relationship dynamics can intensify when living and working in close quarters. For example, college dorms can be an intense social experience as dynamics and potential conflicts emerge between roommates and other dorm mates. These issues can intensify even further within the close confines of cloistered religious communities. From the outside, monasteries may look like peaceful, serene environments with monks or religious sisters' maintaining a constant inner peace and having comfortable relationships with their peers. Sadly, human relationships, even within the cloistered walls of monasteries, are much more complex and often challenging for many who spend their lives within these communities. In addition, those in cloistered communities live and work together in a 24-7 manner for decades. Religious superiors who run these institutions need to negotiate and manage these relationship challenges while living and working in the same environment. Rarely do these religious superiors have the psychological training or professional background to help inform them. Psychologists who are well versed in the lives and traditions of monasteries can act as helpful consultants to work with religious superiors and with individual residents of these facilities to assist in diagnosis, potential treatment, and consultation about relationship dynamics and challenges that unfold.

In one example, a religious novice new to the monastery created significant tensions with other religious sisters. After a consultation with a psychologist, the mother superior decided to ask the novice to participate in a psychological evaluation. Although reluctant to do, the novice agreed to the evaluation. The evaluation process found that the novice had lied about a number of important life events on her application form, and those findings combined with her previous psychological evaluation and the new reevaluation and testing led to a diagnosis of borderline personality. The novice eventually was asked to leave the monastery, and the community returned to a more peaceful environment. Such high-impact evaluations require strong competencies in psychological evaluation and assessment as well as a sophisticated understanding of the contextual factors in monastic life and in religious communities.

## Scenario: Consultation With the United States Conference of Catholic Bishops on Developing National Standards for Child Protection

The clergy abuse crisis in the Catholic Church resulted in the formation of a national review board by the United States Conference of Catholic Bishops (2002). The review board's role was to assist in developing policies and procedures for child protection within the Church as well as strategies for managing offending clerics and victims of abuse, and assisting Church leaders in better understanding the challenges associated with child sexual victimization (see Plante, 2004b, 2015a; Plante & McChesney, 2011). The review board included attorneys and judges, law enforcement professionals, and mental health professionals, including several psychologists with expertise in child victimization and protection. In addition, each religious order (e.g., Jesuits, Dominicans, Franciscan) and each local diocese across the country developed its own committee to advise local bishops and religious provincials (or superiors) on these issues.

Psychologists on these committees at the national and local levels need to be experts on issues involving sex offenders, child sexual abuse, and related topics. They also must understand the workings of the Church, including rules about religious vows, the Church hierarchy, and other matters associated with the faith tradition.

## Scenario: Consultation With Local Churches From Multiple Faiths About Assisting Congregants With Mental Health Issues

Many clerics spend a great deal of time performing pastoral care with congregants who are struggling with mental health, behavioral health, family challenges, life traumas, and so forth. Typically, people who suffer from mental health-related issues within their families approach clerics long before they consider working with mental health professionals. Although most clerics have training in pastoral care and spiritual direction, few have significant training in psychology or mental health issues. Thus, clerics often need to consult with psychologists to better understand and serve their congregants (McMinn & Dominquez, 2005; Plante, 2013). In addition, clerics often need to protect themselves from burnout and from being manipulated by challenging congregants with personality or other psychiatric diagnoses that are difficult to deal with. Consultation with psychologists who are knowledgeable about Church functioning and psychiatric conditions is often invaluable for these clerical professionals.

### Scenario: Consultation With Local Retreat Centers to Assist in Premarital Counseling Preparations Before Marriage—The Pre-Cana Program

Before engaged couples can marry, most religious institutions require them to receive premarital training about marriage and family life within the religious tradition that is hosting their marriage ceremony and celebration. In the Catholic Church, for example, engaged couples are typically asked to meet privately with a priest or deacon and participate in a daylong workshop often referred to as the *Pre-Cana program. Cana* refers to the location of the Gospel account of Jesus' first publicly performed miracle: turning water into wine at a wedding ceremony (John 2:1–11).

Psychologists knowledgeable about Catholic traditions, teachings, and structures are often asked to take part in these trainings to discuss sexuality, family relationship and dynamics, research, and best practices regarding managing intimate marital relationships within a Catholic context. Often these psychologists are made available for individual counseling as needed both before and after the marital ceremony. Other religious traditions also typically require premarital classes or workshops for engaged couples who desire to be married within these church, synagogue, or mosque environments. Psychologists and other mental health professionals working in these environments must know the requirements and specifics of the religious tradition as well as issues relevant to marital and intimate relationships.

### MULTICULTURAL AND ETHICAL ISSUES

Religious institution consultation often means being highly sensitive to multicultural issues. Religious communities by themselves involve multicultural sensitivity based on religious diversity issues. However, many religious communities and institutions are also connected to ethnic, racial, gender, and other forms of diversity. For example, Greek, Russian, and Ukrainian Orthodox Churches are typically closely tied to the ethnic and country of origin identification (e.g., mostly Greek people are associated with the Greek Orthodox Church). Today's Catholic religious sisters typically come from Asian and Latinx backgrounds; most are from Vietnam, the Philippines, Mexico, and

El Salvador. Many Catholic priest applicants also come from these backgrounds as well as several African nations (e.g., Uganda, Kenya, the Congo). Caucasian applicants often come from Polish, Irish, or Italian backgrounds. Thus, religious communities and institutions are often greatly influenced by particular ethnic, cultural, and nationality backgrounds thus adding additional dimensions to these communities. Language, food, and culture are interwoven into religious activities and perspectives. Therefore, psychologists and other mental health professionals need to know not only a great deal about the religious communities, institutions, and traditions with which they work but also about ethnicities and cultures represented within these communities (e.g., Vietnamese, Latino, Greek).

Although ethical issues and conflicts can easily arise in any professional activity, they are especially likely to emerge in consultation activities with institutions and groups that do not follow the same ethical code as psychologists. Different groups may have different points of views about confidentiality, boundaries and dual relationships, and what constitutes ethical and unethical behavior. In addition, there is diversity within religious communities; each shares the same faith tradition. For example, conservative Jews may have different views about a wide variety of ethical issues relative to Reform Jews. This is also true for different Protestant denominations and different Catholic religious communities (e.g., Jesuits, Sisters of Mercy, Opus Dei).

Yet, regardless of the particular issues and concerns of a religious institution or community, those consulting with religious organizations should consider typical ethical challenges. These challenges include issues of competence, confidentiality, professional boundaries, and conflicts with values and behavior expectations (Plante, 2004a, 2007, 2009).

## BEST PRACTICES

In recent years, many effective collaborative relationships have emerged between the religious and psychological communities and institutions, and many examples illustrate impactful and mutually beneficial consultative and collaborative activities (McMinn & Dominquez, 2005; Milstein, Manierre, Susman, & Bruce, 2008; Plante, 2009). These experiences and collaborations have morphed into best practices. Conferences, books, workshops, empirical research, and granting institutions (e.g., The John Templeton Foundation, The Pew Charitable Trusts, The Fetzer Institute) have offered collaborative ways for experts in both science and faith to come together in mutually beneficial and evidence-based ways. Professional organizations such as APA (most especially Division 36) and the Society of Behavioral Medicine (most especially the society's Spirituality and Health special interest group; see Appendix 12.1) are excellent examples of integrating the best evidence-based science with topics of great interest to the religious and spiritual communities.

Consultation activities with religious institutions and organizations have well-established best practices available that often include published and generally agreed on policies and procedures. For example, much research has been conducted and published that highlights a standard psychological screening protocol for evaluating clerical applicants to the priesthood and diaconate for the Roman Catholic and Episcopal Churches (e.g., Plante, 2007; Plante & Boccaccini, 1998; Thomas & Plante, 2015). The United States Conference of Catholic Bishops offers specific guidelines about what constitutes an appropriate and best practices testing protocol for applicants to seminary and religious life (Committee on Clergy, Consecrated Life and Vocations, 2015). Those documents were developed after close collaboration with a number of psychologists and mental health professionals, including the author. Also, the Vatican has issued several documents that specifically outline expectations for collaboration with the psychological community as well as speak to how psychologists can and cannot be used regarding the work and needs of the Church (e.g., Congregation for Catholic Education, 2005).

However, other aspects of consultation with religious institutions and communities may not have well-established and generally agreed on published best practices to refer to and model. Some collaborative activities may be too narrow or too new to have well-established norms, clinical pathways, or best practices available. Under these circumstances, it is likely best to try and partner with a senior colleague or mentor who might provide guidance and possible supervision. For example, some applicants to religious life as priests, religious brothers or sisters, and deacons in the Roman Catholic tradition come from developing countries where traditional background checks (e.g., criminal records, financial checks, recommendation letters) are unavailable. Furthermore, some applicants do not speak English and may be unable to complete psychological testing materials because of language and cultural barriers. Some come from refugee experiences so that whatever records were available are now lost; others have experienced traumas and victimization, which are difficult to fully access. Under these and other circumstances, published or generally accepted protocols for adequate consultation may not be available. During these and other unique circumstances, consultation and potential supervision with a more experienced mentor may be of great value.

## TRANSLATIONAL ISSUES

Psychological language, including that from testing evaluations (e.g., narcissistic, histrionic, repression), must be considered when communicating with religious communities. Misunderstandings regarding technical language can easily occur. Thus, psychologists must be sensitive to issues of translation to easily understandable lay language.

## TRAINING RECOMMENDATIONS

Because consultation with religious institutions and communities likely may be unavailable in most graduate, clinical internship, or postdoctoral training programs, trainees and professionals wishing to ethically and competently provide these services must be proactive and creative in securing suitable training and experience. Seeking out colleagues who may act as mentors is recommended. Several organizations and groups may be of service, too (see Appendix 12.1 for a list, including websites). In addition, a number of quality books and journals are available; many of them are published by APA, but other publishing houses also offer resources (see Appendix 12.1).

## CURRENT STATUS

Consultation between religious organizations and professional psychology has been occurring for decades, but systematic high-quality and evidence-based training in this area at the graduate and postgraduate levels is sorely lacking at present. Most graduate and postgraduate training programs have not engaged the religious communities in an organized and systematic manner, and so few efforts have been made to provide training in consultation services to these institutions.

Fortunately, a number of experts are actively engaged in this area of specialization and can be easily located through organizations, such as APA Division 36 or the Society of Behavioral Medicine. Modern technology that includes videoconferencing, LISTSERVs and emails, and webinars are helpful in connecting with others who can act as mentors, with consultants, and with peers who are interested in further training in and experience with collaborative consultation. Using these and other means, interested professionals and trainees alike should reach out to experts for the guidance they need to ensure that they obtain quality and evidence-based training and experience. Collaboration with religious organizations and professionals is remarkably productive and rewarding and can help to improve the lives of many.

## APPENDIX 12.1
## RESOURCES

### Organizations

- American Psychological Association, Division 36, Society for the Psychology of Religion and Spirituality: http://www.apadivisions.org/division-36/

- Society of Behavioral Medicine, Special Interest Groups, Physical & Mental Health, Spirituality and Health: https://www.sbm.org/membership/special-interest-groups

- International Association for the Psychology of Religion: https://www.iaprweb.org

- Society for the Scientific Study of Religion: https://sssreligion.org/

- Applied Spirituality Institute: https://www.scu.edu/ic/about/affiliated-works/asi/

- The Albert & Jessie Danielsen Institute (Boston University): https://www.bu.edu/danielsen/

- Association for Spiritual, Ethical, and Religious Values in Counseling, American Counseling Association: http://www.aservic.org/

- Association for Transpersonal Psychology: http://www.atpweb.org/

- Christian Association for Psychological Studies: https://caps.net/

## Books

Koenig, H. G., King, D. E., & Carson, V. B. (2012). *Handbook of religion and health* (2nd ed.). New York, NY: Oxford University Press.

McMinn, M. R., & Dominquez, A. W. (2005). *Psychology and the church*. Hauppauge, NY: Nova Science.

Miller, L. J. (Ed.). (2012). *The Oxford handbook of psychology and spirituality*. New York, NY: Oxford University Press.

Pargament, K. I. (2007). *Spiritually integrated psychotherapy: Understanding and addressing the sacred*. New York, NY: Guilford Press.

Pargament, K. I., Mahoney, A., & Shafranske, E. P. (Eds.). (2013). *APA handbook of psychology, religion, and spirituality: Vol. 2. An applied psychology of religion and spirituality*. Washington, DC: American Psychological Association.

Plante, T. G. (2009). *Spiritual practices in psychotherapy: Thirteen tools for enhancing psychological health*. Washington, DC: American Psychological Association.

Plante, T. G., & McChesney, K. L. (Eds.). (2011). *Sexual abuse in the Catholic Church: A decade of crisis, 2002–2012*. Santa Barbara, CA: Praeger.

Richards, P., & Bergin, A. E. (2000). *Handbook of psychotherapy and religious diversity*. Washington, DC: American Psychological Association.

Richards, P. S., & Bergin, A. E. (2005). *A spiritual strategy for counseling and psychotherapy* (2nd ed.). Washington, DC: American Psychological Association.

## Glossary

**bishop:** Also known as *eparchs* in the Eastern Catholic Churches, bishops are priests who are assigned to govern local regions within the Catholic Church known as *dioceses* in the Latin Church and *eparchies* in the Eastern Churches.

**chastity:** Clerical chastity or celibacy is required within some religious traditions meaning that some or all members of the clergy must be unmarried and not sexually engaged with others. The Roman Catholic Church requires clerical celibacy for all clerics except for those in the permanent diaconate; they can be married.

**cloistered:** Religious orders of sisters, brothers, priests, or nuns living in community in a monastery or convent with limited public access

**diocese:** A district or region under the pastoral and managerial care of a bishop in the Christian Church

**novice:** A person formally admitted to a religious institute as a trainee to prepare for eventual religious profession

**orthodoxy:** Authorized or generally accepted theory, doctrine, and beliefs

**orthopraxis:** Correct conduct or practice

**religious order:** A lineage of religious communities and organizations of people who live in some way set apart from society in accordance with their specific religious devotion, usually characterized by the principles of its founder's religious practice

**religious superior:** The person to whom a cleric is immediately responsible under canon (or church) law

**vows:** Promises made by the members of religious communities pertaining to their conduct, practices, and views

## REFERENCES

American Psychological Association. (2003). Guidelines on multicultural education, training, research, practice, and organizational change for psychologists. *American Psychologist, 58*, 377–402. http://dx.doi.org/10.1037/0003-066X.58.5.377

American Psychological Association. (2017a). *Ethical principles of psychologists and code of conduct* (2002, Amended June 1, 2010 and January 1, 2017). Retrieved from http://www.apa.org/ethics/code/index.aspx

American Psychological Association. (2017b). *Multicultural guidelines: An ecological approach to context, identity, and intersectionality.* Retrieved from http://www.apa.org/about/policy/multicultural-guidelines.pdf

Butcher, J. N., Graham, J. R., Tellegen, A., & Kaemmer, B. (1989). *Manual for the restandardized Minnesota Multiphasic Personality Inventory: MMPI–2.* Minneapolis: University of Minnesota Press.

Cattell, R. B., Cattell, A. K., & Cattell, H. E. P. (2002). *Sixteen Personality Factors Questionnaire* (5th ed.). Champaign, IL: Institute for Personality and Ability Testing.

Committee on Clergy, Consecrated Life and Vocations. (2015). *Guidelines for the use of psychology in seminary admissions.* Washington, DC: United States Conference of Catholic Bishops.

Congregation for Catholic Education. (2005). *Instruction concerning the criteria for the discernment of vocations with regard to persons with homosexual tendencies in view of their admission to the seminary and to holy orders.* Vatican City: Author.

Delaney, H. D., Miller, W. R., & Bisono, A. M. (2007). Religiosity and spirituality among psychologists: A survey of clinician members of the American Psychological Association. *Professional Psychology: Research and Practice, 38*, 538–546. http://dx.doi.org/10.1037/0735-7028.38.5.538

Ellis, A. (1971). *The case against religion: A psychotherapist's view.* New York, NY: Institute for Rational Living.

Freud, S. (1961). The future of an illusion. In J. Strachey (Ed. & Trans.), *The standard edition of the complete psychological works of Sigmund Freud* (Vol. 21, pp. 5–58). New York, NY: Norton. (Original work published 1927)

Gonsiorek, J. C., Richards, P. S., Pargament, K. I., & McMinn, M. R. (2009). Ethical challenges and opportunities at the edge: Incorporating spirituality and religion into psychotherapy. *Professional Psychology: Research and Practice, 40*, 385–395. http://dx.doi.org/10.1037/a0016488

Hathaway, S. R., & McKinley, J. C. (1989). ITAL *Manual for the Minnesota Multiphasic Personality Inventory—2 (MMPI–2)*. Minneapolis: University of Minnesota Press.

McMinn, M. R., & Dominquez, A. W. (2005). *Psychology and the church*. Hauppauge, NY: Nova Science.

Millon, T., Millon, C., Davis, R., & Grossman, S. (2008). *Manual for the Millon Clinical Inventory-III*. Minneapolis, MN: Pearson.

Milstein, G., Manierre, A., Susman, V. L., & Bruce, M. L. (2008). Implementation of a program to improve the continuity of mental health care through clergy outreach and professional engagement (C.O.P.E.). *Professional Psychology: Research and Practice, 39*, 218–228. http://dx.doi.org/10.1037/0735-7028.39.2.218

Myers, D. G. (2000). *The American paradox: Spiritual hunger in a land of plenty*. New Haven, CT: Yale University Press.

Plante, T. G. (1999). A collaborative relationship between professional psychology and the Roman Catholic Church: A case example and suggested principles for success. *Professional Psychology: Research and Practice, 30*, 541–546. http://dx.doi.org/10.1037/0735-7028.30.6.541

Plante, T. G. (2003). Priests behaving badly: What do we know about priest sex offenders? *Sexual Addiction & Compulsivity: The Journal of Treatment & Prevention, 10*, 93–97. http://dx.doi.org/10.1080/10720160390230592

Plante, T. G. (2004a). *Do the right thing: Living ethically in an unethical world*. Oakland, CA: New Harbinger.

Plante, T. G. (Ed.). (2004b). *Sin against the innocents: Sexual abuse by priests and the role of the Catholic Church*. Westport, CT: Praeger/Greenwood.

Plante, T. G. (2007). Ethical considerations for psychologists screening applicants for the priesthood in the Catholic Church: Implications of the Vatican instruction on homosexuality. *Ethics & Behavior, 17*, 131–136. http://dx.doi.org/10.1080/10508420701378073

Plante, T. G. (2009). *Spiritual practices in psychotherapy: Thirteen tools for enhancing psychological health*. Washington, DC: American Psychological Association.

Plante, T. G. (2013). Consultation with religious institutions. In K. I. Pargament, A. Mahoney, & E. P. Shafranske (Eds.), *APA handbook of psychology, religion, and spirituality: Vol. 2. An applied psychology of religion and spirituality* (pp. 511–526). Washington, DC: American Psychological Association. http://dx.doi.org/10.1037/14046-026

Plante, T. G. (2014). Four steps to improve religious/spiritual competence in professional psychology. *Spirituality in Clinical Practice, 1*, 288–292. http://dx.doi.org/10.1037/scp0000047

Plante, T. G. (2015a). Four lessons learned from treating Catholic priest sex offenders. *Pastoral Psychology, 64*, 407–412. http://dx.doi.org/10.1007/s11089-014-0623-3

Plante, T. G. (2015b). Six principles to consider when working with Roman Catholic clients. *Spirituality in Clinical Practice, 2*, 233–237. http://dx.doi.org/10.1037/scp0000075

Plante, T. G. (2016). Principles of incorporating spirituality into professional clinical practice. *Practice Innovations, 1*, 276–281. http://dx.doi.org/10.1037/pri0000030

Plante, T. G. (2017). The 4 Ds: Using Ignatian spirituality in secular psychotherapy and beyond. *Spirituality in Clinical Practice, 4*, 74–79. http://dx.doi.org/10.1037/scp0000122

Plante, T. G., & Boccaccini, M. T. (1998). A proposed psychological assessment protocol for applicants to religious life in the Roman Catholic church. *Pastoral Psychology, 46*, 363–372. http://dx.doi.org/10.1023/A:1023020005841

Plante, T. G., & McChesney, K. L. (Eds.). (2011). *Sexual abuse in the Catholic Church: A decade of crisis, 2002–2012*. Santa Barbara, CA: Praeger.

Russell, S. R., & Yarhouse, M. A. (2006). Religion/spirituality within APA-accredited psychology predoctoral internships. *Professional Psychology: Research and Practice, 37*, 430–436. http://dx.doi.org/10.1037/0735-7028.37.4.430

Shafranske, E. P. (2000). Religious involvement and professional practices of psychiatrists and other mental health professionals. *Psychiatric Annals, 30,* 525–532. http://dx.doi.org/10.3928/0048-5713-20000801-07

Thomas, S. N., & Plante, T. G. (2015). Psychological well-being of Roman Catholic and Episcopal clergy applicants. *Pastoral Psychology, 64,* 875–881. http://dx.doi.org/10.1007/s11089-015-0655-3

United States Conference of Catholic Bishops. (2002). *Charter for the protection of children and young people.* Washington, DC: Author.

Watson, J. B. (1983). *Psychology from the standpoint of a behaviorist.* Dover, NH: Frances Pinter. (Original work published 1924)

# 13

# Forensic Consultation

Jeffrey N. Younggren, Michael C. Gottlieb, and Cassandra L. Boness

*Forensic psychology* is a subfield of psychology defined by the American Psychological Association (APA; 2013) in "Specialty Guidelines for Forensic Psychology" as "professional practice by any psychologist working within any subdiscipline of psychology (e.g., clinical, developmental, social, cognitive) when applying the scientific, technical, or specialized knowledge of psychology to the law to assist in addressing legal, contractual, and administrative matters" (p. 7). Forensic psychology helps judicial, administrative, and educational systems make decisions regarding questions when an interface with psychology is involved with legal issues (Neal, 2018). Generally, the psychologist assists to inform adjudication decisions. In this chapter, we use a competency-based approach to identify the requisite knowledge, skills, and attitudes for practice. Some issues addressed in this chapter concern the differentiation of forensic consultation from clinical or administrative and how forensic consultation differs from activities such as supervision, administration, direct care, or all of them. After a review of the literature, we conclude that almost all forensic practice is consultative and should only be conducted by those qualified to do so by training, education, experience, or all three. This conclusion may seem extreme to some; we now explain why we believe this to be the case.

http://dx.doi.org/10.1037/0000153-014
*Consultation in Psychology: A Competency-Based Approach*, C. A. Falender and
E. P. Shafranske (Editors)

## FORENSIC VERSUS CLINICAL PRACTICE: TWO DIFFERENT ROADS

Psychologists who practice in the forensic arena have an ethical obligation to be familiar with the oftentimes confusing world of the law and standards of forensic psychological practice as well as how the two differ from the standards of clinical practice. We contend that this combined familiarity with the law and forensic psychological practice is a necessary foundation for competent forensic practice. In that spirit, we discuss some of these differences to familiarize the reader with the complexity of this role.

First, forensic psychologists do not usually treat patients; they engage in administrative activities, serve the court or attorneys in some capacity or another, or both. In that spirit, they are not intended to be advocates for those they serve—arguably an important role for clinicians—but instead provide scientifically based direction to the judicial or administrative matter at hand, answers to questions related to that matter, or both. Even when called on to provide care, the goal served by the forensic psychologist working in this capacity deals directly with a specific psycholegal issue or question.

Second, forensic psychologists must be sensitive to the differences between emotional truth and forensic truth. APA's (2013) "Specialty Guidelines for Forensic Psychology" states, "Forensic practitioners recognize the adversarial nature of the legal system and strive to treat all participants and weigh all data, opinions, and rival hypotheses impartially" (pp. 8–9). This guideline continues, "Forensic practitioners seek to represent alternative perspectives, including data, studies, or evidence on both sides of the question, in an accurate, fair and professional manner, and strive to weigh and present all views, facts, or opinions impartially" (p. 9). This integration of perspectives is not required of clinicians who usually accept at face value the emotional truth of their patients regardless of whether or not it is factually accurate.

Third, there is an inherent difference between clinical and forensic practice, and role conflicts should be avoided. Greenberg and Shuman (1997) outlined these differences in detail in their seminal article "Irreconcilable Conflict Between Therapeutic and Forensic Roles." In addition, the spirit of this area of concern made its way into the "Specialty Guidelines for Forensic Psychology" (APA, 2013), which states, "Providing forensic and therapeutic psychological service to the same individual or closely related individuals involves multiple relationships that may impair objectivity and/or cause exploitation or other harm" (p. 11). Consider the following example:

> Dr. Blanca Knight was a psychologist who specialized in treating trauma survivors due in part to her own history of childhood mistreatment.[1] Recently, she took on a new female patient, Ivy Landon, who complained of several symptoms of anxiety and depression. In passing, Ms. Landon mentioned mistreatment by a

---

[1]All clinical case material has been altered to protect client confidentiality.

supervisor at work, but this was not the focus of treatment at the time. As a result, Dr. Knight did not pursue the issue. Shortly thereafter, Dr. Knight received a phone call from Ms. Landon's lawyer. The lawyer informed Dr. Knight that Ms. Landon was the plaintiff in a sexual harassment lawsuit and that Dr. Knight would be subpoenaed to testify regarding Ms. Landon's damages. Despite fleeting qualms, Dr. Knight agreed to testify regarding Ms. Landon's damages secondary to the sexual harassment.

The ethical obligations of lawyers and psychologists are extremely similar, but a major difference between the two is the environment in which they work. Clinicians work in supportive and affirming environments in which trust is basic currency, whereas lawyers work within an adversarial system with opponents on the other side of the case. Any statements made by an expert whom lawyers have called to testify must be supported to be entered into evidence. In the preceding example, the adjudicating body would not allow Dr. Knight to testify regarding Ms. Landon's damages because Dr. Knight lacks the data to support such a conclusion and doing so would be a violation of scientific responsibility. Therefore, those who wish to pursue this practice specialty must remain mindful of this difference, be prepared to be vigorously cross-examined if they testify, and develop a thick skin.

We hope this discussion has served the purpose of outlining the complexity of competent forensic practice and how forensic competencies differ from those usually found among psychologists who provide clinical services. Perhaps the best advice one could give a psychologist who lacks a forensic foundation is to make active use of the phrase "I don't know" when asked to opine on a forensic matter in or out of court. That phrase is a perfectly acceptable answer to any question in which the issues are unclear, the answer is beyond those data that are usually found in clinical settings, and the forensic skill set is limited. In the preceding example, when Dr. Knight was asked if Ms. Landon had been sexually harassed at work, an appropriate answer would have been, "I am not a forensic psychologist, and I did not perform a forensic assessment of Ms. Landon. That is what she told me, but I am just her therapist, and I don't know."

## FORENSIC COMPETENCIES

Given that forensic psychology has been recognized as a psychological specialty since 2001 by the APA Commission for the Recognition of Specialties and Proficiencies in Professional Psychology (APA, n.d.), it is fair to say that there are defined competencies required of those who choose to practice this specialty. In their valuable article entitled "Professional Competencies in Forensic Psychology," Varela and Conroy (2012) outlined their view of what is required to competently practice within this specialty. They stated that to practice forensic psychology, a psychologist must have both general and specialized knowledge, skills, and attitudes across a number of specific practice dimensions. Generalized competency skills are applicable across various specialties within the larger field of psychology and are connected to the competencies associated with forensic psychology. In essence, they are the result of broad-based training in the profession of psychology and are skills that the psychologist brings to forensic practice. Specialty competencies are different and are those specific and largely unique skills associated with forensic research and practice. For example, all psychologists should bring with them the general competency of broad knowledge of psychological testing on which they build and develop specialized competencies unique to forensic assessment, such as assessment of recidivism. The dimensions include assessment, intervention, consultation, research, supervision and training, and administration. It is in the specialized category that defined requirements become clear. The reader is referred the various tables included in the Varela and Conroy (2012) article for a clearer understanding of the differences between general competencies and specialized competencies with a specific eye toward the consultation dimension.

## CONSULTATION

*Consultation* is a complex term that can have significant legal and ethical implications. As defined in the *Cambridge Dictionary* (n.d.), *consultation* refers to "meeting to discuss something or to get advice." However, the professional literature contains many definitions of consultation. The exact way in which consultation is operationally defined depends on the consultant's work setting, educational background, and conceptual models (Kurpius & Fuqua, 1993). For the purposes of this chapter, we discuss *expert consultation*, whereby a consultee contracts for the solution to a given problem (Kurpius, 1978). We, therefore, expand the *Cambridge Dictionary*'s definition to include making professional recommendations or giving advice. Therefore, for the purposes of this chapter, *consultants* are individuals who receive and give advice to an identified consultee within a psycholegal context (see also Chapter 1, this volume).

In this regard, it is important to distinguish consultants from supervisors. Consultants are individuals who may have influence but who do not have direct authority to implement the changes they recommend; therefore, they do not have vicarious liability (Falender & Shafranske, 2004; Harrar, VandeCreek, & Knapp, 1990). To draw a parallel from seafaring, a navigation consultant might share information about what is ahead of a ship, the dangers ahead, and where the ship might go but does not steer the ship or have the responsibility for determining the ship's course; that responsibility rests with others. This analogy applies directly to consultation in legal settings and in legal proceedings. That is, a consultant may advise an attorney regarding a certain course of action, but it is the lawyer who makes the final decision and, ultimately, has the responsibility for it. That said, one would be foolish to assume that, because it is not like therapy, consultation does not carry with it exposure for liability and a licensing board investigation.

## FORENSIC CONSULTATION

Recently, forensic psychology as a psychological specialty has become popular. Many clinicians now define themselves as having combined specialties of clinical and forensic practice. However, as with all areas of professional psychology, forensic practice requires specialty training. The purpose of this chapter is twofold. First, we aim to discuss the complexity inherent in this specialty and, second, demonstrate how the competence model proposed by Falender and Shafranske (2004) can help those who want to work as forensic psychologists to do so in a competent fashion with requisite knowledge, skills, and attitudes. (For a general discussion of forensic psychology ethics, see Gottlieb & Coleman, 2011.)

The definition of forensic psychology in the APA (2013) "Specialty Guidelines for Forensic Psychology" given in the introduction to this chapter does not mean that every time a psychologist finds himself or herself in court or dealing with the legal system that he or she is practicing as a forensic psychologist. Psychologists often provide testimony that would not be considered within the practice of forensic psychology. In recognition of this circumstance, the guidelines also state the following:

> Psychological practice is not considered forensic solely because the conduct takes place in, or the product is presented in, a tribunal or other judicial, legislative, or administrative forum. For example, when a party (such as a civilly or criminally detained individual) or another individual (such as a child whose parents are involved in divorce proceedings) is ordered into treatment with a practitioner, that treatment is not necessarily the practice of forensic psychology. In addition, psychological testimony that is solely based on the provision of psychotherapy and does not include psycholegal opinions is not ordinarily considered forensic practice. (p. 7)

This important distinction is best clarified through an example:

> A psychologist has been treating a child who has been caught between two warring parents who are engaged in a custody dispute. This psychologist has been providing psychotherapy with the goal of creating a safe place for the child away from his or her parent's ever-present conflict. This psychologist could easily find himself or herself in court, where it would be permissible to share with the judge the child's diagnosis, the focus of treatment, and, generally, what the child said in therapy. This psychologist could also share with the court his or her clinical treatment plan and opinion about how the child has progressed in therapy. The psychologist, however, should not express specific opinions regarding what caused the child's condition or make any recommendations regarding dispositional matters, such as custody or visitation. And if she or he were to be asked about these matters, he or she should decline because a treating therapist is not entitled to express any forensic opinions.

The key difference is that when playing a forensic role, the psychologist uses his or her expertise in psychology to address and make recommendations regarding legal or administrative issues rather than providing clinical or mental health services to specific individuals.

To make matters more confusing, a psychologist can be working with the legal system yet still be viewed as a clinician. At other times, the psychologist might be providing services that entail the specialized practice of forensic psychology. In addition, all of this could happen within the same employment setting, such as those who work as police psychologists or in correctional settings (see Chapter 13 in Mitchell & Dorian, 2016). In these employment settings, psychologists may provide clinical services yet also be called on to function forensically. For example, within a police department, a police psychologist could be treating an officer after a traumatic event and have the goal of the officer's returning to duty. That psychologist likely will have to file a fitness-for-duty report with that department, something that is a combined clinical and forensic function. Consequently, it is important for psychologists to be aware of their role. The responsibility for being cognizant of these role differences falls on the shoulders of the psychologist who operates in these types of settings.

## PROFESSIONAL ROLE CONFLICTS

The difference between clinical and forensic roles is determined by the retaining party and the purpose of the professional conduct rather than the setting in which it occurs. This distinction requires that the psychologist entering forensic practice understand and manage these differences because the risks of mixing clinical and forensic roles are significant (Greenberg & Shuman, 1997; Varela & Conroy, 2012).

For clinical psychologists, involvement with the legal system can be anxiety provoking and often requires legally sophisticated consultation. But such involvement does not require a separate set of skills or forensic competencies if a clinical psychologist maintains his or her role as a clinician and understands the limitations of that role. However, sometimes things are not so simple. For example, clinicians may be asked to certify a patient for disability or assist in a request for special accommodations in employment or educational settings. Although these activities may become necessary in clinical practice, it is important for clinicians to recognize that these activities are administrative in nature and represent boundary crossings into multiple roles that can damage the clinical alliance if not handled appropriately (Younggren & Gottlieb, 2004).

Consider the following common example of problems that may arise when mixing clinical and administrative activities without clarifying the limitations of the administrative role:

> A psychologist is treating a male patient with significant symptoms of a major depression. The patient is unable to sleep, is not eating, has no energy, and is unable to engage in self-care. This condition has become so serious that he is in trouble at work because he cannot come to work, and even if he could, he could not attend to the job requirements. As a result, the psychologist puts the patient on disability for 2 weeks. However, in 2 weeks, although the patient has improved somewhat, he is still unable to return to work; the psychologist certifies the disability for another 2 weeks. After a month off, the psychologist feels that the patient has improved enough to return to work, but the patient protests. As a consequence of this disagreement, therapy sessions shift from those designed to address the depression to debates about whether the patient should return to

work and why the psychologist is not further certifying the disability. Soon the
patient becomes upset with the psychologist and terminates treatment.

This example demonstrates how mixing clinical and forensic roles, no matter
how necessary, can run the risk of damaging treatment. Although most would
agree that psychologists should be able to put on disability a patient who cannot
work for psychological reasons, the lack of clarity about what the psychologist
is willing and not willing to do regarding disability determinations can be
problematic. In the example, the rupture of the treatment relationship could
have been avoided if the psychologist had defined limits on disability certification (an evaluative forensic activity) and clarified when those determinations would have to be made by someone else after a certain period.

Psychologists who find themselves in legal or administrative proceedings
must constantly ask the questions, What is my role and is there a role conflict?
It is dangerous to assume that these differences are inconsequential? At times,
the conflicts can be serious, such as when a treating therapist renders an opinion as an expert in a proceeding (e.g., a custody recommendation) compared
with times when the roles do not conflict at all, such as when a neuropsychologist testifies in court about the results of an assessment that he or she did
for clinical reasons. For a general discussion of forensic psychology ethics, see
Gottlieb and Coleman (2011).

## FORENSIC PSYCHOLOGY AS A TRAINED SPECIALTY

If one decides to provide forensic services, the psychologist should be able to
substantiate his or her ability to effectively perform in this role by demonstration of education, training, experience, or all three. This substantiation is
necessary because unique competencies are required of those who define
themselves as forensic psychologists (Varela & Conroy, 2012). It was the position of Varela and Conroy (2012) that although all psychologists must have a
generalized set of skills in assessment, intervention, consultation, research,
supervision or training, and management or administration, if they choose to
practice forensically, they also must possess the competencies that are unique
to forensic psychology. The general skill set of a clinically trained psychologist is
simply inadequate.

Competent practice is a requirement of both the professions of psychology
and law. The APA (2017) *Ethical Principles of Psychologists and Code of Conduct*
states, "Psychologists provide services, teach, and conduct research with populations and in areas only within the boundaries of their competence, based on
their education, training, supervised experience, consultation, study, or professional experience" (Standard 2.01[a], p. 4). With specific regard to forensic
practice, Standard 2.01(f) states, "When assuming forensic roles, psychologists
are or become reasonably familiar with the judicial or administrative rules governing their roles" (p. 5). At a minimum, then, forensic psychologists must
have proficient knowledge of how the legal system functions and how their
role fits within that process. Doing so requires the accumulation of specialized

knowledge about forensic practice and the development of a specific skill set based on existing scientific knowledge. Lacking this knowledge and those skills, psychologists are well advised to limit their role in the legal system to clinical matters because failing to understand these differences can expose a psychologist, along with those who have retained their services (e.g., clients), to considerable risk.

## LEGAL KNOWLEDGE FOR THE FORENSIC PSYCHOLOGIST

A fundamental component of competent forensic practice requires some understanding of the law. This does not mean that the forensic psychologist must have had formal legal training, but it does require some understanding of the system within which the forensic psychologist works. It also requires an understanding of the language of the law, which can be different from the language of a clinically focused psychology practice. It requires some understanding of all three types of legal systems, given that forensic psychologists may function within all three: criminal law, civil law, and administrative law.

### Criminal Law

A *crime* is "any act or omission in violation of a law prohibiting the action or omission," and, as such, *criminal law* is defined as that "system of laws concerned with punishment of individuals who commit crimes" (Cornell School of Law, Legal Information Institute, n.d.). It is the people who decide what a crime is as well as the punishments that are appropriate for committing the crime. In most cases, a crime involves intentional or negligent behavior that constitutes a violation of a specific criminal statute punishable by defined standards. Criminal statutes are promulgated by the U.S. Congress and by state or territorial legislatures, and each jurisdiction has its own separate court systems that adjudicate criminal cases. Obviously, this "federal" system of government creates considerable variety in the types of behaviors prohibited and the penalties proscribed such that conduct that is criminal in one jurisdiction can be perfectly legal in another and vice versa. Contemporary examples of these differences include laws regarding carrying concealed weapons, obtaining an abortion, and possessing marijuana. In addition, and contrary to popular thinking, the same criminal act can be prosecuted in more than one jurisdiction. For example, one can be prosecuted at both the state and federal levels for child pornography because these are separate jurisdictions, and the findings of one do not necessarily impact those of another.

Because criminal law is enforced by the considerable power of governmental authority and involves the potential loss of liberty, personal property, or both, criminal defendants are given many more protections than those found in other legal proceedings. For example, a defendant is not required to testify in a criminal proceeding. In addition, criminal law requires the highest level of proof in the legal system—that of a finding that the proof that the defendant committed the alleged crime is "beyond a reasonable doubt." This level of proof is required to minimize false positive findings. In that spirit and as Benjamin Franklin said, paraphrasing a long tradition of English law, "It is better that 100 guilty Persons should escape than that one innocent Person should suffer" ("To Benjamin Vaughan," 1906, p. 293).

## Civil Law

*Civil law* governs how disputes between individuals or organizations, including governmental organizations, are resolved when informal resolution is not possible. Sometimes civil law involves disputes governed by statutes or regulations; other times, not. Civil law has its own complex set of rules and procedures designed to ensure both a fair and neutral process and maximize fairness in outcome. Its standard of proof is generally a "preponderance of the evidence" sometimes defined as more likely than not (Orloff & Stedinger, 1983).

Family law is a subset of civil law. It involves issues that must be decided when a family breaks down, such as dividing of property and assets and establishing child custody, child support, and spousal support among other things (*Legal Dictionary*, n.d.). Separate sets of statutes address these disputes, and some larger jurisdictions have established courts dedicated to adjudicating these matters.

## Administrative Law

*Administrative law* is the system of rules and regulations that are written by regulatory agencies after creation of a law through legislation It governs the activities of administrative agencies of government and can include rulemaking, adjudication, or the enforcement of a specific regulatory agenda. The administrative law system has its own procedures and standards of proof. However, a basic principle of administrative law is that the administrative body is limited by its statutory authority and cannot regulate beyond it. For example, if an administrative body overinterprets its authority through regulation, a dispute about this alleged overinterpretation would have to be resolved legally through litigation. Examples of administrative law exist in the rules and regulations written by licensing boards or other government agencies that specify how the laws passed by state or federal legislatures should be implemented (e.g., State Committee of Psychology, State of Missouri, *Psychology Practice Act and Rules*, 2018).

We highlight these differences to clarify that operating as a psychologist within the legal system can be complex. The legal system is fraught with details and specialized rules that often may appear to conflict with or contradict each other. Consequently, those who find themselves working in that system have an ethical obligation to have a fundamental knowledge about how the legal system works and the necessary skills to successfully apply that knowledge base in psychological practice. Because of this complexity, many forensic psychologists choose to specialize in one area. For example, some may limit their practices to single activities like conducting child custody evaluations, whereas others may specialize only in criminal or civil matters. In so doing, it is easier to remain up to date on the law as it applies to their area of specialization.

## WHAT TO KNOW ABOUT ENTERING FORENSIC CONSULTATION PRACTICE

It is our position that competence is a basic component of effective consultation. Unfortunately, some well-intended psychologists enter the legal arena believing that they know how to operate forensically only to be surprised when they encounter the complexity of the system. The consequences of this well-intended behavior can be serious for both the psychologist and the lawyer and dire for the lawyer's client. In so doing, they fail to recognize that forensic psychology is a broad and complex area of specialized practice that includes, but is not limited to, conducting child custody and parenting evaluations, conducting personal injury evaluations, identifying and treating education disabilities, assessing civil capacities, conducting child abuse and neglect evaluations, assessing competency to stand trial, assessing criminal responsibility, evaluating asylum seekers, assessing risk of future dangerousness, educating the trier of fact on the science of psychology, and evaluating and assisting in jury selection (Weiner & Otto, 2013). Hence, psychologists who are interested in providing forensic services should first define their area of interest and then determine if they have the knowledge and skills necessary to function within that area and, if not, obtain it.

Many who pursue a career in forensic psychology do so by completing a formal postdoctoral training experience. Others may choose to enter the field in a less formal fashion; in that case, interested psychologists must actively pursue mastery of this specialized field of interest in a less structured fashion. They need to familiarize themselves with the complexity of the field and then decide whether they want to be involved in both civil and criminal law or other fields affiliated with the justice system, such as law enforcement or corrections. Then, they need to pursue knowledge about that area through attendance at workshops or conferences, through case supervision, and through self-study. This process is neither a simple nor an easy one, but, as with any subspecialty, a firm knowledge base as well as continuing education in the area are required of each person who chooses to enter forensic practice. These requirements are especially important in forensic practice in which the stakes can be high, given that the outcome often results in extensive financial loss or loss of personal freedom.

A psychologist interested in forensic practice is also well advised to become active in the profession of forensic psychology before accepting a professional assignment. This is an excellent approach for learning about the complexity of the field and can be done in a variety of ways. Affiliating oneself with organizations such as Division 41, APA's American Psychology Law Society, or becoming a member of the American Professional Society on the Abuse of Children would be a good way to learn more about the profession in general and specific areas of interest. It is through organizations such as these that interested psychologists can participate in training experiences and attend presentations that will further prepare them for working as a forensic psychologist.

A psychologist interested in doing forensic work could also pursue a variety of certifications that indicate that the psychologist has met certain standards within the subspecialty. These certifications should be examination based and reflect the opinions of those who already specialize in that area. Perhaps the best credential is certification in forensic psychology by the American Board of Professional Psychology (ABPP). Other types of ABPP certification also stand as evidence that those who hold that status have qualified through examination by peers to practice in those areas. Consequently, an ABPP in clinical neuropsychology, family psychology, or clinical psychology may also stand as evidence of professional competence in forensically related areas. One would be wise to avoid certification through what are commonly called "vanity boards" that provide "board certifications" based on little more than having paid a fee. These boards are well known to forensic psychologists, and putting such credentials forward as having substance in a legal proceeding will likely lead to an embarrassing cross-examination.

The psychologist who is interested in forensic practice would also do well to remember that courtroom work is a world of credentials. When testifying, a psychologist has the responsibility of proving that he or she has the requisite qualifications to testify regarding the matter at hand. For example, one should be able to easily answer such questions as, "Doctor, in what way do you qualify as an expert in . . .?" "What is your experience in . . .?" "How many times have you qualified as an expert in . . .?" Until one can comfortably do so, that person is simply not qualified within the legal context and will not be allowed to testify.

Knowledge, however, is not enough. The new forensic practitioner must learn how to apply that knowledge competently and ethically in the forensic arena. It is here that forensic consultation is vital because it teaches how to apply what is already known in an effective and efficient fashion; it develops applied forensic skills. For example, one might understand the literature on psychopathy and yet not know how to apply the various models to a specific case. Only through consultation with others, coupled with case experience, does the psychologist learn to connect this knowledge to practice by tying it to specific assessment results.

## COMPETENCIES IN FORENSIC PSYCHOLOGY CONSULTATION

Just what are the knowledge, skills, and attitudes required of psychologists who provide consultation in forensic psychology? Given the previous discussion, it becomes rather obvious that forensic psychology is a complex specialty in which the skills of one forensic psychologist may be entirely different from those possessed by another. Some forensic psychologists only consult with others to educate them regarding psychological issues, such as memory, trauma symptomatology, eyewitness research, and coerced confessions research, and never tie those issues to any specific matter or individual (see Reisberg, 2014). They use consultation to educate. Although they may consult to educate in an actual courtroom, this consultation also takes place with others, such as attorneys, in which the forensic psychologist assists them in dealing with and understanding these issues as they apply to a particular case. Other forensic psychologists provide specific evaluative services during which they consult with others regarding a specific set of facts or a specific individual. These forensic psychologists usually have a strong background in assessment and perform evaluations regarding competency or sanity and risk assessment for future dangerousness. Some forensic psychologists consult with nonforensic psychologists on legal and forensic issues, thereby assisting their nonforensic colleagues in addressing forensic questions and challenges, such as how to respond to subpoenas or offer appropriately limited testimony in court.

## CONCLUSION

In this chapter, we discussed various matters that are relevant to clinicians who wish to enter forensic practice; hopefully, we have alerted the reader to the necessity of obtaining specialized training and experience in this complex area of practice. Because the stakes are so high, it is vital that those entering this specialty fully embrace their professional obligations to those who could lose their freedom, financial assets, or their children.

## REFERENCES

American Psychological Association. (n.d.). *Recognized specialties and proficiencies in professional psychology.* Retrieved from https://www.apa.org/ed/graduate/specialize/recognized

American Psychological Association. (2013). Specialty guidelines for forensic psychology. *American Psychologist, 68*, 7–19. http://dx.doi.org/10.1037/a0029889

American Psychological Association. (2017). *Ethical principles of psychologists and code of conduct* (2002, Amended June 1, 2010 and January 1, 2017). Retrieved from http://www.apa.org/ethics/code/index.aspx

*Cambridge Dictionary.* (n.d.). Consultation. Retrieved from https://dictionary.cambridge.org/dictionary/english/consultation

Cornell School of Law, Legal Information Institute. (n.d.). Criminal law. Retrieved from https://www.law.cornell.edu/wex/criminal_law

Falender, C. A., & Shafranske, E. P. (2004). *Clinical supervision: A competency-based approach.* Washington, DC: American Psychological Association. http://dx.doi.org/10.1037/10806-000

Gottlieb, M. C., & Coleman, A. A. (2011). Ethical challenges in forensic psychology. In S. Knapp, M. C. Gottlieb, M. M. Handelsman, & L. VandeCreek (Eds.), *APA handbook of ethics in psychology: Vol. 2. Practice, teaching, and research* (pp. 91–124). Washington, DC: American Psychological Association.

Greenberg, S. A., & Shuman, D. W. (1997). Irreconcilable conflict between therapeutic and forensic roles. *Professional Psychology: Research and Practice, 28*, 50–57. http://dx.doi.org/10.1037/0735-7028.28.1.50

Harrar, W. R., VandeCreek, L., & Knapp, S. (1990). Ethical and legal aspects of clinical supervision. *Professional Psychology: Research and Practice, 21*, 37–41. http://dx.doi.org/10.1037/0735-7028.21.1.37

Kurpius, D. J. (1978). Consultation theory and process: An integrated model. *Journal of Counseling and Development, 56*(7), 18–21.

Kurpius, D. J., & Fuqua, D. R. (1993). Fundamental issues in defining consultation. *Journal of Counseling & Development, 71*, 598–600. http://dx.doi.org/10.1002/j.1556-6676.1993.tb02248.x

*Legal Dictionary.* (n.d.). Civil law. Retrieved from https://legaldictionary.net/civil-law

Mitchell, C. L., & Dorian, E. H. (Eds.). (2016). *Police psychology and its growing impact on modern law enforcement.* Hershey, PA: IGI Global.

Neal, T. M. S. (2018). Forensic psychology and correctional psychology: Distinct but related subfields of psychological science and practice. *American Psychologist, 73*, 651–662. http://dx.doi.org/10.1037/amp0000227

Orloff, N., & Stedinger, J. (1983). A framework for evaluating the preponderance-of-the-evidence standard. *University of Pennsylvania Law Review, 131*, 1159–1174. http://dx.doi.org/10.2307/3311937

Reisberg, D. (2014). *The science of perception and memory: A pragmatic guide for the justice system.* New York, NY: Oxford University Press. http://dx.doi.org/10.1093/acprof:oso/9780199826964.001.0001

State Committee of Psychologists, State of Missouri. (2018, January). *Psychology practice act and rules.* Retrieved from https://pr.mo.gov/boards/psychology/RuleBook.pdf

To Benjamin Vaughan [on the criminal laws and the practice of privateering], March 14, 1785 [Letter]. (1906). In A. H. Smyth (Ed.), *The writings of Benjamin Franklin* (Vol. 9, pp. 291–299). New York, NY: Haskell House.

Varela, J. G., & Conroy, M. A. (2012). Professional competencies in forensic psychology. *Professional Psychology: Research and Practice, 43*, 410–421.

Weiner, I. B., & Otto, R. K. (2013). *The handbook of forensic psychology.* Hoboken, NJ: Wiley.

Younggren, J. N., & Gottlieb, M. C. (2004). Managing risk when contemplating multiple relationships. *Professional Psychology: Research and Practice, 35*, 255–260. http://dx.doi.org/10.1037/0735-7028.35.3.255

# 14

# Custody Case Family Consultation

G. Andrew H. Benjamin and Florence W. Kaslow

Clients often seek psychological assistance to address conflicts in romantic or marital relationships and partnerships and for issues affecting their families. In contrast to individual treatment, consultations with couples and families pose unique challenges. Such challenges arise when consultation concerns dissolutions of relationships, especially when those involve children. Meeting those challenges requires knowledge of family law, specifically about child custody issues and various plausible resolutions.

*Coparent consultation* is an approach we have developed that incorporates knowledge, skills, and attitudes and that explicitly addresses the psychological, emotional, legal, ethical, and financial as well as professional issues involved in family law and custody consultation. We present our model to illustrate a competency-based approach that addresses the many complex issues that are involved when providing family consultation in divorce or separation cases. For instance, some family law cases resist any settlement process and result in poor outcomes without sufficient resolution about the family issues. Such outcomes leave the parties still engaged in high-conflict tactics that often lead to further relational deterioration and family law litigation (see American Psychological Association [APA], 2012). Typically, the negotiations between the parties and their lawyers result in no resolution, and mediation fails. Parties who are engaged in abusive use of conflict tactics do not mediate well or engage in other forms of therapeutic structuring, such as client-centered divorce mediation or divorce therapy (Fieldstone & Coates, 2008; Kaslow, 1990; Schwartz

http://dx.doi.org/10.1037/0000153-015
*Consultation in Psychology: A Competency-Based Approach*, C. A. Falender and
E. P. Shafranske (Editors)

& Kaslow, 1997). As a result, even parent coordination efforts (Nurse & Thompson, 2012) may fail to achieve an acceptable agreement (Brewster, Beck, Anderson, & Benjamin, 2011).

This chapter begins by describing coparent consultation, a competency-based approach to working with families engaged in challenging separations and divorces. Attention is paid to the specific competencies required of the consultant. We then discuss the critical aspects of a standardized protocol that leads to the parents' believing that their concerns are fairly and thoroughly heard and processed. We also highlight specific characteristics of the person of the consultant that must be attended to for such consultations to be effective.

## COPARENT CONSULTATION

As a competency-based model, coparent consultation serves as an alternative to further litigation in complex cases. This model differs from both divorce meditation and parent coordination in several ways. Most notably, both of these approaches often are court ordered in contrast to coparent consultation. We use the coparent consultation model in our practices, as do our colleagues whom we have trained. The model also works well for less conflictual family law cases. Coparent consultation for both parties and their child(ren) can move the family forward. This form of intensive family consultation is structured to build on the strengths of the parents while remediating their communication and parenting deficits. It also diminishes the exposure of the consultant to licensing board complaints by keeping any consultant involved in one role only: focusing on providing consultation with no blurring of this role. Under this model, the consultant recommends and seeks party agreement about how to handle child and family relationship issues in a noncontentious way (see Appendix 14.1). For coparent consultation to occur, both parents must stipulate to the process, and the consultant agrees to engage in the consultation process (see Appendix 14.1). The coparent consultation process rests on treating the family members with respect and transparency as the interventions are launched so that a new, better foundation for the family can be constructed from which to coparent in healthier ways. The consultation process includes working with the couple and sometimes their mature children to delineate their values and goals. The planned changes in behaviors and attitudes are focused on being congruent with their values when the concerns expressed by both parents are addressed (see Appendices 14.2, 14.3, and 14.4).

Research has strongly suggested that a perceived inequitable process rather than a perceived inequitable outcome most likely contributes to dissatisfaction with the final divorce decree (Sheets & Braver, 1996). Lawyers best serve the parties by assisting them to experience a fair process as well as achieve an equitable outcome. As a result, lawyers should refer their clients to coparent consultation before engaging in litigation because litigation often results in a "winner" and a "loser," whereas coparent consultation can lead to addressing the issues without such attributions poisoning the ongoing coparenting.

**Family Custody Issues**

Competence in consultation with high-conflict divorce and separation cases requires an in-depth knowledge of research conducted about such families an addition to skills that facilitate successful processes and outcomes, and awareness of attitudes and *values* that affect the family as well as the consultant. Briefly, divorce for many people usually entails feelings of failure, anger, betrayal, and loss, especially the loss of earlier hopes and dreams for the way the relationship could have been. Furthermore, divorce may present couples and individuals with complex values-based decisions and outcomes. In addition, litigation can produce great distress when compared with other types of professional services. The consequences of the emotional and financial stress on family law litigants can be severe (Hetherington, Cox, & Cox, 1985). Turning to litigation creates negative mental health consequences for children and their parents (Henry, Fieldstone, & Bohac, 2009). A substantial number of children involved in divorce are placed at significant risk of suffering further emotional and behavioral disturbances due to the ongoing exposure to parental conflict and litigation (Brewster et al., 2011).

Although a high-conflict family means different things to different family law professionals (Davis, 2015), such conflict can result in poor outcomes for the child(ren) because of a lack of social support; financial insecurity; and disruptive changes in their routines, schools, and residences. For example, many mediators use the term *high conflict* to define couples with inadequate and possibly damaging communication patterns, whereas judges and court personnel view them as intractable cases that do not settle (Davis, 2015; Pence, Davis, Beardslee, & Gamache, 2012). Parental adjustment problems also can lead to poor outcomes because of grief, impaired conflict resolution skills exacerbated by mental illness or addiction problems, and economic hardship because of financial decline in the residential household of the child (Sbarra & Emery, 2005). Deutsch and Pruett (2009) concluded that

> high conflict between parents is characterized by mistrust, anger, blaming, and disputes over child-related issues. . . . "Conflict" denotes verbal and physical expressions in which both parents are mutually engaged and refuse to submit to one another's rules, requests or demands (Johnston, 2006). At the high end of the continuum, conflict is often associated with physical aggression, where the child is more typically the overt subject of such conflict. (p. 354)

Such adjustment problems often lead the one parent to believe that the other parent is using some of the following tactics (Benjamin, Beck, Shaw, & Geffner, 2017):

- threatens to mistreat or harm my child or me;
- physically or emotionally mistreats or harms my child or me;
- sexually mistreats or harms my child or me;
- tries to control me through finances (e.g., withholding child support);
- tries to control or scare my child or me through damaging property;
- invades my privacy or monitors my whereabouts;
- threatens or actually physically harms himself or herself in front of my child or me;

- creates or uses conflict in a way that creates distress for my child;
- withholds contact or access to my child;
- refuses to comply with the court order regarding adult or child issues;
- refuses to coparent with me (e.g., will not talk with me about parenting issues); or
- makes negative comments about me that make my child confused, upset, or sad.

The abusive use of these conflict tactics distinguishes the clients of coparent consultation from those who divorce more amicably. Settlements and court-ordered resolutions can result in additional litigation without ongoing psychological interventions that address the effects of such tactics, something that does occur during coparent consultation. Also, alternative dispute resolution approaches, such as mediation and parenting coordination to settle disputes involving children, may fail. These approaches are aimed at relieving the high emotional and financial costs of litigation for families and the burden of increased litigation for the courts. But continuing abusive use of conflict tactics can sabotage all such efforts. Coparent consultation provides an approach with the parents that can markedly diminish the communication and parenting deficits of these families. The foregoing provides a summary of critical knowledge about family custody issues. We encourage our readers to continue to build their knowledge about such issues.

### Competencies of the Consultant

This competency-based model for coparenting consultations is predicated on the consultant's competence in the following. Consultants must possess competence in the clinical assessment of motivation and personality as well as in the use of checklists designed to determine current parent or caregiver behaviors (see Appendices 14.2, 14.3, and 14.4). They also should have a systemic understanding of couple and family dynamics and functioning; parent–child relationships; the impact of parental tensions, including arguing and intimate partner violence on children; and children's reactions to separation and divorce. In addition, they need to be competent in forming working alliances with consultees who may be hostile, uncooperative, contentious, tearful, silent, very dependent, or all of these. They remain up-to-date on the divorce literature, research, laws, and legal decisions. Those teaching divorce or supervising or consulting to graduate students, interns, postdoctoral residents, and professionals working in this arena should have the requisite knowledge base, skills, and attitudes to impart them and the belief that this model is relevant and often effective.

## THE COPARENTING CONSULTATION PROCESS

In this section, we delineate the specific seven sequential steps associated with the coparenting consultation process.

## Step 1: Build and Protect the Consultation Alliance

It is imperative that all communications among the parties, their child(ren), and the coparent consultant be confidential *and* privileged from disclosure to build and sustain the consultation alliance. It is in the best interests of the child(ren) and the parents that no one believes that what they process in coparent consultation will be exposed in later legal action. To avoid such a detrimental impact, a court order or a stipulation agreed on by the parties and their lawyers (if the parties are represented by lawyers) mandates that the coparent consultant will not testify at or produce for any proceeding or in any court opinions, records, documents, or recordings formed or created as part of the coparent consultation process. This mandate also reduces the risk of the coparent consultant's being charged with engaging in multiple relationships (*Ethical Principles of Psychologists and Code of Conduct* 3.05; APA, 2017; hereinafter, Ethics Code) because of the mixed roles of service provider and decision maker. Instead, during coparent consultation, the parents create a written record of their own decision making about the communication and parenting issues through ongoing emails.

If coparent consultation cannot result in civil, efficacious communication through this process, the coparent consultant may declare an impasse about the particular issue that is exposed by the thread of emails regarding the decision making or parenting behavior. To not surprise the parties, separate emails are sent to each party that delineate why an impasse may need to be noted. Concrete suggestions are provided to each party about what the party could commit to in an email that would remain congruent to their values. Processing continues with each party separately to see if an agreement can be found. If an impasse occurs, an email is sent to both parties, and the entire thread of only the joint discussions are included below the call for the impasse. In this manner, the consultation is preserved, and the coparent consultant does not engage in a multiple relationship (Ethics Code Standard 3.05; APA, 2017) by also engaging in the additional role of decision maker. An impasse also is declared if one of the following conditions arises:

- noncompliance with the terms of the consultation;
- incomplete or unequal participation by the parties or their child(ren);
- domestic violence, alcohol or drug abuse, or denial of access to the child;
- three coparent consultation sessions with parties have produced no substantial progress; or
- a 3-hour retainer balance for payment—that should be requested before commencing the coparent consultation services—is not maintained.

When an impasse is called, the coparent consultant recommends that one or more of following steps be pursued by the parties:

- ending consultation without any prejudice to either party;

- starting a party or a child in psychological evaluation and treatment with one of three providers recommended by the coparent consultant; or

- arbitrating the impasse through the services of one of three recommended arbitrators, all of whom were agreed on by the parties at the beginning of coparent consultation.

The parties and their lawyers commit the parties to the arbitration decisions remaining mandatory on the parties from the beginning of coparent consultation. The parties also commit by stipulation to additional protections of the arbitration process that will deter abusive use of litigation tactics:

1. If either party appeals an arbitration decision to the court, the party who files the appeal must pay the retainer fees of the other party; and

2. Unless the legal position of the appealing party is significantly improved during the appeal of the arbitration decision to the court, the appealing party must pay all of the legal fees and costs of the court appeal.

### Step 2: Determine if Cases Are Appropriate: How Consultants Engage in Screening Processes

Coparent consultation is an intensive consultation approach to assist chronically conflicted families to develop and implement healthy coparenting. Screening and referring inappropriate cases occur by the determining whether parents are ready for the process and are willing to follow its structure. In most instances, the initial emails between the coparent consultant and the parties provides sufficient evidence about whether a consultation alliance can be formed and the family can engage in the consultation process.

Typically, one parent or that parent's lawyer sends an email or inquire by phone about starting the process. No further contact occurs unless that parent or that parent's lawyer provides the names and email addresses of both parties. Requests for all information sought from either party or their lawyer always is conducted through email so that the written record will show that no ex parte influence occurred. On receipt of both email addresses, the initial contact is written up in an email that is sent to both parties along with the steps of coparent consultation process, disclosure forms, stipulation, and email text rules (see http://depts.washington.edu/petp/coparent.html#process). All of the questions about the process are answered by email to both parties (and their attorneys), but no further work occurs until the first advanced fee is collected, the parents sign the disclosure form and stipulation, and agree to follow the email rules. At that point, the parents are asked to complete allegation or issue forms (see Appendix 14.2) about every single concern that each parent holds about the other parent and how that parent treats their child(ren). No meetings with the parents occur until those forms are returned because the forms help the consultant prepare for the first interview of each parent.

### Step 3: Interview Parents Separately

The consultant should engage in these steps to ensure each parent recognizes the limits of confidentiality during the email interactions and has understood the stipulation and its impact, particularly what will happen if an impasse is called. During the first separate meetings, the consultant takes each parent through the disclosure process carefully. The parties are guided to understand that the stipulation precludes the consultant from providing any consultation notes or testimony about the parents and their child(ren). This part of the process helps the parents stop any posturing. It creates additional readiness to work on improving their communication and remedying their parenting deficits. They also are engaged in formulating their values and begin to consider how their behavior can become consistent with those values (see Appendices 14.3 and 14.4).

As soon as the parent agrees to the terms of coparent consultation, an allegation-focused interview occurs that is based on the documentation submitted by both parties (see Appendix 14.2). Each parent is asked to take the perspective of the other parent when explaining how the other parent could have possibly formed the concerns that were documented (Kohlberg & Turiel, 1971). The details that are provided assist the consultant in understanding more about the parent's judgment and level of insight. At the end of the session, the values homework exercise (see Appendix 14.3) is provided, and questions about the assignment are addressed. We also give them the value-based goal setting list (see Appendix 14.4) and ask them to complete it by the next session along with the coparenting consultation chart (see Appendix 14.5) to reinforce the importance of negotiating their agreement to be predicated on their goals and values. The consultant schedules an appointment for the parent–child(ren) observation (two separate observations: one with one parent and his or her child[ren] and a second with the other parent and his or her child[ren]) and gives instructions for conducting this part of the assessment so that targeted consultation can occur.

## Step 4: Observe Parents and Children

The consultant conducts a structured observation process that involves a digitally video recorded interaction between parent and child(ren). A semistructured process provides examples of parenting strengths and deficits. In the event that a parent comes unprepared for engaging in an hour-long set of play interactions, the consultant provides a container of age-appropriate toys or other items, such as art supplies. All children within the family are observed together with each parent unless the child(ren) are adolescents. (A separate process for adolescents is described later in this section.) How the parent and child interact and talk to one another is observed in terms of relational dynamics, quality of attachment, affection, respect, and voice tone.

Both in oral and written instructions, the consultant explains to the parent the process of the parent–child observations. The parent is first asked to discuss with the child(ren) why they are in this consultation today. Next, the consultant instructs the parent and child(ren) "to do something fun together," first with the child(ren) directing the activity followed by a phase in which the parent is directing the activity. A cleanup phase follows when a structured opportunity occurs for all of the belongings of the party and child(ren) to be collected and the clinic's toys to be put away.

The parent is instructed that he or she should shift to the second phase—the cleanup phase of the observation portion of the meeting—once he or she hears a knock on the one-way mirror or the door. The consultant demonstrates at the time these instructions are delivered how the knock will sound so other building noises will not mislead the party or the child(ren).

The first two phases of the observation continue for 15 to 20 minutes, depending on a natural break point in the activities. The consultant knocks when a period of static activity has continued into this 15- to 20-minute range. Around 50 minutes into the observation, the second and last knock signals the transition to the cleanup phase.

When adolescents are involved, the consultant instructs the parent and adolescent to discuss a series of questions. Each adolescent is viewed with the parent as a dyad. Although the allegations of the case may shape some of the questions, the usual instructions include the following:

- discuss a typical day within the household of the parent,
- outline the family rules and daily tasks the adolescent is expected to carry out,
- discuss the school experience and expectations about homework completion,
- discuss what happens when someone breaks family rules, and
- plan for something fun to do together.

All questions are written in advance and handed to the parent. Each parent and adolescent receives the same set of instructions. The parent is instructed to not discuss the next question until a knock occurs. Often during periods of waiting, parent–child interactions provide telling data.

At the end of the observation, the parent is asked if the interactions are a good representation of typical interactions that occur between the parent and the child(ren). Rarely has a parent declared that the observation was unrepresentative of their typical interactions. If the consultant is not satisfied with the observation, another observation is scheduled, and the parent is asked to send an email to the consultant about what occurred in the first observation that was unrepresentative.

The observation assists the consultant in determining the efficacy of each person's parenting and the relative strengths and weaknesses of each party. In addition, during the review of the digitally video recorded observations, several fundamental parenting behaviors should emerge. The strength of the emotional bond between the parent and the child(ren) is then assessed on the basis of the observed competence of each parent during the interactions, the parent's responses to the child(ren), the child(ren)'s responses to the parent, and the modeling of prosocial behavior by the parent. These observational data deepen the clinical judgments about parental strengths, weaknesses, and the parent–child bond. The consultant also notes parenting behaviors that appear outside the range of expected skills. Molly Reid at the University of Washington (Benjamin,

Reid, Wood, & Gollan, 2012) modified the following operational definitions of expected baseline parenting behaviors from Eyberg's (1974; Eyberg & Bogg, 1989) earlier work about assessing the health of parenting choices and the quality of the relational interactions (Benjamin et al., 2017):

- *Compliance* occurs when the child follows instructions within a short period (a few seconds).

- *Noncompliance* occurs when the child fails to follow instructions within a short period.

- *Inappropriate behavior* occurs when the child whines, sasses, fails to exercise common courtesy, cries, yells, destroys or attempts to destroy an object, hits the parent, or repeatedly asks the same question after it has been answered.

- A *direct instruction* is a clear statement by the parent telling the child to perform some specific behavior. The parent models common courtesy whenever issuing a direct instruction. Direct instructions can also include forced choices (e.g., "Please pick up the toys and put them on the shelf," "Please pick up the blocks and the dinosaurs").

- An *indirect instruction* occurs when the parent's direction to the child is vague or ambiguous, or implies that the child has a choice (e.g., "Let's clean up" but parent actually means, "*You* put the *toys* on the *shelf*"; "Why don't you . . .").

- A *question* is any interrogative statement. Many parents inappropriately use questions when they should use direct instructions ("When will you clean up?" but the parent actually means, "Please put away the toys in the room now").

- A *descriptive statement* is any parental verbalization to the child that describes what the child or parent is doing. Such statements are important because they offer reinforcing attention to the child regarding specific behaviors. These statements also demonstrate for the child that the parent is attuned to the child's needs as well as demonstrate the parent's empathy with child, the ability to encourage the child, and the ability to reflect accurately the child's perspective during play. Descriptive statements are encouraging and validating to the child ("You are really getting the puzzle put together fast"; "Oh, you're stacking the blocks on each other. I'm stacking my blocks, too"). Inappropriate behaviors are not described to avoid negatively reinforcing child behavior.

- *Labeled praise* is a reinforcing statement specifically identifying for the child what child behavior the parent likes or desires ("Well placed, Susan. You stacked those blocks wonderfully"; "Thank you for putting all of the blocks away just as I asked").

- *Unlabeled praise* is a reinforcing statement or phrase that is vaguely unspecific ("Good boy!"; "That's nice."; "Okay").

- *Physical praise* occurs whenever the parent gives the child a hug, a pat on the back, a kiss, or any touching as apparent praise for good behavior.

- *Critical comments* are any negative, apparently punitive statements to the child ("No!"; "You know you are not supposed to do that!"; "What's the matter with you?!"; "Can't you do anything I tell you to?!" "Now, look. You've got the whole room in a mess"; "I don't like that"). Such comments suggest an inability to recognize the child's needs or wants, suggest rigidity and a lack of flexibility when parenting, and show that the parent's agenda comes first—possible evidence of authoritarian parenting.

- *Ignores inappropriate behavior* is noted when the parent makes no verbal or physical response to inappropriate child behavior. Healthy parenting involves finding a balance when helping the child to develop prosocial or effective instrumental behavior. Constant management of the child by the parent is authoritarian and limits independent consequences from arising that are unrelated to the parent involvement. Children are less likely to develop self-efficacy as a result. Instead, they are shaped only by the externalized reinforcement of the parent or, worse, the lack of a parent's ability to regulate their feelings (e.g., anger).

All parenting strengths and deficits are noted for later reporting to the parties when the consultation plan is discussed. Portions of the digitally video recorded may be replayed with the parent(s) to demonstrate a parenting deficit so that the consultant can model better parental options.

## Step 5: Report Findings to Parties

The interview that discusses the consultation plan is broken into two discrete parts (see APA, 2007, for an example of this approach). The first part gains further clarification about any details about the communication or parenting deficits. The second part contains structured statements about communication or parenting deficits that have emerged from emails to date, any records that the parties provided, and the interviews and observations of the parents. The statements present the evidence about the particular deficit.

The consultant also gently challenges any allegations that do not appear to be corroborated by the data. The consultant can use the digital video recording of the parent–child observation to point out parenting knowledge and skills relevant to the specific issues raised by the other parent or skill deficits that require remediation. Each deficit that requires change is concretely described, and the consultant shares options of constructive parental behavior that could replace the problematic actions in a fashion that is more reflective of the parent's values. Examples of alternative constructive behavior are provided that are congruent with the parent's stated values. The parent takes notes about the findings and forwards an email to the consultant that explains the changes that are expected through providing concrete examples. Once agreement through email occurs between the consultant and each parent separately, the consultant forwards a consultation plan to both parties and their lawyers.

## Step 6: Proceed With Consultation

Citing Kelly (2007), Fridhandler and Lehmer (2014) noted, "Outcomes for children are poorest in conflicted coparenting and best in cooperative and parallel coparenting" arrangements, with *parallel coparenting* defined by Sullivan (2008) as the parents' minimizing their communications and interactions. Consultation is launched through the email, with both parents agreeing to no more physical or voice contact with the other parent. Emotional regulation becomes much easier when the parent can engage in problem-solving through simple statements forwarded by email that meet the email rules of coparent consultation and focus on moving forward in ways that are compatible with the parent's values (see Appendices 14.3 and 14.4).

If communication or parenting behavior is outside the range of the what is congruent with the parent's values, specific modeling of the behavior occurs in subsequent session(s) with the parent (and child[ren] as needed). These individual sessions with the consultant assist each parent in developing more constructive communication skills and parenting actions. After each session, the parent describes in an email the behavior that needs to change in a concrete manner and how it relates to a parental value and then sends that note to the coparent consultant. Once an accurate understanding is reached with the coparent consultant, the client also copies the other parent on the note.

## Step 7: Resolve an Impasse Through Immediate Arbitration

In postdivorce situations with little conflict and good communication between the former spouses, changes of circumstances that may affect the needs of either parent or any of the children can be accommodated without requiring additional litigation, even if the parents have significant differences of opinion. Greater trust and an ability to rely on each other grow as communication improves and agreements work well. After the divorce, even a contentious divorce, a gradual transition to a new period of stabilization occurs. It typically takes 2 to 5 years beyond the separation for the instability in the children's lives to settle out and the psychological functioning of the parties to improve significantly (Kaslow, 1991).

New stability, however, can again be threatened by any major change. Stabilization may be disrupted by remarriage, family relocations, new developmental stages in the children (e.g., an adolescent who no longer wants to be bound to a regular visitation schedule), emerging behavioral problems in one or more of the children, a child's refusal to visit the nonresident parent, or major changes in financial circumstances. Poor outcomes are more likely when parties remain or become emotionally disturbed, engage in drug or alcohol abuse, or are hostile toward each other, and so forth (Brewster et al., 2011).

Coparent consultation can establish a constructive parallel coparenting context in which the processing of any new conflict can avoid ensnaring the children in the problem. Impartial assistance through postdivorce coparent consultant can help resolve any emerging issues. When conflict is high, it is helpful if communication about decision making is restricted to written documentation of an email. Such a manner of communication dampens conflictual tactics, provides a more leisurely response period that allows for the quieting of impulsive outbursts, and, if necessary, provides a written evidentiary record of improper communication. If such communication continues, it may warrant a change to sole decision making.

Persistent parental conflict is strongly associated with poor child adjustment. The level of conflict is more likely to be reduced and the quality of parenting increased if the embattled parties work with an impartial, well-trained professional who is astute in behavioral and relational dynamics, stages of divorce and postdivorce, and legal issues regarding custody, divorce, and remarriage.

If during coparent consultation the written record shows an unequal bargaining relationship exists between the parties or that one or both parties appear incapable of resolving conflicts in good faith based on the written email record, the conflict is resolved quickly by mandatory arbitration. Mutually agreed-on arbitrators should remain available to the parties for at least 3 years following the settlement agreement or court order. Quick, inexpensive resolution of further impasses then occur. Binding or mandatory arbitration can result in rapid resolution (fewer than 2 weeks) at considerably less cost than returning to court. Many jurisdictions in this nation have enabled arbitration as a dispute resolution process for family law cases. All impasses are arbitrated.

## THE PERSON OF THE CONSULTANT

In addition to the consultation-related knowledge, skills, and attitudes delineated earlier, several other personal factors are relevant in determining whether the professional is competent and proficient to serve as a coparent consultant. Psychologists need to be mindful of the influence of their own personal values, including attitudes toward separation, divorce, family unification, or other beliefs that could potentially lead to bias. The consultant's personal history, for example, as having been the child of a divorce, the parent of a divorce, or personally divorced, will likely affect their personal values. Psychologists need to be aware of how these personal experiences affect the "person" of the consultant. Are they able to be an unbiased consultant? Have they resolved their own issues so that they do not have a negative or positive countertransference reaction to either or both parties in the separation or divorce process (Kaslow, 2018)?

Sometimes having a coconsultant conduct the consultation process can help mitigate such potentially biased reactions. Another concern is that the consultant's personal beliefs may lead to thinking that the divorce is wrong or a sin, and this is likely to preclude maximum objectivity.

## CONCLUSION

Divorce is a time of heightened psychological stress and disequilibrium for most couples. It continues to affect many family members long after the legal documents are signed. These divorces require a restructuring of parental rights and responsibilities with respect to the children that can have great impact if not carried out effectively.

Coparent consultation can end destructive parental conflict and move the parents into parallel coparenting. It keeps the child(ren) out of the conflict zones so that they can focus their full attention on age-appropriate activities, social interactions, and their academic or vocational activities. It also increases adaptive parental communication and improves parenting skills and the lives of all postdivorce family members.

---

## APPENDIX 14.1
## STIPULATION FORM

IN THE SUPERIOR COURT OF THE STATE OF WASHINGTON
FOR KING COUNTY

In re Parentage of ?:                )

                                      )

                                      )

?                                     ) No. ? SEA

                                      )

Petitioner,                          ) Stipulation Regarding Coparent Consultation
                                      )      Conducted by
and                                   ) G. Andrew H. Benjamin, JD, PhD, ABPP

                                      )

?                                     )

                                      )

Respondent.                          )
_____ )

THIS STIPULATION is entered into between the Petitioner ? and the Respondent ?, and they each declare and agree to the following:

1) All communications among the parties, their child, and the coparent psychotherapist will be confidential and privileged from disclosure. Both parties stipulate that Dr. Benjamin will not be required to testify at or to produce for any proceeding or in any court opinions, records, documents, or recordings formed or created as part of the coparent consultation process.

2) It is in the best interests of the child and the parties that no one feels influenced by any possible later legal action when involved in coparent consultation. Without both parties entering into this type of stipulation, the therapeutic alliance would be affected detrimentally.

3) This stipulation does not preclude obeying the statutory requirements to report information about: child, adult dependent person, or elder abuse, neglect, or exploitation; an actual threat of violence against a reasonably identifiable victim(s); or mental illness that requires involuntary commitment because of danger to self or others or grave disability.

4) Each participant must provide releases of information to other professionals who are evaluating or treating the parties or their child, if any, to facilitate the coparent consultation process with the Dr. Benjamin.

5) The parties, or child of the parties, may require evaluation and treatment by another mental health professional. If Dr. Benjamin recommends such a course of action, he will provide or approve the names of three qualified mental health professionals. The parties or child of the parties then must seek additional services.

6) The coparent consultation process will be determined to be at an impasse if:
   a. Dr. Benjamin declares it because of
      1. Noncompliance with the terms of the consultation;
      2. Incomplete or unequal participation by the parties or their child;
      3. Lack of the parties' or the child's personal readiness;
      4. Domestic violence, alcohol or drug abuse, or denial of access to the child;
      5. Failure to maintain a 3-hour retainer balance for payment of the Consultation services.
   b. A party or their child may declare an impasse and Dr. Benjamin agrees because of one of the preceding reasons.
   c. Three coparent consultation sessions with parties have produced no substantial progress.
   d. The parties mutually agree.

7) An impasse will be handled in one or more of following ways as designated by Dr. Benjamin:
   a. Ending treatment by Dr. Benjamin without any prejudice.
   b. Starting a party or a child in other psychological evaluation or treatment as specified above.
   c. Resuming the consultation process after a sufficient period of time not to exceed 90 days, and the parties have followed the interim recommendations of Dr. Benjamin during this period of time.
   d. Arbitrating the impasse through the services of ??, ??, or ??. Any arbitration decision shall remain mandatory on the parties. If either party appeals an arbitration decision to the Court, the party who files the appeal must pay the retainer fees of the other party. Unless the legal position of the appealing party is significantly improved, the appealing party must pay the entire fees and costs of the action in the Court.

8) These stipulations have been explained to us, and we agree to abide by them. We have been provided ample opportunity to inquire into the experience and credentials of Dr. Benjamin. We have consulted with our attorneys about these stipulations and are fully satisfied with proceeding under the proposed approach.

9) We certify under penalty of perjury under the laws of the State of Washington that the foregoing is true and correct and mutually agreed upon.

_____   _____

Date_____   Date_____

---

## APPENDIX 14.2
## ALLEGATION FORM

### LIST OF ALLEGATIONS ABOUT PARENTS OR CARETAKERS

Adults involved in custody disputes often express strong concerns about the welfare and behavior of other adult parents and caretakers. This questionnaire asks you to do three things:

1. Read the list of divorce-related allegations below.

2. Please write down the name of the adult caretaker you are referring to and check off one allegation. <u>Please choose one person and check one allegation per sheet</u>. If you think the same allegation applies to two or more adults, then fill out separate sheets for each adult. Writing one allegation per adult per sheet helps the consultant track your specific concerns.

3. Please check off one of the allegations that best describes your concern.

**NAME OF PARENT OR ADULT**: _____

**TYPE OF ALLEGATION**: Check <u>one</u> of the allegations below.

_____   Threatens to mistreat or harm me

_____   Physically mistreats or harms me

_____   Emotionally mistreats or harms me

_____   Sexually mistreats or harms me

_____   Tries to control me through finances (e.g., withholding child support)

_____   Tries to control or scare me through damaging property

_____   Invades my privacy or monitors my whereabouts

_____    Uses alcohol to excess

_____    Uses drugs to excess

_____    Uses alcohol or drugs in my presence

_____    Threatened to harm himself or herself in front of me

_____    Physically harms himself or herself in front of me or the child(ren)

_____    Creates or uses conflict in a way that creates distress for my child(ren)

_____    Withholds contact or access to the child(ren)

_____    Refuses to comply with the court order regarding adult issues

_____    Refuses to coparent with me (e.g., will not talk with me about parenting issues)

_____    Says negative things about me that make me confused, upset, or sad

_____    Has a long-term emotional impairment (e.g., mental illness)

_____    Doesn't have parenting skills or experience, which makes it hard for me to parent

_____    Other A: _____.

_____    Other B: _____.

**EVIDENCE TO SUPPORT ALLEGATION**: Please write down brief and specific descriptions of the situation that supports the allegation that the other adult or parent has affected you. Please try to include factually correct and detailed information about the event that supports your assertion. Please describe the <u>two most recent examples and the worst example</u> (e.g., most troubling) for each allegation on three separate sheets. If you have questions, please ask your consultant for more explanation. *Remember:* Use one sheet per allegation. You may use the back of a sheet if you need more space.

<u>Date, Time, and Place of Event or Situation:</u>

<u>Who was present?</u> (Include name, phone number, relationship to the child(ren).)

<u>What happened exactly?</u>

<u>What did you do before, during, and after this event or situation?</u>

<u>What did the other adult do before, during, and after the event or situation?</u>

<u>Did you talk with anyone about the event or situation? Did anyone witness the event?</u> (Include name, phone number, and date of conversation.)

<u>If we were to talk to these witnesses, what would they say about what happened?</u>

<u>What were the negative effects of this specific event or situation on you?</u>

## LIST OF CHILD-FOCUSED ALLEGATIONS

Children involved in custody disputes may experience problems as a result of the behavior of their parents or caretakers. This questionnaire asks you to do three things:

1. Read the list of child-focused allegations below.

2. Please write down the name of the parent or caretaker you are concerned about, and check off one allegation. <u>Please choose one person and check one allegation per sheet</u>. If you think the same allegation applies to two or more adults, then fill out separate sheets for each adult. Writing one allegation per adult per sheet helps the consultant track your specific concerns.

3. Please check off one of the allegations that best describes your concern.

**NAME OF PARENT OR ADULT**: _____

**NAME OF CHILD WHO HAS BEEN HARMED:**

_____

**TYPE OF ALLEGATION**: Check <u>one</u> allegation.

_____ Threatens to mistreat or harm my child

_____ Physically mistreats or harms my child

_____ Emotionally mistreats or harms my child

_____ Sexually mistreats or harms my child

_____ Tries to control my child through finances (e.g., bribes or withholds allowance)

_____ Tries to control or scare my child through damaging property

_____ Invades my child's privacy or monitors my child's whereabouts

_____ Uses alcohol to excess in front of the child

_____ Uses drugs to excess in front of the child

_____ Uses alcohol or drugs or both while responsible for parenting

_____ Threatened to harm himself or herself in front of the child

_____ Physically harms himself or herself in front of the child

_____ Creates or uses conflict in a way that creates distress for my child

_____ Withholds contact or access to the child

_____ Refuses to comply with the court order regarding parenting (e.g., misses child visits)

_____   Refuses to coparent with me (e.g., will not talk with me about parenting issues)

_____   Says negative things about me that make my child confused, upset, or sad

_____   Has a long-term emotional impairment (e.g., mental illness)

_____   Doesn't have parenting skills or experience, which impacts my child's well-being

_____   Other A: _____.

_____   Other B: _____.

**EVIDENCE TO SUPPORT ALLEGATION**: Please write down brief and specific descriptions of the event or situation that supports your allegation. We are interested in how this event affected your child. Please try to include factually correct and detailed information about the event that supports your assertion. Please describe the <u>two most recent examples and the worst example</u> (e.g., most troubling) for each allegation on three separate sheets. If you have questions, please ask your consultant for more explanation. Remember: Use one sheet per allegation. You may use the back of a sheet if you need more space.

<u>Date, Time, and Place of Event or Situation:</u>

<u>Who was present</u>? (Include name, phone number, relationship to the child(ren).)

<u>What happened exactly</u>?

<u>What did you do before, during, and after this event or situation</u>?

<u>What did the other adult do before, during, and after the event or situation</u>?

<u>Did you talk with anyone about the event or situation</u>? <u>Did anyone witness the event</u>? (Include name, phone number, and date of conversation.)

<u>If we were to talk to these witnesses, what would they say about what happened</u>?

<u>What were the negative effects of this specific event or situation on you</u>?

---

## APPENDIX 14.3
## TRUE-SELF VALUES

As you reflect about how to engage the values task, consider the best decisions and the best relationship interactions that you have had during the course of your life. Please consider that they went so well because you were acting congruently with these deeply felt values. The assignment is to help you articulate those values and to make them quite concrete for each of the 16 competencies

that are set out in the worksheet below. *Note.* An example in first-person present tense is included under each competency (values should always be listed
in an affirmative manner). Please do not use the example—you have your
own values. Each example demonstrates the expected form and specificity
required. Remember to delete the sample value and provide three of your own
values for each competency. Please bring two hard copies of your 48 values
with you.

## NURTURING

*Example: I express appreciation when an individual enters my presence.*

1.

2.

3.

## COMMUNICATION:
### SENDING

*Example: I am clear and specific in my verbal communication.*

1.

2.

3.

### RECEIVING

*Example: I detect underlying themes and patterns in others' communication.*

1.

2.

3.

## ATTITUDES

*Example: I focus on the likely positive outcomes in given situations.*

1.

2.

3.

## PHYSICAL HEALTH

*Example: I get sufficient exercise to promote physical fitness.*

1.

2.

3.

**ETHICS**
*Example: I act with integrity.*

1.

2.

3.

**EMOTIONAL HEALTH**
*Example: I diligently clarify the actions of others that generate strong feelings.*

1.

2.

3.

**MANNERS**
*Example: I am silent about others' shortcomings unless there is a good reason to bring them up.*

1.

2.

3.

**WORK HEALTH**
*Example: I diligently use a time management system in my daily life.*

1.

2.

3.

**SPIRITUALITY**
*Example: I evaluate how I pursue my values in the context of my faith.*

1.

2.

3.

**RECREATION**
*Example: In my recreational activities, I pursue intellectual stimulation.*

1.

2.

3.

## ROMANCE/MARRIAGE

*Example: I engage in full partnership by being assertive about my needs.*

1.

2.

3.

## MONEY

*Example: I plan how to save and spend money with my partner.*

1.

2.

3.

## SEX

*Example: Whenever I feel uncomfortable, I redirect my partner to touch me in another way.*

1.

2.

3.

## CHILDREN

*Example: I am available to my children.*

1.

2.

3.

## FRIENDSHIP

*Example: I am dependable and faithful to my friends.*

1.

2.

3.

---

## APPENDIX 14.4
## VALUE-BASED GOAL SETTING IN COPARENTING CONSULTATION

*Check all that apply:*

I.  Define Your Values—Powerful goals are built on your core values. What is important to you in the following areas?

1. ____ Children's well-being postdivorce

2. ____ Coparenting in a healthy, cooperative manner

3. ____ Promoting collaborative child-rearing arrangements

4. ____ Being in charge of my behavior, my thoughts, my feelings

II.  Fashion Your Future Self—Decide who and what future you want. Ask yourself the following questions:

1. ____ What does my future ideal self look like and feel like?

2. ____ What is the quality of my relationships? What do I need to change to obtain this quality, particularly in the coparenting and child–parent relationships?

3 ____ What do I want to strive for as my highest potential?

4. ____ Will I act with integrity and consideration of others, especially my children or ex-partner?

III. Write Out Predetermined Goals (for your postdivorce life, particularly in relation to your ex-spouse, child(ren), and ex–in-law family). A goal is most compelling when written with the following characteristics:

1. **Positive:** Articulate what you <u>will</u> create. A goal is what you <u>will</u> do. It is an affirmation of intention.

2. **Set Target Date:** Always state the date by which you plan to achieve your goal.

3. **Present Tense:** Write your goals in the here and <u>now</u>.

4. **Be Specific:** Clarity adds vision.

5. **Evaluate:** Define how you will know you have reached your goal(s).

6. **Self-Reflection:** Jot down what usually impedes your goal realization and how you can overcome the obstacles or traits.

**APPENDIX 14.5**
**COPARENTING CONSULTATION CHART**

Name:

Age:

Date Partnered/Married

Current Residence: Parent 1

Current Residence: Parent 2

| Values | Major goals for consultation | Steps to be taken | Target dates | Self-reflections (What might keep you from reaching goals? Be specific.) How might you overcome obstacles? How might you know when you reach goals? |
|---|---|---|---|---|
|  |  |  |  |  |
|  |  |  |  |  |
|  |  |  |  |  |
|  |  |  |  |  |
|  |  |  |  |  |
|  |  |  |  |  |
|  |  |  |  |  |

## REFERENCES

American Psychological Association (Producer). (2007). *Child custody* [DVD]. Available from https://www.apa.org/pubs/videos/4310753

American Psychological Association. (2012). Guidelines for the practice of parenting coordination. *American Psychologist, 67*, 63–71. http://dx.doi.org/10.1037/a0024646 Retrieved from http://www.apa.org/practice/guidelines/parenting-coordination.pdf

American Psychological Association. (2017). *Ethical principles of psychologists and code of conduct* (2002, Amended June 1, 2010 and January 1, 2017). Retrieved from http://www.apa.org/ethics/code/index.aspx

Benjamin, G. A. H., Beck, C. A., Shaw, M., & Geffner, R. (2017). *Family evaluation in custody litigation: Promoting Optimal outcomes and reducing ethical risks* (2nd ed.). Washington, DC: American Psychological Association.

Benjamin, G. A. H., Reid, M., Wood, B., & Gollan, J. K. (2012). Psychological aspects of divorce. In D. J. Radin (Ed.), *Washington family law deskbook* (2nd ed., Vol. 1, Chapter 1 [CD]). Seattle: Washington State Bar Association.

Brewster, K. O., Beck, C. J. A., Anderson, E. R., & Benjamin, G. A. H. (2011). Evaluating parenting coordination programs: Encouraging results from pilot testing a research methodology. *Journal of Child Custody: Research, Issues, and Practices, 8*, 247–267. http://dx.doi.org/10.1080/15379418.2011.620926

Davis, G. (2015). A systematic approach to domestic abuse-informed child custody decision making in family law cases. *Family Court Review, 53*, 565–577. http://dx.doi.org/10.1111/fcre.12173

Deutsch, R. M., & Pruett, M. K. (2009). Child adjustment and high conflict divorce. In R. M. Galatzer-Levy & L. Kraus (Eds.), *The scientific basis of custody decisions* (2nd ed., pp. 353–374). New York, NY: Wiley.

Eyberg, S. (1974). *Manual for coding dyadic parent–child interactions.* Unpublished manuscript, Department of Medical Psychology, Oregon Health Sciences University, Portland.

Eyberg, S., & Bogg, S. (1989). Parent training for oppositional-defiant preschoolers. In C. E. Schaefer & J. M. Briesmeister (Eds.), *Handbook of parent training: Parents as co-therapists for children's behavior problems* (pp. 105–132). Oxford, England: Wiley.

Fieldstone, L. B., & Coates, C. A. (Eds.). (2008). *Innovations in interventions with high conflict families.* Madison, WI: Association of Family and Conciliation Courts.

Fridhandler, B., & Lehmer, M. (2014). Ethical issues in coparent counseling. *Journal of Child Custody, 11*, 139–158. http://dx.doi.org/10.1080/15379418.2014.921590

Henry, W. J., Fieldstone, L., & Bohac, K. (2009). Parenting coordination and court relitigation: A case study. *Family Court Review: An Interdisciplinary Journal, 47*, 682–697. http://dx.doi.org/10.1111/j.1744-1617.2009.01281.x

Hetherington, E. M., Cox, M., & Cox, R. (1985). Long-term effects of divorce and remarriage on the adjustment of children. *Journal of the American Academy of Child Psychiatry, 24*, 518–530. http://dx.doi.org/10.1016/S0002-7138(09)60052-2

Johnston, J. R. (2006). A child-centered approach to high-conflict and domestic-violence families: Differential assessment and interventions. *Journal of Family Studies, 12*, 15–35. http://dx.doi.org/10.5172/jfs.327.12.1.15

Kaslow, F. W. (1990). Divorce therapy and mediation for better custody. *Japanese Journal of Family Psychology, 4*, 19–37.

Kaslow, F. W. (1991). The sociocultural context of divorce. *Contemporary Family Therapy, 13*, 583–607. http://dx.doi.org/10.1007/BF00890595

Kaslow, F. W. (2018). Countertransference in couples therapy. In J. Lebow, A. Chambers, & D. C. Breunlin (Eds.), *Encyclopedia of couple and family therapy* (pp. 1–10). Cham, Switzerland: Springer. http://dx.doi.org/10.1007/978-3-319-15877-8_2-1

Kelly, J. B. (2007). Children's living arrangements following separation and divorce: Insights from empirical and clinical research. *Family Process, 46*, 35–52. http://dx.doi.org/10.1111/j.1545-5300.2006.00190.x

Kohlberg, L., & Turiel, E. (1971). Moral development and moral education. In G. S. Lesser (Ed.), *Psychology and educational practice* (pp. 410–465). Chicago, IL: Scott Foresman.

Nurse, A. R., & Thompson, P. (2012). Collaborative divorce: A family-centered process. In J. H. Bray & M. Stanton (Eds.), *The Wiley-Blackwell handbook of family psychology* (pp. 475–486). Walden, MA: Wiley-Blackwell.

Pence, E., Davis, G., Beardslee, C., & Gamache, D. (2012, June). *Mind the Gap: Accounting for domestic abuse in child custody evaluations.* Minneapolis, MN: Battered Women's Justice Project. Retrieved from https://www.courts.wa.gov/programs_orgs/gjc/documents/Mind_the_Gap_Accounting_for_Domestic_Abuse_in_Child_Custody_Evaluations.pdf

Sbarra, D. A., & Emery, R. E. (2005). Coparenting conflict, nonacceptance, and depression among divorced adults: Results from a 12-year follow-up study of child custody mediation using multiple imputation. *American Journal of Orthopsychiatry, 75,* 63–75. http://dx.doi.org/10.1037/0002-9432.75.1.63

Schwartz, L. L., & Kaslow, F. W. (1997). *Wiley series in couples and family dynamics and treatment. Painful partings: Divorce and its aftermath.* Hoboken, NJ: Wiley.

Sheets, V. L., & Braver, S. L. (1996). Gender differences in satisfaction with divorce settlements. *Family Relations: Interdisciplinary Journal of Applied Family Studies, 45,* 336–342. http://dx.doi.org/10.2307/585506

Sullivan, M. J. (2008). Coparenting and the parenting coordination process. *Journal of Child Custody, 5,* 4–24. http://dx.doi.org/10.1080/15379410802070351

# 15

# Consultation in Police and Public Safety Psychology

Cary L. Mitchell and Edrick H. Dorian

Modern law enforcement agencies are complex organizations that employ a broad range of professionals and serve increasingly diverse and vocal constituencies. Once considered rare birds in the law enforcement landscape (Reiser, 1972), today's psychologists are integral to the effective functioning of both large and small police departments. Growing numbers of psychologists pursue training and develop consultation practices in police and public safety psychology (PPSP). For example, as many as 4,500 psychologists in the United States annually participate in conducting preemployment psychological evaluations of police officer candidates (Cuttler, 2011), which is just one area of police psychology practice. Major professional organizations have formally recognized PPSP as a specialty (Trompetter, 2017), which will likely spur the development of additional training and practice opportunities. Police psychologists also appear uniquely positioned to help strengthen the trust between law enforcement agencies and the communities they serve, something the President's Task Force on 21st Century Policing identified as a critical need (Mitchell & Dorian, 2017).

In this chapter, we summarize the development of this vital, emerging area of psychological practice, which offers a broad range of full- and part-time consulting opportunities. We consider different models of consultation in PPSP while exploring the requisite knowledge, skills, and attitudes that compose a competency-based approach. Our goals are to illuminate best practices, introduce avenues for participation in the specialty, and highlight important resources.

http://dx.doi.org/10.1037/0000153-016
*Consultation in Psychology: A Competency-Based Approach*, C. A. Falender and
E. P. Shafranske (Editors)

## HISTORY AND DEVELOPMENT

According to Kitaeff (2011b), Hugo Munsterberg was arguably the first police psychologist in that he explored psychological aspects of crime detection and related themes in an influential book titled *On the Witness Stand* (Munsterberg, 1908). Other early examples of psychological consultation to law enforcement included Terman's use of psychological testing to assist the San Jose Police Department in California in its selection of police officers (Terman et al., 1917). By the 1970s, the provision of direct psychological services to law enforcement personnel was more common and included individual therapy for police officers, substance abuse recovery groups, and postcritical incident debriefings (Kitaeff, 2011b). Important to the development of police psychology was a number of federal commissions that advocated for reforms in areas such as police officer selection and training (Trompetter, 2017), including The President's Commission on Law Enforcement and Administration of Justice (President's Commission, 1967). These political and social forces, along with the accumulated wisdom of police psychologists and the fruit of psychological research, led to the expansion of police psychology to include four domains: assessment, intervention, operational support, and organizational consultation (Aumiller & Corey, 2007).

The maturing of police psychology into a distinct practice area was formalized by two important events. In 2011, the American Board of Professional Psychology (ABPP) recognized PPSP as its 14th specialty board (ABPP, n.d.). This meant that PPSP took its place among other specialties, such as clinical neuropsychology and clinical health psychology, as a practice area in which psychologists could seek advanced certification. Trompetter (2011) described this achievement as the most important development to date in the history of police psychology. In 2013, the American Psychological Association (APA) officially recognized PPSP as a specialty (APA, n.d.-b). Professional milestones such as these do not occur by accident; they are the hard-won successes of visionary professionals working together.

## CONTEMPORARY DEFINITION

APA (n.d.-a) describes PPSP as follows:

> Police and public safety psychology is concerned with assisting law enforcement and other public safety personnel and agencies in carrying out their missions and societal functions with effectiveness, safety, health and conformity to laws and ethics. It consists of the application of the science and profession of psychology in four primary domains of practice: assessment, clinical intervention, operational support, organizational consultation. ("Police and Public Safety")

The four domains and other definitional aspects of PPSP have been described in detail elsewhere (e.g., Aumiller & Corey, 2007; Trompetter, 2017) and are explored more fully later in this chapter.

## MODELS AND PATHWAYS OF CONSULTATION IN POLICE AND PUBLIC SAFETY PSYCHOLOGY

PPSP has grown impressively since 1968, when the Los Angeles Police Department became the first major law enforcement agency in the United States to hire a full-time, in-house police psychologist (Corey, Cuttler, Cox, & Brower, 2011). The pioneering psychologist with the groundbreaking distinction was Martin Reiser, and his enormous contributions to the specialty included books, articles, and conference presentations on police psychology. An early survey by Parisher, Rios, and Reilly (1979) showed a pattern that has continued: Large police departments, especially those serving communities of at least 500,000, are more likely to employ in-house psychologists than smaller departments, but most police psychologists in the United States operate as paid outside consultants rather than in-house employees. According to Davis (2011), either of these approaches can be effective, and each presents its own advantages and challenges.

The types of law enforcement agencies for which contracting or employed police psychologists provide services include municipal police departments; county sheriff's departments; police departments in educational institutions (e.g., school districts, colleges); state agencies, such as highway patrol departments; and federal law enforcement agencies. Some police psychologists develop contractual relationships with several law enforcement agencies and weave together a variety of professional commitments and roles. Some combine full- or part-time employment at one agency with external consulting relationships at one or more other law enforcement departments. Psychologists who work as external consultants may operate as solo practitioners or in group practices. Regardless of whether police psychologists work as in-house employees or as paid external consultants, they are expected to practice ethically, legally, and within the limits of their professional competence. As in all specialty areas of psychology, a commitment to lifelong learning and professional development is essential in PPSP.

## LICENSURE AND BOARD CERTIFICATION

Police psychologists are doctoral-level clinicians who are licensed as psychologists in the state or states where they practice. However, in most jurisdictions, the psychology license is generic and confirms only that a psychologist has the education, knowledge, and skills for the general practice of psychology (Corey et al., 2011). In addition to generalist training and licensure, police psychologists must have specialized supervision, training, and experience in PPSP to practice competently.

Advanced certification in police psychology is now available through ABPP; the certification is a developmental process that involves evaluation through multiple methods or stages (Corey et al., 2011). In addition to the basic knowledge requirements of approved doctoral education, clinical training, and licensure, ABPP candidates in PPSP need at least 3,000 hours of relevant experience, must submit a practice performance sample, and must undergo both peer and expert panel review. An ongoing challenge to the field is the widespread adoption of this pathway for demonstrating competence. Although thousands of psychologists in the United States participate in one or more aspects of police psychology practice in any given year, just 71 had obtained ABPP certification as of this writing (N. Holland, personal communication, December 11, 2017). However, given that PPSP was so recently recognized, this tally should be viewed as the proverbial glass that is half full. The number of board-certified police psychologists can be expected to grow. Moreover, there are multiple ways to demonstrate competency in police psychology. In the following sections, the educational foundation and training experiences necessary to practice police psychology are described, as are some of the essential knowledge, skills, and attitudes that combine to form competence (see Chapter 2, this volume) in this specialty area of consultation.

## EDUCATION AND TRAINING GUIDELINES FOR POLICE AND PUBLIC SAFETY PSYCHOLOGY

The Council of Organizations in Police Psychology has developed a set of aspirational guidelines and recommendations regarding education and training in PPSP (Brewster et al., 2016). From the council's perspective, at present, the preparation for a career in police psychology typically begins with successful completion of an APA-accredited doctoral program (or its equivalent) in one of the "core PPSP disciplines," that is, clinical, counseling, educational, or industrial-organizational psychology (Brewster et al., 2016, p. 172). Although a few graduate psychology programs may specialize or provide concentrations in PPSP (see http://www.policepsychology.org for the Society for Police and Criminal Psychology's list of educational and clinical training opportunities in police and criminal psychology), the vast majority of psychologists practicing in police psychology earned their doctorates in one of the aforementioned four areas. It is through such doctoral programs that police psychologists develop the primary, foundational competencies expected of all practicing psychologists.

Doctoral programs in clinical or counseling psychology typically require an internship, and postdoctoral fellowships or residencies allow for further professional development and help meet licensing requirements. Relatively few internships and postdoctoral programs focus on PPSP at present (Brewster et al., 2016), although that number should grow. Whenever possible, those who are interested in police psychology should take related coursework and obtain supervised clinical experience in PPSP as part of the educational and professional experiences that lead to their doctorates and their licensure as psychologists (Brewster et al., 2016). Postdoctoral continuing education is required to maintain licensure in psychology, and a variety of continuing education programs in PPSP are available. Continuing education programs and on-the-job training represent pathways for psychologists without exposure to PPSP in their doctoral programs, internships, or postdoctoral fellowships to gain relevant knowledge and insight into PPSP.

## KNOWLEDGE, SKILLS, AND ATTITUDES

In the following sections we present the knowledge, skills, and attitudes essential in consultation with police and public safety departments and officers.

### Knowledge Domains in Police and Public Safety Psychology

From the authors' perspectives, the foundational knowledge obtained in an APA-accredited doctoral program in clinical or counseling psychology is highly relevant to the practice of PPSP. Generalist training in areas such as psychopathology, psychological assessment, evidence-based intervention, socio-cultural factors in human behavior, ethics, research, and program evaluation, when combined with a clinical internship and postdoctoral training, establishes a strong foundation on which to build the specialized competencies for PPSP. Other important areas of core knowledge include the effects of trauma, biological bases of behavior, the physiological impacts of acute and chronic stress, couple and family systems, and adult career development.

The areas of specialized knowledge for PPSP include an understanding of the laws, statutes, and case law that impact the practice of PPSP in each setting in which a psychologist intends to practice (Corey & Borum, 2013). Psychologists need in-depth knowledge and insight regarding law enforcement culture, which is different than the culture and values in traditional mental health treatment settings (Cordner, 2017; Kirschman, Kamena, & Fay, 2014). They also need knowledge of the nature and duties of law enforcement job classifications as well as the stressors and occupational hazards in law enforcement careers. The four domains of PPSP incorporate a total of 57 distinct areas of practice and consultation, and each is associated with specific knowledge competencies that cannot all be covered in one chapter. Clearly, most police psychologists focus their professional activities in a relatively limited number of the 57 areas (Brewster et al., 2016). However, broad awareness of the many possible roles that police psychologists assume is important and helps ensure that appropriate referrals are made and that law enforcement agencies' treatment and consultation needs are met.

### Skill Domains in Police and Public Safety Psychology

A number of books produced in recent years describe the specific skills involved in PPSP (e.g., Clevenger, Miller, Moore, & Freeman, 2015; Kitaeff,

2011a; Mitchell & Dorian, 2017). Consistent with a competency-based approach to consultation, evidence-based approaches to assessment and intervention are favored in police psychology. Regarding the assessment domain, pre-employment psychological evaluations of police officer candidates (Mitchell, 2017) and psychological fitness-for-duty evaluations of incumbent officers (Corey, 2011) are two of the most frequent forms of assessment in PPSP. The Police Psychological Services Section of the International Association of Chiefs of Police (IACP) has developed guidelines for the performance of each of these types of assessment, which are available on the IACP website (see https://www.theiacp.org). The California Commission on Peace Officer Standards and Training (POST) has developed a comprehensive, evidence-based approach to the preemployment psychological evaluation of police officer candidates. The POST screening manual produced by psychologists Spilberg and Corey (2017) represents a state-of-the-art achievement in this area and has impacted the practice of police psychology in much of the United States. In addition, APA offers professional practice guidelines for occupationally mandated psychological evaluations (APA, 2017b). It is expected that police psychologists who perform evaluations be thoroughly familiar with such APA guidelines. The professional guidelines and recommendations developed by APA, IACP, and other authoritative organizations, such as POST, shed light on the assessment-related skills necessary for contemporary practice in PPSP and help steer professionals toward best practices.

Essential skills for the intervention domain include the capacity to provide individual, group, couples, and family therapy to law enforcement personnel, their families, or both. Police psychologists who provide direct services also need the skills to perform critical incident interventions for police officers, including psychological first aid, defusing, and debriefing (Aumiller & Corey, 2007). The IACP Police Psychological Services Section has developed resources relevant to the intervention domain, including officer-involved shooting guidelines and peer support guidelines, which can be viewed on the IACP website. The Commission on the Accreditation of Law Enforcement Agencies has developed standards that are relevant to police psychology intervention efforts, including standards for employee assistance programs (Standard 22.2.6), fitness and wellness programs (Standard 22.3.3), and personnel support services (Standard 22.2.3; Gupton et al., 2011).

Police psychologists' operational support activities often involve special-ized skills in areas such as criminal profiling, criminal intelligence, and crisis and hostage negotiation (Aumiller & Corey, 2007). Police psychologists par-ticipate as consultants to, or members of, crisis negotiation teams and crisis intervention teams. Such activities typically require competence in crisis intervention, crisis de-escalation techniques, mediation, risk assessment, and postincident debriefing (McMains & Mullins, 2015). Research has indicated that the use of mental health professionals as consultants to hostage negotia-tion teams is associated with better outcomes, that is, more negotiated sur-renders and fewer injuries (Butler, Leitenberg, & Fuselier, 1993). For decades, psychologists have used their expertise to assist police in developing more effective ways to respond to persons in crisis who have mental health problems. A promising development has been psychologists' role in creating, evaluating, and implementing police officer resilience and sustainability programs (e.g., Papazoglou & Andersen, 2014).

The consulting domain of PPSP refers to specialized activities and roles that contribute to organizational development; assist law enforcement agencies in designing, implementing, or improving aspects of organizational performance; or both. The consulting domain involves the implementation of higher order skills to benefit law enforcement organizations and personnel through activities that include management consultation, mediation, and development of performance appraisal systems (Aumiller & Corey, 2007). The IACP Police Psychological Services Section's guidelines for consulting psychologists are an essential resource and include regularly updated literature references and case law citations (IACP, 2016).

## Attitudes in Police and Public Safety Psychology

One of the more unique considerations for working in police psychology is the goodness-of-fit between the consulting psychologist's attitudes and values and those of the law enforcement profession and its personnel. Consider that, at a minimum, psychologists have been exposed to law enforcement in idiosyncratic ways throughout their lives, if even only indirectly via books, television, or the movies. Perhaps more significantly, some psychologists (or their family members) have had their own interactions with law enforcement either during their professional activities (e.g., with patients in crisis) or in their personal lives (e.g., traffic violations, arrests). Therefore, working with law enforcement officers requires a willingness to reflect on one's own pre-conceived notions (i.e., biases) about police officers and law enforcement culture and to maintain an openness (better yet, a healthy curiosity) to learn how the mental health professional is perceived by law enforcement personnel. Although there are certainly a wide range of within-group attitudinal differences among both law enforcement professionals and psychologists, the authors offer the following themes of relevance to the consulting psychologist. Due to the limited academic research in this area, the following is an amalgamation of the authors' observations and those of other seasoned police psychologists.

### Appreciation for the Law Enforcement Profession

Perhaps unlike any other profession, people tend to have strong beliefs about law enforcement. After all, police are often the only face of government with whom people interact directly. With the powers to arrest, use force (including deadly force), and place limits on other civil liberties, it is understandable that members of society would have strong, if not harsh, judgments about law enforcement organizations and their personnel. The consulting psychologist is tasked with reconciling any such negative attitudes about the law enforcement profession with an appreciation for the complex paths that lead to such perceptions. There is wisdom in the oft expressed gripe by officers that "everyone hates the cops—until they need one." Kirschman et al. (2014) wrote, "The number one error clinicians make treating cops is failing to understand what they do, why they do it, and the culture in which they operate" (p. 5). Fortunately, almost anyone can develop a better appreciation for the profession by pursuing opportunities to gain a greater understanding of the training, performance standards, and occupational hazards that police officers face, all within the context of working for a paramilitary organization.

### Perception of the Law Enforcement Officer
Similarly, it is important to recognize that serving as a police officer is not just a job choice but an identity that often pervades into personal life (Kirschman et al., 2014). It is an identity that typically begins with a desire to make a positive difference in the world that is gradually shaped through training, modeling, field experiences, and organizational dynamics into one that is highly adapted to a negatively skewed version of the world (Kirschman et al., 2014). Unfortunately, traits that are adaptive in preserving life and career as a police officer (e.g., suspiciousness, guardedness, rigidity, commanding, controlling), can be maladaptive in relationships, both personal and professional. It is imperative that the consulting psychologist not reflexively pathologize all such characteristics as negative personality traits but instead aims to achieve a contextualized understanding. Of course, the consulting psychologist must also contend with how police officers' experiences and characteristics impact their perceptions of mental health professionals.

### Perception of the Mental Health Professional
Much in the same way that the consulting psychologist's initial impressions of the law enforcement profession can be shaped by fiction or overgeneralized experiences, police officers often hold distorted views of the mental health professional as the stereotypical "shrink" they have seen in the movies and television (Herndon, 2000). Reiser (1972) was among the first to point out that "there tends to be some suspiciousness, resistance, and negative feelings between mental health professionals and men [and women] in police work" (p. 67). He theorized then that this may be due in part to the perception that the mental health professional is overly-permissive, too forgiving, and less practical. Fortunately, even in 1972, Reiser concluded that younger, better educated officers did not evidence these impressions as much and that "the net result over time will be the diminishing of the perceived distance between the psychologist and the policeman [or policewoman]" (p. 68). The present authors propose that the gap in perception has yet to be closed, but it is certainly smaller than ever.

In addition, the first direct experience with a mental health professional for many officers is at the time of the preemployment psychological screening—

an experience that can make or break their law enforcement career. Unfortunately, this association to the psychologist as an "evaluator" can sometimes be carried long into their careers in the form of believing that going to see "the doc" will get them in the "rubber gun squad." It must be acknowledged that a significant degree of stigma about seeking psychological services persists among many law enforcement officers as does a concern about the perceived weakness that such services might imply.

### Suggested Steps for Addressing Attitudes

The successful consulting psychologist must make a sustained effort to counteract the aforementioned attitudinal discrepancies and challenges. The present authors propose what we call the *3-E approach* to an enhanced perspective: exposure, education, and experience.

### Exposure

The psychologist must be a known entity to both the command staff and the rank and file. In small organizations, this exposure may involve some type of direct experience with every employee. In larger law enforcement agencies, the psychologist might only interact with a representative sample via the occasional roll call attendance or meeting for supervisors (i.e., sergeant ranks and above). For the consulting psychologist to be perceived as "one of us," "the more, the better" is a safe assumption regarding contact with department personnel. It is the authors' experience that this is the most foreign and therefore challenging of the 3-Es for new consulting psychologists. Psychologists are trained to maintain boundaries and reinforced for demonstrating their knowledge and expertise. Early in the second author's career, just "being present" at police stations or at department events triggered his concern that he would be perceived as having nothing better to do or not knowing his place. Only later did he learn that he was instead perceived as being committed, interested, and approachable by doing so. Ongoing exposure to the police psychologist breeds familiarity, familiarity breeds comfort, and comfort breeds trust, permitting, one might say, the *real* work to begin.

### Education

As previously discussed, many of the challenges for the police psychologist stem from police officers' misunderstanding of and preconceived notions about the role and value of not only the psychologist but also the field of psychology itself. By delivering educational presentations, the psychologist has the opportunity to overcome these challenges. There are countless opportunities to provide education in the form of traditional training in the academy and departmental in-service training days, but perhaps more important, in brief, semicasual settings, such as roll calls, supervisor meetings, and even in individual interactions, particularly with command staff (e.g., captains, commanders, deputy chiefs.). We must caution that a psychologist's *approach* to the training can be as, or more important than, the *subject* of the training.

Police officers are not fans of psychobabble, and care must be taken to ensure that the practical value of educational content is clear and well emphasized; otherwise, the consulting psychologist inadvertently reinforces the very stereotypes he or she sought to defeat. Examples of practical educational topics include communication strategies to de-escalate emotionally disturbed subjects, approaches to effectively manage shift work and sleep needs, and tips for officers on what and how to share their work experiences with their significant others or families.

### Experience

If one is looking for a litmus test for a police psychologist's genuine interest in the police officer's experience, it can likely be found here. Policing does not easily lend itself to verbal description, nor do some of the dynamics among police officers and their peers, or between officers and their superiors. Only so much about law enforcement culture can be understood from afar. The police officer's transformation begins long before his or her badging ceremony. The journey begins with a job application, typically followed by a yearlong process of exams, screenings, interviews, and background checks as a candidate, followed by many months of intensive academy experience as a recruit, all of which is chock full of pressure and uncertainty. If fortunate enough to graduate from the academy, the new officer begins life as a probationer who is beholden to the incessant evaluations of his or her field training officers. Even after field training is complete, officers again find themselves at another "beginning" of their careers. It is unlikely the consulting psychologist can participate in all aspects of these early experiences, but this review highlights the importance of pursuing a breadth of experiences in law enforcement ranging from interaction with the most newly-trained officers to the most seasoned, as well as contact with those who work in patrol or in specialized units, such as homicide, gangs, or vice. Accessible and recommended experiences include learning to shoot a firearm, going on patrol vehicle or helicopter ride-alongs, participating as a consultant (or observer) at crisis negotiation team callouts, and even participating in some of the training officers receive. Of course, the ultimate immersion experience would be for a consulting psychologist to complete his or her own reserve officer training. Pursuit of the 3-Es helps police psychologists develop the attitudes necessary for competent practice.

## ETHICAL STANDARDS AND CONTEXTUAL ISSUES

The *Ethical Principles of Psychologists and Code of Conduct* (APA, 2017a) contains the key ethical concepts and guidelines that inform and shape all aspects of psychological practice in the United States, including police psychology. The practice of PPSP entails distinctive characteristics and poses unique ethical challenges and considerations (McCutcheon, 2017). For example, police psychologists who provide consultation services need to be clear about who is the client and who are the stakeholders or involved parties whose interests and rights need to be considered (Archibald, 1995). In the case of preemployment psychological evaluations of police officer candidates, the client is typically the law enforcement agency that engaged the psychologist to perform the service. However, the rights of the police officer candidate are also important as are the interests of the community served by the hiring agency. Obtaining informed consent becomes especially important when multiple parties are involved, stakes are high, and competing interests may be at play. Spilberg and Corey (2017) provided an excellent example of a disclosure and informed consent statement for use in preemployment psychological evaluations. Their consent document addresses issues such as the nature of the evaluation, the limits of confidentiality, the party to whom the results of the evaluation will be communicated, whether the candidate may access the written report and testing records, matters of payment, and possible outcomes and uses of the exam results. This systematic approach to informed consent helps ensure that the appropriate ethical principles, legal standards, and guidelines have been considered.

Issues of confidentiality need careful consideration in PPSP practice due to the sensitive and private nature of psychological services and because of the unique characteristics of law enforcement settings. Police departments have to ensure that the police officers in their organizations are mentally and emotionally capable of carrying out their duties (Corey, 2011). For in-house police psychologists, most therapy referrals from police officers are self-initiated, yet management-initiated or mandated therapy referrals often occur as well (Sweet, 2011). In mandated referrals, the psychologist is usually required to provide limited feedback to the referring executive in the department. Moreover, such feedback could have bearing on a police officer's employment status. Therefore, the limits to confidentiality need to be carefully explained and must be understood by everyone involved.

Police psychologists must be particularly adept at managing the multiple relationships that often emerge in the course of PPSP practice. For example, a consulting psychologist who provides various services to multiple agencies may, over the course of time, interact with the same persons in different contexts and roles (McCutcheon, 2017). As one police psychologist observed, "In what [other] clinical or work environment would a therapist expect to see his/her patient in the office on Monday, in a classroom on Tuesday, at a crime scene on Wednesday, and at a SWAT callout on Saturday night?" (Sweet, 2011, p. 341). Police psychologists refrain from entering into any multiple relationships that might compromise their objectivity or cause harm to others (APA, 2017a). The IACP (2016) guidelines for consulting psychologists address how to proceed when the requests or demands of a law enforcement agency conflict with psychologists' ethical standards or practice guidelines. Police psychologists strive to respect the rights of all the individuals or parties impacted by the services they provide and, in all situations, are expected to conduct themselves in accordance with the APA Ethics Code (APA, 2017a). Despite the complexities, it is possible for police psychologists to balance the disparate needs so that the interests of all involved parties, including the community, are advanced (Sweet, 2011).

A key tenet of the ethical principles for psychology is that psychologists practice within the limits of their professional competence. Moreover, psychologists must ensure that they take the steps necessary to retain and develop their competence. According to Johnson et al. (2011), psychologists who participate in *in extremis practice*, that is, who "practice in settings where exposure to trauma—both personally and vicariously—is high," face particular challenges or threats to the maintenance of their competence (p. 95). Johnson et al. (2011) posited that consistent exposure to intense or overwhelming stress in the workplace may compromise a psychologist's ability to evaluate her or his own competence. Therefore, psychologists who work in such settings, including many police psychologists and military psychologists, are advised to engage in professional communities with similarly tasked colleagues who, together, can help ensure that competence is maintained and appropriate self-care practices are followed (Johnson et al., 2011).

The principles in the APA Ethics Code identify important priorities and aspirations, including that psychologists seek to benefit others and not do harm; demonstrate respect for the dignity of all persons, including those in vulnerable communities; and strive to eliminate the destructive effects of bias or prejudice on their work (APA, 2017a). Similarly, police psychologists often have the opportunity to partner with law enforcement agencies to strengthen efforts to improve the fairness and effectiveness of policing efforts. Competency-based consultation in such areas may be enriched through consideration of research findings that speak to contemporary issues in policing. For example, implicit bias has been identified as one of the likely causes of racially discriminatory practices in policing (Spencer, Charbonneau, & Glaser, 2016). Many police departments require police officers to complete intervention programs designed to reduce bias, although the evidence regarding the enduring benefits or effectiveness of such interventions is not impressive (Paluck & Green, 2009). However, Spencer et al. (2016) indicated that promoting nonnegative intergroup contact is an especially promising method for reducing the negative impacts of implicit bias on policing. They stated that intergroup contact can be facilitated through efforts such as increasing the diversity of police department personnel and encouraging the use of community-oriented policing. Equipped with this type of knowledge, police psychologists have the opportunity to help effect positive change.

## VIGNETTES AND EXAMPLES OF CONSULTATION DOMAINS

Consultation in police psychology can vary greatly. The police psychologist's roles and responsibilities can be in one or all four domains of practice: assessment, clinical intervention, operational support, or organizational consultation.

Moreover, psychologists might provide services in one or more domains while working either as outside consultants or as in-house employees. Gallo and Halgin (2011) described steps that psychologists without formal training in police psychology can take to gain the competence needed to perform preemployment psychological evaluations of police officer candidates. In all areas of PPSP, mentoring and supervision from seasoned police psychologists is essential to acquiring competence.

What follows are examples[1] of police psychology activities in three practice domains. The first involves a psychologist functioning as an outside consultant, and the other two examples involve employed, in-house psychologists.

## Assessment Domain

Mr. Ang is a 53-year-old married man who worked successfully for 27 years in a police department that served a major metropolitan area. After a brief retirement, he sought employment as a senior-level investigator in a different law enforcement agency. He passed all aspects of the selection-related written exams, interviews, and physical ability tests, after which he cleared his background investigation and polygraph exam. The hiring agency gave him a conditional offer of employment that was contingent on passing the mandatory medical and psychological exams. The criteria used for the psychological exam included meeting minimum qualification standards in regard to the 10 psychological screening dimensions established by POST (2019).

Dr. Paredes, a consulting police psychologist, conducted the preemployment psychological evaluation. Consistent with best practices, the psychological evaluation included an extensive background questionnaire and two self-report inventories: the Minnesota Multiphasic Personality Inventory—2 (MMPI–2; Butcher, Graham, Tellegen, & Kaemmer, 1989), a 567-item measure of psychopathology, and the Sixteen Personality Factors Questionnaire (Cattell, Cattell, & Cattell, 2002), a 187-item measure of normal personality traits. Dr. Paredes carefully reviewed the written psychological test results and the background investigation report before conducting a 50-minute, face-to-face interview with the candidate, Mr. Ang. The candidate's relevant history included that he and his family left their country of origin when he was 12, after which they spent 3 years in a refugee center before settling permanently in the United States. English was the candidate's third language, which he mastered within 2 years of his arrival. His family faced economic hardships, and the candidate began working part time at a gas station when he was 16. He later completed an associate's degree at a community college, after which he became a police officer in his city. He was promoted multiple times in his career, and all of his former coworkers and supervisors recommended him for the new position. The candidate's background showed impressive resilience and grit. He had also maintained a positive, stable marriage of 19 years. The

---

[1]All clinical case material has been altered to protect client confidentiality.

written psychological test results indicated validity problems, including a tendency to respond "False" to test items regardless of item content and socially desirable responding. Several elevations on the substantive clinical scales were also noted, suggesting depressive symptoms, health concerns, and cynicism. The MMPI–2 results raised possible questions about POST Screening Dimension 7, Emotional Regulation and Stress Tolerance, and Dimension 1, Social Competence. During Dr. Paredes's psychological interview, the candidate related in a socially appropriate, assertive, and self-confident manner. The observed behavior in the interview and the reported history, including the background records, showed no evidence of mental health problems or substance abuse issues. Dr. Paredes explored themes from the written psychological test results, and it appeared the candidate may have struggled with some of the test items keyed in the "False" direction. The candidate did not show any of the job-relevant behavioral problems that might be expected from the elevated clinical scales. Dr. Paredes concluded that Mr. Ang fully met psychological qualification standards for employment as a peace officer and recommended the candidate.

## Clinical Intervention Domain

Officer McDaniel is a 17-year veteran of a large metropolitan police department. She currently works as a field training officer for new officers still under probation. Two months ago, she and her partner responded to a "disturbance" radio call involving a man yelling and throwing objects from the second story balcony of an apartment building. Officer McDaniel and her partner witnessed the subject as they approached the building. They stopped about 15 yards from the building's stairway and commanded the individual to stop what he was doing, turn around, and put his hands on his head. Meanwhile, Officer McDaniel unholstered her handgun and the probationer, his Taser (i.e., nonlethal weapon that fires dartlike electrodes that deliver an incapacitating electroshock). Instead of complying, the individual suddenly charged down the stairs and ran toward the officers. The probationer, fearing for his and his training officer's lives, fired the Taser, and the darts struck the suspect. Although the electrical shocks found their target, there was no noticeable effect on the suspect. Officer McDaniel was overwhelmed by the suspect's sudden approach and fell backward as she tried to maintain the gap between them. Although quickly back on her feet, she found herself struggling with the suspect for her gun. Meanwhile, the probationer abandoned the Taser and readied to fire with his handgun but could not immediately do so without placing Officer McDaniel at risk. Officer McDaniel's handgun was thrown in the struggle, and as the suspect ran for it, the probationer fired two rounds, striking and incapacitating the suspect, who immediately collapsed.

Per the agency's protocol after officer-involved shootings, Officer McDaniel was required to meet with the police psychologist within a few days of the incident, as recommended by the IACP's officer-involved shootings guidelines. Dr. Anderson obtained informed consent from Officer McDaniel and introduced the rationale for the meeting, emphasizing that she was not singled out, but, instead, that the protocol is for all officers involved in shootings or other critical incidents, including the probationer, to meet with a psychologist. Dr. Anderson further clarified that the meeting was a confidential communication between Officer McDaniel and the psychologist. No information regarding the content of the meeting would be released to her command staff without McDaniel's written authorization, save for her attendance and apart from the usual legal exceptions to confidentiality. Officer McDaniel asked Dr. Anderson if the meeting was a fitness-for-duty evaluation, and Dr. Anderson clarified that it was not, explaining that the meeting was primarily educative with the aims of supporting the officer's resilience and individual coping abilities. Dr. Anderson further clarified that if either of them had concerns about the officer's ability to return to field duties as a result of this incident, they would work together to identify the best course of action to ensure the safety and well-being of her, other officers, and the community they serve. Dr. Anderson invited Officer McDaniel to "walk through" the incident from the start of the radio call through the end of her shift that evening. Officer McDaniel agreed and provided a play-by-play of the incident while Dr. Anderson interjected validation, education, and inquiries about her emotional status.

Toward the end of the meeting, Dr. Anderson evaluated Officer McDaniel's adjustment after the incident, focusing on sleep quality, family and coworker support, and any maladaptive coping, particularly excessive or increased alcohol use. The officer indicated she felt confident about returning to work but acknowledged feelings of guilt about placing her probationer in a difficult situation by allowing the suspect to close the gap on her so quickly. She also revealed a previous incident with a different probationer about which she felt some guilt and regret. Dr. Anderson provided the feedback that although Officer McDaniel reported feeling ready to return to work, it was recommended that she return for follow-up on a self-referred basis with the psychologist to better understand and address her feelings of guilt about the incident. In addition, it would provide both of them the opportunity to monitor her adjustment back to field duty and provide additional support. Officer McDaniel asked if her commanding officer would learn of this feedback, and Dr. Anderson indicated that although the commanding officer would receive feedback that the required protocol was completed, the clinical recommendations and other content of the session would remain confidential. Officer McDaniel successfully returned to her field duties after the incident but continued to attend sessions with Dr. Anderson for the next several weeks on a self-referred basis. Officer McDaniel subsequently reported that before this incident, she had always feared having to meet with a police psychologist, but afterward, she had recommended Dr. Anderson to several of her peers as someone who "gets us."

## Operational Support Domain

It was shortly after 1 a.m. on a Tuesday when Dr. Vaughn, the on-call police psychologist, received a phone call from the department command post. The officer notified Dr. Vaughn that there was a SWAT call-up involving a barricaded suspect who had fired a weapon inside his apartment and was threatening to kill himself and any police who came near the building. Dr. Vaughn deployed from his home with a police radio, body armor vest, and his department identification; he arrived on scene to be briefed by the officer in charge. The psychologist connected with the specially trained primary and secondary SWAT officers who would serve as the crisis negotiators during the incident. Dr. Vaughn obtained the available background information on the subject from the intelligence officer, who had learned that the suspect, Jesse, was a 24-year-old, unmarried man with a history of misdemeanor theft and drug possession convictions. Dr. Vaughn met the suspect's mother, who showed up on scene after receiving a text from her son that read, "Whatever happens, tonight is all your fault." Dr. Vaughn spoke with the mother, who stated that Jesse had never been willing to see a therapist but did sometimes hear voices and would threaten family members to "stop playing games" with him. She confirmed that he had been using illicit substances, including methamphetamine, for the past 6 months. She was uncertain if he had used drugs that evening.

Dr. Vaughn provided operational support to the police department with the goal of resolving the barricaded suspect situation in the most peaceful manner possible. Consistent with the agency's protocol of serving as the consulting mental health professional on the crisis negotiation team, Dr. Vaughn was an integral part of the agency's operational response to a crime (i.e., negligent discharge of a firearm and potentially criminal threats) involving a barricaded suspect who was possibly suicidal. As a psychologist, Dr. Vaughn had to consider all of his actions from the perspectives of the laws and ethics that govern his professional activities; the needs of the law enforcement agency he is there to support; and the potential impact of the entire operation on the community. Guideline 4.2 of the IACP (2016) *Consulting Police Psychologist Guidelines* addresses this matter:

> In their professional actions, consulting police psychologists seek to safeguard the welfare and rights of those with whom they interact professionally and other affected persons (e.g., vulnerable third parties) and agencies. Ethical concerns are at their highest when psychological expertise is employed to protect third parties but might also cause harm to the subject(s) of an intervention. The awareness, expectation, or intention of inflicting harm is in direct tension with the core ethical principles of beneficence and nonmaleficence. In such circumstances, consulting police psychologists must exercise reasonable judgment to minimize the harm to a subject while providing consultation designed to protect third parties (e.g., potential victims of the subject/society at large). Because police enforce the law and regulate behavior, consulting police psychologists are inexorably linked to police actions, so diligent attention to ethical obligations to both the potential victim(s) and the subject must be assiduously maintained.

Dr. Vaughn's activities ranged from evaluating the mood and behavior of the suspect, recommending negotiation strategies, monitoring the team's stress, monitoring stress in the suspect, and consulting with command staff regarding the variables involved and the progress of negotiations (McMains & Mullins, 2015). Once on scene, Dr. Vaughn and the two sworn negotiators huddled to discuss the available intelligence, and Dr. Vaughn emphasized the possibility that Jesse would be in an agitated state, perhaps even evidencing symptoms of psychosis due to methamphetamine intoxication, a serious mental illness, or the combination. As a result, he recommended the negotiator speak calmly and slowly to increase the likelihood that Jesse could attend to the communications. As Dr. Vaughn and the secondary negotiator listened in, the primary negotiator made contact with Jesse's cell phone and spent the next 90 minutes attempting to build trust and understanding with him—with intermittent call breaks when Jesse would hang up after saying he needed to think. Throughout the conversation, Dr. Vaughn communicated feedback to the negotiator via notes and interviewed the mother to determine if she was a good candidate to make an audio recording that could be played for Jesse. The officer in charge asked Dr. Vaughn to provide a briefing on the status of negotiations to the command staff who gathered outside the SWAT crisis negotiation team truck. Dr. Vaughn indicated that Jesse appeared to become calmer and more rational over time and that he demonstrated greater openness with the negotiator, indicating the possibility of improved trust and rapport. Per Dr. Vaughn's feedback and the absence of exigent circumstances, the officer in charge determined that negotiations would proceed without tactical intervention, ultimately allowing sufficient opportunity for Jesse to surrender without further incident.

## PROFESSIONAL TRAINING AND RESOURCES IN POLICE AND PUBLIC SAFETY PSYCHOLOGY

Steps that interested graduate students and psychologists can take to grow in their understanding of PPSP include getting involved with the professional organizations that have shaped the development of the specialty. Those groups include the Police and Public Safety Section of APA Division 18 (Psychologists in Public Service), the IACP Police Psychological Services Section, and the Society for Police and Criminal Psychology. These organizations hold annual meetings, sponsor workshops and continuing education, and in some cases, produce regular journals or periodicals. Some state-level organizations, such as POST, likewise develop PPSP resources, offer workshops, and maintain an active presence on the web. An increasing number of professional and trade books address themes of PPSP, and many psychological journals include useful articles on police psychology and related subjects. The professional practice guidelines the IACP Police Psychological Services Section regularly produces and updates are critically important resources that are freely available on the IACP website.

## CONCLUSION

Police psychology is a growing specialty that offers unique challenges and opportunities. It is especially well suited to initiative-taking, culturally competent psychologists who appreciate the singular role that peace officers occupy in our complex world. Police psychology blends direct service and consultation in powerful ways that directly impact the lives of individuals and the functioning of our communities. Considerable work remains to be done in fleshing out the development of PPSP as a clinical specialty, including more doctoral programs, internships, and postdoctoral fellowship that emphasize it. However, competency-based approaches to police psychology show great promise for the critical tasks of supporting first responders and contributing to the well-being and safety of community life.

## GLOSSARY

**critical incident:** For law enforcement purposes, this term generally refers to an out-of-the ordinary event that involves serious threat, harm, or loss.

**debriefing:** An individual or group session in which a mental health professional educates about the effects of trauma, assesses the impact of an incident, explores coping mechanisms, processes feelings about an incident, identifies resources, and plans for next steps, if any

**peer support program:** An organized network of agency personnel who are trained to assist their peers in coping with a broad range of challenges, stressors, or experiences and who are typically available to offer this type of informal assistance on a 24-hour basis

**psychological first aid:** An evidence-guided approach that seeks to facilitate coping, resilience, and well-being in the immediate aftermath of a disaster, traumatic event, or critical incident (sometimes also referred to as a *psychological defusing*)

**psychological fitness-for-duty evaluation:** A formal psychological evaluation of an incumbent officer about whom there is evidence of possibly compromised ability to safely and effectively carry out the duties of a police officer presumably due to psychological reasons

**SWAT:** Stands for *special weapons and tactics* and refers to highly trained law enforcement units that use specialized or military equipment and tactics—and often a crisis negotiation team—in responding to barricaded suspects, hostage-takings, and other high-risk events

**sworn officer:** Refers to law enforcement personnel with police training whose duties include the power to arrest and lawfully use force and who usually have taken an oath to carry out their duties faithfully and in accordance with all relevant laws

## REFERENCES

American Board of Professional Psychology. (n.d.). *Police & public safety psychology*. Retrieved from https://abpp.org/Applicant-Information/Specialty-Boards/Police-Public-Safety-Psychology.aspx

American Psychological Association. (n.d.-a). *Police and public safety*. Retrieved from https://www.apa.org/ed/graduate/specialize/police

American Psychological Association. (n.d.-b). *Recognized specialties and proficiencies in professional psychology*. Retrieved from https://www.apa.org/ed/graduate/specialize/ recognized

American Psychological Association. (2017a). *Ethical principles of psychologists and code of conduct* (2002, Amended June 1, 2010 and January 1, 2017). Retrieved from http://www.apa.org/ethics/code/index.aspx

American Psychological Association. (2017b). *Professional practice guidelines for occupationally mandated psychological evaluations*. Retrieved from http://www.apa.org/ practice/guidelines/psychological-evaluations.aspx

Archibald, E. M. (1995). Managing professional concerns in the delivery of psychological services to the police. In M. I. Kurke & E. M. Scrivner (Eds.), *Police psychology into the 21st century* (pp. 45–54). New York, NY: Erlbaum.

Aumiller, G. S., & Corey, D. (2007). Defining the field of police psychology: Core domains & proficiencies. *Journal of Police and Criminal Psychology, 22*, 65–76. http:// dx.doi.org/10.1007/s11896-007-9013-4

Brewster, J., Stoloff, M. L., Corey, D. M., Greene, L. W., Gupton, H. M., & Roland, J. E. (2016). Education and training guidelines for the specialty of police and public safety psychology. *Training and Education in Professional Psychology, 10*, 171–178. http://dx.doi.org/10.1037/tep0000122

Butcher, J. N., Graham, J. R., Tellegen, A., & Kaemmer, B. (1989). *Manual for the restandardized Minnesota Multiphasic Personality Inventory: MMPI-2*. Minneapolis: University of Minnesota Press.

Butler, W. M., Leitenberg, H., & Fuselier, G. D. (1993). The use of mental health professional consultants to police hostage negotiation teams. *Behavioral Sciences & the Law, 11*, 213–221. http://dx.doi.org/10.1002/bsl.2370110210

California Commission on Peace Officer Standards and Training. (2019). *Peace officer psychological screening manual*. Retrieved from http://lib.post.ca.gov/Publications/ Peace_Officer_Psychological_Screening_Manual.pdf

Cattell, R. B., Cattell, A. K., & Cattell, H. E. P. (2002). *Sixteen Personality Factors Questionnaire* (5th ed.). Champaign, IL: Institute for Personality and Ability Testing.

Clevenger, S. M. F., Miller, L., Moore, B. A., & Freeman, A. (Eds.). (2015). *Behind the badge: A psychological treatment handbook for law enforcement officers*. New York, NY: Routledge.

Cordner, G. W. (2017, February). Police culture in the 21st century. *Police Chief, 84*, 50–51.

Corey, D. M. (2011). Principles of fitness-for-duty evaluations for police psychologists. In J. Kitaeff (Ed.), *Handbook of police psychology* (pp. 263–293). New York, NY: Routledge.

Corey, D. M., & Borum, R. (2013). Forensic assessment for high-risk occupations. In R. K. Otto & I. B. Weiner (Eds.), *Handbook of psychology: Vol. 11. Forensic psychology* (2nd ed., pp. 246–270). Hoboken, NJ: Wiley. http://dx.doi.org/10.1002/ 9781118133880.hop211011

Corey, D. M., Cuttler, M. J., Cox, D. R., & Brower, J. (2011, August). Board certification in police psychology: What it means to public safety. *Police Chief, 78*, 100–104.

Cuttler, M. J. (2011). Pre-employment screening of police officers: Integrating actuarial practice models with practice. In J. Kitaeff (Ed.), *Handbook of police psychology* (pp. 135–163). New York, NY: Routledge.

Davis, J. A. (2011). Police-specific psychological services: Using behavioral scientists as consultants to public safety. In J. Kitaeff (Ed.), *Handbook of police psychology* (pp. 63–66). New York, NY: Routledge.

Gallo, F. J., & Halgin, R. P. (2011). A guide for establishing a practice in police preemployment postoffer psychological evaluations. *Professional Psychology: Research and Practice, 42*, 269–275. http://dx.doi.org/10.1037/a0022493

Gupton, H. M., Axelrod, E., Cornell, L., Curran, S. F., Hood, C. J., Kelly, J., & Moss, J. (2011, August). Support and sustain: Psychological intervention for law enforcement personnel. *Police Chief, 78*, 92–97.

Herndon, J. S. (2000). The police psychologist on the silver screen: Reviewing the roles on the reels. *Journal of Police and Criminal Psychology, 15*, 30–40. http://dx.doi.org/10.1007/BF02802663

International Association of Chiefs of Police, Police Psychological Services Section. (2016). *Consulting police psychologist guidelines*. Arlington, VA: Author.

Johnson, W. B., Johnson, S. J., Sullivan, G. R., Bongar, B., Miller, L., & Sammons, M. T. (2011). Psychology in extremis: Preventing problems of professional competence in dangerous practice settings. *Professional Psychology: Research and Practice, 42*, 94–104. http://dx.doi.org/10.1037/a0022365

Kirschman, E., Kamena, M., & Fay, J. (2014). *Counseling cops: What clinicians need to know*. New York, NY: Guilford Press.

Kitaeff, J. (2011a). (Ed.). *Handbook of police psychology*. New York, NY: Routledge.

Kitaeff, J. (2011b). History of police psychology. In J. Kitaeff (Ed.), *Handbook of police psychology* (pp. 1–59). New York, NY: Routledge.

McCutcheon, J. L. (2017). Emerging ethical issues in police and public safety psychology: Reflections on mandatory vs. aspirational ethics. In C. L. Mitchell & E. H. Dorian (Eds.), *Police psychology and its growing impact on modern law enforcement* (pp. 314–334). Hershey, PA: IGI Global. http://dx.doi.org/10.4018/978-1-5225-0813-7.ch016

McMains, M. J., & Mullins, W. C. (2015). *Crisis negotiations: Managing critical incidents and hostage situations in law enforcement and corrections* (5th ed.). New York, NY: Routledge.

Mitchell, C. L. (2017). Preemployment psychological screening of police officer candidates: Basic considerations and recent advances. In C. L. Mitchell & E. H. Dorian (Eds.), *Police psychology and its growing impact on modern law enforcement* (pp. 28–50). Hershey, PA: IGI Global. http://dx.doi.org/10.4018/978-1-5225-0813-7.ch002

Mitchell, C. L., & Dorian, E. H. (Eds.). (2017). *Police psychology and its growing impact on modern law enforcement*. Hershey, PA: IGI Global. http://dx.doi.org/10.4018/978-1-5225-0813-7

Munsterberg, H. (1908). *On the witness stand*. Garden City, NY: Doubleday.

Paluck, E. L., & Green, D. P. (2009). Prejudice reduction: What works? A review and assessment of research and practice. *Annual Review of Psychology, 60*, 339–367. http://dx.doi.org/10.1146/annurev.psych.60.110707.163607

Papazoglou, K., & Andersen, J. P. (2014). A guide to utilizing police training as a tool to promote resilience and improve health outcomes among police officers. *Traumatology: An International Journal, 20*, 103–111. http://dx.doi.org/10.1037/h0099394

Parisher, D., Rios, B., & Reilly, R. R. (1979). Psychologists and psychological services in urban police departments: A national survey. *Professional Psychology, 10*, 6–7. http://dx.doi.org/10.1037/h0078197

The President's Commission on Law Enforcement and Administration of Justice. (1967). *The challenge of crime in a free society: A report by The President's Commission on Law Enforcement and Administration of Justice*. Washington, DC: U.S. Government Printing Office. Retrieved from https://www.ncjrs.gov/pdffiles1/nij/42.pdf

Reiser, M. (1972). *The police department psychologist*. Springfield, IL: Charles C Thomas.

Spencer, K. B., Charbonneau, A. K., & Glaser, J. (2016). Implicit bias and policing. *Social and Personality Psychology Compass, 10*, 50–63. http://dx.doi.org/10.1111/spc3.12210

Spilberg, S. W., & Corey, D. M. (2017). *POST peace officer psychological screening manual* (Rev. ed.). Sacramento, CA: California Commission on Peace Officer Standards and Training.

Sweet, G. (2011). Isn't this against the law? Boundary problems in police psychology. In W. B. Johnson & G. P. Koocher (Eds.), *Ethical conundrums, quandaries and predicaments in mental health practice: A casebook from the files of experts* (pp. 335–343). New York, NY: Oxford University Press.

Terman, L. M., Otis, A. S., Dickson, V., Hubbard, O. S., Norton, J. K., Howard, L., . . . Cassingham, C. C. (1917). A trial of mental and pedagogical tests in a civil service examination for policemen and firemen. *Journal of Applied Psychology, 1,* 17–29. http://dx.doi.org/10.1037/h0073841

Trompetter, P. S. (2011, August). Police psychologists: Roles and responsibilities in a law enforcement agency. *Police Chief, 78,* 52–53.

Trompetter, P. S. (2017). A history of police psychology. In C. L. Mitchell & E. H. Dorian (Eds.), *Police psychology and its growing impact on modern law enforcement* (pp. 1–26). Hershey, PA: IGI Global. http://dx.doi.org/10.4018/978-1-5225-0813-7.ch001

# 16

# Consultation Within the Military Setting

Christina L. Schendel and Carrie H. Kennedy

onsultation to the military is an essential function of psychologists who serve in or provide services to the military, and psychologists have been an integral part of the U.S. military since World War I. During that war, a critical need arose to assess men for military service, and psychologists created psychometric assessment instruments to screen the nation's military recruits (Yerkes, 1921).[1] In conjunction with psychological research, the primary function of military psychologists was known as assessment and selection (A&S)—now known as an operational psychological role.[2] Consultation provided during World War I to the military largely encompassed making recommendations regarding which men were qualified for military service or specific jobs and which men were not.

In World War II, psychologists expanded their research footprint, continued their A&S role, and began to focus on new areas of practice, such as human factors in aviation, as military technology and capability expanded (Olson, McCauley, & Kennedy, 2013). However, the largest impact on the field of

---

[1]These efforts evolved into today's most popular intelligence test, the Wechsler Adult Intelligence Scale (Boake, 2002; Wechsler, 1981).

[2]*Operational psychology* is that psychology subspecialty in which the focus is on the "operational activities of law enforcement, national intelligence organizations, and national defense activities" (Kennedy & Williams, 2011, p. 4).

The views expressed in this chapter are those of the authors and do not reflect the official policy or position of the Defense Health Agency, the Department of the Navy, the Department of Defense, or the United States Government.

http://dx.doi.org/10.1037/0000153-017
*Consultation in Psychology: A Competency-Based Approach*, C. A. Falender and E. P. Shafranske (Editors)

psychology occurred at the end of the war when psychologists were needed to meet the psychological health care needs of veterans, and the clinical contributions of psychologists took root. This shift led to a massive expansion of clinical psychology as a profession, and the nation's first psychology internships were established within the Department of Veterans Affairs system in 1946 to train clinical psychologists (Kennedy & Zillmer, 2012; McGuire, 1990). Since World War II, military psychology has adapted and evolved but continues to have three primary functions: clinical, operational, and research/experimental. This chapter focuses on the clinical and operational domains of military psychological practice as they pertain to consultation and recognizes that research guides empirically based practice.

## MILITARY PSYCHOLOGICAL CONSULTATION DEFINED

Today's military psychologists perform a multitude of roles, and each of these roles has a concomitant consultation function. In this chapter, we define *consultation in the military setting* as the provision of expert opinion, analysis, and recommendations to support informed decisions made by military leadership for the purpose of improving military functioning and effectiveness.

Psychologists are thus required to be psychological subject-matter experts, educators, leaders, researchers, psychological health care providers, policy analysts, and, often, commissioned officers in the military while providing critical consultation in each role. The military psychologist provides guidance, potential courses of action, and recommendations to commands, other health care providers, and policymakers. With this knowledge, the decision makers are then empowered to take action based on the widest array of information and subject-matter expertise.

The importance of this consultation function in the military setting cannot be overemphasized. Ill-informed military consultation can be dangerous given the stakes involved in military environments and may be harmful to individuals, military missions, and society (see more on mixed agency later in the chapter). Military psychologists make routine recommendations regarding such issues as weapons handling, flight status, security clearances, the readiness of units, and suitability for special missions. The aim of this chapter is to provide a brief overview of the knowledge, skills, and attitudes (KSAs) required to succeed as a military psychological consultant; provide real-world examples of appropriate and effective responses to common challenges; and discuss the pathways to obtain these KSAs in both of the domains of focus.

## CLINICAL AND OPERATIONAL MILITARY PSYCHOLOGY PRACTICE

An overview of psychological practice in the military environment provides context for the KSAs required for military psychological consultation. What follows is a brief description of clinical and operational psychology and the settings in which these two domains are practiced. It is notable that both civilian and active duty military psychologists function in all of the roles noted in this chapter, although it is unlikely that civilians will find themselves in hostile, deployed environments.

## Clinical Military Psychology

Within the domain of clinical military psychology are two practice models: (a) the *traditional model* in which the psychologist works within a military treatment facility (i.e., clinic or hospital) and (b) the *embedded model* in which the psychologist is integrated within a military command (e.g., infantry, logistics, special operational unit; ship; training command). In both models, the clinician is simultaneously placed in the dual roles of consultant and psychological health care provider. The traditional model is practiced on hospital ships, in overseas clinics and hospitals, and in clinics and hospitals in the continental United States in addition to hospitals set up in combat zones. The primary goal of the traditional model is to evaluate and treat the individual and, whenever possible, achieve symptom resolution and return the service member to normal duties.

Within the embedded clinical model, which is also termed *expeditionary psychology*, clinical psychology is practiced directly within a military unit to support both the individual service members and overall psychological health of that unit. The psychologist is an organic asset who is always with the unit, whether the unit is in garrison, on a training exercise, or deployed. The psychologist is viewed as a member of the unit who understands the unique culture and inner workings of that specific group. This understanding allows the psychologist to function in several different roles, including providing organizational consulting on the health and readiness of the unit, implementing prevention and early intervention strategies, detecting psychological health problems early, accelerating access to care, and decreasing the stigma associated with seeing a psychological health care provider. In contrast to the traditional model, embedded psychologists spend much of their time performing needs assessments of their unit such that the emphasis is on prevention, early intervention, and short-term treatment with an eye toward the readiness of the entire unit. Less emphasis is placed on traditional psychological health care (e.g., one-on-one appointments for long-term care or individuals requiring multidisciplinary treatment). When an individual's needs are better met in the traditional model of care, that care is provided at the nearest military treatment facility, which can meet more complex health care needs.

Clinical psychology practice in the combat zone and other deployed environments may be provided either traditionally (e.g., a combat stress clinic, combat hospital) or via an embedded model. Treatment capabilities in the war zone may be different than those available in the continental United States, but the goals of evaluation and treatment are the same. Consultation, however, becomes more complicated due to the need for rapid return to duty decisions in an actively hostile area where weapons are more readily accessible and life and death decisions are imminent.

It is notable that each time a psychological health care provider sees an active duty patient, that provider has just assumed a consultation role. The provider is now responsible for making a determination regarding fitness for duty; determining what, if any, treatment is required; and determining how to provide access to that treatment within the individual service member's constraints (e.g., available services, deployed environment.). Although these responsibilities can be difficult for providers given the potential lethality of each individual service member, an interaction with any medical provider may result in duty status changes or a necessary breach of confidentiality, or both (see more on confidentiality and mandatory disclosures in the Military-Relevant Ethical Standards section).

### Operational Psychology

Within the domain of operational psychology, the thrust of the duties is geared toward applying the science of military psychology to national security functions. The primary role here is not the clinical care of individuals or the psychological health of any given military unit but the operational support of specific units and missions. Psychologists working in this capacity apply psychological science to real-world problems that impact the effectiveness of military missions and the security of the nation (e.g., terrorism, espionage).

As in the clinical domain, psychologists consulting in this capacity may be hired specifically to perform particular consultation functions to support a specific project or mission. However, many are embedded into such commands as special operational units; survival, evasion, resistance, and escape schools; and commands with highly specialized missions (e.g., embassy security guards). Many of these psychologists are highly mobile; they go wherever the mission takes them and are integral members of the team. Examples of areas of psychological consultation in the operational psychology domain include crisis negotiation, hostage reintegration, security clearance evaluation, insider threat detection, intelligence, counterintelligence and counterterrorism activities, and A&S of service members for high-risk duties (e.g., special operational forces, astronauts).

## KNOWLEDGE, SKILLS, AND ATTITUDES NECESSARY FOR MILITARY PSYCHOLOGICAL CONSULTATION

Effective consultation in the military setting requires a comprehensive understanding of the fundamental KSAs necessary to provide empirically supported and useful recommendations. Knowledge of military psychological consultation describes the contextual information (factual and procedural) needed to provide effective consultation. The skills noted in this section include the ability to practically apply this knowledge to meaningful consultation and to communicate findings and recommendations effectively to the military command.

In addition, the attitudes described in this section outline the necessary mind-set required to be an effective consultant in the military.

## Knowledge of Military Psychological Consultation

A consulting psychologist must be able to provide an evidence-supported opinion in the context of the military culture and in a manner that is consistent with applicable laws, military policies, and the profession's ethical standards. In the clinical domain, consultation and recommendations must be usable by the command and implementable in a way that facilitates the maximum chance of treatment success for the service member and minimum disruption to command functioning. In the operational domain, consultation must effectively translate psychological science into information useful for mission success (e.g., detection of an insider threat, selection of the best candidate for a job). A necessary first step for both domains is to gain an understanding of the culture and subcultures within the military.

### Military Culture

The military is a culture all its own with its own language, rites, values, code of conduct, and even its own set of laws (Reger, Etherage, Reger, & Gahm, 2008). Although the American Psychological Association's (APA's) *Multicultural Guidelines* (APA, 2017b) were not constructed with the military's distinctive culture in mind, these guidelines may be effectively applied to military practice. Military culture may be divided further into subcultures represented by the individual branches of service and occupational communities (e.g., infantry, artillery, aviation). A few of the critical areas in which psychologists must pursue education, experience, or both, are military rank, military occupational specialties, and military language.

A service member's rank, for example, determines his or her level of responsibility and authority. With higher rank comes greater responsibility for the preparedness, training, conduct, and performance of subordinate service members. Rank is an omnipresent force in the military that contributes to the smooth operation of various missions by facilitating a concrete understanding of exactly who does what and when. Essentially, the military rank structure conveys organization to any task and sets clear expectations. However, although the rank structure is of serious benefit to military operations, it can also complicate psychological consultation—making military rank an issue that needs to be recognized, respected, and finessed.

Understanding the various jobs that individual service members perform is integral to psychological assessment. Each time a service member sees a psychological health care provider, that provider has to determine if the individual is able to continue to perform his or her job safely and effectively. Understanding the core requirements of the specific jobs in the military is key to providing effective consultation. There are vast differences, for example, between an infantryman and an aviator in job function, physical and psychological demands, and reporting requirements.

As another example of the need for military cultural competence, psychologists require an understanding of military language, jargon, and the ever present acronym use. Without this understanding, the psychologist risks making an ill-informed decision. If a military patient says, for example, that his or her PRD is next year but he or she is being PCS'd early due to an NJP, what do you know? All three of these acronyms are used as basic words by service members. The translation is that your patient is moving out of the area unexpectedly (permanent change of station, or PCS) instead of on schedule (projected rotation date, or PRD) because he or she got into some kind of trouble (nonjudicial punishment, or NJP), which suggests that his or her job duties may have changed because of the disciplinary action.

### Research

To develop, maintain, and remain current in the academic knowledge base of military psychology, psychologists must keep up with pertinent military-related research that pertains to both active duty service members as well as veterans in the areas of mental health, consulting, A&S, combat-related disorders as well as other role-specific topics. This is not an easy task because thousands of journal articles have been published on military posttraumatic stress disorder (PTSD) and suicide alone in the past few years. Managing this volume of information requires a systematic approach and continuous consumption of current research. Although consultations regarding military personnel must be evidence based, decades' worth of research is available to assist consultants on a variety of topics, such as personnel selection processes and psychological health treatments most beneficial to military members and veterans, among others.

A psychologist's specific consultation role drives which topics to follow. However, as an example, specific topics for clinicians include empirically supported treatments and the Department of Veterans Affairs and Department of Defense (DoD) clinical practice guidelines for disorders seen in the military population (e.g., PTSD, suicide risk, major depressive disorder), psychological health trends and prevalence rates, and an understanding of trending psychological health treatments that may or may not have evidence to support their use.

### Department of Defense and Service-Level Policies

The recommendations of consultants are often predicated on what the DoD and service-level policy dictate. For the purpose of this chapter, *policy* is a broad term that describes regulations, directives, memoranda, instructions, legislation, and executive orders that may impact the work of the military psychological health consultant. Table 16.1 outlines the many sources to consult for pertinent information. What follows is greater detail about key policy areas, including confidentiality and mandatory disclosure (see the Military-Relevant Ethical Standards section), mental health evaluations for members of the military, and sexual assault.

Commanders have a responsibility to promote a culture of well-being by providing access to psychological health care evaluations and treatment for

**TABLE 16.1.  Department of Defense and Service-Level Policy Sources and Repositories**

| Organization | Location | Types of policies |
|---|---|---|
| Congressional and executive | • U.S. Government Publishing Office https://www.gpo.gov<br>• The White House https://www.whitehouse.gov/presidential-actions | • Congressional publications: Laws, such as the National Defense Authorization Acts<br>• Executive orders released by the White House |
| DoD | • DoD issuances from the DoD Directives Division, Executive Services Directorate http://www.esd.whs.mil/DD/DoD-Issuances<br>• Office of the Assistant Secretary of Defense for Health Affairs policies and guidelines https://health.mil/Reference-Center/Policies | • DoD directives, or DoDD<br>• DoD instructions, or DoDI<br>• DoD manuals, or DoDM<br>• Directive-type memoranda, or DTM<br><br>• Office of the Assistant Secretary of Defense for Health Affairs memoranda<br>• Defense Health Agency procedural instructions<br>• DoD and service-specific issuances |
| United States Air Force | • Air Force E-Publishing http://www.e-publishing.af.mil<br>• Air Force Medical Service (or AFMS) policies https://kx2.afms.mil | • Air Force instructions, or AFI<br>• Air Force policy directives, or AFPD<br><br>• Medical policies |
| United States Army | • Army Publishing Directorate http://www.apd.army.mil<br><br>• U.S. Army Medical Command, Office of the Surgeon General (or OSTG, MEDCOM) policies https://www.army.mil/armymedicine | • Army regulations, or AR<br>• Army activities messages, or ALARACT (All Army Activity)<br>• Medical policies |
| United States Navy | • Department of the Navy issuances https://www.secnav.navy.mil/doni/default.aspx<br><br>• Navy Medicine directives http://www.med.navy.mil/directives | • Secretary of the Navy, or SECNAV, and Chief of Naval Operations, or OPNAV, instructions, notices, manuals; and Navy, or ALNAV (All Navy), regulations<br>• Bureau of Medicine and Surgery, or BUMED<br>• Instructions, notes, and Navy Medicine, or NAVMED, forms<br>• Bureau of Medicine and Surgery (or BUMED)–sponsored instructions (Chief of Naval Operations, or OPNAV)<br>• Secretary of the Navy, or SECNAV<br>• Bureau of Naval Personnel, or BUPERS |

*(continues)*

**TABLE 16.1.  Department of Defense and Service-Level Policy Sources and Repositories (*Continued*)**

| Organization | Location | Types of policies |
|---|---|---|
| United States Marine Corps | • Marine Corps Publications Electronic Library http://www.marines.mil/News/Publications/MCPEL/Custompubstatus/3000 | • Marine Corps orders, or MCO<br>• Navy and Marine Corps policies, directives |
| United States Coast Guard | • Coast Guard Directives and Publications Division http://www.dcms.uscg.mil/Our-Organization/Assistant-Commandant-for-C4IT-CG-6/The-Office-of-Information-Management-CG-61/About-CG-Directives-System | • Commandant instructions, or COMDTINST<br>• Commandant notices, or COMDTNOTE |
| U.S. Department of Veterans Affairs | • Veterans Affairs Publications https://www.va.gov/vapubs | • Veterans Affairs–wide policies and procedures |

*Note.* DoD = U.S. Department of Defense.

service members. Evaluations in the military are dictated by DoD Instruction (DoDI) 6490.04 *Mental Health Evaluations of Members of the Military Services* (U.S. DoD, 2013) as well as service-level policies that establish procedures for the referral, evaluation, treatment, and medical and command management of service members who may require assessment for psychological health problems or psychiatric hospitalization or are at risk of danger to self or others. These evaluations includes command-directed evaluations that assess for "fitness for duty, occupational requirements, safety issues, significant changes in performance, or behavior changes that may be attributable to possible mental status changes" (U.S. DoD, 2013, DoDI 6490.04, section 3(c)). The locations or repositories of service-level policies (addressing mental health evaluations) can be found in Table 16.1.

Sexual assault deserves special mention and is an important topic in the military; as such, it is guided by specific policies and procedures. In recent years, legislation[3] has impacted military policies and has had the aim of broadening sexual-assault–related counseling options and improving the response to sexual assault of men, in particular. Psychological health care providers and consultants should be familiar with DoDI 6495.02 *Sexual Assault Prevention and Response Program Procedures* (U.S. DoD, 2017), which establishes specific health care

---

[3]Legislative updates include Section 538 of the National Defense Authorization Act for Fiscal Year 2016, "Improved Department of Defense prevention and response to sexual assaults in which the victim is a male member of the Armed Forces" ("H.R. 1735—National Defense Authorization Act for Fiscal Year 2016," 2016).

processes and procedures for service members and their adult family members regarding a sexual assault, including reporting procedures for a restricted (confidential) and an unrestricted report. This DoDI outlines the duties of psychological health care providers, additional layers of confidentiality, and the reporting process. Psychological health care providers are routinely called on as consultants in these cases to provide recommendations on a variety of factors related to both the individual and the command response.

**Military-Relevant Ethical Standards**

In any environment in which a psychologist is consulting to a government agency regarding individuals in positions of social trust or with individuals whose actions can endanger others when they are unsuitable for duty, there are numerous ethical considerations. The primary ethical dilemmas identified in military practice are multiple relationships, professional and cultural competence, informed consent, mixed agency, and confidentiality. The exploration of all of these dilemmas in both clinical and operational practice may be found in more comprehensive sources (e.g., Kennedy, 2012; Kennedy & Williams, 2011). However, the two that are considered most pertinent to the current discussion are mixed agency and confidentiality, both of which are described in detail here.

Mixed agency is encountered by psychologists working in both military and other government organizations on a daily basis. Generally, any military psychologist or psychologist consulting to the military can have three clients at any given time, including the patient or individual service member, the organization, and society. When decisions are being made, for example, as to whether or not a military aviator may control tactical aircraft, the individual certainly has a stake (health, career, identity), as does the command/military (safe and successful mission accomplishment), and society (safety from mistakes made regarding weapons and aircraft accidents). Fully understanding who the "client" is in each situation is imperative to providing ethical, legal, and meaningful consultative work. Within APA's (2017a) *Ethical Principles of Psychologists and Code of Conduct* are three pertinent ethical standards to consider regarding the dilemma of mixed agency: 1.02, Conflicts Between Ethics and Law, Regulations, or Other Governing Legal Authority; 1.03, Conflicts Between Ethics and Organizational Demands; and 3.11, Psychological Services Delivered to or Through Organizations. These standards help to build a foundation of internal processes that will prevent significant dilemmas from occurring as well as provide guidance in addressing problems when they do arise.

Conflicts involving confidentiality are also encountered on a routine basis and can be fairly complicated in military practice because information inside the psychologist–patient relationship is frequently not confidential (Hoyt, 2013). The concept of confidentiality and mandatory disclosure (the need of commanders to have sensitive information about their service members) must pass the test of determining if the information impacts the unit or individual's fitness (ability to perform his or her job duty safely). Based on the Health Insurance Portability and Accountability Act of 1996, both civilian and military health care providers are legally able to disclose confidential information for such purposes as fitness for duty, special duty assignments, and negative impact to mission.[4]

In addition to the Health Insurance Portability and Accountability Act of 1996, there is other guidance regarding confidentiality practices in military psychological health. Specifically, DoDI 6490.08, *Command Notification Requirement to Dispel Stigma in Providing Mental Health Care to Service Members* (U.S. DoD, 2011) outlines in a more concrete manner the exceptions to service member/patient–provider confidentiality. Generally, these exceptions include issues related to harm to self, others, or mission; high-risk, high-demand personnel status; mental health hospitalization; substance use treatment; command-directed evaluations, and fitness-for-duty concerns. The aim is to provide a balance between patient confidentiality and the commander's right to know so that he or she can make informed operational and risk management decisions. Counterintuitively, although confidentiality is considered a key component of effective psychological health treatment, in the military, disclosure to the command in some instances can help to better meet patient needs and allow access to command resources.

The following is a vignette that depicts a clinical case in which the symptoms cannot be effectively addressed in a treatment situation without the involvement of the command:

> A 20-year-old female Seaman (i.e., an E3, a junior enlisted sailor) is currently serving on shore duty and living in the barracks.[5] She presents to a psychologist for psychological treatment of insomnia. She has been referred by her primary care physician after failing several trials of sleeping medication. No physiological cause has been found for her current sleep difficulties. After a comprehensive evaluation, including ruling out a psychological health diagnosis, substantial inter-personal stressors, poor sleep-related habits, substance abuse (including energy drinks, caffeine, nicotine), and so forth, the only significant finding is that the sailor shares a barracks room with another sailor who works on an opposite shift. You discover that the sleep problems did not arise until this opposite work schedule commenced. Essentially, each night that your patient is trying to sleep, the roommate has the light on and is doing normal awake activities in the room. Will this sailor benefit from your empirically validated treatment of insomnia or implementation of a wide variety of compensatory sleep aids (e.g., eye mask, ear plugs, white noise)?

No matter how skilled a psychologist is in the implementation of psychological treatment of insomnia, it is unlikely that this sailor will be helped significantly by a course of treatment. An environmental change is indicated—one that is only in the purview of the command to implement. By instruction (DoDI 6490.08; U.S. DoD, 2011), the psychologist has no legal requirement to

---

[4]The specific exception is documented in Title 45 of the *Code of Federal Regulations* (CFR), §164.512(k) and DoD Regulation 6025.18-R *DoD Health Information Privacy Regulation* (U.S. DoD, 2003).
[5]All clinical case material has been altered to protect client confidentiality.

report information about this sailor to the command because there has not yet been mission degradation (although it is fair to say that mission degradation has either not yet been noticed or will occur in the short term). The "treatment" of choice in this case would be to call the sailor's chief and recommend a change in living situation to a barracks room with someone on the same shift schedule.

Military psychologists are confronted with these types of scenarios as a normal course of business. and the best solution is often to facilitate communication with the command. Various solutions to this problem are to encourage the patient to talk to the command herself or to get written permission from the sailor for the psychologist to talk to the command. This approach has the greatest likelihood of solving her sleep problems. Keep in mind that the command tends to have more resources than the psychologist, and these resources can be used to substantial benefit to military patients. Beyond the preceding guidance, it is recommended that a psychologist consultant review service-specific polices and have open discussions with peers, supervisors, and legal, if necessary, to determine appropriate courses of action with regard to patient confidentiality when complications arise.

## Skills in Military Psychological Consultation

In addition to the core skills learned in the course of the psychology doctoral degree and subsequent training opportunities, being a skilled military consultant requires two other key components. First, the psychological consultant needs to be able to apply the knowledge (see the Knowledge of Military Psychological Consultation section) of sound psychological assessment within the context of the military culture. Second, once a way forward has been determined, the psychologist then needs to be able to present that information in a clear, succinct, confident, and professional manner so that information is usable by the command.

## Application of Psychological Science in the Military

Applying the previously discussed knowledge, which is more comprehensively covered by other sources (e.g., Kennedy & Zillmer, 2012), is truly both science and art. When assessing a military member clinically or for operational duties, information about the individual's job responsibilities must be integrated into any fitness, suitability, special duty, or treatment recommendations. Does the individual have weapons-handling responsibilities? Does the individual have flight status? Is the individual getting ready to deploy or move overseas? If there are restrictions on military service, is there a waiver process that can or must be adhered to? Given the specific constellation of symptoms, do you need to report them and, if so, to whom? Each of these types of questions brings additional requirements to the evaluation and consultation function to determine if the service member can continue to safely perform existing functions or to be selected for additional specialized duties.

The first vignette dealt with the application of confidentiality rules in the case of an active duty patient. This second vignette addresses an operational psychological evaluation pertaining to a security clearance issue:

> An Army Sergeant (E5) applied for a high-risk, high-demand position that required a top secret security clearance.[6] He was provided an in-depth background check, and the operational psychologist performed a full complement of A&S procedures, including psychometric assessment, interview, and behavioral observation. Because one of the primary areas of concern in this case is the security clearance, the psychological assessment focused on known risk factors related to unsafe handling of classified information. As examples, the following areas were assessed: What are his finances like? Does he live beyond his means? What is his approach to spending money and accumulating or managing debt? Does he have any sexual behaviors that could be considered problematic, such as hiring prostitutes or engaging in aberrant sexual practices? What are his alcohol use patterns? Is there a history of alcohol or other substance abuse? How often does he become intoxicated? Is there any evidence of poor decision making while drinking? The security clearance psychological evaluation necessarily covers some areas that are not typically covered in a standard psychological evaluation.
>
> His evaluation unearthed no concerns; he was selected for the job and was provided a security clearance. He completed the required course of training and was deployed overseas. Eight months later, the psychologist received a request via the command security manager for a second assessment because of new information that the Sergeant had physically threatened his friends, family, and coworkers who were interviewed as a part of the security clearance process conducted by the government agency overseeing that process. The threats were specifically related to protecting information related to long-standing transvestic behavior (i.e., cross-dressing). During his reassessment he disclosed his transvestism and acknowledged threatening his collateral sources for his background investigation.

The psychologist in this case was asked to provide an assessment for redetermination of the Sergeant's access to classified material. Essentially, does the Sergeant have a diagnosis? If so, what is the treatment? What is the prognosis? Are there any concerns related to his ability to safeguard classified material?

Ironically, the issue is not that the Sergeant may engage in cross-dressing or even have a transvestic disorder, because neither is necessarily disqualifying for a security clearance.[7] The issue is his approach to keeping it a secret and the poor judgment he displayed, which are the concerns related to the clearance. Had the Sergeant been open in the course of the first evaluation, he would have likely been provided the clearance anyway. His decision and poor judgment to threaten people to keep his secret caused him to lose both the clearance and the job. This makes sense for jobs in which honesty, trustworthiness, problem-solving, decision making, and integrity are required core components.

---

[6]Note that when service members apply for or are working in special duty assignments, they expressly waive standard confidentiality.

[7]Fewer than 1% of people applying for a clearance who acknowledge a mental health history are denied a clearance.

It should be noted that the psychological evaluation for anyone seeking a security clearance is only one component of that process, and the operational psychologist has no say in whether or not someone is granted one.

## Interpersonal Skills and Communication

Interpersonal skills in military psychological consultation mirror those skills necessary to be an effective psychologist in any environment, including the abilities to build rapport and communicate recommendations in a method that can be easily understood and implemented. One of the most important skills a psychologist can learn is how to effectively communicate with commands. Commanders are more able to accept and implement clinical recommendations when those recommendations take into account the capacity of the command to support them, their adherence to military policies, and mission impact. Although the psychologist is the subject-matter expert on psychological health, the commander is the expert on how the unit functions, the resources available to the unit, and how he or she can support the service member.

Successful psychological consultants take this information into account and are creative in meeting the needs of the service member/patient (as well as the command) so that in the optimal scenario, the service member/patient is able to retain his or her job and meet military requirements. Working with a commander requires a team approach and a willingness to accept that the command holds almost all of the cards and is ultimately responsible for all decisions.

With regard to military members who may need or be in psychological health treatment, the commander assumes all risks in allowing an individual access to firearms, classified information, or control of aircraft, for examples. Thus, any refusal to work with the command will make the treatment of a patient much more difficult. Because psychological health care providers and military commanders often do not speak the same language, the following are recommendations for successfully communicating with any given command:

- Build rapport with local commands and develop a good working relationship; doing so will bolster the psychologist's recommendations.

- Be organized in the approach to any communication and know ahead of time what you are trying to accomplish. Military commands appreciate a succinct and unambiguous communication.

- Never provide information that the command cannot use or does not need to know to make an informed decision about the topic at hand.

- Do not provide vague or ambiguous recommendations; otherwise, you place the command in the position of having to make a medical decision. For example, either a service member is considered safe—from a psychological health perspective—to handle firearms or not. Do not hedge on your recommendations.

- Always remember that the command has most of the control over what happens with his or her service member. To optimize positive outcomes for military patients, psychologists must be able to adapt their recommendations so that they enable treatment while still meeting mission, do not drain command resources, and take into account the limitations of the command.

- When interacting with military officers, take care to be respectful, use appropriate titles when addressing or discussing individuals, and observe other components of military etiquette. Failure to do so can present an appearance of low professional competence, which is contrary to good patient outcomes.

- When you are going to communicate with a command, decide who to call. Because the commander is the individual generally permitted to receive confidential communications, the commander is often the person that psychologists default to calling. Unfortunately, the commander frequently is not the best choice, particularly in large commands in which he or she may not know the service member in question. In such cases, calling the commander will result in the input's being conveyed down the chain to the designated action officer. Psychologists should have a discussion with patients, outline the information that needs to be passed or discussed, and let the patient decide (through written permission) which person he or she is most comfortable with being contacted. Make sure that the person is someone who has some decisional authority in either the enlisted or officer chain.

## Attitudes in Military Consultation

When examining your approach to psychological consultation in the military, it is important to first be mindful of, and acknowledge your own biases about, the military, war, and service members. Also consider how your personal beliefs, including political beliefs, may impact your consultation activities. Through family experiences, newscasts, friends, and so forth, everyone develops beliefs and attitudes about the military as they grow up. APA's (2017b) Guideline 2 in the updated *Multicultural Guidelines* specifically addresses psychologists' personal attitudes and beliefs:

> Psychologists aspire to recognize and understand that as cultural beings, they hold attitudes and beliefs that can influence their perceptions of and interactions with others as well as their clinical and empirical conceptualizations. As such, psychologists strive to move beyond conceptualizations rooted in categorical assumptions, biases, and/or formulations based on limited knowledge about individuals and communities. (p. 4)

For those with potentially negative views of the military or of any given war or combat operation, attempting to consult to the military can be complicated. It is critical that psychologists never communicate negative views to a patient or service member because, as we know from service member experiences during the Vietnam War, these views can negatively affect psychological health (e.g., Levenberg, 1983). Service members join the military for a lot of reasons but primary among them are patriotism, family tradition, personal improvement opportunities (e.g., job training, educational benefits), and a sense of adventure. For most service members, their identities are defined by their military roles and experiences.

Unfortunately, some myths about service members persist in our society. For example, it is not uncommon to see jokes about supposed lower intellectual abilities in the military population, which, ironically, is one of few organizations in the nation that requires 100% of its non–college-educated work force to take the equivalent of an IQ test and meet specific standards to join. Recent comparisons of male and female veterans to nonveterans found that veterans of both genders have higher rates of employment and higher earnings rates, and, for females, higher educational levels (U.S. Department of Veterans Affairs, 2017, 2018). Erroneous beliefs also persist about the psychological health of service members. Astonishingly, a poll by the George W. Bush Institute (2016) found that 40% of respondents believed that more than half of post-9/11 veterans had mental health problems![8] Monitoring your own thoughts and beliefs regarding service members in the context of military consulting is critical.

Continual introspection, education, supervision, and awareness of any biases help you to minimize the impact they play in your consultation with a military command as well as your professional recommendations. As an ambassador for the profession, it is important to continually dispel myths about military personnel and stigma surrounding psychological services. Reinforce that most service members and veterans are well-adjusted, high achievers who are dedicated to serving their country.

## TRAINING

Psychologists working with members of the military do so in a variety of capacities: as active duty officers; contract or government civilians; or as community providers working in civilian hospitals, clinics, or in private practice. For those who are serving on active duty as psychologists, the most common route is to compete for a military internship with the United States Air Force, United States Army, or United States Navy via the Association of Psychology Postdoctoral and Internship Centers selection process. Others come into the military via the Health Professions Scholarship Program, which funds the majority of an approved civilian doctoral program in exchange for military service. Still others gain acceptance into the Uniformed Services University of Health Sciences (https://www.usuhs.edu), during which students become commissioned officers and spend the first 5 years of active duty service as graduate students. Fully licensed psychologists meeting military entrance requirements may accept direct commissions to serve.

Although psychologists who are active duty or veterans have an edge on developing the cultural expertise necessary to work with service members, for those with no prior military experience, several resources are available for civilians to learn military culture, particularly as it pertains to psychological health.

---

[8]The real number is between 10% and 20%.

The Center for Deployment Psychology (https://deploymentpsych.org) provides online and in-person training that specifically address cultural competence as well as evidence-based treatments. The Department of Veterans Affairs (https://www.va.gov) provides training with the aim of better understanding military culture and the role psychological health plays in the lives of service members and their families. The National Center for PTSD (https://www.ptsd.va.gov/index.asp), a center within the Department of Veterans Affairs, provides PTSD-focused continuing education and resources, including a clinical consultation service for providers who treat veterans with PTSD. Within the DoD, the Psychological Health Center of Excellence (https://www.pdhealth.mil) provides information for clinicians and researchers working with military populations, including information on empirically supported treatments and clinical practice guidelines, current psychological health disorder prevalence trends, expert-reviewed evidence briefs on existing and potential treatments for psychological health conditions, and general resources for clinicians and patients regarding psychological health. In addition, there is a small but growing number of graduate programs that primarily focus on military psychology and a rapidly increasing number of universities that have campus chapters of APA Division 19 (Society for Military Psychology).

The operational psychology domain requires additional formal and experiential training and, depending on the specific job, the psychologist may also require a security clearance and a psychological A&S process. All branches of service have training pipelines for their active duty population to follow, which include formal courses in topics such as A&S and formal mentorship programs, and the Navy has a 1-year postdoctoral fellowship devoted to operational psychology. Criminal justice, forensic psychology, ethics and multicultural training, psychological assessment, sports psychology, consulting psychology, and police psychology are all relevant areas of advanced training for operational psychologists.

## BOARD CERTIFICATION

Board certification through the American Board of Professional Psychology remains the highest credential for U.S. psychologists, and military psychologists are no exception. Military psychologists achieve board certification in the array of specialty areas, but those that are particularly relevant to military consultation are Clinical Psychology, Police & Public Safety, and Organizational & Business Consulting Psychology. Although the clinical domain has no areas of practice that are unique to military psychology, this board in particular strives to provide senior military mentors and military board members for candidates, thus resulting in substantial professional development for psychologists who work within military settings (Kennedy, 2012). The Police & Public Safety and Organizational & Business Consulting Psychology boards are newer boards for military psychologists to pursue but have direct relevance toward developing and establishing competence in the field given the extreme overlap in these areas of practice (Kennedy, 2016).

## CONCLUSION

As the mission set of the military changes and adapts to address the nation's priorities, so, too, will the consultation responsibilities of military psychologists. Both clinical and operational psychology practice in the military are great examples of the high-impact value of psychology, and an increasing number of training pipelines and opportunities are available to psychologists. Within the domains of practice in the military, psychologists are able to directly apply their consultation expertise to improve the lives of individual service members, the functioning of military units, and the security of the nation.

## GLOSSARY

**assessment and selection:** Formal psychological procedures used to determine individuals who are best suited for a specific military occupation or mission

**clinical military psychology:** The practice of clinical psychology in the military; evaluation and treatment may be provided in a traditional, clinic- or hospital-based model or an embedded or expeditionary model.

**command-directed evaluation:** An evaluation governed by military instruction in which an individual service member is referred for mental health evaluation by his or her commander due to concerns related to psychological health symptoms impacting the safety and well-being of the individual service member in the military environment

**embedded clinical psychology:** Psychologists are integrated within a military command or unit to optimize the psychological health of the entire unit.

**expeditionary psychology:** See *embedded clinical psychology.* The terms *embedded clinical psychology* and *expeditionary psychology* are used interchangeably.

**military psychological consultation:** The provision of expert opinion, analysis, and recommendations to support informed decisions made by military leadership for the purpose of improving military functioning and effectiveness.

**mixed agency:** An ethical dilemma experienced by psychologists who have a responsibility to multiple parties

**operational psychology:** A psychology subspecialty in which the focus is on the operational activities of law enforcement, national intelligence organizations, and national defense activities

## REFERENCES

American Psychological Association. (2017a). *Ethical principles of psychologists and code of conduct* (2002, Amended June 1, 2010 and January 1, 2017). Retrieved from http://www.apa.org/ethics/code/index.aspx

American Psychological Association. (2017b). *Multicultural guidelines: An ecological approach to context, identity, and intersectionality.* Retrieved from http://www.apa.org/about/policy/multicultural-guidelines.pdf

Boake, C. (2002). From the Binet–Simon to the Wechsler–Bellevue: Tracing the history of intelligence testing. *Journal of Clinical and Experimental Neuropsychology, 24,* 383–405. http://dx.doi.org/10.1076/jcen.24.3.383.981

George W. Bush Institute. (2016). *Confronting the invisible wounds of war: Barriers, Misunderstanding, and a Divide.* Retrieved from the George W. Bush Presidential Center website: https://gwbcenter.imgix.net/Resources/GWBI-invisiblewoundsperceptionssurvey.pdf

Health Insurance and Portability and Accountability Act of 1996, Pub. L. No. 104-191, Aug. 21, 1996, 110 Stat. 1936 (1996).

Hoyt, T. (2013). Limits to confidentiality in U.S. Army treatment settings. *Military Psychology, 25*, 46–56. http://dx.doi.org/10.1037/h0094756

H.R. 1735—National Defense Authorization Act for Fiscal Year 2016: ["Text" tab:] Sec. 538. Improved Department of Defense prevention and response to sexual assaults in which the victim is a male member of the Armed Forces. (2016). Retrieved from https://www.congress.gov/bill/114th-congress/house-bill/1735/text

Kennedy, C. H. (2012). ABPP certification for military psychologists. *Military Psychology, 27*, 19–20. Retrieved from http://www.apadivisions.org/division-19/publications/newsletters/military/2012/04/military-psychologists-certification.aspx

Kennedy, C. H. (2016). Board certification for military psychologists: A new option through the American Board of Police and Public Safety Psychology. *Military Psychology, 31*, 6–7. Retrieved from http://www.apadivisions.org/division-19/students-careers/board-certification.aspx

Kennedy, C. H., & Williams, T. J. (Eds.). (2011). *Ethical practice in operational psychology: Military and national intelligence applications*. Washington, DC: American Psychological Association. http://dx.doi.org/10.1037/12342-000

Kennedy, C. H., & Zillmer, E. A. (Eds.). (2012). *Military psychology clinical and operational applications*. New York, NY: Guilford Press.

Levenberg, S. B. (1983). Vietnam combat veterans: From perpetrator to victim. *Family & Community Health: The Journal of Health Promotion & Maintenance, 5*(4), 69–76. http://dx.doi.org/10.1097/00003727-198305040-00009

McGuire, F. L. (1990). *Psychology aweigh! A history of clinical psychology in the United States Navy, 1900–1988*. Washington, DC: American Psychological Association.

National Defense Authorization Act for Fiscal Year 2016. Pub. L. 114–92, Nov. 25, 2015, 129 Stat. 726 (2016).

Olson, T. M., McCauley, M., & Kennedy, C. H. (2013). A history of aeromedical psychology. In C. H. Kennedy & G. G. Kay (Eds.), *Aeromedical psychology* (pp. 1–15). Farnham, England: Ashgate.

Reger, M. A., Etherage, J. R., Reger, G. M., & Gahm, G. A. (2008). Civilian psychologists in an Army culture: The ethical challenge of cultural competence. *Military Psychology, 20*, 21–35. http://dx.doi.org/10.1080/08995600701753144

U.S. Department of Defense. (2003). *DoD health information privacy regulation* (Department of Defense Regulation 6025.18-R). Washington, DC: Author.

U.S. Department of Defense. (2011, August). *Command notification requirement to dispel stigma in providing mental health care to service members* (Department of Defense Instruction 6490.08). Washington, DC: Author.

U.S. Department of Defense. (2013, March). *Mental health evaluations of members of the military services* (Department of Defense Instruction 6490.04). Washington, DC: Author.

U.S. Department of Defense. (2017, May). *Sexual assault prevention and response program procedures* (Department of Defense Instruction 6495.02). Washington, DC: Author.

U.S. Department of Veterans Affairs. (2017). *Women veterans report*. Retrieved from https://www.va.gov/vetdata/docs/SpecialReports/Women_Veterans_2015_Final.pdf

U.S. Department of Veterans Affairs. (2018). *Profile of veterans: 2016*. Retrieved from https://www.va.gov/vetdata/docs/SpecialReports/Profile_of_Veterans_2016.pdf

Wechsler, D. (1981). *WAIS-R: Wechsler Adult Intelligence Scale–Revised*. New York, NY: Psychological Corporation.

Yerkes, R. M. (Ed.). (1921). *National Academy of Sciences memoirs: Vol. XV. Psychological examining in the United States Army*. Washington, DC: Government Printing Office.

# Afterword

## Advancing Consultation Practice

Carol A. Falender and Edward P. Shafranske

Although consultation and its analogue, interprofessional collaboration, have long been recognized professional competencies (Arredondo, Shealy, Neale, & Winfrey, 2004; see also Fouad et al., 2009; Kaslow et al., 2004; Chapter 5, this volume), the complexity of the roles across the various settings, demand characteristics, worldviews, and contexts had not been fully addressed. To fill this gap, we invited leaders in the respective fields of consultation to prepare chapters with the objective of providing an integrated, innovative competency-based approach for individuals in training or those considering expansion of practice.

## A NECESSARY PARADIGM SHIFT

Although provision of direct services is well within the bailiwick of psychologists, providing consultation to other health care professionals, participating on interprofessional teams, and functioning within community, school, and government agencies to bring psychological knowledge and skills require a shift in functions and roles. Furthermore, implicit in the role of consultant is the shift in value orientation to examine assumptions often attached to clinical work and to adopt a lens that addresses the values, culture, societal norms, and organizational mores of the consultee, setting, context, and organization (see Chapters 5 and 6, this volume). Although what is required complements the functional

http://dx.doi.org/10.1037/0000153-018
*Consultation in Psychology: A Competency-Based Approach*, C. A. Falender and
E. P. Shafranske (Editors)

competencies associated with assessment, prevention, and psychological treatment, a spectrum of other competencies and worldviews are required. Moving from direct service with clients to providing professional-to-professional consultation to a multitude of disciplines requires a distinct paradigm shift. The consultant frames the problem, defines it, and posits proposed solutions all in coordination with the consultee. The consultant has expertise in a particular area, but competence goes beyond that to understanding the process of how the issue arose and is sustained, empowering and facilitating processes of consultees to move toward potential solutions, identifying aspects of organizational functioning to determine when interventions should be made and where, providing clarity regarding who is the client and who holds the decision power, and addressing more complex ethical issues, as discussed by Barnett in Chapter 3, this volume. A consultant may shift roles from collaborator to thought leader to the individual who finalizes the consultation confident that he or she has confronted the issues and is moving forward to address them.

Some of the distinctive elements of the process include the consultant's adopting and maintaining professional distance and objectivity regarding the consultation question or issue. The process of framing the consultation request so that it is accurate, understandable, and actionable is a competency. Underlying the consultation process is the distinct understanding that the consultant offers input and suggestions, but it is the sole responsibility of the consultee to decide whether and how to implement those suggestions. The entire consultation process occurs with direct attention to ethical and legal standards and codes (see Chapter 3).

Consultation is increasingly a high-frequency event, as is reflected in the *Standards of Accreditation for Health Service Psychology* (American Psychological Association, Commission on Accreditation, 2018), which identifies consultation as a professionwide competency. Core competencies for interprofessional collaborative practice (Interprofessional Education Collaborative, 2011, 2016) have also been elucidated by professionals of multiple disciplines with representation from the American Psychological Association. However, a 2015 survey of service provision by psychology health service providers indicated that although respondents valued collaborative practice, consultation was a low-frequency event and was grouped with other human services or "other," which, in totality, amounted to less than 5% of their work activity (American Psychological Association, Center for Workforce Studies, 2016). It is projected that the frequency of consultation will increase quickly, and thus guidance in the provision of consultation is a high priority.

## COMPETENCY-BASED CONSULTATION TRAINING

Designing learning environments for the health care professionals of tomorrow will be incomplete unless those environments include interprofessional education within a competency-based approach (Barr, 2013). At the heart of this effort are collaboration and communication across disciplines—essential components of consultation—and an understanding that the consultant exerts social influence that is implicit in his or her every action (Erchul & Martens, 2010). Psychology training programs differ in the emphasis placed on the complex issue of consultation competence. As highlighted by the contributors to this volume, momentum is increasing to formalize consultation training across specialties.

As each of the chapters connotes, multicultural competence is a factor that is essential to all consultation but may not have been adequately addressed within consultation. Basic challenges entail providing language and context-specific understanding; addressing generalizations and stereotypes, authenticity, cultural humility, power dynamics, and diversity in leadership customs; and recognizing hierarchical versus collaborative structures (Cooper, Wilson-Stark, Peterson, O'Roark, & Pennington, 2008) as well as the multicultural intersections of individuals and organizations (see Chapter 6, this volume). A survey of syllabi for school psychology consultation training revealed attention to the cultural identities of the clients in consultation, but few mentioned in the syllabus the impact of the consultant's culture on the process or directly addressed consultee's culture or social position (Hazel, Laviolette, & Lineman, 2010). Incompatibilities in perspectives or agendas, including worldviews among the referring teams, leaders and consultees, and the consultant's practices, present potential barriers to the process (Doll et al., 2005).

When consultation training is provided (although only 25% of doctoral programs in school psychology offer two consultation courses; most offer one), the experience is often without supervision of the actual experience (Anton-LaHart & Rosenfield, 2004; Hazel et al., 2010). And although some supervision of the consultation experience may occur in consultation training, it has generally been without live or video review of the actual practice. *Metacompetence,* that is, not knowing what one does not know, is a significant deterrent to achieving greater competence because the consultation trainee does not receive the requisite feedback or evaluation to enhance practice. Dedicated course work, exposure to consultation models with in depth exposure to at least one, and supervision without total reliance on self-report all increased confidence of early career school psychologists in their roles (Barrett, Hazel, & Newman, 2017). Blanton (2014) surveyed consulting and industrial–organizational psychology doctoral programs and concluded that supervision varied greatly across programs and no particular model predominated. Unless formal supervision does occur, though, graduates will be ineligible for licensure in multiple states.

Formal course work in consultation and supervised experience are essential components. Suggested topics for greater efficacy of training include preparing for entry into systems and balancing expertise with collaboration (Klose, Plotts, & Lasser, 2012). However, without supervision, the developing consultant is left without reflective process, feedback, and targeted development of specific competencies and assessment of whether those competencies were achieved.

Unfortunately, assessment of outcomes of consultation has not been a general practice. It needs to be elevated to a standard of practice because it is essential to the consultation process, including increasing the efficacy of current and future consultation efforts, and to the educational process. Outcomes could be assessed throughout the consultation process, at completion, and at later time intervals to assess change and continued value and impact as well as limitations and barriers. Selection of outcome parameters is a significant consultant role because he or she is in a position to identify measurable variables that may or may not be obvious to the organization. Examples include employee satisfaction, turnover, demographics and diversity of management, outcomes of various sectors, and the impact of these variables on organizational efficacy (Lowman, 2014).

Using a multiple-baseline, single-case study design of a school consultation project, Lepage, Kratochwill, and Elliott (2004) reported that clients improved as did skills and knowledge of consultants, but attitudes did not change. Their paradigm with ongoing assessment and evaluation of knowledge, skills, attitudes, and satisfaction as well as self-assessment by consultants (graduate students) provides an excellent model of formative and summative assessment strategies.

The future of consultation in psychology training requires specific attention to it as a competency. A competency-based approach must focus on knowledge, skills, and attitudes. As with most of psychology training, knowledge, and to a lesser extent with consultation, skills, are at the forefront, but attitudes may have been neglected.

Moving forward, training at the graduate level should contain a meta-approach to consultation, preferably through a competency-based frame. Introduction to the multiple consultation areas, processes, functions, and career opportunities is essential. Graduate students should have supervised consultation hands-on experience and the opportunity to discuss the multiple settings, consultation questions and issues, and the multitude of factors that play a role in determining appropriate interventions or approaches. Models have been proposed to revisit consultation and use it as a mechanism for change toward social justice in graduate training (Grapin, 2017) in line with Parham (see Chapter 6, this volume). By addressing both the foundational and functional aspects of consulting, the supervisee will have a framework from which to build competence in consultation practice.

## IMPLEMENTATION

Consultation is increasingly described as an implementation strategy for evidence-based practice (e.g., Funderburk et al., 2015; Jackson, Herschell, Schaffner, Turiano, & McNeil, 2017; Nadeem, Gleacher, & Beidas, 2013) as a means to instill and support acquisition and application of knowledge, skills, and adherence to the model and to enhance fidelity (Schoenwald, Sheidow, & Letourneau, 2004). Generally, encouraging outcome data are emerging on the use of consultation in evidence-based treatment implementation (Edmunds et al., 2017).

Consultation provides continued targeted training in conjunction with the skill implementation; a problem-solving format for addressing barriers; and a means for engaging, adapting the treatment, providing skill-building, and planning for long-term sustainability. Consultation also may entail supportive video review of the implemented practice—a promising approach. A skillful consultant who has knowledge of the organization—and thus can interface with multiple levels, can target organizational contexts, and can consult directly with organizational leadership while placing high value on interpersonal relationships, a form of collaboration—may also facilitate a favorable implementation climate. A high level of accountability is required both on the part of the consultant and the organization. The authors of chapters in this volume have described a critical part of consultation: planning for sustainability when the consultant is no longer involved. Thus, a valued role of the consultant in this setting is to ensure that other individuals are available to provide the supportive and myriad roles that the consultant had provided. A consultant should not be indispensable but should always be planning for sustainability postconsultation.

Because attitudes are bellwethers of change in organization, the role of consultants as agents of attitude change may be powerful and provide the perspective that the organization is an adaptive system (Aarons, 2005). Thus, consultants would assess attitudes toward evidence-based practice. They could assist leaders to address the promotion of evidence-based practice by enhancing supportive attitudes in organizations, increasing communication of enthusiasm and positive experiences of early adopters of the change, creating increased channels of communication, and bridging the gap between the adopters and the less eager employees (Aarons, 2005).

As the role and efficacy of consultation are more widely understood and valued, training to address specific competencies is essential. Through a combination of course work attending to foundational (Part I, this volume) and functional (Part II, this volume) competencies and supervised experience in the field, psychology will enter a new era of expanded roles and competence in consultation.

## REFERENCES

Aarons, G. A. (2005). Measuring provider attitudes toward evidence-based practice: Consideration of organizational context and individual differences. *Child and Adolescent Psychiatric Clinics of North America, 14*, 255–271, viii. http://dx.doi.org/10.1016/j.chc.2004.04.008

American Psychological Association, Center for Workforce Studies. (2016). *2015 survey of psychology health service providers*. Retrieved from http://www.apa.org/workforce/publications/15-health-service-providers/index.aspx

American Psychological Association, Commission on Accreditation. (2018). *Standards of accreditation for health service psychology*. Retrieved from http://www.apa.org/ed/accreditation/about/policies/standards-of-accreditation.pdf

Anton-LaHart, J., & Rosenfield, S. (2004). A survey of preservice consultation Training in school psychology programs. *Journal of Educational and Psychological Consultation, 15*, 41–62. http://dx.doi.org/10.1207/s1532768xjepc1501_2

Arredondo, P., Shealy, C., Neale, M., & Winfrey, L. L. (2004). Consultation and inter-professional collaboration: Modeling for the future. *Journal of Clinical Psychology, 60,* 787–800. http://dx.doi.org/10.1002/jclp.20015

Barr, H. (2013). Enigma variations: Unraveling interprofessional education in time and place. *Journal of Interprofessional Care, 27*(Suppl. 2), 9–13. http://dx.doi.org/10.3109/13561820.2013.766157

Barrett, C. A., Hazel, C. E., & Newman, D. S. (2017). Training confident school-based consultants: The role of course content, process, and supervision. *Training and Education in Professional Psychology, 11,* 41–48. http://dx.doi.org/10.1037/tep0000128

Blanton, J. S. (2014). Supervision practices in consulting and industrial-organizational psychology doctoral programs and consulting firms. *Consulting Psychology Journal: Practice and Research, 66,* 53–76. http://dx.doi.org/10.1037/a0035681

Cooper, S., Wilson-Stark, K., Peterson, D. B., O'Roark, A. M., & Pennington, G. (2008). Consulting competently in multicultural contexts. *Consulting Psychology Journal: Practice and Research, 60,* 186–202. http://dx.doi.org/10.1037/0736-9735.60.2.186

Doll, B., Haack, K., Kosse, S., Osterloh, M., Siemers, E., & Pray, B. (2005). The dilemma of pragmatics: Why schools don't use quality team consultation practices. *Journal of Educational and Psychological Consultation, 16,* 127–155. http://dx.doi.org/10.1207/s1532768xjepc1603_1

Edmunds, J. M., Brodman, D. M., Ringle, V. A., Read, K. L., Kendall, P. C., & Beidas, R. S. (2017). Examining adherence to components of cognitive-behavioral therapy for youth anxiety after training and consultation. *Professional Psychology: Research and Practice, 48,* 54–61. http://dx.doi.org/10.1037/pro0000100

Erchul, W. P., & Martens, B. K. (2010). *School consultation: Conceptual and empirical bases of practice* (3rd ed.). New York, NY: Springer. http://dx.doi.org/10.1007/978-1-4419-5747-4

Fouad, N. A., Grus, C. L., Hatcher, R. L., Kaslow, N. J., Hutchings, P. S., Madson, M. B., . . . Crossman, R. E. (2009). Competency benchmarks: A model for understanding and measuring competence in professional psychology across training levels. *Training and Education in Professional Psychology, 3*(4, Suppl.), S5–S26. http://dx.doi.org/10.1037/a0015832

Funderburk, B., Chaffin, M., Bard, E., Shanley, J., Bard, D., & Berliner, L. (2015). Comparing client outcomes for two evidence-based treatment consultation strategies. *Journal of Clinical Child & Adolescent Psychology, 44,* 730–741. http://dx.doi.org/10.1080/15374416.2014.910790

Grapin, S. L. (2017). Social justice training in school psychology: Applying principles of organizational consultation to facilitate change in graduate programs. *Journal of Educational and Psychological Consultation, 27,* 173–202. http://dx.doi.org/10.1080/10474412.2016.1217489

Hazel, C. E., Laviolette, G. T., & Lineman, J. M. (2010). Training professional psychologists in school-based consultation: What the syllabi suggest. *Training and Education in Professional Psychology, 4,* 235–243. http://dx.doi.org/10.1037/a0020072

Interprofessional Education Collaborative. (2016). *Core competencies for interprofessional collaborative practice: 2016 update.* Washington, DC. Interprofessional Education Collaborative. Retrieved from https://nebula.wsimg.com/2f68a39520b03336b41038c370497473?AccessKeyId=DC06780E69ED19E2B3A5&disposition=0&alloworigin=1

Interprofessional Education Collaborative Expert Panel. (2011). *Core competencies for interprofessional collaborative practice: Report of an expert panel.* Washington, DC: Interprofessional Education Collaborative. Retrieved from https://nebula.wsimg.com/3ee8a4b5b5f7ab794c742b14601d5f23?AccessKeyId=DC06780E69ED19E2B3A5&disposition=0&alloworigin=1

Jackson, C. B., Herschell, A. D., Schaffner, K. F., Turiano, N. A., & McNeil, C. B. (2017). Training community-based clinicians in parent–child interaction therapy: The inter-action between expert consultation and caseload. *Professional Psychology: Research and Practice, 48,* 481–489. http://dx.doi.org/10.1037/pro0000149

Kaslow, N. J., Borden, K. A., Collins, F. L., Jr., Forrest, L., Illfelder-Kaye, J., Nelson, P. D., . . . Willmuth, M. E. (2004). Competencies Conference: Future Directions in Education and Credentialing in Professional Psychology. *Journal of Clinical Psychology, 60,* 699–712. http://dx.doi.org/10.1002/jclp.20016

Klose, L. M., Plotts, C., & Lasser, J. (2012). Participants' evaluation of consultation: Implications for training in school psychology. *Assessment & Evaluation in Higher Education, 37,* 817–828. http://dx.doi.org/10.1080/02602938.2011.576310

Lepage, K., Kratochwill, T. R., & Elliott, S. N. (2004). Competency-based behavior Consultation training: An evaluation of consultant outcomes, treatment effects, and consumer satisfaction. *School Psychology Quarterly, 19,* 1–28. http://dx.doi.org/10.1521/scpq.19.1.1.29406

Lowman, R. L. (2014). Social justice in industrial-organizational and consulting psychology. In J. Diaz, Z. Franco, & B. K. Nastasi (Eds.), *The Praeger handbook of social justice and psychology: Vol. 3. Youth and disciplines in psychology* (pp. 165–182). Santa Barbara, CA: Praeger.

Nadeem, E., Gleacher, A., & Beidas, R. S. (2013). Consultation as an implementation strategy for evidence-based practices across multiple contexts: Unpacking the black box. *Administration and Policy in Mental Health and Mental Health Services Research, 40,* 439–450. http://dx.doi.org/10.1007/s10488-013-0502-8

Schoenwald, S. K., Sheidow, A. J., & Letourneau, E. J. (2004). Toward effective quality assurance in evidence-based practice: Links between expert consultation, therapist fidelity, and child outcomes. *Journal of Clinical Child & Adolescent Psychology, 33,* 94–104. http://dx.doi.org/10.1207/S15374424JCCP3301_10

# INDEX

## A

ABPP. *See* American Board of Professional
    Psychology
Academic needs, in school-aged
    population, 204
Accountability, 118, 323
    in client-focused interprofessional
        practice, 18
    and competence in consultation, 38
    in education and training programs, 122
    and leadership coaching, 176
Accreditation standards, 38, 282, 283. *See
    also Standards of Accreditation for Health
    Service Psychology, 2018* (APA)
Acculturation, 92. *See also* Culture
Adherence (compliance)
    in consultation for chronic diseases,
        159–160
    in coparent consultation, 261
    defined, 137
    pediatric consultation in, 137
Administration
    health service psychology in, 81–82
    leadership vs., 170–171
Administrative law, 247–248
Adolescents, in coparent consultation, 260
Agreement, consultation. *See* Consultation
    contract
Allegation Form (coparent consultation),
    267–270

Alliance, consultation, 62, 257–258
Alternative right movement, 117
American Association of Applied
    Psychology, 29–30
American Association of Clinical
    Psychologists, 30
American Board of Professional Psychology
    (ABPP), 249, 280–282, 316
American Counseling Association, 113
American Professional Society on the
    Abuse of Children, 248–249
American Psychological Association
    (APA), 316
    Commission for the Recognition of
        Specialties and Proficiencies in
        Professional Psychology, 241
    Commission on Accreditation, 54
    on consultation with religious
        institutions, 224, 231
    doctoral programs accredited by,
        282, 283
    *Ethical Principles of Psychologists and Code of
        Conduct, 2017,* 23, 39, 56–57, 61, 63,
        65, 66, 74, 163, 226, 245, 257, 288,
        290, 309
    *Guidelines for Education and Training at the
        Doctoral and Postdoctoral Level in
        Consulting Psychology (CP)/Organizational
        Psychology (OCP), 2017,* 189, 203

*Guidelines on Multicultural Education,*
  *Training, Research, Practice, and*
  *Organizational Change for Psychologists,*
  *2003,* 97, 103, 112, 226
  on health service psychology, 72, 74,
    78, 79
*Implementing Regulations,* 77
"Model Act for State Licensure of
  Psychologists," 72
*Multicultural Guidelines: An Ecological*
  *Approach to Context, Identity, and*
  *Intersectionality, 2017,* 87, 88, 91–93,
    110, 162, 226, 305, 314
  on multiculturalism, 112
  on police and public safety psychology,
    280, 284, 295
  "Record Keeping Guidelines," 65
  "Specialty Guidelines for Forensic
    Psychology," 239, 240, 243
*Standards of Accreditation for Health Service*
  *Psychology, 2018,* 37–38, 55, 76, 77,
    169, 187, 320
American Psychology Law Society, 248
APA Ethics Code. *See Ethical Principles of*
  *Psychologists and Code of Conduct, 2017*
  (APA)
*APA Thesaurus of Psychological Index Terms,* 12
Application-based competency, 133
Applications, smartphone, 80–81
Applied psychology
  clinical, 30
  competence in, 38
  history of consultation in, 29–30
  KSA domains in consultation vs., 37
Appreciation, for law enforcement
  profession, 285–286
Arbitration, in coparent consultation,
  263–264
Arnault, S., 163
Arredondo, P., 12, 90–92, 112–113, 204,
  206
A&S. *See* Assessment and selection
Assessment(s)
  in health service psychology, 73–75
  in leadership development programs,
    175
  in medical settings consultation, 158
  in military psychological consultation,
    311–313
  in organizational consultation, 194–195
  outcome, 321–322
  in police and public safety psychology,
    284, 291–292
  in school-based consultation, 209–210
Assessment and selection (A&S), 301, 304,
  316
Assimilationist model, 92–93
Association of Multicultural Counseling
  and Development, 113

Attitudes
  in competence consultation model, 39,
    42, 322
  for consultation with religious
    institutions, 225–227
  in military psychological consultation,
    305, 314–315
  for multicultural competence, 118
  in organizational consultation, 188–189
  in police and public safety psychology,
    285–288
  in school-based consultation, 202–203,
    205–206, 208, 209, 211
Authentic leadership model, 172
Avoiding Harm (Standard 3.04), 56
Aylward, B. S., 133

**B**

Background checks, for seminary
  applicants, 232
Baker, T. B., 76
Barlow, D. H., 81
Barnett, J. E., 59
Bases for Scientific and Professional
  Judgments (Standard 2.04), 56
Beck, C. A., 255–256
Behavioral anchors, for pediatric primary
  care, 141
Behavioral consultation, 207–208
Behavioral needs, in school-aged
  population, 204
Behavioral problems
  in coparent consultation, 261, 262
  pediatric consultation for, 131, 132
Behavioral research, biomedical and,
  79–80
Belar, C., 18, 141, 155
Beliefs
  explicit, 120
  of military psychology consultants,
    314–315
  of police and public safety psychologists,
    285–286
Benjamin, G. A. H., 255–256, 260–262
Biases
  and critical pedagogy, 119
  implicit, 120, 122, 290
  of military psychology consultants,
    314–315
Bioecological theory, 110
Biomedical research, behavioral and, 79–80
Biopsychosocial model, 74, 152–153
Birkman method, 175
Blanton, J. S., 321
Blattner, J., 31
*A Blueprint for Training and Practice III, 2006*
  (National Association of School
  Psychologists), 203

Board certification
  in forensic psychology, 249
  in military psychological consultation,
    316
  in police and public safety psychology,
    281–282
Boundaries of Competence (Standard
    2.01), 23, 56, 57
Brain development, poverty and, 80
Bronfenbrenner, U., 87, 92, 110
Brown, R. T., 72
Burnout, 144, 230
Butler, S. K., 112

**C**

Campbell, D. T., 82
Capacity, competency vs., 157, 158
Caplan, G., 11–12, 19, 21, 30
Caplan, R. B., 19
Care methods, disagreements over, 164–165
Carter, B. D., 135–136, 138, 144
Case consultation. *See* Clinical case
    consultation
Catholic Church
  clergy abuse crisis in, 229
  diversity of communities within, 231
  ethnic diversity of clerics in, 230–231
  premarital counseling in, 230
  psychological screening and testing for
    applicants, 227, 232
Center for Deployment Psychology, 316
Changing systems, pediatric consultation
    in, 138
Chen, H. T., 82
Child custody issues. *See* Coparent
    consultation
Child sexual victimization, 229
Chronic diseases, consultation for, 159–160
Civil Rights legislation, 90
Claus, R. E., 59
Clerical professionals
  knowledge about, 224
  with mental health issues, 222, 228
  psychological evaluation screenings for,
    221, 225, 227, 232
  referrals to mental health professionals
    from, 221, 222
Client, defined, 4. *See also* Consultees
Client-focused clinical case consultation,
    14–17
Client-focused community organizational
    consultation, 14–15, 21
Client-focused interprofessional practice,
    14–15, 18
Clifton, Donald O., 195
Clinical case consultation (clinical
    consultation)
  client-focused, 14–17

competence consultation model for, 39,
    42–46
  consultee-focused, 14–16, 18–19
  formal, 20
  ongoing, 20
  in primary care settings, 154–155
Clinical interventions. *See* Interventions
Clinical military psychology, 302–305,
    315–316
Clinical neuropsychology, 30
Clinical psychology
  clinical child psychology, 133
  clinical health psychology, 152
  forensic consultation vs., 240–241
  history of consultation and, 29
  social justice as training topic for,
    115–116
Clinical Psychology certification, 316
Clinical roles, forensic vs., 244–245
Clinical supervision
  for consultants, 46
  consultation vs., 24–26
  knowledge about professional issues
    in, 53
C-L (consultation-liaison) model, for
    pediatric consultation, 134–135
Cloistered monasteries, conflicts in,
    228–229
C-L (consultation-liaison) psychologists,
    135–136, 143–145
Coaching
  definitions of, 176
  leadership, 176–180
  in school-based consultation, 211
Coequal relationships, 206
Collaboration. *See also* Interprofessional
    consultation
  complexity of, 319
  for pediatric consultation, 132, 138,
    140–141
  in school-based consultation, 206
Collaborative leadership framework, 172
Collins, C. J., 27
Command-directed evaluations, 308
*Command Notification Requirement to Dispel
    Stigma in Providing Mental Health
    Care to Service Members, 2011*
    (DoD), 310
Communication
  with command, 311
  competency benchmark related to, 41
  in consultation with religious
    institutions, 225
  and culture, 101
  in health service psychology, 74
  by interprofessional collaborators, 105
  in military psychological consultation,
    313–314
  in pediatric consultation, 138, 143

Community organizational consultation
  client-focused, 14–15, 21
  consultee-focused, 14–15, 21–22
Community psychology, 30
Competence constellation, 58
Competence consultation model, 22,
    37–49
  application of, 47
  attitudes in, 39, 42
  benchmarks in, 39–41
  consultation contracts in, 48–49
  education, training, professional
    development and, 47–48
  knowledge in, 42–43
  and relevance of competence in
    consultation, 38–39
  skills in, 44–46
The Competencies Conference, 95–96
Competency(-ies)
  application-based, 133
  benchmarks of, 39–41
  capacity vs., 157, 158
  for clinical consultation in primary care
    settings, 154–155
  for consultation with religious
    communities, 231
  for coparent consultation, 256
  cultural, 162–163
  defined, 38–39, 121
  for forensic consultation, 241–242,
    249–250
  foundational, 37, 75, 121–122
  functional, 75, 121–122
  in health service psychology, 73–76, 133,
    135, 169
  for industrial-organizational psychology,
    189
  for interprofessional practice, 155
  in leadership, 169–171
  for medical settings consultation,
    152–156
  metacompetence, 19, 28, 44, 321
  multicultural, 204–205, 226, 230–231,
    321
  from multicultural training in
    consultation, 121–122
  for organizational consultation, 189
  for pediatric primary care, 141
  for pediatric psychologists, 133–135
  in police and public safety psychology,
    282, 290
  profession-wide, 55–57, 77
  relational, 74
  for school-based consultation, 201–211
  self-assessments of, 58–59
  social justice, 88
  specialty, 242
Competency-based consultation,
    fundamental principles in, 5–6

Competing demands, in pediatric
    consultation, 144
Compliance. *See* Adherence
Confidentiality
  in consultation with religious
    communities, 228, 231
  informed consent about, 62
  in medical settings consultation, 164
  in military psychological consultation,
    304, 309–310
  in pediatric consultation, 142
  in peer consultation, 22
  in police and public safety psychology,
    289
  as professional issue, 63–64
Conflict of Interest (Standard 3.06), 66
Conflicts
  high conflict, 255
  of interest, 65–67
  in monasteries, 228–229
  role, 244–245
Congregants, psychological services for,
    222, 229–230
Conjoint-behavioral consultation model,
    207
Conroy, M. A., 241–242, 245
Consciousness raising, 115
Consultant, definition of, 12
Consultation alliance, 62, 257–258
Consultation contract (consultation
    agreement)
  informed consent and, 62–63
  legal liability and, 27
  and legal liability in consultation, 68
  sample, 48–49
Consultation, definitions, 11–13
Consultation in the military setting,
    defined, 302
Consultation-liaison (C-L) model, for
    pediatric consultation, 134–135
Consultation-liaison (C-L) psychologists,
    135–136, 143–145
Consultation models. *See also* Competence
    consultation model
  for pediatric consultation, 132, 134–135
  in police and public safety psychology,
    281
  for school-based consultation, 201–204,
    207–208
Consultation relationship, 5
  attending to, 42
  informed consent in, 61–63
  in organizational consultation,
    195–196
  in school-based consultation, 206
Consultation request, framing of, 320
Consultation, types of, 13–23
Consultations (Standard 4.06), 63
Consultee, definition of, 12

Consultee-focused clinical case consultation, 14–19
Consultee-focused community organizational consultation, 14–15, 21–22
Consultee-focused consultation involving law/ethics, 16
Consultee-focused corporate consultation, 16
Consultee-focused interprofessional practice, 16, 18
Consultee-focused professional development, 14–16, 19–21
*Consulting Police Psychologist Guidelines, 2016* (IACP), 294
Consulting psychology, 11
  health service psychology vs., 71
  history of, 29–31
Context
  in consultation, 114
  leadership coaching for contextual difficulties, 177–178
  life realities as contextual variables for clients, 116–117
Continuing education, 78, 282–283
Contract, consultation. *See* Consultation contract (consultation agreement)
Coparent consultation, 253–275
  Allegation Form for, 267–270
  chart for, 275
  competencies for, 256
  family custody issues in, 255–256
  personal factors for consultant, 264
  requirements for successful, 254
  steps in process of, 256–264
  Stipulation Form for, 265–267
  True-Self Values worksheet for, 270–273
  Value-Based Goal Setting worksheet for, 274
*Core Competencies for Interprofessional Collaborative Practice, 2011* (Interprofessional Education Collaborative), 18, 75
Corey, D. M., 284, 289
Corporate consultation, consultee-focused, 16. *See also* Organizational consultation
Cottone, R. R., 59
Countertransference, 19, 59
Cox, T. H., Jr., 91, 92
Craske, M. G., 81
Criminal law, 246–247
Crises
  organizational, leadership coaching in, 178–179
  pediatric consultation in, 136
Crisis intervention, 284–285, 294–295
Critical comments, in coparent consultation, 262

Critical incidents, 284
Critical pedagogy, 119–120, 122
Cultural competence, 162–163
Cultural considerations
  in health service psychology, 74
  in medical settings consultation, 162–163
  in school-based consultation, 204–205
Cultural divergence, 100–101
Cultural humility, 42, 205
Cultural responsiveness, 115
Cultural self-awareness. *See* Interprofessional consultation
Culture
  attention paid to, 116–118
  consultant's understanding of, 55
  defined, 109
  definitions of, 89
  frameworks of, 110–113
  internalizations of, 110
  and interprofessional consultation, 90–95
  Latinx, 96–99, 230–231
  law enforcement, 283, 288
  military, 305–306, 315–316
  in organizations, 89
  of religious community, 224
Culture-centered organizations
  blueprint for, 102–104
  psychologists on, 91–92
Custody case family consultation. *See* Coparent consultation

**D**

Davis, D. E., 205
Davis, J. A., 281
Decisional capacity, 157–158
Decision making
  in consultation, 43, 46
  informed consent about, 62
  models of, 59
  in pediatric settings, 143
  return to duty decisions, 303
Defendants, 246–247
Deficit-based approach, 205
Delaney, H. D., 226
Delegation of Work to Others (Standard 2.05), 56
Delgado-Romero, Ed, 98–99
Demand, for health service psychology, 81
Department of Defense (DoD), 306–310, 316
Department of Veterans Affairs, 302, 306, 308, 316
Depression, 79–80
Deutsch, R. M., 255
Dimensions of personal identity model, 93–94
Direct instructions, in coparent consultation, 261

Direct service provision, 16, 319–320
Discipline-specific knowledge and
    experience, 30, 77
Disclosure, mandatory, 309–311
Divided responsibilities, in pediatric
    consultation, 144
Doctoral programs, 77, 282
Documentation
    informed consent about, 62
    in medical settings consultation, 164
    in postconsultation phase, 46
    as professional issue, 64–65
    as risk management strategy, 60
Documentation of Professional and
    Scientific Work and Maintenance of
    Records (Standard 6.01), 65
DoD (Department of Defense), 306–310,
    316
Drotar, D., 132
Dual relationships, 231
Duty status changes, military, 303, 304

**E**

Ecobehavioral consultation model, 207
Ecological systems theory, 110, 115
Education
    and competence consultation model,
        47–48
    competency in, 75
    in health service psychology, 76–78
    in pediatric consultation, 133–135
    for police and public safety psychology,
        282–283, 295
    in 3-E approach, 287–288
Effectiveness of consultation, 5
Electronic media, 64
Elliott, S. N., 322
Ellis, Albert, 226
Embedded clinical psychology, 303
Emotional problems, pediatric consultation
    for, 131, 132
Emotional truth, 240
Employment settings, working in, 243
English language learners, 203
Environmental context
    culture as part of, 113
    in health service psychology, 79
    in organizational consultation, 111,
        190–191
Episcopal Church, 227, 232
Epstein, R. M., 38
Equity, 111, 113, 117, 162
Ethical challenges and considerations
    in consultation, 6, 16, 27–28
    in consultation with religious
        communities and institutions, 226, 231
    decision-making models for addressing,
        59

in forensic consultation, 244–245
in medical settings consultation, 163–165
in military psychology consultation,
    309–311
in pediatric consultation, 142–143
in police and public safety psychology,
    288–290
and responsibilities in consultation, 43
*Ethical Principles of Psychologists and Code of
    Conduct, 2017* (APA), 23, 39, 56–57,
    61, 63, 65, 66, 74, 163, 226, 245, 257,
    288, 290, 309
Ethics committees, of children's hospitals,
    142–143
Ethnic minority populations
    religious clerics/congregants from,
        230–231
    school-aged, 203, 204
Evidence-based approach
    consultation as implementation strategy
        for, 322–323
    for consultation with religious
        institutions, 231
    in health service psychology, 74, 82
    in police and public safety psychology,
        284
    treatments using, 4, 16, 19–20
Executive policy, 307
Expeditionary psychology, 303
Experience
    discipline-specific, 30, 77
    with religious institutions, 223–224
    specialization-specific, 30
    in 3-E approach, 288
Expert consultation, 242
Explicit beliefs, 120
Exposure, in 3-E approach, 287
External consultants, police psychologists
    as, 281
External validity, 82
Eyberg, S., 261

**F**

Face-to-face training, 20
Fairness, in policing, 290
Falender, C. A., 27, 38, 39, 47, 53–56, 62,
    242, 243
Family custody issues, 255–256
Family law, 247
Farah, Martha, 80
Fears, about stereotype threat, 121
Fees, 62
Fifield, P. Y., 163
Fingerhut, R., 57–59
Fit, person-organization and person-group,
    193
Fitness-for-duty evaluations, police officer,
    284

Five-step ethical decision-making model, 59
Flores, M. P., 114–115
Follow-up consultations, 46
Forensic consultation, 239–250
    beginning practice of, 248–249
    clinical practice vs., 240–241
    competencies in, 241–242, 249–250
    defined, 243–244
    and definition of consultation, 242–243
    legal knowledge for, 246–248
    professional role conflicts in, 244–245
    training for, 245–246
Forensic psychology, 239
Forensic truth, 240
Formal case consultation, 20
Fouad, N., 39, 92
Foundational competencies
    and competence consultation model, 37
    in health service psychology, 75
    from multicultural training in
        consultation, 121–122
Freeman, E. L., 141
Freud, Sigmund, 226
Fridhandler, B., 263
Functional competencies, 75, 121–122
Fundamental Interpersonal Relations
    Orientation-Behavior measure, 175
Funding challenges, in pediatric
    consultation, 144–145

**G**

Gallo, F. J., 291
Gallup, George, 195
Geffner, R., 255–256
Gillman, J., 132
GLOBE study, 100–101
Goals-related challenges, in pediatric
    consultation, 143
Gonsiorek, J. C., 226
*The Good Behavior Game*, 214, 215
Goodman, L. A., 115
Goodworth, Marie-Christine, 99–100
Goodyear, R. K., 54, 64
Gottlieb, M. C., 59, 63, 67
Graduate programs
    consultation with religious institutions
        in, 223, 233
    in health service psychology, 77
    and interprofessional collaboration/
        consultation, 97–100
    multicultural training in, 122
Greenberg, S. A., 240
Group, fit of person and, 193
Group-level consulting, in organizations,
    191–192
Guidelines for Education and Training at
    the Doctoral and Postdoctoral Level in
    Consulting Psychology (CP)/

Organizational Psychology (OCP),
    2017 (APA), 189
*Guidelines for Education and Training at the
    Doctoral and Postdoctoral Level in
    Consulting Psychology (CP)/Organizational
    Psychology (OCP), 2017* (APA), 203
*Guidelines for Education and Training in
    Industrial-Organizational Psychology,
    2016* (SIOP), 189
*Guidelines on Multicultural Education,
    Training, Research, Practice, and
    Organizational Change for Psychologists,
    2003* (APA), 97, 103, 112, 226

**H**

Habitat for Humanity, 99
"Half-life" (of professional knowledge), 20
Halgin, R. P., 291
Hall, G. Stanley, 29
Halo effects, 28
Handelsman, M. M., 63, 67
Harbeck, C., 132
Hargrove, D. S., 141
Harrar, W. R., 242
Health care measures, in HSP, 75
Health care teams
    interdisciplinary research with, 96–97
    medical settings consultation for, 161
    organizational consultation for, 191–192
Health conditions, pediatric consultation
    for, 131–132
Health disparities, 160–162
Health Insurance Portability and Account-
    ability Act (1996), 45, 309–310
*Health Practitioner Regulation National Law
    Act 2009* (Psychology Board of
    Australia), 23
Health Professions Scholarship Program,
    315
Health promotion, 73
Health service delivery, 190–191
Health service psychology (HSP), 20, 72–82
    APA Ethics Code requirements in, 56–57
    competencies in, 73–74, 133, 135, 169
    confidentiality in, 63–64
    consultation in, 3–5, 11
    defined, 3n1, 71, 72
    determining when to seek consultation
        in, 57–59
    documentation in, 64–65
    education and training in, 76–78
    establishment/maintenance of
        competencies in, 75–76
    features of consultation in, 23
    future of, 79–82
    history of consultation in, 29, 30
    knowledge base required for, 73–74
    leadership as core competency in, 169

legal and ethical issues in consultation
for, 28
pediatric consultants in, 132
professional issues in, 53
risk factors for psychologists in, 60
scope of, 72–73
training in, 135
types of consultation in, 21
Health Service Psychology Education
Collaborative (HSPEC), 72, 74–77,
135
Heteropatriarchy, 90
High conflict (term), 255
High health care utilizers, 158–159
Hoffman, M. A., 114
Hofstede, G., 89–91
Homicidal risk assessment, 158
Hook, J. N., 205
Hospital-based consultation, 13
Hospitalist psychologists, pediatric, 135
Hostage negotiation, 284
HSP. *See* Health service psychology
HSPEC. *See* Health Service Psychology
Education Collaborative
Hudgins, C., 163
Humility, cultural, 42, 205
Hundert, E. M., 38


I

IACP. *See* International Association of
Chiefs of Police
Identity(-ies)
in civil rights movement, 117
and intersectionality in organizations,
93–95
of law enforcement officers, 286
of participants in consultation, 114
role of culture in, 109–110
*Implementing Regulations* (APA), 77
Implicit bias, 120, 122, 290
Inappropriate behavior, in coparent
consultation, 261, 262
Inclusive leadership approach, 172
Inclusivity, multicultural training in
consultation for, 116
Independent functions model, 132
Indirect instructions, in coparent
consultation, 261
Indirect psychological consultation model,
132
Individual-level consulting, in
organizations, 191
Industrial-organizational (I/O) psychology,
30–31
competencies in, 189
social justice as training topic for,
115–116
supervision in, 321

Inequity
health disparities, 160–162
and multicultural training in
consultation, 111, 113, 117
In extremis practice, 290
Informed consent
and consultation relationship, 61–63
in medical settings consultation, 163–164
in pediatric consultation, 142
in police and public safety psychology,
289
as risk management strategy, 60
Informed Consent (Standard 3.10), 63
Ingraham, C. L., 115, 205–206
In-house employees, police psychologists
as, 281
Initiation of consultation (stage), 44
Institutional context, 43
Institutional policies, 145
Instructional consultation model, 207
Instructions, in coparent consultation, 261
Integrated practice
in health service psychology, 3, 4
in pediatric primary care, 140–142
Integrative validity, 82
Interdisciplinary care, 79–80, 96–97
Internal validity, 82
International Association of Chiefs of Police
(IACP), 284, 285, 290, 293–295
Internships, 78, 122, 223
Interpersonal problems and skills
leadership coaching for, 178
in military psychological consultation,
313–314
Interprofessional consultation, 87–105
blueprint for culture-centered
organizations, 102–104
client-focused, 14–16, 18
complexity of, 319
context for, 43
core competencies for, 155
and culture, 89–95
defined, 18
inclusive scenarios in, 95–102
in medical settings consultation, 155
in school-based consultation, 206
seeking, 57
skills and activities in, 45
Intersectionality, 93, 95, 109, 110, 122
Interventions
crisis, 284–285, 294–295
in health service psychology, 73
in organizational consultation, 20,
194–195
in police and public safety psychology,
284, 292–293
in school-based consultation, 210–211
Interviews, in coparent consultation,
258–259

**J**

Jackson, Y., 133
Johnson, W. B., 59, 290

**K**

Kahn, R. L., 190
Kaslow, N. J., 5, 121
Katz, D., 190
Kilburg, R. R., 30
Kirschman, E., 286
Kitaeff, J., 280
Kluckhohn, C., 89
Knapp, S. J., 57–59, 63, 67, 242
Knowledge, skills, and attitudes (KSAs). *See
    specific domains*
Knowledge domain
    in competence consultation model,
        42–43
    for consultation with religious
        institutions, 224–225
    for health service psychology, 73–74
    for medical setting consultation, 152–155
    for military psychological consultation,
        305–311
    for multicultural competence, 118
    for organizational consultation, 188–192
    for pediatric consultation, 133
    for police and public safety psychology,
        283
    for school-based consultation, 202–203,
        205–206, 208, 211
Kratochwill, T. R., 322
Kroeber, A. L., 89
Kullgren, K. A., 144

**L**

Labeled praise, 261
La Greca, A. M., 133–134
Language
    for consultation with religious
        institutions, 225, 232
    military, 306
Latinx culture, 96–99, 230–231
Law enforcement agencies, 279. *See also*
    Police and public safety psychology
    (PPSP)
Law enforcement officers
    experiences of, 288
    officer-involved shootings, 292–293
    POST screening for, 284, 291–292, 295
    preemployment psychological evalua-
        tions for, 279, 284, 286–287, 289
    psychologists' perceptions of, 286
    training about PPSP for, 287–288
    views of mental health professionals by,
        286–287

Law enforcement profession, 285–286
Lawyers, ethical obligations of, 241
Leadership
    culture-centered, 100–102
    definitions of, 170
    management and administration vs.,
        170–171
    organizational consultation for, 193
    paternalistic, 101
    servant, 172–173, 175
    in VUCA world, 173
Leadership coaching, 176–180
    addressing specific challenges in,
        177–179
    case example of, 179–180
    components of, 177
    definitions of, 176
    outcome data from, 179
    process of, 176–177
Leadership consultation, 169–181
    approaches to, 171–173
    best practices for, 173–179
    competency in leadership, 170–171
    training program case example,
        179–180
Leadership development programs,
    174–176
LEAP (Longitudinal Education for
    Advanced Practice) model, 20–21
Legal expertise and knowledge
    for forensic consultation, 246–248
    for police and public safety psychology
        consultation, 283
Legal issues and considerations
    in consultation, 6, 27–28, 54
    consultations involving, 16
    as professional issue, 67–68
    and responsibilities in consultation, 43
    with supervision vs. consultation, 54
Lehmer, M., 263
Lepage, K., 322
Liaison activities, in health service
    psychology, 73
Licensure
    and documentation requirements, 65
    and legal liability in consultation,
        67–68
    in police and public safety psychology,
        281–282
Liebowitz, B., 31
Lifelong learning, 78
Life realities, as contextual variables for
    clients, 116–117
Local churches, consultations with,
    229–230
Longitudinal Education for Advanced
    Practice (LEAP) model, 20–21
Looser, J., 208
Lowman, R. L., 113, 115–116

## M

Maintaining Competence (Standard 2.03), 56
Maintaining Confidentiality (Standard 4.01), 63
Management, leadership vs., 170–171
Mandated consultation
  by licensing boards, 67–68
  with police and public safety psychologists, 289
Mandatory disclosure, 309–311
Marginalized populations, 117, 121. *See also* Minority populations
Martens, B. K., 207
Mason-Sears, C., 54
Matsumoto, D. R., 89
Mayberg, Helen, 79–80
McCullough, J. R., 112
McDaniel, S. H., 141
McDavis, R., 112–113, 204
McMinn, M. R., 226
Medical decision making, 143
Medical settings, consultation in, 151–165
  areas of knowledge for, 152–155
  common types of, 156–165
  competencies for, 152–156
  cultural considerations in, 162–163
  ethical considerations, 163–165
  pediatric consultation, 132, 145
  typical structure of, 157
Meeting facilitation, 196
*Mental Health Evaluations of Members of the Military Service, 2013* (DoD), 308
Mental health needs
  clerical professionals with, 222, 228
  pastoral care for congregants with, 229–230
  in school-aged population, 204
Mental health professionals
  in clinical military psychology, 303
  ethical obligations of lawyers vs., 241
  police officers' perceptions of, 286–287
Mental health services, demand for, 81
Mentorship, 176, 224, 233
Metacompetence, 19, 28, 44, 321
Military
  application of psychological science in, 311–312
  consultant's attitudes about, 314–315
  as setting for consultation, 302
Military culture, 305–306, 315–316
Military psychological consultation, 301–317
  attitudes in, 314–315
  board certification in, 316
  clinical military psychology, 302–304
  defined, 302
  knowledge of, 305–311
  operational military psychology, 302–304

skills in, 311–314
training for, 315–316
Miller, G. A., 209
Millon Clinical Inventory-III, 225, 227
Minnesota Multiphasic Personality Inventory—2 (MMPI–2), 225, 227, 291
Minority populations
  religious clerics/congregants from, 230–231
  school-aged, 203, 204
  schools' deficit-based approach to serving, 205
Mission, organizational, 189–190
Mixed agency, 309
MMPI–2. *See* Minnesota Multiphasic Personality Inventory—2
"Model Act for State Licensure of Psychologists" (APA), 72
Monasteries, conflicts in, 228–229
Monitoring, of multicultural training, 118
Morgan, G., 91
Motivation, work, 193
Mullins, L. L., 132
"Multicultural and Social Justice Counseling Competencies" (Ratts et al.), 88, 112
Multicultural competence, 321
  in consultation with religious institutions, 230–231
  in school-based consultation, 204–205, 207
"Multicultural Competencies and Standards" (Sue, Arredondo, & McDavis), 112–113
Multicultural consultation model, 207
Multicultural Guidelines (APA). *See Guidelines on Multicultural Education, Training, Research, Practice, and Organizational Change for Psychologists, 2003* (APA)
*Multicultural Guidelines: An Ecological Approach to Context, Identity, and Intersectionality, 2017* (APA), 87, 88, 91–93, 110, 162, 226, 305, 314
Multicultural issues and considerations
  with consultation, 43
  in consultation process, 45
  in medical settings consultation, 160–161
  in organizations, 116–117, 194
  with religion, 226
  in school-based consultation, 203–206
Multicultural training in consultation, 109–123
  aspects of, 118–119
  and critical pedagogy, 119–120
  current state of, 117–118
  foundational and functional competencies in, 121–122

and frameworks of culture, 110–113
and history of multicultural issues in
organizations, 116–117
and implicit bias, 120
and importance of context in
consultation, 114
inclusivity of, 116
monitoring and accountability for, 118
and stereotype threat, 120–121
training models of, 114–116
Multiple relationships, 65–67, 231,
289–290
Multiple Relationships (Standard 3.05), 66
Munsterberg, Hugo, 280
Myers–Briggs Type Indicator, 175

**N**

Nassar-McMillan, S., 112
National Association of School
Psychologists, 203
National Center for PTSD, 316
National Health Council, 159
National Institute of Mental Health
(NIMH), 79–80
National security, 304
Neale, M., 12
Needs
of clerical professionals, 222, 228
of congregants, 229–230
in school-aged population, 204
Negotiation, 259
Newell, M., 113–116, 203, 204, 207, 208,
210, 212
Newell, T. S., 208, 210, 212
Newman, D., 113–114, 116, 208,
210, 212
NIMH (National Institute of Mental
Health), 79–80
Nine-step ethical decision-making model,
59
Noncompliance, in coparent consultation,
261
Novices, clerical, 228–229

**O**

Objectivity, 320
Observation, in coparent consultation,
259–262
Occupational specialties, military, 305
Officer-involved shootings, 292–293
Ongoing clinical consultation, 20
*On the Witness Stand* (Munsterberg), 280
Operational psychology, 301–304
evaluation related to security clearance
in, 312–313
KSAs in, 305
training in, 316

Operational support, from police and public
safety psychologists, 284, 294–295
Oppression, 111, 113, 117, 178
Organizational & Business Consulting
Psychology certification, 316
Organizational consultation, 187–197
assessments and interventions in, 20,
194–195
community, 14–15, 20–21
consultation process in, 195–196
culture as framework in, 111–112, 114,
118
focal issues in, 193–194
knowledge, skills, and abilities in,
188–189
legal and ethical considerations in, 28
levels for, 191–192
multiculturalism in, 122–123
and organizational mission/purpose,
189–190
organization–environment relationship
in, 190–191
with religious institutions, 222, 229
and structure/subparts of organizations,
192
supervision for, 46
Organizational crises, leadership coaching
in, 178–179
Organizational performance, for law
enforcement agencies, 285
Organizations
attraction-selection-attrition cycle in,
191
consultants as agents of change in, 323
cultural paradigms in, 89
mission and purpose of, 189–190
multicultural issues at, 116–117, 194
person-organization fit, 193
power and politics in, 194
relationship of environment and,
190–191
structure and subparts of, 192
view of culture by, 109–110
Orthodox Christian Churches, 227,
230–231
Outcome assessments, 321–322
Owen, J., 205
Ownership, problem, 112

**P**

Pain management, 159
Palermo, T. M., 134–135
Parallel coparenting, 263
Parallel play, 18
Pargament, K. I., 226
Parisher, D., 281
Pastoral care, 229–230
Paternalistic leadership, 101

Peace Officer Standards and Training
　(POST) screening, 284, 291–292, 295
Pediatric consultation, 131–145
　burnout in, 144
　communication challenges in, 143
　competencies for, 133–135
　divided responsibilities or competing
　　demands in, 144
　education and training in, 133–135
　ethical challenges to, 142–143
　funding challenges for, 144–145
　models of, 132
　in other domains, 145
　and pediatric primary care, 140–142
　referral question and goals challenges
　　to, 143
　role of psychologists, 135–140
Pediatric primary care (PPC), 140–142
Pediatric psychology, 30
　competencies in, 133–135
　conceptualizations of field, 131–132
　core competencies within, 134
Peer consultation, 14–15, 22–25
"The People Make the Place" (Schneider),
　191
Person-group fit, 193
Person-organization fit, 193
Physical praise, 262
Physician extenders, 81
Plante, T. G., 226
Police and public safety psychology (PPSP),
　279–296
　attitudes in, 285–288
　consultation models in, 281
　defined, 280
　education and training for, 282–283, 295
　ethical standards, 288–290
　history and development of, 280
　knowledge domains in, 283
　licensure and board certification in,
　　281–282
　resources in, 295
　skill domains in, 283–285
　vignettes, 290–295
Police officers. *See* Law enforcement officers
Police & Public Safety certification, 316
Policing practices, improving, 290
Policy, defined, 306
Politics, in organizations, 194
Postconsultation phase, 46
Postgraduate programs
　consultation with religious institutions
　　in, 223, 233
　in health service psychology, 78
　in police and public safety psychology,
　　282–283
Postlicensure, 54
POST screening. *See* Peace Officer Standards
　and Training screening

Posttraumatic stress disorder (PTSD), 306,
　316
Poverty, 80, 203
Power, 115, 194
PPC (pediatric primary care), 140–142
PPSP. *See* Police and public safety
　psychology
Praise, in coparent consultation, 261–262
Preemployment psychological evaluations,
　279, 284, 286–287, 289
Premarital counseling, 230
President's Commission on Law
　Enforcement and Administration
　of Justice, 280
Prevention, primary and tertiary, 72, 73
Primary care, pediatric, 140–142
Primary care psychology, 152
Primary prevention, 73
Problem ownership, 112
Problem-solving consultation model, 207
Procedural knowledge, 20–21
Professional boundaries, with religious
　communities, 231
Professional development
　and competence consultation model,
　　47–48
　consultee-focused, 14–16, 19–21
Professionalism, 74, 78
Professional issues, 53–68
　confidentiality, 63–64
　conflicts of interest, 65–67
　consultation as area of competence,
　　55–57
　determining when to seek consultation,
　　57–59
　documentation and record-keeping,
　　64–65
　ethical dilemmas, 59
　informed consent, 61–63
　legal liability, 67–68
　multiple relationships, 65–67
　risk management, 60–61
　and supervision vs. consultation,
　　54–55
Professional knowledge, durability of, 20
Professional practice, consultation as,
　42–43
Profession-wide competencies, 55–57, 77
Program-centered administrative
　consultation, 21
Program development, 46
Program evaluation, 73, 81–82
Project Consultation Liaison in Mental
　Health and Behavior, 142
Pruett, M. K., 255
Psychological applications, competency in,
　41, 74–75
Psychological Clinical Science Accreditation
　System, 76, 77

Psychological evaluation screenings
    for clerical applicants, 221, 225, 227, 232
    for law enforcement candidates, 279,
        284, 286–287, 289
Psychological fitness-for-duty evaluations,
    284, 286
Psychological health, of service members,
    315
Psychologist extenders, 81
Psychology, attitudes about knowledge and
    practices of, 42
Psychotherapy, with clerical professionals,
    228
PsyD doctoral programs, 77
PTSD (posttraumatic stress disorder), 306,
    316
Public health, 145
Public safety psychology. *see* Police and
    public safety psychology

**Q**

Qualitative research, 82
Questions, in coparent consultation, 261

**R**

Racial minority populations, school-aged,
    203, 204
Rae, W. A., 143
Rank, military, 305
Rank and file, exposure to, 287
Rapport building, 313
Ratts, M. J., 112
Recommendations of consultant, 5, 12,
    313–314
Record-keeping, 64–65
"Record Keeping Guidelines" (APA), 65
Referrals
    from clerical professionals, 221, 222
    competency benchmarks related to, 40
    in pediatric consultation, 143
    to police and public safety psychologists,
        289
    soliciting, 44
Reid, Molly, 260–261
Reilly, R. R., 281
Reiser, Martin, 281, 286
Relational competency, 74
Relationships
    coequal and collaborative, 206
    critical pedagogy for learning about,
        119–120
    dual, 231
    multiple, 65–67, 231, 289–290
    organization–environment, 190–191
    of religious communities and
        professional psychologists, 226
Religion, 59, 226

Religious clients, decision-making mode
    with, 59
Religious institutions, consultation with,
    221–235
    best practices for, 231–232
    competency in, 223–227
    current status of, 233
    examples of, 227–230
    multicultural and ethical issues in,
        230–231
    opportunities for, 221–223
    resources on, 223, 233–235
    training for, 233
    translational issues, 232
Religious rules, 227
Reporting findings, in coparent
    consultation, 262–263
Research
    biomedical and behavioral, linking,
        79–80
    in health service psychology, 73, 78–80
    military consultant's knowledge of, 306
    qualitative, 82
    team, 79–80
Research consultation, pediatric, 145
Reserve officer training, 288
Resilience and sustainability programs,
    police officer, 285
Respect, in consulting, 42
Responsibility(-ies)
    in consultation, 5, 23, 26, 43, 54
    informed consent about, 62
    in pediatric consultation, 144
    in supervision vs. consultation, 43, 54
Responsiveness, 62, 115
Retreat centers, 230
Return-to-duty decisions, 303
Richards, P. S., 226
Rios, B., 281
Risk assessment, for suicide or homicide,
    158
Risk factors, for health service
    psychologists, 60
Risk management, 59–61, 65
Roberts, M. C., 132, 133
Rodolfa, E., 75, 121
Role clarity, 5
Role conflicts, forensic consultation and,
    244–245
Roman Catholic Church. *See* Catholic Church
Rose, S., 163
Rousmaniere, T., 54
Rudisill, J. R., 54
Russell, S. R., 226

**S**

Sánchez-Johnsen, Lisa, 96–97
Sandoval, J. H., 210

Schneider, B., 92, 191
School-based consultation, 201–216
    assessment in, 209–210
    classwide behavioral case example,
        212–215
    coequal, collaborative relationships in,
        206
    competencies for, 202–211
    defined, 202
    with diverse, multicultural population,
        203–206
    engaging consultees in, 208–209
    intervention design for, 210–211
    model flexibility in, 207–208
    multicultural competence in, 113–114,
        116
    multicultural training in models for, 115
    training for, 211–212
School psychology, 321
Schools
    as cultural entities, 92
    as loosely coupled systems, 206
Schroeder, C., 140, 141
Screening process
    for clerical applicants, 221, 225, 227, 232
    in coparent consultation, 258
    for cultural diversity/representation,
        104–105
    for law enforcement candidates, 279,
        284, 286–287, 289
    Peace Officer Standards and Training,
        284, 291–292, 295
Sears, R. W., 54
Secular psychology, 225–226
Security clearance, 312–313
Self-assessments of competence, 58–59
Self-awareness, 115
Self-initiated referrals, 289
Self-reflection
    for consultants with religious
        institutions, 226–227
    at initiation of consultation, 44
    on multiculturalism in organizational
        consultation, 122–123
    in postconsultation phase, 46
Seminary applicants, 221, 225, 227, 232
Servant leadership, 172–173, 175
Servant Leadership Assessment
    Instrument, 175
Servant Leadership Survey, 175
Service-level policies, military, 306–309
Service members, attitudes/beliefs about,
        314–315
Service provision consultation, 16
Sexual assault, 308–309
*Sexual Assault Prevention and Response*
    *Program Procedures, 2017* (DoD),
        308–309
Sexual victimization, child, 229

Shafranske, E. P., 27, 38, 39, 47, 53–56, 62,
        226, 242, 243
Sharing power, 115
Shaw, M., 255–256
Shealy, C., 12
Shuman, D. W., 240
Singh, A. A., 112
SIOP (Society for Industrial and
        Organizational Psychology), 189
Sixteen Personality Factors Questionnaire,
        225, 227, 291
Skills
    in competence consultation model,
        44–46
    for consultation with religious
        institutions, 225
    development of, for medical providers,
        161
    of health service psychologists, 73–74
    implementation of, consultation with,
        323
    in military psychological consultation,
        304, 311–314
    for multicultural competence, 118
    in organizational consultation, 188–189
    in police and public safety psychology,
        283–285
    in school-based consultation, 202–203,
        205–206, 208, 209, 211
Skinner, B. F., 226
Smartphone applications, 80–81
Socialization, 92
Social justice, 88, 115–116, 322
Social justice consultation, 114–115
Societal context, for consultation, 43
Society for Industrial and Organizational
        Psychology (SIOP), 189
Society for Police and Criminal Psychology,
        282, 295
Society of Behavioral Medicine, 224, 231
Society of Pediatric Psychology (SPP),
        133–134
Specialization-specific experience, 30
Specialty competencies, 242
"Specialty Guidelines for Forensic
        Psychology" (APA), 239, 240, 243
Spencer, K. B., 290
Spencer-Oatey, H., 89
Spilberg, S. W., 284, 289
Spirito, A., 134
Spirituality- and religion-integrated
        psychological health care, 223
SPP (Society of Pediatric Psychology),
        133–134
*Standards of Accreditation for Health Service*
    *Psychology, 2018* (APA), 37–38, 55, 76,
        77, 169, 187, 320
Stanley, J. C., 82
Stereotype threat, 120–122

Stigma, with service seeking, 287
Stipulation Form (coparent consultation), 265–267
Strengths-based approach, 205
Stressors, for clerical professionals, 227
Subject area knowledge, consultant's, 43
Sue, D. W., 112–113, 204
Suicide, 158, 306
Supervision
  clinical, 24–26, 46, 53
  in competency-based consultation training, 321–322
  competency in, for health service psychology, 75
  for consultants, 46
  consultation vs., 24–26, 43, 54–55
  legal and ethical duties of supervisor, 28
  for organizational consultation, 46
  responsibility in consultation vs., 43, 54
Sustainability planning, 323
Sweet, G., 290
Systems-oriented model, 132

**T**

Talmi, A., 142
Team research, 79–80
Technology
  confidentiality when using, 64
  for health service psychology, 80–81
  informed consent about, 62
  for peer consultation, 22
Terman, L. M., 280
Terminating Therapy (Standard 10.01a), 57–58
Tertiary prevention, 72
Theme interference, 19
*The Theory and Practice of Mental Health Consultation* (Caplan), 30
Thomas, J. T., 62
3-E approach to enhanced perspective, 287–288
Traditional model, of clinical military psychology, 303
Training
  and competence consultation model, 47–48
  for competency-based consultation, 320–322
  for consultation with religious institutions, 233
  for forensic consultation, 245–246, 248
  in health service psychology, 76–78, 188
  leadership consultation for, 179–180
  for medical settings consultation, 156
  of military psychological consultants, 315–316

multiculturalism consultation training models, 114–116
  in pediatric consultation, 133–135
  in police and public safety psychology, 282–283, 287–288, 295
  for primary pediatric care, 141–142
  responsibility and legal liability in, 54
  for school-based consultation, 201, 211–212
  in team or organizational psychology, 187
  in U.S.-centric models of multiculturalism, 192
Transactional approach, 171
Transformational approaches, 172–173
Translational issues, in religious institutions and communities, 232
Trompetter, P. S., 280
True-Self Values worksheet (coparent consultation), 270–273
Trust building, 225, 279
Truth, emotional vs. forensic, 240
Turning Point Collaborative Leadership Self-Assessment Questionnaires, 175

**U**

Undergraduate education, in health service psychology, 76–77
Uniformed Services University of Health Sciences, 315
United States Conference of Catholic Bishops, 229, 232
Unlabeled praise, 261
U.S. Air Force, 307, 315
U.S. Army, 307, 315
U.S. Coast Guard, 308
U.S. Congress, 246, 307
U.S. Marine Corps, 308
U.S. Navy, 307, 315, 316
Utsey, S. O., 205

**V**

Validity, 82
Value-Based Goal Setting worksheet (coparent consultation), 274
Values
  national and organizational, 90–91
  of religious communities, 226
VandeCreek, L., 57–59, 242
"Vanity boards," 249
Varela, J. G., 241–242, 245

**W**

Watson, John, 226
Web-based training, 20

Winfrey, C. C., 12
Witmer, L., 29, 131
Women's leadership development
    programs, 174
Work motivation, 193
Work performance, 193–194
Work-related difficulties, 45
World Health Organization, 137

Worthington, E. L., Jr., 205
Wright, L., 131, 132
Wu, Y. P., 133

**Y**

Yarhouse, M. A., 226
Younggren, J. N., 59

# ABOUT THE EDITORS

**Carol A. Falender, PhD,** is coauthor, with Edward P. Shafranske, of *Supervision Essentials for the Practice of Competency-Based Clinical Supervision* (2017), *Clinical Supervision: A Competency-Based Approach* (2004), and *Getting the Most Out of Clinical Training and Supervision: A Guide for Practicum Students and Interns* (2012). She is coeditor, with Edward P. Shafranske, of *Casebook for Clinical Supervision: A Competency-Based Approach* (2008) and, with Edward P. Shafranske and Celia J. Falicov, *Multiculturalism and Diversity in Clinical Supervision: A Competency-Based Approach* (2014). In 2018, Dr. Falender received the American Psychological Association's (APA's) Distinguished Contributions to Education and Training in Psychology award. She was a member of the Supervision Guidelines Group of the Association of State and Provincial Psychology Boards and chaired the Supervision Guidelines Task Force of APA's Board of Educational Affairs. For more than 20 years, she directed APA-approved internship programs at child and family guidance clinics and has served as a consultant to multiple organizations and trained consultants. Dr. Falender is a Fellow of APA and was president of APA's Division 37, Society for Child and Family Policy and Practice. She is an adjunct professor at Pepperdine University in Los Angeles, California; clinical professor in the Department of Psychology at the University of California, Los Angeles; and chair of the California Psychological Association Continuing Education Committee.

**Edward P. Shafranske, PhD, ABPP,** is a professor of psychology, Muriel Lipsey Chair in Clinical and Counseling Psychology, and director of the PsyD program in clinical psychology at Pepperdine University in Los Angeles, California. He serves on a number of editorial boards and has published widely in the fields of clinical training and supervision and the applied psychology of religion. Dr. Shafranske is coauthor, with Carol A. Falender, of books related to clinical training, including *Clinical Supervision: A Competency-Based Approach* (2004), *Getting the Most Out of Clinical Training and Supervision: A Guide for Practicum Students and Interns* (2012), and *Supervision Essentials for the Practice of Competency-Based Clinical Supervision* (2017). He is coeditor, with Carol A. Falender, of *Casebook for Clinical Supervision: A Competency-Based Approach* (2008) and, with Carol A. Falender and Celia J. Falicov, *Multiculturalism and Diversity in Clinical Supervision: A Competency-Based Approach* (2014). Dr. Shafranske is a Fellow of the American Psychological Association (APA) Divisions 12, 29, and 36 and has served twice as president of APA Division 36. The California Psychological Association has recognized him for his contributions to psychology. He also is associate clinical professor of psychiatry, School of Medicine, at the University of California, Irvine; maintains a private clinical practice; and has served as a consultant to clinicians, academic programs, and religious institutions.